Afro 🍁 Texans

SERIES EDITORS: WILL GUZMÁN, KIMBERLY D. HILL, AND WILLIAM T. HOSTON

Also in the series:

Emmett J. Scott: Power Broker of the Tuskegee Machine
by Maceo C. Dailey Jr.; edited by Will Guzmán and David H. Jackson Jr.

Images in the River: The Life and Work of Waring Cuney
by Cynthia Davis and Verner D. Mitchell

Their Stories, Our Stories: Four Presidents of Huston-Tillotson University
by Rosalee Martin

The Water Cries: Uncovering the Slave Auction Houses of Galveston, Texas
by Anthony Paul Griffin

THEIR STORIES, OUR STORIES

FOUR PRESIDENTS OF
HUSTON-TILLOTSON
UNIVERSITY

DR. ROSALEE MARTIN

TEXAS TECH UNIVERSITY PRESS

Copyright © 2025 by Rosalee R. Martin

All rights reserved. No portion of this book may be reproduced in any form or by any means, including electronic storage and retrieval systems, except by explicit prior written permission of the publisher. Brief passages excerpted for review and critical purposes are excepted.

This book is typeset in [XX The paper used in this book meets the minimum requirements of ANSI/ NISO Z39.48-1992 (R1997). ♾

Designed by Hannaah Gaskamp
Cover design by Hannah Gaskamp
Dr. King photo courtesy of Mr. Stuart King; Dr. McMillan photo © Larry Kolvoord–USA TODAY NETWORK; Dr. Earvin and Dr. Pierce Burnette photos courtesy of Huston-Tillotson University

Library of Congress Cataloging-in-Publication Data

Names: Martin, Rosalee, 1944– author. | Title: Their Stories, Our Stories: Four Presidents of Huston-Tillotson University / Rosalee Martin. Description: Lubbock, Texas: Texas Tech University Press, 2025. | Series: Afro-Texans | Includes bibliographical references and index. | Summary: "An institutional history of Huston-Tillotson University, shown through portraits of four past presidents who shaped its trajectory"—Provided by publisher.
Identifiers: LCCN 2024031789 (print) | LCCN 2024031790 (ebook) |
ISBN 978-1-68283-232-5 (paperback) | ISBN 978-1-68283-233-2 (ebook)
Subjects: LCSH: Huston-Tillotson University—Presidents—Biography. | Huston-Tillotson University—History. | King, John Q. Taylor (John Quill Taylor), 1921–2011. | McMillan, Joseph Turner, Jr., 1944–2017 | Earvin, Larry L., 1949– | Burnette, Collette Pierce, 1957–
Classification: LCC LC2851.H89 M37 2024 (print) | LCC LC2851.H89 (ebook) |
DDC 378.764/310922 [B]—dc23/eng/20240821
LC record available at https://lccn.loc.gov/2024031789
LC ebook record available at https://lccn.loc.gov/2024031790

Texas Tech University Press
Box 41037
Lubbock, Texas 79409-1037 USA
800.832.4042
ttup@ttu.edu
www.ttupress.org

This book is dedicated to my mother, Lucille Martin, who taught me the importance of education; to my children and grandchildren who choose to become educated; and to all the presidents, students, faculty, and staff of Huston-Tillotson College/University, past, present, and future for understanding the power of education. Additionally, it is dedicated to all HBCUs; our institutions are still needed.

Contents

TABLES	ix
FOREWORD	xi
PREFACE	xv
ACKNOWLEDGMENTS	xxiii

	Prologue HUSTON-TILLOTSON UNIVERSITY BRIEF HISTORY BEFORE 1965	3
CHAPTER 1:	Dr. John Q. Taylor King Sr. A LEADER EXTRAORDINAIRE	7
CHAPTER 2:	Dr. Joseph T. McMillan Jr. THE DASH BETWEEN "I LOVE HT"	53
CHAPTER 3:	Dr. Larry L. Earvin ACCOMPLISHMENTS VS. ABSENTEEISM	139
CHAPTER 4:	Dr. Colette Pierce Burnette PRESIDENT OF GENIUSES	199
CHAPTER 5:	Historically Black Colleges and Universities (HBCUs) Still Needed	299
	Epilogue NEW BEGINNINGS	325
	APPENDIX: COMPARISON OF FOUR PRESIDENTS	327
	NOTES	337
	BIBLIOGRAPHY	363
	INDEX	371

Tables

194	Table 1. Student Enrollment, 2010–2015
240	Table 2. Student Enrollment, 2015–2022
303	Table 3. Comparison of HBCU and HT Professors
309	Table 4. Internal Difficulties/Problems
313	Table 5. Financial Stability Survey

Foreword

UNDERSTANDING HUSTON-TILLOTSON *AND* ITS HISTORY WILL help both the current and the next generations of leaders transform education as well as create equity in the education system. Giving an objective and firsthand account of Huston-Tillotson (HT) is critical to that understanding.

Of all the people who could write a book on four presidents of Huston-Tillotson University, Professor Rosalee Martin is the most qualified, for many reasons. Two of those reasons that I have witnessed firsthand over nearly forty years of friendship are her leadership and her judgment. A third possible reason is that Professor Martin was employed at Huston-Tillotson University longer than any professor in its 149-year history. During her fifty years at HT, she has been and continues to be unwavering in her pursuit of reformation and transformation in higher education.

I met Professor Martin in 1985 when I started teaching at HT and was fortunate enough to get the office adjacent to hers in the Jackson Moody (JM) building. JM has been a hub for faculty in Humanities, Social and Behavioral Sciences, and Criminal Justice. But perhaps more important, JM is also a center for student support services where students assemble throughout the day. The faculty in our building interact with each other and with students in very real ways as we live out the mission of our university each and every day in the halls of JM.

As colleagues over so many years, Professor Martin and I have shared numerous experiences (both pleasant and unpleasant) working on several committees and projects for the institution. What brought us together was, and still is, our love for teaching and our unified commitment to the growth and sustainability of HT. Most of our students come from highly marginalized backgrounds, and Professor Martin has dedicated her career to fighting for them. That fight, that we shared, meant at times we had to push back against a president of our institution. You can go to chapter 2 for relevant stories (including one in which we were branded "snakes" by the then president). Through red tape and "politics" over the years, Professor Martin has remained dedicated to our students, faculty, and community.

She possesses not only academic training and excellent teaching skills but also professional expertise as a licensed counselor and social worker. Moreover, she has served as a division chair (sixteen years), department chair (three years), and dean (three and a quarter years).

Again, Dr. Martin is, without hesitation, the most appropriate and qualified person to write this book. My tenure at HT spans the four presidencies (from Dr. King to Dr. Pierce Burnette) that Professor Martin covers, so I can attest to how accurate and important this book is.

Let me give you a quick idea of how and why to use Their Stories, Our Stories.

For a comparative study of the four presidents' leadership effectiveness, an inquisitive reader might want to start with a review of the appendix. Here you can examine how presidential performance might be linked to comparative measures that Professor Martin has suggested. If your focus is on promoting productive performance at a small private HBCU like HT, you might go to chapter 2 for insights on behaviors that can *derail* well-thought-out strategic plans at the institution. This book delineates for the reader methods both to avoid and to implement.

Among other things, this book notes the importance of raising the profile of the HBCU among various segments of the community. The point is that anything that can diminish the standing of HT is a liability. Why is this consideration important? For a good answer I suggest that the reader go to chapter 4. The broader and more pertinent question is this: What lessons about financial stability can one learn from this book?

I share Professor Martin's conviction that HT, as the oldest institution of higher learning in Austin, is a historic anchor institution established as a center of learning and transformation for marginalized racial minorities. We believe that the historic mission is as true now as it ever has been. HT today stands as evidence of that historic struggle. It was our belief in, and commitment to, its mission that a reader of *Their Stories, Our Stories* must grasp to appreciate why three professors challenged threats to the sustainability of the institution. You can read a good amount of the narrative of that struggle in chapter 2. As you might have read, at one point the chair of the Board of Trustees asked if we were trying to close the college by opposing the president's appointment of personnel. We saw our response differently. We witnessed those presidential decisions conflicting with the goals and objectives of the institution. We demanded a course correction—by organizing an underground group, Save HT—that placed sustained pressure on the president and board. When the board verified that the trajectory of the president's performance was off course, they made the necessary change.

FOREWORD

As one who participated in the struggle between the president and faculty for the direction of the institution (a challenge that led to the president's resignation), I want to offer some suggestions that might be of interest to readers of *Their Stories, Our Stories*:

- First, each chapter has spoken and implied lessons for the reader. These lessons might include presidential leadership style, goals for institutional outcomes, presidential-student and president-faculty relationships, and community engagement.
- Second, if you want to learn about behaviors and approaches to decision-making that promote presidential effectiveness, you might elect to read chapters 1 (King), 3 (Earvin), and 4 (Pierce Burnette).
- Third, if your focus is on financial stability and academic innovation, you might want to pay particular attention to chapters 3 and 4.
- Fourth, for growth and enhancement of community relationships, you might focus on chapter 4.
- Fifth, for approaches to effective decision-making during times of uncertainty, faculty, administrators, and students must apply insights on how to manage disruptors as allies, not as enemies to be isolated and defeated. This management approach is reflected under two presidents, Earvin and Pierce Burnette.
- Sixth, on the basis of what I observed and read in *Their Stories, Our Stories*, I conclude that what makes the greatest difference in their leadership, in terms of their decisions, temperament, focus, and accomplishments, lies in their background.
- Seventh, one general question to consider is this: How will this book benefit students, faculty, administrators, trustees, and communities not only at HT but other Historically Black Colleges and Universities (HBCUs)? A review of chapter 5 provides some insight.
- Eighth, analysis of external forces that influence HBCUs' financial stability and their future can be found in chapter 5.

Directly or indirectly, Professor Martin has given us challenges in framing research questions dealing with such issues as fiscal soundness and the quality of community relationships; patterns of presidential decision-making and the significance of the background variable; the predictive influence of faculty cohesiveness and administrative performance; and others. The research questions raised related to HT might help constituents at other HBCUs grappling with similar issues.

I believe that with this book, Professor Rosalee Martin has made a valuable contribution to the evolving rich history of Huston-Tillotson University on the Bluebonnet Hill of East Austin, and indirectly to that of other HBCUs.

Dr. Paul Anaejionu
Professor of Political Science, Huston-Tillotson University

Preface

Why I Wrote This Book

The question might be asked, "Why write a history of Huston-Tillotson University (HT) covering the years 1965 to 2022?" The simple answer is that so little was written about that period of HT's existence. Currently there are only a few volumes that describe HT history, of which one comprehensive work is *Reminiscences of Huston-Tillotson College* by Chrystine Shackles, who taught at HT for forty years.[1] Her book is a chronological account of Tillotson, and later Huston-Tillotson College, from 1928 to 1968. *Huston-Tillotson University Legacy: A Historical Treasure* (2007) is a publication prepared by alumni Dr. Wilhelmina Perry and Dr. Gus Swain for HT International Alumni. Perry and Swain's book is limited to alumni history, including information on faculty and staff only if they were also alumni. Dr. Bronté Jones's dissertation, "Restoring Accreditation in Two Private Texas Historically Black Colleges," focuses on Huston-Tillotson University and Texas College and, although valuable, provides only accreditation history.[2] A recent book, *The Abolitionist's Journal: Memories of an American Antislavery Family*, is the story of George Richardson, the founder of Samuel Huston College. Although that book devotes only a dozen pages to Huston-Tillotson, it provides environmental/social/historical context of the post–Civil War time. All four works are referenced throughout this book. Notwithstanding the works mentioned, there is no comprehensive history of HT written after 1968.

Another reason for writing this book was the awareness that I had a unique body of knowledge derived from fifty years of lived experience at HT; that knowledge should be formally documented. My experiences differed depending on the president: Dr. John Q. Taylor King, Dr. Joseph McMillan, Dr. Larry Earvin, or Dr. Colette Pierce Burnette. Therefore, I decided to explore HT's story through the tenures of those four presidents and through the lens of faculty, students, and alumni.[3] Some important historical voices had already been lost before I began this book, and I regret not having interviewed them. Staff perspective will be mostly missing, although the work they do is critical for the effective operation of HT. That will be a limitation of this research. I hope that someone from student affairs or other staff positions will write from their perspective. Only then will we see the true complexities and greatness of Huston-Tillotson College/University.

Goals and Objectives of Research

This research on HT required dedicated time and committed effort. Having one year's sabbatical, and with the assistance of those mentioned in the acknowledgments, I moved the project forward. Initially, I grappled with the recurring question: "What do you want the reader to know after having read your book?" This can be the most difficult aspect of a research project and in fact was the most important question for me to answer, as it determined how I designed interviews and surveys and analyzed documents. I knew that I did not want this to be simply an HT history book guided by timelines. I saw my work as a historical memoir over four presidencies, with their concomitant faculty and students. I initially thought I wanted readers to understand the importance of familial-type relationships at HT. This thought was not created in a vacuum but rather from face-to-face and telephone interviewees who inevitably said that HT had a family environment, which resulted in lifelong friendships, sometimes even marriages, and enduring lessons. Yet, many also highlighted that the lack of resources, inadequate facilities, and limited curriculum negatively impacted their view of HT.

These latter views changed what I wanted readers to get from the book. Although the sense of family was important, a more significant theme emerged, which was the relationship of HT's financial status to the stability of the institution. Consequently, two additional surveys were sent with questions about perceptions of HT's financial stability and, if perceived as secure, how respondents would like to see HT's resources used. The information gathered was vital for understanding the many presidential challenges related to students' academic success not only for HT but for most HBCUs facing financial challenges, some of which are related to limited governmental funding.[4] According to Edelman, "As early as 1890, many states refused to match federal funds provided to Black colleges, as required by law. This inequity persists today: a 2022 analysis by Forbes found that HBCUs have been underfunded by at least $12.8 billion over the last three decades compared to their predominantly white peers."[5]

Therefore, after much thought, I decided to focus on the following goals and objectives:

Goal 1: To write the history of HT through the lens of four presidents (Drs. King, McMillan, Earvin, and Pierce Burnette) and their respective faculty, students, and alumni during the years 1965–2022.
   a. Collect data about the four presidents and important constituent groups, primarily faculty and students/alumni under those presidents.[6] Data to be collected through interviews, surveys, and existing documents.
   b. Share my perspective as one who worked at HT for fifty years.

Goal 2: To uncover themes that emerged from respondents' data and to represent them as fully and accurately as possible.

Goal 3: To compare the four presidents in several areas including financial stability, accreditation, family environment, recruitment/retention, visibility, and others.

Goal 4: To examine HT as an HBCU by comparing HT with other HBCUs.
   a. Survey other HBCUs by email and in person at conferences.
   b. Analyze why HBCUs are in constant struggle for recognition and financial stability by using the "Success to the Successful" archetype.[7]

Goal 5: To render the research into a published book.
   a. Submit a proposal to, and be accepted by, a publisher.
   b. Sign a contract.
   c. Make requested edits toward a publishable manuscript.

Gathering Data for This Book

Originally, the research was to take place between June 2017 and December 2018. The time was extended to June 2022 because of Covid-19, and Dr. Pierce Burnette's June 30, 2022, retirement to include HT's Covid experience and Dr. Pierce Burnette's entire presidency. The book was submitted to the publisher in July 2022; I received comments from peer reviewers and the press acquisitions editor in January 2023. A revised document submitted for publication in July 2023 contained a few 2023 events.[8]

Personal Experience

As an author with lived experience at HT, I had to decide how to refer to myself in the book. Should I call myself "the researcher," or Dr. Martin, or use first-person nouns and pronouns? I decided to employ "I/me/my" as opposed to my formal title, Dr. Rosalee Martin, or "the researcher." I believe that rather than diminishing

PREFACE

the integrity of the work, this approach highlights the integral part I, as the person who was at HT the longest, played in its history. I recognized that my firsthand information is subjective, although often supported by objective, real-time data and documents.

Qualitative Data—Interviews

Qualitative data was gathered from faculty, staff, current students, and alumni in three ways. Two of these ways were in-depth face-to-face and phone interviews. I conducted fifty such interviews with alumni, current and former faculty, current and former staff, a former and current president, and former and current board members. I also interviewed community members such as ministers because of HT's historical connection to community leaders. Interviewees were identified in numerous ways: old employee lists, word of mouth, solicitation at class reunions, alumni associations, my contacts, Facebook, and other social media channels. All face-to-face and phone interviews were recorded by either audio or video. Not all respondents gave permission to be videotaped, so they were only audiotaped. All face-to-face interviewees signed a consent form that was needed to place their interviews into HT's archive. There were other people I would have liked to have interviewed who critically impacted a president's legacy but were unable to do so.

I was strategic in identifying face-to-face interviewees, as I wanted to include those persons who were most familiar with Dr. King's administration. My notion was that many of them were older and least adept at, or comfortable with, online surveys. Since Dr. King was deceased, I wanted to hear as many voices about him and his administration as possible. Key interviews were conducted with his children, Dr. Stuart King and Mrs. Marjon King Christopher. I sought out Dr. Lenora Waters, Dr. King's Vice President for Academic Affairs (VPAA), and Dr. McMillan's VPAA and later Senior Vice President. Retired at the time of the interviews, Mr. K. J. Buyers had multiple positions under both Dr. King and Dr. McMillan and was an important source.[9] Mr. Terry Smith, who was known on campus as its historian, was employed by Dr. King in 1987 and worked closely as a senior administrator for both Dr. McMillan and Dr. Earvin. Mr. Smith retired in July 2015, in the first year of Dr. Pierce Burnette's administration. His memories of dates, places, and experiences were invaluable, resulting in two interviews and many calls. I also interviewed Dr. Kathy Schwab, biologist, who after forty years of teaching at HT brought a unique perspective to the research.[10]

Another key interviewee was Dr. Bronté Jones. She was brought to HT by Dr. McMillan to fix the financial aid difficulties that HT was having with the federal government. I interviewed her by phone and included direct quotes from our conversation and her dissertation in this book. Dr. Jones was also a consultant to Dr. Earvin, providing him with extremely valuable information about the financial status of HT.

Critical perspectives were gained through face-to-face interviews with HT's current and past presidents. Three months prior to his death, I interviewed Dr. Joseph T. McMillan Jr., the fourth president of HT.[11] It might be the last interview he gave. At the time of that exchange, he agreed to any follow-up interviews needed, but when I called him to schedule such a follow-up, he informed me that he was in the hospital. He died five days later. At an informal meeting prior to his death, he agreed to give his presidential papers to the HT Archives. However, that did not happen, nor did his adopted son give them to HT. The majority of documents used in this research came from my personal collection, later placed in HT Archives.

Dr. Larry Earvin, the fifth president of the merged college, now lives in Atlanta. I made multiple attempts to secure an interview with him to no avail. I had hoped that a visit to Atlanta might result in an interview with him, but it did not. Thus, my data on him consists of analysis of board reports and other written material, along with informant responses to surveys and my own experiences with him and his administration. I also had access to several *Rams* magazines that featured the presidential message, along with videos online.

The sixth president of HT, Dr. Colette Pierce Burnette, is also the first woman president to serve after the merger of Sam Huston and Tillotson. I interviewed her twice, believing that she was in a unique situation—a female sitting president. Additionally, when I served as the University Marshal, we had informal discussions between lineup and the procession on Charter Day, Honors Convocation, and commencements.[12] I also had access to her by text, email, and phone. A frequent user of social media platforms, Dr. Pierce Burnette had a large footprint containing her vision, beliefs, skills, and knowledge on Facebook, in newspaper and journal articles, and in podcasts and video interviews. These sources were used extensively.

I wanted to incorporate the voices of board members as well.[13] They constitute the presidents' bosses and influence HT through presidencies and policies. I interviewed Board President Jim George (an attorney), a key player discussed in McMillan's chapter, and Board President Albert Hawkins, who, along with other board members, hired Dr. Pierce Burnette. These were critical and important interviews.

Quantitative Data—Online Surveys

The responses from the face-to-face and phone interviews provided such valuable information that these answers were used to develop a series of tailored online surveys. I developed online surveys for the following constituent groups: students/alumni, faculty (current and former), staff (current and former), and board members (current and former). The initial tailored surveys were sent to ALL current students, faculty, and staff via HT email. Requests for HT alumni participation were made through mail from the alumni office, word of mouth, HT Alumni Facebook page, WhatsApp, Messenger, text messages, institutional activities on campus, and old student lists. I also invited respondents to forward the survey to their alumni friends and followers on their social media platforms.

The number of respondents to the initial comprehensive surveys were sixty-six students, ninety-nine alumni (they were given the same survey), twenty-eight faculty, twenty-two staff, and twelve board members. Two follow-up surveys were later developed yielding forty-one and 123 respondents, respectively. The follow-up surveys were sent to all potential respondents and not developed for each constituent group as were the initial surveys. These surveys were created to answer questions that were raised after analyzing the initial surveys.

Long before this book was conceived as a project, students in various HT classes conducted their own surveys during Dr. King's and Dr. McMillan's presidencies. These 1987 and 1992 surveys, designed by students for student respondents, provided me with valuable real-time information about academics, living arrangements, social life on campus, and other topics. Additionally, I looked at 2018 online survey data hosted by Niche that provides academic, campus, health and safety, housing, party scene, and student life and values information about many colleges and universities.[14] These data go back to 2011, covering Dr. Earvin's and Dr. Pierce Burnette's presidencies.

The platform I used for the online surveys was SurveyMonkey, which provides data analysis for the instruments administered through its platform. I chose to use both open-ended and closed-ended questions.[15] There were standard questions in all surveys as well as different questions tailored to the following categories: student/alumni, faculty, staff, board member, and community. Prior to sending the survey to potential participants, I sent them to a colleague for her input. As a safeguard, once a survey respondent completed the survey, the individual could not change answers.

SurveyMonkey analysis option allows for cross tabs between questions, such as comparing data according to the four presidents or comparing data between constituent groups. Its reports were able to list the responses of all participants on a given question, as well as saving individual responses, so that each participant's response to the entire survey was available for analysis.

Content Analysis

From June 2017 to 2022, I conducted content analyses on existing written material, e.g., board reports, yearbooks, bulletins, programs, newspaper articles, *Ram* magazines, letters and memos, etc., some found in Huston-Tillotson's archives and others found in my personal collection. Pictures and previous audio and videos were also collected from various HT offices. Written material was not available equally for all four presidents due to limited archival material, limited or no social media presence, and length of time as president. King did not have much access to social media; his work is written and found in HT Archives. McMillan used some social platforms, but mainly wrote letters, memos and articles for *Ram* magazines, most of which I collected and gave to the archives. Earvin's documents were generally written, but he had many online videos. Pierce Burnette used social media extensively, which material became the primary source for her chapter. I felt that when most sources of available data were used, enough information was sufficient for a comprehensive representation of each president.

Acknowledgments

THERE IS NO WAY THAT I COULD HAVE CONDUCTED THIS EXTENsive project on Huston-Tillotson University (HT) by myself.¹ Although it was twenty-one years in the making, it was only in the last six years that it became a priority. During that time, it was clear to me that authoring this book was my final way of honoring the great institution to which I committed fifty years of my professional life. Coming to and remaining at Huston-Tillotson University was an act of obedience to God's calling on my life; the research and this book are the final phase of that calling. Thus, my overwhelming acknowledgment first goes to my Lord and Savior, Jesus Christ, for He not only called me but sustained me through many challenging times at HT.

Dr. John Q. Taylor King (1965–1988) was the first president with whom I worked.² It was during his 23-year presidency, and with funds secured from United Negro College Fund (UNCF), that I received my PhD. I am grateful to Dr. John Q. Taylor King's son, Mr. Stuart King, and his daughter, Mrs. Marjon King Christopher, for firsthand information about their deceased father.³ They enhanced my understanding of his vision, motivation, and love for HT. Most of the documents on him came from the HT Archives. He was not a president during the era of social media, thus no emails, Facebook, or LinkedIn.

Thanks to Dr. McMillan (1988–2000), who gave me an interview three months prior to his death.⁴ Our varied interactions, although sometimes disagreeable, helped to mold me into the strong warrior that I am. I knew that I would write about his presidency and, therefore, kept most documents related to him and his presidency.

Although Dr. Larry Earvin (2000–2015) did not agree to an interview, I'm thankful to him for the many articles he wrote and videos he made regarding HT that were available for this research.

My thanks to President Colette Pierce Burnette (2015–2022) who approved my sabbatical leave for 2017–2018. This research could not have been done without that leave. As the immediate past president of HT, Dr. Pierce Burnette allowed me to interview her twice and to contact her through text and email.

Thanks to my HT colleagues and those who helped me flesh out my thoughts and assisted with editing this document. They are:

- Dr. Paul Anaejionu, tenured professor of political science: We were not only colleagues but friends who were bound by our mutual struggle to keep HT open. His interest in research methodologies and statistical knowledge buttressed the help he gave me. More important, we spent hours talking about each president, as he too worked under each of them, and was the first to read my draft. He provided invaluable information and support throughout the process. He wrote the foreword to this volume.
- Mrs. Harriet Buxkemper, now deceased, and her daughter, Alexa, an HT alum (2000), were in the trenches when our beloved institution looked like it was failing.[5] Mrs. Buxkemper's letters live after her death; her daughter gave me permission to include them in this document.
- Dr. Theodore Francis, professor of history, helped me to think through the questions that would undergird this research.[6] He also shared his knowledge on oral history techniques.
- Dr. Alaine Hutson, professor of history, taught a class on historical research and shared with me some of those methodologies.
- Dr. Juli Fellows pored over my rough drafts, making suggestions and corrections to the early document. She deemed editing my work "an act of love." I am profoundly grateful to her editing and encouragement.
- Dr. Yvette Wingate reviewed my draft for organization and readability. Thanks to her for valuable recommendations.
- Mrs. Betty Etier, although deceased at the writing of this book, taught at HT for thirty-six years.[7] She taught on Friday and died on Sunday in 2016. It was her sudden death that motivated me to move my thinking about writing HT's history to doing it. Her unspoken stories made me realize that I needed to capture those of the living because of the uncertainties of life.

My thanks to specific alumni for their invaluable help. They include:

- Ms. Lillie Beth Jones ('11) who taught me how to develop an online survey using SurveyMonkey. With her help, I developed surveys for all HT constituents except for presidents.

- Ms. Tisha Christopher ('92) was the VP for HT's International Alumni Association and a past alumni representative to HT's Board of Trustees. She posted the student/alumni survey on its Facebook page. As a second-generation graduate (her daughter was a third-generation student at one time), Ms. Christopher spent countless hours sharing her perspectives, while also referencing the views of her father, Dr. Reginald Christopher.
- Ms. Devan Spence ('99), for not only being one of the interviewees but also for reviewing various drafts of my work. Our conversations resulted in a broader and deeper understanding of Dr. McMillan, the president she valued and under whom she matriculated.
- Ms. Tishana Lands ('92), for sharing her story about the UNCF incident and for giving her perspective on how to encourage alumni participation. Her relationship with Dr. McMillan is addressed in more detail in McMillan's chapter.

Finally, I am deeply grateful to New York University for providing me with a 2017 Summer Scholar-in-Residency where I got access to two consultants to assist me. Dr. Alton Borst, a curriculum specialist, and Mrs. Janet Bunde, NYU's head archivist, pushed me to think about my purpose and methodology. Mrs. Joan Dim, an author of NYU's history, also shared with me critical information about the networking, researching, and preparation needed prior to the first page being written.

My face-to-face participants provided exceptional information about their time at HT.[8] Although their interviews were extensive, with a few requiring two or three sessions, most of their names will not be mentioned in the book, but their sentiments are included. Thanks to each of you for your time and transparency.

Online survey participants provided such rich information; without their input and those of my interviewees, the findings of this research would be far different. All complete interviews and survey data are available in HT's archives for future research.

This major research project was completed without institutional funds. The following persons contributed financially to the project: attorney Jim George, former president of the Board of Trustees; Louis Henna, former Board Member, of Henna Chevrolet; Tammy Terry (alum, '84), federal bankruptcy attorney; Mrs. Carolyn Collins, a fellow member of my church[9]; and my church, David Chapel Missionary Baptist Church.

Their Stories, Our Stories

Prologue

Huston-Tillotson University Brief History Before 1965

THE INSTITUTION OF SLAVERY SYSTEMATICALLY DEPRIVED slaves of receiving formal education. Slaves, counted as three-fifths of a state's population as per an agreement reached during the 1787 US Constitutional Convention, were valued for their ability to increase their masters' economic wealth and political power, for sexual exploitation, and for their birthing of more slaves. White masters feared that an educated slave would be dangerous, as noted by Frederick Douglass in his autobiography.[1] Although not formally educated, many newly freed slaves had extraordinary skills due to their forced work ethic and passed those skills to the young. Formal education was needed and desired for the newly freed masses. During Reconstruction, many White religious leaders from established religious organizations were moved by the plight of newly freed slaves and their children. Educating them became a priority for these religious leaders—but not at already established White schools. It was within this environment of fresh wounds from slavery and systematically demeaning Blacks through societal oppressive policies and actions that Tillotson College and Sam Huston College found their Austin roots.[2]

Wanting to move south, George Jeffrey Tillotson of Connecticut had a vision to establish a school for "Negro" women who would educate "their kind."[3] A White former pastor affiliated with the American Missionary Association, he founded Tillotson Collegiate and Normal School in 1875 in Austin, Texas, twelve years after Emancipation and twenty-one years prior to legalized segregation embedded in *Plessy v. Ferguson* (1896). This first "Negro" school in Austin, Texas, was chartered in 1877 and the first 200 students were admitted in 1881, under the White leadership of Rev. William E. Brooks. The school was renamed in 1893 to simply "Tillotson." Dr. Isaac Agard changed the educational character of the institution from a collegiate and normal school to a college in 1909; a campus building is named after him. Mr. J. T. Hodges was appointed as the first Black president of Tillotson (1924–1930). Following him was the appointment of the first Black woman president, Ms. Mary E. Branch (1930–1944).[4] In 1925, this small, private, Black liberal arts college was recognized as a junior college by the State of Texas. In 1926 it became a women's college and then co-ed in 1935. In 1931 Tillotson became a senior college, receiving an "A" classification by the Southern Association of Colleges and Secondary Schools (SACS), an accreditation organization.[5] In 1946, under its last president prior to the merger—William H. Jones—student enrollment was 650 for the long session, and the faculty numbered thirty-five.[6] Tillotson had twelve presidents from 1881 to 1952, with only the last three being Black. The presidents held office from one to sixteen years, with the mean being 5.9 years.

Rev. George Warren Richardson, from a White abolitionist family in Minnesota, was the chaplain for a colored Union Army regiment posted in Memphis.[7] According to his great-great-grandson, James Richardson, George Richardson saw "his life mission as the salvation of African Americans from bondage, ignorance, poverty, sickness, and racial caste."[8] Fulfilling his mission, Richardson established a "Negro" school first in Dallas (1875) with the help of a Black pastor, Reverend Jeremiah Webster. In its first year the school was burned down by the KKK. Undeterred, both Richardson and Webster rebuilt the one-room schoolhouse. However, the City of Dallas did not want a 'Negro" school and created an examination process for the teachers guaranteeing their failure, justifying the closing of the school. Consequently, the school, affiliated with the Texas Conference of the United Methodist Church, was relocated to Austin in 1876 without Pastor Webster, who had died. The school, then named the West Texas Conference School, was opened at Wesley Chapel Methodist Episcopal Church in Austin, now Wesley United Methodist Church. Land was purchased in 1887 by Samuel Huston, at an estimated worth of $10,000, with the expectation that the school would bear his name. Years passed with minimal education offered due to insufficient funds. The school was later closed for a decade until the Methodist Freedmen's Aid Society found the money to reopen it.[9] In 1900, with a name change, the school was opened, with Reuben S. Lovinggood being its first Black president.[10] The school was on bush land and it took years to be cleared by students and staff, who later planted bluebonnets—thus came the name Bluebonnet Hill.[11] In 1910, the school was chartered as a private educational corporation under the laws of Texas. Within ten years, the school had nineteen teachers, 507 students, eighty-seven graduates, five buildings, and $87,000 worth of property. In 1926, Sam Huston was recognized as a Class A senior college by the Texas Department of Education. During that time it had football, baseball, track, tennis, and basketball teams, the same teams as now in 2024 except football. Occasionally, there is some nostalgia about not having a football team.

Renowned athlete Jackie Robinson lettered in four sports (football, basketball, track, and baseball) at UCLA in 1941. In 1944, the twelfth president of Samuel Huston, Karl E. Downs (1943–1948), asked Jackie Robinson to coach Samuel Huston's men basketball team. During his short time as basketball coach, the team was undefeated within the Southwestern Athletic Conference. Robinson left the college to play baseball with the Kansas City Monarchs baseball team, the most successful Negro league. Then in 1945, Robinson integrated Major League Baseball teams, breaking the color line when he signed with the Brooklyn Dodgers in 1945.[12] According to Linda Jackson, Robinson also served on the Board of Directors at Samuel Huston.[13]

During their individual and collective historical timelines, both Tillotson and Sam Huston were focused on their students, academic offerings, teachers, sports, and culture. Partially shaped by their religious traditions, the fact of Austin's segregated community also impacted life on HT. These two schools were located in East Austin. Ironically, in 1928 Austin City Council enacted a new Negro District in East Austin. The city forced all Black businesses, churches, schools, and families to relocate to East Austin to avoid duplication of schools and other services during the Jim Crow era. This ordinance was enforced with the threat of cutting off municipal utilities to Blacks who refused to move, meaning that African Americans choosing to remain in areas like Clarksville would not have access to city utilities like water and sanitation.

This recommendation would change the demographics of the entire city of Austin; by the 1940s almost all African Americans had relocated to East Austin.[14] Due to their East Austin location, neither Samuel Huston nor Tillotson had to move. Constituent groups in the college became a close family within the social mecca of the Black Austin community. Students were embraced by the East Austin community, often being "adopted" by Black families and Black churches. Referencing her first year (1928) at Sam Huston, Shackles stated that "there were a bond of friendship and love among the members of the faculty group so that we were a family unit on Bluebonnet Hill. This feeling of closeness and cordiality has maintained through the years."[15] Faculty members' closeness was reflected in the lives of their students. In a 1930 reference to students, Shackles stated, "We [faculty] see among them [students] a concern for those in the community who were less fortunate than them. Each year the students accompanied by some faculty members carried Thanksgiving baskets to the folk in the city."[16] One alumna's love for Samuel Huston can be seen in her poem:

We leave you truly with hearts bowed down
Because in you a friend we've found
Our hearts and thoughts will always be
With you until eternity

—Mrs. G. W. Norman (1930)[17]

The histories of Samuel Huston College and Tillotson College were parallel in their curricula, the majors they offered, and the importance of their instruction in moral values. Both had their origins in religious traditions, and both were in Austin. Both experienced periods of financial instability. Given these similarities, a discussion of merging the two institutions began in the 1940s, initiated by Dr. Fred L. Brownlee, Executive Secretary of the American Missionary Association of the Congregational Church, and Dr. I. Garland Penn, Secretary of the Methodist Board of Education.[18] In 1945 the trustees of Tillotson approved the proposal; the trustees of Samuel Huston suggested a joint committee to investigate its feasibility. Trustees of Samuel Huston College and Tillotson College met jointly on January 26, 1952, and agreed to merge the two institutions on the site of Tillotson College, Bluebonnet Hill.[19] The new Charter of Incorporation for Huston-Tillotson College was signed on October 24, 1952. The merged institutions adopted "In Union, Strength" as their motto.[20] Neither of the presidents from the former colleges was appointed as president; instead, Dr. Matthew S. Davage was chosen as interim president of the newly merged college. On September 1, 1955, Dr. John Jarvis Seabrook became the first permanent president of Huston-Tillotson College. Upon Seabrook's retirement in 1965, Dr. John Q. Taylor King Sr. was named the second permanent president.

Prior to his presidency, Dr. John Q. Taylor King summed up HT's history this way: "Huston-Tillotson College is a living example of the fact that 'In Union there is Strength.' The College[21] today is a tribute to those who 'labored in love' through the years so that we today might dream our dreams and have them come true tomorrow."[22] Two years later he added, "We must pause often to reflect and look from whence we have come. We must thank God for the wonderful and increasing blessings through which this institution has been led, for the blessings which she has been permitted to receive, and the blessings which she has been able to bestow. We must thank God for our glorious past and for the wonderful and exciting possibilities of the future. Each day we write the history of the College and each day the Divine Hand touches the pen."[23]

This brief history prepares us for the focus of this book, the continuation of HT's history through four presidents, beginning with Dr. John Q. Taylor King Sr.

Chapter 1

Dr. John Q. Taylor King Sr.

A Leader Extraordinaire

AT JUST 44 YEARS OLD, DR. JOHN Q TAYLOR KING SR. BECAME the third president of the merged Huston-Tillotson College. He was a giant of a man, prepared for a life of service on many fronts. At Huston-Tillotson College, we knew him as president (1965–1988). In United Methodism, they knew him as lay minister and chairman of the Committee on Higher Education. In the military he was known as a three-star lieutenant general. In the community he was known as a servant leader/humanitarian. In the funeral world he was known as a mortician. And in his family he was beloved as son, husband, father, uncle, and cousin. King was more than his education, more than his accomplishments, more than his relationship with others: he was who he was because of the faith he embraced. A life well lived can be more fully understood through the lens of King's own words, which will be sprinkled throughout this chapter.

CHAPTER I

Who Is Dr. John Q. Taylor King?

A family man, Dr. King was born to John Quill Taylor, MD, and Alice Clinton Woodson Taylor on September 25, 1921, in Memphis, Tennessee. His father was an ear, nose, and throat specialist who was in the "Negro" 368th Infantry Regiment where he experienced the harsh reality of military segregation. Dr. Taylor died young from complications of being gassed in France during World War I. King's mother, an elementary school teacher, later married Charles B. King Sr., an insurance executive. King and his older sister Edwina took their stepfather's surname because "he was the father I knew best."[1] The family moved to Austin, Texas, in 1933 and opened the King Funeral Home, now known as King-Tears Mortuary. King went to local Austin schools, Blackshear Elementary and L. C. Anderson High School, graduating at age 15.

In an interview with David Williams, King shared memories of his teen years at L. C. Anderson.

> The former Anderson High School was the second Anderson High School. The original Anderson High School was over on Pennsylvania Avenue where Kealing Middle School is now. There were, at that time, only two high schools in Austin. There was Austin High School and Anderson High School. Regardless to where African Americans lived, whether it was in Clarksville, which is West Austin, or South Austin, North Austin, or East Austin, when they graduated from junior high school, they went to Anderson High School. I mean the one over on Pennsylvania Avenue. That's where I started in the first year of high school. It was not called L. C. Anderson High School then, just called Anderson High School. People refer to it now as the Old Anderson High School. I don't put the "old" in front of it. I always say "the" Anderson High School because that was my school.
>
> I had very good teachers in all of my subjects, very, very good teachers. I learned a lot. One thing I must say about those teachers, if they thought that a student had the ability to do more than the student was doing, they would call the student in and sort of push the student. That's what they did to me. They said, "Now, you're not doing your best, and we know you can do better than you are doing. I'm sure you want to go to college," which I did want to go to college. "In order to get in college, you've got to have some good grades from high school, and not only that, but your college courses will also depend upon what you have learned through your education career, particularly in high school."
>
> I look back upon my English teachers, and they were just great. Miss A. M. Reed and Miss Frances Reeves, two of my great English teachers, taught me a

lot. And my math teacher, Mr. C. R. Stewart, taught me my first course in high school algebra, and Mrs. Countee taught me algebra, and then Mr. Pickard, Mr. M. L. Pickard, taught me general science. Mr. Stewart also taught me general science, but Mr. Pickard taught me the second part of general science, and then he taught me chemistry, and I learned a lot. Mr. T. C. Calhoun taught me geometry, and I learned a lot from them.

Not only did I learn academically from them, but I learned a lot from them because of their personalities. They tried to weave themselves into the lives of their students so that the students would see in them something important and sort of see them as role models. I did. I saw my teachers as role models. . . . I learned a lot. So when I graduated from the Anderson High School and went to Fisk University in Nashville, Tennessee, I was academically prepared because there were students at Fisk from the great high schools across the country, particularly the schools in Boston. You may remember they even referred to the schools in Boston as the Boston Latin schools. And the big schools in Chicago, schools in certain parts of upper state New York and in Cleveland and Philadelphia, as well as Atlanta and other places. So academically, I was prepared for college at Fisk University.

It was not only because of my high school teachers but because of my elementary school teachers. I learned how to build on what I had already developed. Elementary school prepared me for high school, and high school prepared me for college, and college prepared me for graduate school. So I pay in my own mind a deep debt of gratitude to all of my teachers but particularly to my high school teachers.[2]

In 2001, reflecting back to the closing of L. C. Anderson, Dr. King said:

I'd been out of high school for a very long time. I'd been out of college for a very long time. I had been in World War II, and I continued to serve in the Army Reserve. When it was announced that Anderson High School was going to be closed, I felt pretty badly about that because I felt it would have been much better had they put more emphasis on Anderson High School to try to encourage students from all over the city to come here. Say the magnet school concept. If this facility, this Anderson High School, had had the magnet concept, that would have encouraged young people from all across the city to come here and participate in the programs that were available. But they didn't do that. They closed the school and tried to scatter the kids across to the other schools which are around. I felt very badly about that.[3]

CHAPTER I

I found it incredible that at the age of 70, King remembered the names of his high school teachers; he did so because of the profound impact they had on him. King's experiences with great teachers, character-builders, provided him with an extraordinary foundation for future education and life choices. They were the forerunners of what he wanted the teachers at HT to be to their students. As president of HT, he expected no less.

After high school, King left Austin to go to Nashville to attend Fisk University following his family tradition. His mother and grandmother graduated from Fisk in 1872 and 1912, respectively. King met and later married (June 28, 1942) Marcet Alice Hines, a Fisk music major. The Fisk tradition was passed down to the Kings' three children, as three out of four, (John Quill Taylor King Jr., MD; Clinton Allen King, MD; Marjon Alicia King Christopher) graduated from Fisk. Stuart Hines King, the youngest, started there but graduated from Huston-Tillotson College during his father's presidency.

King recalls his grandmother's reflection on her education at Fisk. "'They [the teachers] taught us how to think, they taught us how to be proud, and how to conduct ourselves with dignity.' They were always true to their Christian commitment. When the Whites in Nashville spat upon them, they neither fought nor turned the other check. They walked away, straight-backed and with dignity."

After earning a BA at Fisk in 1941 and completing mortuary school, King received a BS in math in 1947 from Samuel Huston. In 1950 he completed an MS degree from DePaul University in Chicago. In 1957 he earned a PhD in mathematics and statistics from the University of Texas at Austin. King became a math teacher at Huston-Tillotson in 1947 and then a dean in 1960. He was promoted to president of Huston-Tillotson by the Board of Trustees on March 18, 1965. His wife, Marcet Hines King, also became an instructor at Samuel Huston in 1947, teaching music. In order to avoid the appearance of a conflict of interest, she was asked to resign by the Board of Trustees when her husband became president.[4]

King was raised in Wesley Chapel Methodist Episcopal Church, Austin, which later became Wesley United Methodist Church. Wesley was and is very important in the history of Huston-Tillotson, as Samuel Huston had its beginnings in the basement of that church. King followed the tradition of bringing HT's constituents to Wesley's annual College Day worship, and he would be the guest speaker. King served as a delegate to each of the General and Jurisdictional Conferences of the United Methodist Church from 1956 until 1988 and was the president of the General Council on Ministries of the United Methodist Church (the highest policymaking Board of Trustees of UMC) from 1972 to 1980. King was also the president of the United Methodist Black College Presidents. In his multiple governance roles, he encouraged the church leadership to support the twelve HBCUs organized by its conferences, including Huston-Tillotson which in 1978 received 7.8 percent of its budget from UMC. King was a frequent speaker at local, state, and national Methodist church activities as well as social and political functions with the intent to share the history of his beloved Huston-Tillotson and to raise desperately needed funds.

King was drafted into the segregated army in November 1942 (during WWII) as a private. He served as captain in the Pacific theater of operations and carried out duties in Alaska, Japan, Korea, Okinawa, Germany, Hawaii, and at many US posts. As a reservist King rose to the rank of three-star lieutenant general in 1985. In his early army days, King lived in two worlds, one segregated and another integrated. He understood that duality well. King recalled when he was assigned to an all-White unit in Utah that he was received as an individual with foreign extraction by his commanding officer, resulting in multiple dialogues about his color. The commander wanted to consider him as "colored," but King insisted on "Negro," as he remembered his grandmother telling him never to "pass" and never accept the racial designation of "colored." Having these racial encounters as a backdrop, King's elevation to the position of Special Assistant for Minority Affairs to the Chief, Office of Reserve Components, at the Pentagon in Washington, DC, was poetic justice. In that capacity he traveled throughout the world as a speaker and educator, often highlighting the achievements of Martin Luther King Jr. and elevating the position of Blacks.

Hal Drake interviewed Dr. King, then the highest-ranking Black reservist, on the topic of race. In that interview, Drake included these quotes from John King: "The army is 'way ahead' in breaking down racial fences. . . . It would take a war to force Black and White soldiers into total togetherness. . . . Unfortunately, only crisis situations draw people together." Maj. Gen. John Q. T. King further said, "People are drawn closer together because of the idea and the desire for survival. . . . I've been in combat situations, and there is a closeness which this brings in a realization that while gosh, I'm going to survive, I've got to depend on the other folk, and they've got to depend on me."

"That never lasts," said King. "When that abates, and that situation is no longer in existence, people sort of drift back into previous patterns of thought." Would it be the same during and after another war, asked Drake? "Right. And certainly, I don't want a combat situation or a crisis situation to develop to bring people together. I think it's terrible that we have to resort to those kinds of situations."[5]

CHAPTER I

Integration was in the forefront of King's life, but segregation shaped his existence. Although he could have passed as a member of several different ethnic groups, King knew who he was; he owned it and moved comfortably in his skin. Experiencing segregated Austin as it was transforming to a more inclusive society and seeing the remnants of Jim Crow in every institution, King had a heavy heart for his community, society, and the nation, recognizing the need for change. A humanitarian concerned about all aspects of human life, King's keynote speech at the 48th Annual Forum on Social Welfare held in Mississippi was titled "To Serve the Future Hour." King wanted action to replace words, action that changed the quality of life for the masses. This 1975 speech could well be one spoken in 2023 and certainly contains a blueprint for change in current US politics:

> Change is the modus operandi, the "order of the day" of our world. The striking fact of the twentieth century is that more aspects of the future of humankind lie in the hands of people than ever before. People have arrested the spread of many potent diseases, created the capability to destroy the world, discovered methods and resources for increasing our full potential, and are working yet to control the rain.
>
> The thorny question is where we as a nation will place our priorities. We will have priorities, whether they are by public *choice* or by public *apathy*. What will we do about conflicts between energy conservation and individual growth? What will we do with social welfare and where on the ladder of expenses will apply? Social policymakers are increasingly recognizing that society pays for people's lack of access to services at one end of the age spectrum or the other. That is, those who are permitted to suffer malnutrition as babies will cost society in one of several ways: the most basic is the loss of adult potential, which is loss of human resources, but also society has to bear the cost of supporting, training, institutionalizing, and providing for the lack of access, which should have been offered during childhood. Malnutrition during childhood can result in early old age, crippled physical disorders, and many other debilitating conditions. Thus, society is obligated to provide for those who cannot or will not provide for themselves.
>
> I read in a recent issue of *U.S. News & World Report* the following lines which I quote: "Becoming Americanized has resulted in much of the strain, harassment, and devaluation of human life in the last two decades." This is a tremendous indictment against an effort purported to make humans' existence more real, more meaningful, and more satisfying. . . . No wonder then that we speak of

this as a "time of crisis!" It is a dangerous time! But a time of crisis is also a time of opportunity! Out of sickness can come health! Out of a world catastrophe can come progress towards human betterment.

Our country today has no lack of challenges. The list is long and frightening. It includes inflation, foreign competition, unsatisfactory productivity, urban rebuilding, minority opportunities, pollution control, and many other things. We no longer enjoy the technological edge over the advanced countries. Now we must decide whether or not this is important! We must rethink the social responsibilities of the business community. We must all work ever so much harder to create a climate of understanding, a climate of encouragement, a climate of confidence, and a climate of growth so that there will be expansions of job opportunities for the millions of new workers who are entering the labor force; so that there will be useful jobs at useful wages, useful products at fair prices, and earnings from business which will pay its proper share of taxes and still pay adequate dividends to investors, large and small. The entire educational program—K through college—must be revamped in order to provide the kind of training necessary to meet the challenges in the age of scarcity.[6]

Bestowed Honors

A true Renaissance man, Dr. John King was awarded honorary doctorate degrees by Southwestern University (Doctor of Laws, 1970), St. Edwards University (Doctor of Laws, 1976), Austin College (Doctor of Humane Letters, 1978), Fisk University (Doctor of Humane Letters, 1980), and Huston-Tillotson College (Doctor of Science, 1988). He was given honorary citations from such organizations as the National Conference of Christians and Jews; the Distinguished Service Award from Texas Lutheran College; the Roy Wilkins Meritorious Award from the NAACP; the Arthur B. DeWitty Award from the NAACP; the Martin Luther King Jr. Humanitarian Award; the Frederick D. Patterson Award; the Minority Advocate of the Year Award from the Austin Chamber of Commerce; the Military Education Award from the San Antonio League of the National Association of Business and Professional Women's Clubs, Inc.; the Whitney M. Young Jr. Award from the Austin Area Urban League; the 1990 Distinguished Alumnus Award from the University of Texas at Austin; the 1991 Philanthropist of the Year in Austin Award from the National Society of Fundraising Executives, Austin Chapter; the 1994 Man of the Year Award from the Independent Funeral Directors of Texas, Inc.; and many more. Huston-Tillotson's King-Seabrook Chapel, built under his presidency, is named after the institution's second and third presidents, a personal and family honor he accepted with deep gratitude.

Dr. King's educational contributions included authoring several books: *Silhouettes of Life* (on J. Mason Brewer) and, with his wife, *Stories of Twenty-Three Famous Negro Americans* (1967) and *Famous Black Americans* (1975). He authored a booklet, *Mary McLeod Bethune: A Woman of Vision and Distinction* (1977), published by the United Methodist Church. He collaborated on four textbooks on mathematics. Dr. King also contributed a number of articles to professional and religious journals.

Dr. John Q. Taylor King's Appointment

King became HT's third president one year following the Civil Rights Acts of 1964, in the year of the Voting Right Act of 1965, both signed into law by President Lyndon B. Johnson. The first law outlawed discrimination based upon race, color, religion, sex, or national origin, and the second made voters' poll taxes and grandfather clauses unconstitutional. Laws are not easily or readily implemented; therefore, during the beginning and throughout much of King's presidency, some form of discrimination existed against Blacks in the Austin community. Furthermore, King became president only thirteen years after the merger of Samuel Huston and Tillotson Colleges in 1952.

As he rose up through the ranks to become president, his peers became his subordinates, but their long-term supportive relationships made it easy for them to embrace King as their leader and were conducive to student and institutional success. King understood the roles and value of each constituent group and readily engaged many in his administration. As is detailed earlier, King experienced great teachers himself and knew that's what he wanted for his students. The discipline he gained from the military, business knowhow from family, academic experience as a professor, and deep religious ethics all prepared him for becoming the president of the religious affiliated institution, Huston-Tillotson.

As a heart and mind educator, King was a dignified man who drew allegiance not by threat or aggression but by his gentle spirit, his reverence for history, and his sense of purpose.[7] His presidency was privileged by having distinguished alumni and professors that maintained their connections to HT during his administration. Listed below are only a few of those alumni; far more are included in *Huston-Tillotson University Legacy: A Historical Treasure*.[8] Providing the names of inherited alumni and faculty under every president is critical to demonstrate the quality of persons graduated and their multiple, diverse careers that might even include teaching at Huston-Tillotson. These are the backs administrations are built on.

Inherited Distinguished Alumni and Faculty[9]

- Charles Akins ('54) was respected in the Austin community after his serving in the Austin Independent School District as classroom teacher, coach, dean of students, principal of Anderson High School, and district-wide administrator.[10] Akins was deeply involved in the controversial Austin school desegregation in the 1970s. He retired from AISD in 1984. Later, W. C. Akins High School (Austin) was named in his honor.[11] He was active in Wesley United Methodist Church, Austin, and worked closely with HT on many levels through his church and his personal efforts. He also served in, and retired from, the military.
- Ada Anderson ('41) graduated from Tillotson College under President Mary Branch.[12] She was a civic leader and philanthropist who was highly acclaimed for her civil rights work. In 1951, she became co-owner of the real estate and insurance firm Anderson-Wormley with her husband, Andy Anderson. In 1953 she co-founded the Austin chapter of Jack and Jill of America, a social and recreational civic organization for youth, and worked as both a National Corresponding Secretary and as its South-Central Regional Director. She is a lifelong member of Alpha Kappa Alpha (AKA) sorority. During President Larry Earvin's administration, Ms. Anderson gave HT $3,000,000 towards the Sandra Joy Anderson Community Health and Wellness Center located on HT's campus. The center was opened under President Pierce Burnette's administration in 2015. The health center, under the auspices of CommunityCare, provides the East Austin community with access to health care.
- Dr. Herman A. Barnett III ('49, Biology) went to Austin public schools and to Sam Huston for a biology degree after being a fighter pilot from 1944 to 1946. He was the first African American admitted to the University of Texas Medical School in Galveston in 1949 and was licensed to practice medicine in 1950.
- Maxine Kelly Boles ('44 Home Economics and Natural Sciences). After an illustrious teaching career, she was awarded an honorary doctoral degree from Huston-Tillotson in 1995, under McMillan. Boles gave HT more than $250,000.

- Dr. June H. Brewer ('53, English)[13] was among the first five African Americans admitted to the University of Texas (1950) after the landmark *Sweatt v. Painter* case opened the previously White-only university to African American students.[14] For thirty-five years she was professor of English at Huston-Tillotson under the presidencies of King and McMillan. For part of that time she was chairperson of the English department. Her commitment to her students was legendary, preparing students for graduate school entry exams and following them for academic success. When grants were not available, Brewer used her own money for student programs.
- Dr. Reginald Christopher ('60) was a retired serviceman, dentist, and director of alumni affairs at HT.[15] Dr. Christopher was an outspoken, loyal HT alum who authored descriptive articles in 1992 and 1999 in *NOKOA* (a Black-owned Austin newspaper) on the state of HT under Dr. McMillan. His love for and commitment to the success of HT was seen in the fact that Dr. Christopher encouraged his daughter and granddaughter to attend HT. Dr. Christopher was brother-in-law to Dr. John King's daughter, Marjon Christopher.
- E. E. Hill ('31) earned his bachelor of arts degree from Samuel Huston College. He was a WWII veteran who lived to be 109 years old. Mr. Hill enjoyed a prestigious career in education, beginning in 1931, resulting in a high school in Henderson, Texas, being named after him.
- Dr. Marvin Kimbrough ('52, English), a native Austinite, received her PhD from UT Austin while teaching at HT under President King.[16] She was an excellent French and English teacher, and her students held her in esteem because of her knowledge, skills, and genuine interest in their success. She introduced poetry chapbooks to her students, resulting in many students becoming serious poets. HT still hosts the annual Poetry on the Patio event that she started. Kimbrough was the recipient of numerous teacher excellence and poetry awards. Her poems have been published nationally and internationally. Her *On Writing Hat Poems* was animated by Francesca Talenti and screened at the Guggenheim theater in New York.
- Willie Mae Kirk ('47) was recognized for her years of service to the community as a civil rights advocate, political activist, and library commissioner. The Oak Springs Branch Library (3101 Oak Springs Dr. in Austin) was renamed Willie Mae Kirk Library. She retired as an AISD teacher.

- Dr. Bertha Sadler Means ('45) married HT professor James Means in 1941 while she was still an HT student.[17] She was an entrepreneur (owner of Austin Cab Company) as well as an educator and philanthropist. She was one of the pioneers who fought segregation and was accepted into the University of Texas at Austin to earn her master's in education. She retired from the Austin Independent School District (AISD) and was awarded the W. Charles Akins African American Heritage Award in 2002 for her exemplary character, leadership, and community service. HT's Bertha Sadler Means African American Resource Center, located in the Anthony and Louise Viaer Administrative Building, was named in her honor for her generosity and support. Additionally, HT gave her an honorary doctorate.
- Dr. James Means (HT 1938–1980) taught mathematics and physics, headed the Department of Mathematics, and was chairman of the Physical Science Division during his 42-year tenure at HT.[18] He chaired or belonged to regional and national mathematics and science societies. He co-authored a college algebra textbook with Dr. King and published in the *American Mathematical Monthly*. Before the institutional merger, Means coached football, basketball, and track for Samuel Huston. He was elected president of the Gulf States Coast Athletic Conference. In 1991 Means was inducted into Huston-Tillotson College's Hall of Fame.
- Azie Taylor Morton ('56, Commercial Degree) was in the inaugural class of HT's merged institution. When she was a child in Dale, Texas, her family worked as sharecroppers. Despite not being blind, deaf, or an orphan, Taylor attended high school at the Texas Blind, Deaf and Orphan School because her home community didn't have a high school that would admit Blacks. After receiving her HT degree, she was refused admission to UT Austin ostensibly because she "was not prepared," but probably due to discriminatory policies.[19] After working at other jobs, including the Texas AFL-CIO, she later was invited to serve on President John F. Kennedy's Committee on Equal Employment Opportunity and did so for twenty years. From September 12, 1977, to January 20, 1981, Azie Morton-Taylor served as the 36th Treasurer of the United States under the Carter administration. Her signature was printed on US currency during her tenure in that position. She remains the only African American who held that office.[20] Upon retiring, she returned to HT to volunteer in various areas. Her daughter, Virgie Morton, has had three

positions at HT: at the bookstore 1999–2002, in the President's Office 2002–2019, and in the Provost Office, 2019 to the present.

- Dr. Wilhelmina Perry ('44, Sociology) was the daughter of a former HT dean.[21] She was a retired sociologist and Professor Emerita from Rowan University in southwestern New Jersey who also taught at Texas Southern University. After her retirement she volunteered at HT, working closely with the librarian to ensure that HT's legacy be told. As noted, Perry and Swain co-authored *Huston-Tillotson University Legacy: A Historical Treasure* Book (2007).

- Dr. Charles Urdy ('54, Chemistry) received his HT degree and then served in the army as a chemical laboratory staff member. In 1962, he received his PhD in chemistry and later became a professor at HT from 1972 to 1993, leaving HT to become manager of Environmental Science and Technology Development at the Lower Colorado River Authority (LCRA). Concurrently, from 1981 to 1993 he served on the Austin City Council as a way to move his civil rights agenda forward. He was the first chairperson of the Austin Revitalization Council and is Chairman Emeritus. Urdy was the recipient of numerous awards, including an honorary doctorate from HT in 1994, and the East 11th Street corridor was named the Dr. Charles E. Urdy Plaza.[22]

- Rev. Cecil Williams ('52, Sociology) was the organizer and is Pastor Emeritus of Glide Memorial United Methodist Church (1963–2000) in San Francisco, as well as community leader, author, lecturer, and spokesperson for the poor. Two of his brothers and a sister also graduated from HT. He was one of five African American graduates of Perkins School of Theology in Dallas (1955), and afterwards he co-founded the Council on Religion and the Homosexual in 1964. Political activist Angela Davis, members of the Black Panthers, and even Billy Graham spoke at council meetings. Glide Memorial UMC was the largest provider of social services in the San Francisco area, having the mission of being radically inclusive, just, and a loving community mobilized to alleviate suffering and break the circles of poverty and marginalization. Williams has been a Charter Day speaker at HT and has given back in many other ways.

- James Wilson ('57) was a faculty member, coach, and athletic director from 1960 to 2004.[23] He recalls having to be strategic in planning and transporting his students to basketball games, as in the earlier days they were not allowed to stay at hotels nor eat at many segregated restaurants.

Students and coaches stayed in family homes identified prior to traveling. Student athletes were recruiters and excellent representatives of the family quality of HT. Coach Wilson's sense of humor was legendary—sharing jokes was truly his gift. Even after retiring from HT, he was a referee for highly visible sports competitions.

Dr. King's Moral Compass

Integrity, humaneness, humility, and servant leadership were deeply ingrained in Dr. King's character and paramount to how he served HT. He used all his skills and knowledge that came from his varied life experience toward the execution of his role of president. This included his love for God. The following scriptures aptly described Dr. King as he lived according to God's will for his life.

> Jeremiah 29:11–13 (NIV) states: [11]"For I know the plans I have for you," declares the Lord, "plans to prosper you and not to harm you, plans to give you hope and a future. [12]Then you will call on me and come and pray to me, and I will listen to you. [13]You will seek me and find me when you seek me with all your heart."
> . . .
> Romans 8:28 (NIV): And we know that in all things God works for the good of those who love him, who have been called according to his purpose.

King's focus was on fulfilling God's plan for his life, which was to become the best possible leader of Huston-Tillotson, doing what was necessary to keep its doors open to educate both the minds and hearts of students through capable and competent teachers and programs. He was passionate about all that he did. In his March 11, 1970, report to the Board of Trustees, he reaffirmed his total commitment to Huston-Tillotson:

> When I joined this faculty in 1947, there was a romance between me and the College which has grown, matured, and developed into a deep love and affection. I am committed to this institution and am determined to work to the end that it will continue to grow and be a viable institution, making maximum contributions to the students it serves.[24]

His love for HT, dependence on God, and acknowledgment of his ancestors were always evident in his introductory comments in his reports to the Board of

Trustees. Below are excerpts from his November 3, 1979, report:

> Greetings: Huston-Tillotson College is in its hundred-fourth year of service to humanity—to the young people of the Austin community, the state of Texas, the nation, and the world! There have been years of devotion, of caring and sharing of faith in the now and in the tomorrow! The record is quite clear for thousands of young men and women; young women and people of all ages have had their minds stretched and their hearts warmed at this historic institution. The truly great men and women who have sacrificed, who have given their all to the mind-stretching and heart-warming experiences which students across the years have enjoyed, the unsung heroes whose memories should never fade. They made today possible, and that commitment should encourage all who are here now to make commitments so that tomorrow will surely come for Huston-Tillotson College. As your president, my commitment has been made and that commitment is renewed and strengthened each year. The renewal of that commitment accompanies my twenty-ninth report to the Board of Trustees, and I submitted it with great pleasure![25]

In this report, King provided the Board of Trustees with descriptions of events and activities of the school along with problems, primarily financial. However, he ended his report stating:

> No one contributes without the support of the family. I am grateful to my family for their love and understanding and support. Marcet, our four children and their families (which include four grandchildren), and mother, (who is now 88) and my sister and her family give me the encouragement and inspiration needed to go ever forward. But I owe much to God who gave them to me, for He is good, and His love will keep and sustain us and Huston-Tillotson College!

King loved his family, and likewise his second family, Huston-Tillotson College, now University. His love was manifested in his mission for HT as its president.

Dr. King's Mission / Vision

King's humanitarian viewpoints loom large in my contact with him and from the research gathered. He recognized that he came from a privileged background and used the biblical principle "to whom much is given, much is required" (Luke 12:48) to guide his life. Many of his actions indicated that his love for family extended to his HT family. These principled values influenced his leadership as president of Huston-Tillotson College. He saw himself as a team-building president. In March 1969 Board Report King stated:

> No administration can be successful without the assistance of cooperation of his colleagues. There must be teamwork if there is to be progress. We have developed the team approach to administration here and it is paying dividends. There will be no empires or little islands. Each administrator must assume his/her responsibility with commensurate authority and perform as a member of the team. I can assure the Board that we work within this framework. I congratulate my colleagues, and I commend each of them to the Board. They are a fine team, and we are growing together.[26]

King engaged his team in advancing his mission for HT. His vision and mission closely align with HT's mission. Dr. King's vision of education for HT can be found in his numerous undated papers.

> One of the major objectives of education should be to provide an atmosphere in which students can learn to think logically, to reason clearly, and to speak and write plainly and forcefully. In addition to having competent men and women, we must have leaders whose training extends beyond some specialty into the broad areas of human understanding contained in history, literature, and philosophy, and who can draw upon the great versatility of the human mind rather than capitalize upon the minutiae of some technicality. . . . We must create in our people the desire to become intellectually independent and mature; to be socially useful, informed, and conscious of matters outside the specific problem of earning a living, or [we] will have wasted the great educational opportunity which our theoretical ideals have created. . . . There is a vast and almost boundless store of unused human energy and versatility in our midst, the resources of which we have not begun to tap. Many people have potential abilities far beyond their meager development of intellect and skill. . . .[27]
>
> Huston-Tillotson is almost a hundred years old: it has served three generations of freedmen in their efforts toward self-discovery and in the struggle to make the American ideal real and meaningful for themselves and their children. Not only has it been the embodiment of that struggle and of the idealism and sacrifice of the many who have given their hearts and substance to it over the long hard years, but it—and the many institutions like it which we have come to

call the Predominantly Black College—have been a major vehicle of the struggle itself. When no other recourse was possible, when the doors of the common society remained fiercely closed, when no form of power—political, economic, or moral—was at hand to wage the battle for equal opportunity, education was the vehicle, the solitary slow and plodding train to the promised land. The source of our strength and the certainty of our purpose today lie not in ourselves, however, but in the example of those whose dreams and labors made Samuel Huston and Tillotson Colleges a reality . . . although they were founded to provide educational opportunities for Negroes, neither had clauses of exclusion in its charter. Similarly the charter of Huston-Tillotson College makes no references to such mundane irrelevances as race, creed, or ethnic origin of students, faculty, nor trustees. . . . The future of HT is bright! However, it is only as bright as you, the Church, will help it to be. If it reaches its true potential, you, the Church, must play a significant role in its further development. As its president, I commit my total self to this future and I call on each of you, Ministers and Laymen, to help me in this great task. You can help in many ways—tell others about the College and the good work which it is doing. Encourage more United Methodist young people to attend the College. Share your material resources with the College, especially through the KARL EVERETT DOWNS PROFESSORSHIP FUND. Pray for the College! God will answer prayers. Do these things and Huston-Tillotson College will have an eternal life.[28]

In a 1969 report to the Board, Dr. King wrote, "Huston-Tillotson College is a living example of the fact that 'In Union there is Strength.' The College today is a tribute to those who 'labored in love' through the years so that we today might dream our dreams and have them come true tomorrow."[29]

These excerpts from Dr. King's writings were embedded in Huston-Tillotson's mission statements, which guided institutional operations and activities. Although the language of the mission statements changed slightly during his presidency, their essence remained constant. Below are two mission statements in their entirety.

Mission Statements from the 1978–1980 College Bulletin:[30]

The mission of HT is to enhance the abilities of particularly African American and other minority students, to be critical thinkers, and to function successfully in society. It will be accomplished through a modified liberal arts curriculum which will provide for:

1. The development of understandings and skills.[31]
    a. In reading, oral/written communication and computation which are required to function successfully in society.
    b. For effective cognitive processing including comprehension, analysis, synthesis, evaluation, problem-solving and decision-making in a complex society.
    c. Which are required for the maintenance of a strong sense of personal development and personal control over one's life space.
    d. Which help persons develop ethical standards and spiritual awareness, thus enabling them to lead full productive lives.
    e. In human relations which promote satisfactory interpersonal relations.
    f. Which will permit one to engage in lifelong learning and to be gainfully employed.
    g. Which are required to function effectively in complex social organizations.
2. The development of an understanding and appreciation of the Black experience in America.
3. The development of an orientation toward the future which will permit one to operate effectively in society.

The purpose of Huston-Tillotson College is to provide varied undergraduate educational experiences such that individuals of various racial, national, and socioeconomic backgrounds can develop to full levels of maturity and maximize their human potential for scholarly achievement. The College operates on the assumption that education is an experience, not simply a body of data.

Huston-Tillotson College is an intellectual church-related community guided by Christian tradition and commitment. The curricular framework of this community is general education within a modified liberal arts structure.

The College assumes as its responsibility the promotion of liberal education within the framework of ethical and moral principles. It seeks to provide its students opportunities for intelligent and creative participations in contemporary living and to develop and maintain in its faculty and student body excellence in scholarship, character and self-expression.

Mission Statements from Multiple (1983–1987) College Bulletins:[32]

The Mission of Huston-Tillotson College is to provide educational opportunities to Black Americans and other ethnic groups who possess the desire and capabilities for achieving intellectual growth. The College has a special concern for students with high potential, some of whom may have been educationally, economically and/or socially disadvantaged. The educational experiences provided by the College seek to identify the strengths and weaknesses of individual students in order to encourage their highest achievements. Included in the broad educational experiences are programs and services designed to stimulate the total growth of students, including concern for their social, cultural, moral, and spiritual growth. The College seeks to provide opportunities for responsible and creative participation in community life and expects its students to excel.

This mission statement had an emphasis on educating Black Americans not only intellectually but holistically. Efforts to achieve this mission can be seen in educational programs, student activities, strong relationships, and institutional morale. Inadequate funds, low student enrollment, and institutional problems, however, sometimes lead to difficulties and conflicts, despite the mission statement.

Fulfilling Its Mission: Student Experiences Under His Leadership
King did what he did because of his hopes and dreams for young men and women. He reached out to all nationalities, diverse religious groups, and genders. His presidency boasted a higher international student body percentage than that of any president who proceeded him, at times with over 200 (31 percent) of the student body comprised of international students. He reached out to youth in the Gary Job Corps, a federally funded program. In fall 1980, Job Corps funded sixty-seven students to attend HT by paying for full tuition, room and board, books, and a stipend.[33] These youth came to the college three weeks into the semester, but faculty worked closely with them to get them up to speed in their classes. This investment in low-income students paid off by providing the foundation for one of the graduates to become a federal bankruptcy attorney, and others were equally successful.

Given the diversity of the student body and of faculty and staff, King's intention was to create an atmosphere conducive to social acceptance, caring, learning, and teaching. He frequently said that the heart was engaged with the mind. He was intentional in creating an environment where all students knew that they mattered from a holistic perspective.

Lacking today's numerous social media platforms, King's communications channels were limited. Still, he addressed students in the annual yearbooks and via letters to them and their family. Upon his appointment as president, his very first message went to the alumni and ex-students, highlighting their importance (only the first and last paragraphs are quoted here):

July 19, 1965

My Dear Friends

I am very pleased to greet you in my new assignment, which began officially on June 1, 1965. On March 18, 1965, the Trustees of our Alma Mater voted to entrust the destiny of the college to our joint care—yours, mine, theirs, with a real sense of trust being given to our students. This expression of confidence places upon us all a special responsibility to carry forward our mission on the level of the highest Christian purposes. The faith that has been placed in us and the growing enthusiasm for our work means that we must continually rededicate ourselves to our Christian educational objectives. . . .

As we said to our Board of Trustees, in my brief but honest and sincere statement of acceptance on March 18, 1965, "We must dream new dreams and translate these dreams to positive action." We are the architects of the future of Huston-Tillotson. With a real and genuine interest in our college, and with the abundance of Divine grace available to us, we can and we will participate in the exciting venture of making the Huston-Tillotson of today the College of tomorrow. May God continue to richly bless each of you.

Most sincerely yours,
John T. King
President

This letter also demonstrated his emphasis on the need to continue to seek excellence, the inevitability of change, and his awareness of the blessing of having a good faculty.

King's initial letter to his students was found in the 1965 yearbook:

October 28, 1965

My Dear Fellow Students:

It is a real pleasure to greet you. We have come together this year as in other years, to enjoy and to enrich Huston-Tillotson College. Life in this community is effective, rich, and varied. It provides a foundation for the development of Christian character, effective leadership and building of sound scholarship. You are a vital part of this community.

John T. King
President

CHAPTER I

In the 1967 yearbook, President King wrote this letter to students:[34]

> My Dear Fellow Students:
>
> Life has again granted me the marvelous privilege of greeting you through this medium. Through it we express our sincere appreciation to you for your continued loyalty and support in the program of education, by which you are given the chance to prepare yourselves for an active, fruitful life. Huston-Tillotson College is your college, which represents you in all things, and which you represent in all your areas of activity and endeavor. Since it is your college, I implore you to avail yourselves of its offerings, to support it in all ways as it continues to grow, develop, and succeed. It is through you, its students, that your college will live to be a monument to human progress.
>
> To those who have joined us this year for the first time, we welcome you into a family of friends; we charge you to cherish these familial bonds, and to return to us, bringing with you others to enlarge and enhance our family traditions.
>
> To all the students of Huston-Tillotson College, we enjoin you to continue with us in our search for the highest good obtainable, in our devotions to the cause of higher education, higher ethical and moral standards and stronger allegiance to those Christian principles by which we purport to live.
>
> Very sincerely yours,
John T. King
President

Dr. King's Effectiveness via Student Assessments

King was viewed with high esteem by faculty and staff. Yet, his effectiveness is best determined by the students who matriculated during his presidency. Although not all attribute credit for their success to King, credit given to faculty, staff, and the HT culture indirectly reflects his leadership.

During each graduation, the fiftieth-year class is also celebrated. Those alumni are asked to reflect on their experience at HT. In 2017, the class of 1967 provided their reflections of life at college under King's leadership.[35]

- "Mostly, I enjoyed meeting, living, and learning with classmates from other cities and states in a wholesome, constructive, and safe environment. These experiences and fond memories led us to forming our values, beginning our careers, and best of all, establishing lifelong friendships."

- "The other fond memory is of Dr. John King. When my twin sister and I lost our mother in 1963, Dr. King made it possible for us to receive a grant that enabled us to complete college. This is why I work so hard for HT."
- A student from Chicago remembers that he received a basketball scholarship and was picked up from the bus station by the coach who then took him to practice. He immediately felt the "love and bond of family. When one asks me what stands out in my mind about Huston-Tillotson it is a genuine feeling of family and caring."
- Another 1967 student, who met her life partner at HT and sent one of her three daughters to the college, said in 2017: "I thank HT for all of our college experiences that made us the compassionate, courageous, enthusiastic, fierce, optimistic, innovative, risk takers, determined, responsible adults with integrity that we became. We never forget Mrs. McCracken's statement that 'attitude equals altitude.' . . . Thank you, HT!!!"

Echoing the sentiments of the 1967 alums, thirty-three students, who attended HT during King's tenure as president, responded to an online survey I created and administered in 2017 and 2018.[36] In response to a question about their impressions of King, some of the responses included:

- He was very professional, intelligent, practical, personal, humble, kind, had tenacity, integrity and good work ethics.
- His preparation for leadership responsibilities were noted along with his business skills.
- He was student oriented, willing to listen and offer advice. He knew us by name. He was articular [sic] and progressive with a quiet dignity.
- He always was there and made each student feel a part of HT's close family environment.
- He was like a father figure.
- He had an open-door policy, not making students make an appointment.
- He donated his own resources to HT.
- He communicated well with students and expected students to do their best.
- Even though he was a general in the US Army, he was never a dictator.
- He was a people person but probably overextended.
- He was a master showman.

- He was always on TV to raise funds for HT.
- He was engaged in the community.
- He encouraged growth through recruitment programs and community involvement.
- He made me feel valuable.
- He was "one of the best!"
- He had too many strengths to mention.
- He created change with VIGOR and always had a smile and kind words.

Overall, these student respondents signaled that King led with authority and passion; he was a "top-notch professional" who was hands-on, leading by example. He created an environment to enhance students' involvement with each other and with other constituents. He was also perceived as candid, as he shared institutional problems and encouraged HT stakeholders to become part of the solution.[37] Alumni were urged to assist him in achieving the primary institutional goal of educating current students to become brilliant world shakers and powerful influencers in local, state, and national policies.

Some students also mentioned the HT staff and faculty who taught them during King's presidency.

- Staff and faculty were dedicated to helping students obtain a college degree and they worked to obtain financial assistance for students.
- Faculty was always available for mentoring.
- HT prepared me for the workforce with the federal government.
- Because I was immature coming out of high school, I needed the family atmosphere that HT offered. The constant support and encouragement were good for me.
- Dr. Arberenia Malone was my favorite professor and mentor.[38]
- The HT student life experience galvanized and fused lifetime personal relationships.
- Huston-Tillotson educated me so that I was able to gain employment and later get a master's degree and further my education with an educational administration which afforded me the privilege to teach.
- My educational experience prepared me to be an excellent teacher and served as a basis for my counseling job and finally an administrator who retired with 31 years of service.
- I was a Cooperative Education Student while at HT which laid the

foundation for a 36-year career with the federal government from which I recently retired.

Some students indicated that HT grew them from a child to an adult by instilling in them lifelong learning skills, compassion, and social justice concerns.

Face-to-face and phone interviews (2017) with alumni from King's era concurred with comments from the fiftieth-year class and the online surveys. A family of alumni had high praise of King, as indicated in my interviews with them. "He was highly respected and did an excellent job managing the college," said 1977 graduate, Billy Harden, a retired teacher, and high school principal, as well as a musician, actor, and director.[39] Two of Harden's siblings, a niece, and his mother graduated from HT. The latter, Ada Harden, a well-known Austin actor, public speaker, and educator had her first child at age 16. She returned to college as an older student, against the advice of her children. She ended up graduating with one of her daughters in 1978 and said that was "one of her proudest moments." She said, "Dr. King exemplified leadership; when he spoke, people would listen. Dr. King was 'an original' who knew everyone's family." She further stated that we "knew where he came from, knew his expectations, and he was sensitive to our needs. He had a lot of pride for HT, knew its history. Even though I didn't interact with him much, his presence was felt."[40]

A 1975 graduate said King was highly respected and did an excellent job managing the college. Most saw him as genuinely loving HT and its students. They would support the statement made by journalist Julie Hutchinson that "It is impossible to know where the college ends and King begins."[41]

In addition to these personal reflections of esteem, King's effectiveness is illuminated through alumni career and other accomplishments. Many graduates received advanced degrees in education, counseling, law, business, sociology, and others. Their careers range from licensed professional counselor to federal government bankruptcy attorney and included K–12 teachers and university professors, federal employee workers, and private business owners. Alumni volunteers, continuing the legacy of HT's emphasis on excellence and service, evinced their loyalty to HT and indirectly to King.

Although the online surveys and phone and face-to-face interviews indicated King had few weaknesses, the one that came up most frequently was that he was often not at HT. Others said that he was present and available—a matter of perspective. King addressed his absences this way: "There are those who, perhaps, feel that there is some conflict between duties at and responsibilities to the College, the military and various positions in the church. There is no conflict! HT comes first, others complement presidential duties. Valuable contacts for the College are made and the visibility of the College is enlarged."[42]

In response to the question "How did he deal with conflicts?" responses included "he talked to you"; "he listened and asked for solutions"; "he managed all problems and was objective, handling people with utmost respect"; "he made public addresses in open meetings." He was both kind and firm, while managing conflict in a personal and confidential manner with all persons involved. Many people said that they were not aware of conflicts or how he managed them.

These favorable attitudes about Dr. King existed despite students' major concerns regarding the institution that resulted in a student boycott in 1976.[43] During that weeklong boycott, students complained about issues related to education, business practices, and student-administration communication. More specifically, their complaints referenced dormitory repairs, the dining hall, recreation facilities, and campus security. King acknowledged problems, giving financial instability as reasons for institutional problems. Students in my 1988 Community class surveyed HT students on a wide variety of issues including academics, extracurricular activities, housing, and food issues.[44] One hundred thirty-six HT students from different majors responded to the class survey. These data, compared to the data collected in 2018, are "real time" rather than retrospective. There were forty-four multiple choice questions and nine open-ended questions. To each question students were to answer either poor, fair, average, good, excellent, or no comment.

The areas that had the highest "poor" responses were:

- laundry facilities (72 percent)
- food (68 percent)
- accessibility to telephones in the dorms (67 percent)
- dormitory facilities (58 percent)
- campus security (57 percent)
- school newsletter (55 percent)
- maintenance services (52 percent)
- campus social life (50 percent)
- involvement in Austin community (poor and fair totaling 68 percent).

For positive responses in that same survey, students said:

- course offerings were at least average (average (39 percent), good (14 percent), excellent (5 percent) with a total of 58 percent
- teaching methodology was at least 70 percent or above
- liked HT class size (68 percent) and generally liked assemblies
- indicated that student services (Learning Assistance Center, co-operative education, student placement, student emergency funds, etc.) each had 68 percent average or above
- responses to preparation for future employment yield an average or above of 59 percent
- students saw low involvement of faculty members outside the classroom but saw slightly above average in the area of communication among HT constituents.

The first open-ended question was, "What do you see as the strongest point of HTC?" The majority of the students said teachers—having concerned teachers, positive student/teacher relationship, faculty going out of their way to help students, a caring faculty, and professors taking time out after class to assist students. The second most frequent strength response was small classes. The second open-ended question was, "What are the weaknesses of HT?" Weaknesses identified were lack of student involvement, campus social life, low standards, long lines at registration, food, student apathy, student morale. A few students said everything was a weakness or too many to mention.

These perceived weaknesses do impact student retention. King identified student recruitment and retention as critical objectives for the financial health of Huston-Tillotson. The need for a strategic plan for HT recruitment and retention was seen in the up-and-down enrollment at the college, fluctuating primarily in the 500–600 range with one or two years in the 700s. In 1973 King organized a committee on recruitment and retention. Under his leadership an Office of Admission was organized, funded externally. During his 23-year presidency, tuition, room, and board were raised more than five times as a way of securing funds to improve education and students' outcomes.

Dr. King's Struggle with HT's Financial History
Securing Institutional Funds
King's presidency was plagued with underfunded programs, low faculty/staff salaries, fluctuating student enrollments, and limited student programming. King was an effective fundraiser for Huston-Tillotson, raising a little over $5 million,

but he still could not procure enough funds for non-restricted expenses. At one point when the college was in a precarious cash-flow position, he obtained a second-lien mortgage on his family home to meet the school's payroll.[45] King viewed himself as a "professional beggar" on behalf of the college.[46] In a 1985 *Austin American-Statesman* article, journalist Hutchinson stated, "Dr. King daily stalks the hearts and pocketbooks of a nationwide bounty of benefactors, aiming his solicitous arrows with shamelessly perfect marksmanship."[47] This statement described his entire presidency. His love for HT, along with his passionate desire to keep HT's doors open for future generations, placed him on a 23-year path to find funds for student services, curriculum building, securing and retaining competent professors/staff, and building and maintaining strong relationships with other institutions.

Huston-Tillotson College's funders included but were not limited to US government Title III annual funds,[48] Upward Bound (a pre-college program), TRIO,[49] Texas Educational Agency, NASA, United Methodist Church (a major source of income that fluctuated annually), United Church of Christ, and UNCF.[50] Lou Rawls telethon,[51] and individual philanthropists (including political leaders,[52] friends, businesspersons, and alumni). King traveled extensively to raise funds and to recruit students. He was creative in his "begging." He would take HT's choir to woo congregants and organizations; he brought along professors who would tell the HT story. He would take the best ambassadors of HT—its students—on fundraising trips. King would deliver powerful speeches to groups within the United Methodist Church and any organizations that would listen to him. He reached out to the Baptist Ministers Union for funding; some of its churches provide small scholarships. He met with heads of foundations and government leaders. He gave honorary doctorates to community and political leaders, including Senator Barbara Jordan, because of their humanitarian accomplishments and the potential for them to make large contributions (which didn't always happen). King pushed his administrative team, faculty, and staff to develop grants for curriculum building, faculty development, remodeling facilities, supplies, and other needed items. Large matching grants were won, requiring HT to provide equal funds or a combination of funds and/or in-kind services. Examples of matching grants are the Mellon and Ford Foundation grants. The Pilsen Education Foundation and others gave scholarship funds.

In 1966, the first full year of his presidency, King sought money to assist two students to go to Africa sponsored by the Methodist Board of Trustees of Education. The general Board of Trustees contributed $2,000, and HT helped the students raise the additional money.[53] In a 1971 Higher Education Report, King indicated that there was an urgent need for at least 100 four-year full scholarships, which at that time would be $950 each. According to him, "Our job is to educate these givers to comprehend the significance and importance of the specialized educational experiences that small Black colleges offer, and to persuade them that it is in their long-term interests to support Black colleges in more realistic terms."[54] Pitching the value of HT's current students and alumni was the basis of his message to businesses, organizations, religious communities, and other potential grantors. Students were his greatest asset in securing funds.

Although not all the above resources and funding existed throughout his presidency, these funding partners were very valuable in providing needed resources that the college could not provide. Always heavy on his heart, King did everything he could to make HT financially stable. Not having the use of the internet to the extent we have today, King relied on newspapers, word of mouth, and speeches to get HT's story out.

During King's tenure, Huston-Tillotson did not stand alone in its financial instability, as there were tier one universities that, in 1970, were in financial trouble as well. A Carnegie Commission engaged in a five-year study of American Higher Education.[55] In its December 1970 report, "The New Depression in Higher Education: A Study of Financial Conditions at 41 Colleges and Universities," colleges and universities were placed in three financial categories: "Not in Trouble," "Heading for Financial Trouble," and "In Financial Trouble." HT was among eleven institutions considered to be In Financial Trouble—also in this category were Boston College, New York University, Stanford University, University of California, Berkeley, and Tougaloo College, among others.[56]

Throughout his presidency, King pressed his Board of Trustees to establish multiple endowments. In his October 1969 Board of Trustees report he recommended that Huston-Tillotson engage in an "endowment campaign to acquire $10,000,000 over 5 years, plus annual gift grants of at least $200,000."[57] He stated at that time the need for a strong board developmental committee that would establish endowment building as a priority. This did not happen. In 1980, eleven years later, King reported to the Board of Trustees the purpose of such endowments: "The greatest need is for general endowment which will provide hard money—money to pay faculty salaries, utilities, library resources, material, instructional supplies, equipment and maintenance."[58] He asked each board member to contribute $1,000 to HT's nonrestrictive funds. King was perplexed as to why the Austin community did not support HT capital campaigns even when outstanding Austin personalities were part of the campaigns. He felt that he always had to justify the continued existence of HT and other HBCUs.

Each year continued to be financially challenging. In his March 1983 Board of Trustees report, King stated that he must be realistic: "These are difficult times for Huston-Tillotson College," as the financial condition for the college had not been "this precarious" at any other time of his presidency.[59] Even with some increase in funding, the levels had not kept up with inflation. On many occasions, King told the Board of Trustees that he "can't do this alone."

Under his leadership, in both 1970 and 1980, HT was reaccredited by the Southern Association of Colleges and Schools (SACS). In each case its reaccreditation carried with it numerous recommendations, many of which were related to HT's financial situation. The 1980 accreditation report recommended that faculty credentials and general curriculum be addressed. Still, HT's reaccreditation continued to raise a beacon of hope, as without accreditation the college would lose all government funding, student enrollment would decline, and the institution could even close, as was the case with other HBCUs that lost accreditation during this period.

King kept an eye on Texas and national legislation that might benefit or harm Huston-Tillotson. He visited Capitol Hill in Washington as well as the Texas Capitol to try to influence legislative outcomes. In 1971, King and other private higher educational institutions lobbied for the passage of two bills that originated in the Texas 62nd legislative session that would have positive outcomes for Huston-Tillotson.[60] One bill, known as the Tuition Equalization Grant (TEG), would provide direct grants, not to exceed $600 per student per year, based on need, to students electing to attend nonpublic institutions of higher education (this measure would increase enrollment).[61] It was approved in 1971, but appropriation for the bill was passed later. The second bill was a "contract bill" that would permit the state to contract with independent colleges for production of degrees and educational services, providing $1,000 for each bachelor's degree awarded to Texas residents, excluding degrees in religion and theology. Further information about this bill was not included in his archival records. Being able to package attractive financial aid for students increased enrollment, retention, and revenue. With more than 85 percent of the HT student body requiring some sort of financial aid, HT needed alternative sources of funding. Students who failed classes or did not complete their matriculation at HT resulted in high default rates on financial aid loans, which had a negative impact on the college and for providing adequate financial aid packages for future students. On several occasions, King informed the board about students who defaulted on their loans and asked for permission to hire a lawyer to secure loan payment to reduce HT's default rate. This request was granted.

In the November 1982 alumni news brochure, King told alums what they could do to help the college:[62]

> Love it, help portray it in a positive image, send your children, your relatives, and your friends to the College, help to recruit students, including some who do not need financial aid, and support the College with your financial resources.... Additionally, there are several ways you can support the institution as part of your legacy:
> 1. Give your home or other real property to the College as a bequest or as a "living gift," in which you retain live tenancy.[63]
> 2. Give a monetary gift and reserve the income from the principal for yourself or others, for the lifetime of the beneficiary or for a designated period.
> 3. Establish a "trust" to pay beneficiaries for a stated number of years or the duration of their lives with the remainder going to Huston-Tillotson College.
> 4. Make the College the beneficiary of a life insurance policy, in which case the premiums are tax deductible.

In 1985, the extremely poor financial status of Huston-Tillotson College might have been one reason for King's recommendation to his Board of Trustees that HT merge with Wiley and Texas Colleges, with the three colleges to be housed on Huston-Tillotson's campus. According to King, "It is your President's honest opinion that the Board of Trustees must vote for the merger under certain conditions. Merger is never easy! Everyone has to give up something in a merger; however, it is far better to merge in history than to die in history! It is much better to let the pages of history record the merge of an institution than the death of an institution!"[64] A second reason for his recommendation was based on the findings of a merger study funded by the United Methodist General Board of Trustees of Higher Education.[65] Those findings indicated that the financial needs of the three institutions could best be met if a merger occurred. Although the merger didn't happen, there was talk of merger for the remainder of King's time as president. The Board of Trustees of Wiley and Texas Colleges rejected the proposal; I was unable to find any record of HT's vote.

In his March 1987 board report, King told the trustees about changes in the guaranteed institutional funds for student financial aid.[66] He quoted from an article stating that the US Senate had inserted into its trade bill a provision allowing guaranteeing agencies to bar such institutions from the program.[67] Another person in the article stated, "Loss of federal student loan funds in most cases force an institution to close its doors." Furthermore, that article stated, "Students who would be hurt the most are the ones who have least access to education." In the same board report King noted, "Some trustees can remember when our default rate exceeded federal standards, and the College received no additional capital contributions because of it. The College must exercise care in implementing the GSL."[68] He urged the trustees to maintain serious concern about the student default rate. Dr. King summed up HT's financial health this way: "The College does not have a sufficient financial base. An inadequate endowment, insufficient annual gifts and grants, small enrollment, outstanding (uncollected) student accounts, unrealized income and unanticipated and/or unbudgeted expenditures contribute to the College's financial situation. . . . [T]he College must find additional stable sources of support."[69]

In a 1987 newspaper article, King asserted that HT survival was threatened by cash-flow problems linked to declining enrollment (520), federal cutbacks, and shrinking income from private donations.[70] Despite financial problems throughout his presidency, King's love for and allegiance to Huston-Tillotson College never wavered. Most years he created a family environment with high morale, overall acceptance of his leadership, and committed long-term faculty and staff. In a 1988 interview, King answered the question, "In your opinion, what makes Huston-Tillotson College unique?" by stating:

> I guess one of the unique things about this institution is its size, which provides for what we call a closeness of people. It's a small institution in terms of the number of people: it's small enough for everybody to get to know everybody else. We have had for many, many years the family concept, and I don't mean patriarchal type things. I'm talking about the family concept in its finest where people respect one another as human beings, one another as people of value and of worth. We have an excellent faculty. This College has a great school spirit, and I think that is the uniqueness of the small institution, and, particularly, the Historically Black College.[71]

Partnerships and Consortia[72]

Partnerships and consortia with other colleges and universities during King's tenure provided needed services and financial resources. These consortia included but were not limited to:

1. *Consortiums for Research Training (CRT)*, consisting of seven institutions—Clark College, Dillard University, Fisk University, LeMoyne College, Talladega College, Tougaloo, College, and HT—all HBCUs.[73] CRT had many goals, including but not limited to engaging both faculty and students in research that will serve to create a more stimulating academic climate on campus and to encourage the development of shared resources of the seven institutions. The programs were under the leadership of Fisk University's Amistad Research Center (1967).
2. *Texas Association of Developing Colleges*, incorporated in 1967, consisted of Bishop College, Jarvis Christian College, Huston-Tillotson College, Paul Quinn College, Texas College, and Wiley College. Today (2024) that association consists of Jarvis Christian College, Huston-Tillotson University, Paul Quinn College, Texas College, and Wiley College. Bishop College no longer exists.
3. *Cooperative arrangement with UT Austin*. HT's accrediting agency Southern Association of Colleges and Schools (SACS) required credentialed faculty (at least one professor with a PhD) in all majors offered by the college. In 1970, such was not the case for sociology and business administration and economics. To correct this deficiency, HT entered into a cooperative arrangement whereby UT would provide HT with two visiting professors, one in each area. . . .
4. *Texas Methodist Association*. HT and Wiley (1970) were the only two HBCUs affiliated with the association, which continues as of 2024 to support only these two. That association provided limited unrestricted funds to HT.
5. *Social Welfare Consortium*. Established in 1970, St. Edwards, UT-Austin, and HT formed a consortium in which HT students could take courses at both of the other institutions that would be transferred to HT. This relationship expanded HT's course offerings for students at no cost to HT.
6. *Consortium for Curriculum Change (CCC)*. Numerous HBCU faculty members participated in a six-week summer curriculum development training program resulting in manuals on many subjects such as writing across the curriculum. The curriculum of this training was broad and deep, highlighting teaching strategies for engaging both underprepared and prepared students.

The dedicated faculty who engaged in these trainings produced excellent academic documents but did not publish their work. Much of their strategies ended up in research papers of PWI professors. An ongoing discussion at HT was about the need to publish our work before usurped by others.

7. *Moton Development Consortium* assisted the college in doing some long-range thinking and planning and in developing basic data for a "case piece." The data were used in planning the Centennial Campaign (1975). Strategic planning was needed to better understand HT's assets and liabilities and best practices for managing them.
8. *College Industry Cluster* was established in 1975 to initiate, develop, and expand a cooperative relationship among colleges, universities, and business. Businesses such as IBM and Capital Metro spoke at business classes to provide mentoring and advice to students, allowing HT students to receive firsthand information and training from people in the field. Visits to companies and internships also strengthened the business program.
9. *Black Executive Exchange Program* (BEEP), organized in 1968–69, was a semester-long program supported by the National Urban League. "The program involved Black representatives from business, industry, and government. The program was designed to create opportunities for dialogue in an academic setting and between practitioners from the real work world, and students and faculty with current theoretical knowledge."[74]
10. *United Methodist Black Colleges Consortium*, renamed United Methodist Black College Fund (1972), comprised twelve HBCUs founded by the American Methodist Association (AMA). King was the president of this consortium for a period. UMC annually discussed the viability of continued support for the twelve colleges, floating the idea of eliminating some, recommending mergers for some, or even giving money to any colleges and universities that enrolled Black students. In his numerous capacities in the UMC organizational structure, King's was a consistent and forceful voice that encouraged the organization to continue, and even increase funding.[75]
11. *Austin Community College relationship*. In 1977, Dr. King allowed Austin Community College to hold classes at HT for a fee, reducing the space for HT classes. Although the money was needed, ACC was asked to leave in 1978.[76]

Although many of these consortia resulted in increased financial resources, some of them also created opportunities for improvements in academic curriculum and student success.

Huston-Tillotson's Faculty Held in Esteem

King was a professor at HT, later a dean, and then president, all of which roles made him sensitive to the needs of faculty. He appreciated the commitment of his faculty and encouraged longevity. King provided leadership to the academic deans who in turn provided faculty leadership. Yet, he was not a top-down president but interacted with faculty and staff freely. Still, his board report had little information about faculty, as the dean gave the faculty overview. In his March 1966 Board of Trustees report, King stated,

> We have a good faculty, but we must develop a better faculty . . . the recruitment and retention of a faculty of recognized professional and scholarly quality are a major concern for us. Our ability to attract students of high ability and to prepare them for significant contributions to their professions depends, to a large extent, upon the quality of faculty which we continue to attract and retain. We must increase our fringe benefits, especially concerning insurance. A plan which includes hospitalization and major medical coverage is an urgent need.[77]

King made this happen. As early as 1966, one year after his presidency began, he recommended to the trustees a tuition-free plan for sons and daughters of all college employees. Although this recommendation didn't have the same impact as a salary raise, that benefit, if used, would save employees thousands of dollars for their children's education.

Additionally, King never cut salaries, as did some of the other HBCU presidents, as a way to save money. However, as an economic measure, he instituted an increased faculty load to fifteen hours beginning in 1975–76. Faculty were asked to write letters when possible rather than use the phone, as long-distance calls cost more. During that academic year, to help manage expenses, King also recommended an increase in class size. Over the years he apprised his trustees of the need to raise salaries for current and potential new faculty even within HT's financial shortfall. He would inform the faculty that salary increases were merited but financial restraints prohibited those increases.

Faculty development was a vital concern to the college during King's tenure. Efforts were made to obtain financial assistance for additional faculty members to study each year: "We must meet the standards of the Southern Association of Colleges and Schools regarding quality of faculty and faculty improvement."[78] Early in his administration and throughout its duration, King understood that a well-trained faculty would help him achieve his goal of academic excellence. In the March 1967 Board of Trustees report, King indicated that Title III provided several members release time from part or all of their teaching assignments to pursue further study at the University of Texas. Faculty members also received foundation grants to use for study. For example, one faculty member received an Esso Education Foundation Faculty Fellowship that paid for half of his regular salary for one year, his tuition, cost of books, and incidentals. The inter-College Faculty Exchange Program allowed for professors to teach at different colleges.[79] In October 1967, eleven faculty were engaged in study, partially from a Ford Foundation grant for faculty development and Title III. Efforts were also made to provide funding for faculty to attend professional meetings. Some interviewed faculty stated that they received their doctorate during King's administration. I was one of them.

Faculty members who were interviewed and surveyed shared their insights about teaching at HT under King. Themes among those insights included: King was a highly professional academician who operated from a place of honor and dignity. He knew no stranger, was warm and accepting yet disciplined. He used a collaborative leadership style, delegating responsibilities when needed. A man of integrity, King was transparent with both bad and good news about the life of the college. Deeply rooted in historical knowledge, King encouraged institutional self-examination to improve students' outcomes and collegiate interactions. Faculty indicated that they looked up to King. Modeling after him, many professors readily made sacrifices for the institution. Faculty members did not note any weaknesses for King.

King believed that faculty members should be acknowledged for personal accomplishments and retirements. Faculty awards were noted, and their sponsoring professional student organizations were commended. The president and the Board of Trustees gave retirees a ceremony commemorating their longevity and contribution to the college. Despite low salaries, an atmosphere of trust fostering a strong relationship with his faculty often resulted in their staying and providing students with an excellent education. According to Dr. Lenora Waters, "Dr. King let you do your job because he had confidence in your ability. He had an open-door policy which built and strengthened relationships. He recognized that faculty could go anywhere, and deeply appreciated that they stayed at HT."[80] Waters saw him as transparent, warm, and gentle; he always promoted excellence. Dr. King would explain why a raise was not possible in such a way that hostility was not the result. Waters, VP for Academic Affairs, gave several examples of how faculty and staff had to put their personal life on hold to work on behalf of HT.

She and her husband (also an HT faculty member) had planned on going on vacation when King called her and told her he really needed her to assist him with a critical report. The couple postponed their vacation to help out. Waters said she did this without regret, because of who Dr. King was, a person committed to HT. In a similar vein, Coach Charles Dubra (a pianist and music major) accompanied Dr. King to churches to provide the music.[81] His connection with Dr. King went deep, retaining a relationship with him after King's retirement.

An education professor, responding to the online survey, stated the following about her time at Huston-Tillotson:

> I jumped at the opportunity to teach at HT (a smaller institution) to allow me to better mentor students over 4–6 semesters, assuring thoroughness of training to become effective classroom teachers. My prior teaching experiences at the University of Texas proved a tad disheartening due to the enormous class sizes and typically, I only taught students for 1 to 2 courses. At HT, I not only served as their course advisor but also as instructor and supervisor of student teachers. Also, this opportunity allowed me greater say in important decisions about curriculum and training. I laughingly warned my students, "If you don't like me, choose another major at HT, because to stay in this department we must totally trust each other." I stayed 27 years because I continued to learn so much from the students. . . . I LOVED IT! Teaching at HT is my proudest and favorite life-accomplishment beyond raising my three children and eight grandchildren. I highly value my continued friendships with colleagues and the lessons I learned being at HT. Of course I believe the Education Department was highly effective under Dr. Davies and Dr. Loredo's supervision. Both cared about high standards of academics and morality, personal attention to students, and building relations with other HBCU institutions as well as the flagship universities in Texas. I was always proud to represent HT at state and national conferences.

Teachers were central to keeping HT's legacy alive. Caring, committed, and prepared professors were integral to the academic success of students, a truth held by King. The positive aspects of education far outweighed the negative, and all students said that if they had it to do over again that they would go to HT. In fact, some reflect that their poor academic performance was due to their own lack of effort. The caring environment went beyond just academics. A faculty online survey participant stated, "[King] made sure that students who did not go home for Thanksgiving or Christmas holidays were not left on campus and often invited them to his own home to share his family's holiday dinner." At times some even stayed with him. This was true for many international students who had nowhere to go. Other faculty/staff members were encouraged to bring students into their homes when the dormitories were closed. Many HT employees readily did that.

Importance of Strong Curriculum

Not only were teaching style and professors' genuine commitment to education important, so was the curriculum they taught. Under King's administration, academics were divided into three divisions, each having many departments.

- Division of Education (Education and Kinesiology). Under King, the Education Department was the stellar department, educating and matriculating most of the Black teachers in Austin and surrounding areas.
- Division of Natural Sciences (biology, chemistry, physics, and mathematics); later the department of computer science was added.
- Division of Social Sciences (sociology, history, government, religious studies, social sciences, English, communication, music, business), which was the largest division. I was division chairperson from 1983 to 1999.

Survey results already highlighted indicate that students were prepared to pursue advanced and professional studies. The curriculum and professors who taught it were critical to students' success. Curriculum review and revision were ongoing, as was reviewing professors' credentials. Both were part of self-study evaluations and assessments, also done to maintain academic excellence.

King had specific ideas about curriculum. In his March 1971 article, "Serving the Disadvantaged," he said, "The most pressing need in curriculum is to focus upon some specific area of educational training not generally engaged in by larger colleges, or the more affluent state-supported institutions."[82] This statement refers to his goal of having a flagship curriculum that drew students. In that article, King highlighted the need to relax the rigid curriculum in place. He wrote, "Each department prescribes a set number of hours for a major. These hours need to be revisited." He further stated, "[A] student survey conducted by the Test and Guidance Office has revealed that a considerable number of our non-returning better students have repeatedly listed curriculum rigidity as one of the reasons for transferring to another college or university." King used the survey as partial justification for requesting faculty revision of the curriculum.

In 1980, King added a 3–2 engineering partnership with UT, where students studied at HT for three years and took their engineering courses at UT the final two years.[83] Five years later a similar partnership was created with Prairie View A&M. Later ROTC articulation agreements were made with both Prairie View A&M and with UT. Students who completed ROTC graduated as a lieutenant. Both the engineering and ROTC partnerships continue to this day.

Another valuable program created under King was Cooperative Education. This office provided students with paid and unpaid internships needed to reinforce academic program goals. Additionally, the office provided students with opportunities to apply principles and techniques learned in the classroom to real-life problems and problem-solving. The goals of the Office of Cooperative Education were switched to academic majors' internship courses after King's administration.

In 1974, a Guided Reading and Study Precepts Laboratory (GRASP) was established to meet the needs of students, faculty, and staff. It was operated under the Consortium for Curriculum Change (CCC) program in which interdisciplinary courses were developed and team-taught. Library cooperative agreements with other universities/colleges were established to enhance students' resources. This was important in the pre-computer era. HT also had TRIO pre-college programs.[84] TRIO is not an acronym; rather it then stood for three programs, Upward Bound, Talent Search, and Student Support Service. Upward Bound was a program for high school students from grades 10 to 12, ending with a pre-college summer program. Not all Upward Bound students matriculated at HT, but some did.

During the early 1970s, only Teacher Education and sociology had a course requiring students to do studies outside the classroom. Teacher Education required students to do practice teaching in public school systems. The sociology curriculum required students to complete 157 hours in a field placement/internship.[85] I, the sociology professor, allowed students to identify their vocational passion and then found agencies and supervisors who would simultaneously meet educational and students' goals. The internship became the course that most education and sociology majors looked forward to, as it either reinforced their career goals or helped them to redefine their goals based upon their experiential learning. Experiential learning and internships later became the norm for most HT majors, and under Presidents Earvin and Burnette an office of Career Services was created to assist all students to get paid and unpaid internships either as part of the major requirement or for personal development.

During King's presidency a new major in communication and a minor in art were created. The art minor had a studio for visual art production. Majors in gerontology and hotel and restaurant management were also created by special funding. Art and gerontology were dropped as minor/major when external funding ended. Hotel and restaurant management was dismantled by McMillan, the president who followed King. Communication had bouts of being dismantled and then reinstated in different formats. It is now a major.[86]

Occasional curriculum changes were made based on trends in the discipline, Texas educational codes, HT's multiple accrediting organizations, professors' specialties, workforce needs, and students' recommendations.[87] Regular evaluation of curriculum was standard practice; however, King noted that there were some territorial strongholds when it came to serious discussion about curriculum change.

Huston-Tillotson Continuing Education Department, using faculty's specialties, provided short-term courses, seminars, and workshops for community members. It also brokered agreements with UT Austin in the area of HIV education and programming.[88] Mrs. Gloria Black, the initial director, solicited my assistance to work with UT and Planned Parenthood to create, develop, and disseminate HIV materials to community partners. We did this by establishing Project REACH (Regional Education on AIDS for Community Health), a collaboration between Huston-Tillotson College and the University of Texas (1987–1990). Project REACH, in partnership with Planned Parenthood, existed from 1990 to December 1994 under Dr. McMillan's presidency. As the coordinator of this program, I trained HT students and community youth to be HIV peer educators. Some trained students were placed at Planned Parenthood and MH-MR (mental health organization) and other HIV/AIDS organizations for their internships. My extensive HIV/AIDS involvement continued under McMillan's presidency, but with less presidential support.

Student Activities, Dean of Student Affairs Office

Although this book is not intended to fully cover all the details of students' extracurricular activities, Huston-Tillotson offers more than just academic education. Much of the education that students received was outside the classroom and could be found in every aspect of the college, embedded within a family-like environment. Student "Organizations which stimulate the intellectual life, satisfy the spiritual life, or advance the social life of their members are encouraged. Participation in campus organization offers experiences in assuming responsibilities and leadership, in developing desirable character and personality in the pursuit of worthy goals."[89] Life on campus was important on many levels: Greek life; spiritual development; student life programming; interpersonal relationships; community involvement; athletics; and other campus activities.

Campus took on a different ambience during the time of induction into Greek system organizations. Students would walk across campus lined up, dressed alike, marching to the drum beat of the upperclassmen or women. It was not unusual to see the pledgees in outlandish costumes, like men dressed as babies in diapers holding their bottles and speaking in unison to orders given. Students' academic life was held at bay until they crossed over and became full-fledged members. These fraternities and sororities provided members with lifelong friendships and even marriage partners for some. The sororities were Alpha Kappa Alpha, Delta Sigma Theta, and Zeta Phi Beta. Fraternities were Kappa Alpha Psi Phi Beta Sigma, and Omega Psi Phi. There were other social groups on campus; many students who didn't pledge might participate in such groups as the Zodiac Club, Guys and Dolls, Distinguished Brothers, Chic 26, and the Superb Club. Some of these groups continue to exist today, although the rituals for induction have changed over time.

Students participated in academic and professional organizations such as the history club, Student National Education Association, College Choir, and Pre-Law Society. Additionally, many students who maintained a GPA of 3.3 or higher for at least five semesters participated in national honor societies such as the Kappa Xi chapter of Alpha Kappa Mu. A chapter of Beta Kappa Chi Honor Scientific Society was on campus. Phi Beta Lambda Honor Society drew memberships from Business Administration and Economics.[90]

Student Government Association (SGA) was an active organization that often had direct contact with the administration through its elected leaders. Every HT student is automatically a member of SGA and encouraged to become an active participant. The success of the SGA is correlated with the proportion of students' participation and the relationship of its leaders with key administrators. The greater the student support, the more likely students can influence institutional policies. Unfortunately, not enough students are active participants. This organization was, and still is, a visible force on campus and acts on behalf of students' welfare.

Athletic teams brought pride and support from faculty, students, staff, and administrators. In 1978, there were six competitive varsity groups on campus: men's basketball, women's basketball, women's track, men's baseball, tennis, and golf. Some athletes describe their team as forming their "family" and intimate connections. These team members are close to their coaches and to each other due to their frequent and intense contact before and after games. The HT Rams, or HT's Intercollegiate Athletic program, was and continues to be under the guidance of the National Association for Intercollegiate Athletics (NAIA).

During his tenure, King obtained funds for a part-time chaplain to address students, faculty, and staff spiritual needs. Often the chaplain did more than that as he worked with students during family crises and was the point person to be notified when death occurred within the HT community. The chaplain's position was funded by the United Methodist Church through a shared arrangement with UT Austin. Religious life provided reinforcement for HT's religious values for all constituents. Programming under religious life was far-reaching and established a worship day and time on HT's calendar when no other sponsored activities could occur. Additionally, students went on religious retreats and engaged in community service activities.

King realized that student life activities were extremely important for retention and recruitment. He established the position of Dean of Student Affairs, which had the primary responsibility of overseeing non-academic activities such as Ms. HT (popularity, issue-driven contest) and Miss UNCF (fundraising competition). The Dean of Student Affairs and other campus offices, along with student organizations, created and sponsored extracurricular programs. Campus programming included meetings, seminars, guest speakers, student step shows, cultural activities, and others. The real challenge was marshaling student participation at administrative and faculty-sponsored programs, while encouraging students to create and support their own social and educational programs. Even with numerous campus activities, students often complained that there was nothing to do on campus. This was (is) not always true, as many campus activities were sparsely populated. That Student Affairs Office also supervised dormitory employees responsible for managing students while in the dorms.

While students' concerns were taken seriously, financial restraints often posed barriers to meeting those concerns. Students sometimes resort to non-hostile protests with the goal of broadcasting their concerns. Some of the protesting students, now alumni, remember the conflicts as less significant than the family environment created by all constituents—president, faculty, staff, students, board members, and community.

Fostering HT as a Family

Under Dr. King's leadership, research suggests, most students, faculty, and staff viewed HT as a family. In the student/alumni survey, thirty-three alumni who matriculated under Dr. King provided remarks containing elements of what a family is expected to be—nurturing, caring, intimate, strong relationship, and character-building.[91] These elements are found in students' responses to such questions as: What do you want others to know about HT? In what ways HT is a family? Many students stated that other family members attended and encouraged them to matriculate; in some cases the student was a third-generation HT graduate. That fact alone demonstrates that for many families HT was trusted for the education it provided, and for the positive environment it fostered. Other students identified their fraternity/sorority and/or athletic team as family. Those groups provide students with an identity and lifelong friendships. Below are responses about HT's family environment from the online survey.[92]

- While at HT you develop lifelong friendships with both students and faculty. Whenever you step back on campus you feel the experience no matter how long ago it was.
- "It's a Family Affair"
- How I got along with people shows what kind of school HT was for me.
- My experience at HT was a wonderful experience. I met people that will be my friends forever. The classes were small and were conducive to my learning experience which helped me to get on the Dean's List. The parties were always so much fun. The students and faculty became more like family. I love HT.
- It was hard but worth it.
- I would like everyone to know that HT is more than an academic environment. The environment provided a safe place for me to grow and mature as an individual, without having to deal with the blessed burden of being an African American Young Woman. My Blackness was nurtured with love. My Womanly ways were groomed. And before I knew it, the child that arrived on campus left a grown ass woman prepared to take on the world. But what I did not realize at the time was how much I would be cheered on after I graduated. My HT cheering section continues to this day. And for that I am grateful. And for HT, I thank God.
- I had very smart, intelligent, caring, approachable instructors. Every adult made you their responsibility.
- I enjoyed the "small town" atmosphere. While I did not know everyone in town, there was always someone to "go to" for my concerns be they school-related or personal. I learned that it was my choice to ferret out who could assist me. While channels were not always specific, there was always a specific person who could assist me.
- I love HTU; however, [we] are going to have to think outside of the

> proverbial box in order to survive. We need to utilize our younger alumni sooner rather than later. I understand that younger alumni are setting up their careers, life, families and are often busy but they are also the wage earners, networkers, movers and shakers. Find a way to remember HT more.
>
> – My time at Huston-Tillotson I would not trade for anything in this world. I have developed true and dear relationships, some thru pledging Kappa Alpha Psi, and others who helped mode and shape the man I am today and to them I say, "thank you."

These online comments were similar to those in face-to-face interviews conducted for this study. Faculty and staff said remarkably similar things about the atmosphere and attitude of those involved at HT during King's administration. Although financial problems plagued his administration, most alumni selectively remembered the atmosphere created and the nurturing environment that existed.

Major Strengths and Accomplishments

Based on both my research and personal experience, King's major strengths were his availability and straightforwardness; he created an environment of respectability and excellence. His persistence was seen as strength, as he did what was necessary to keep HT's doors open; he solicited financial support and academic resources. Paying salaries was a priority, as for instance placing his house up for collateral to get funds to pay faculty and staff. Additionally, he supported faculty growth by funding faculty development via conferences and advanced degrees. His writing and his actions indicated that he wanted the best for his students and believed that a well-trained faculty was essential to reach that goal.

Another indicator of his dedication to student success is the success of alumni and their continued support of HT. As already mentioned from the surveys and interviews, alumni from King's era often credit their first degree from HT as the basis for future degrees and life careers. Many constituents perceived King's spiritual leadership as a key strength. King instilled in students, faculty, and staff a spiritual commitment through mandatory chapel and by modeling his spiritual life. His prayer at the Joint Dinner Meeting of the General Council on Ministries and the General Council on Finance and Administration, December 2, 1977, clearly highlights his spirituality.

> Most merciful God, our Heavenly Protector, we ask ourselves often, "What does a person possess?" It appears that one really possesses only the moments of time,

each called now, granted successively to each of us. In these moments one helps to create memories of the past and to build the hope of the future. We are here now creating memories of yesterdays and building hopes for the tomorrows.

We come to Thee now, as always, with our troubles and our sorrows, that we might find light for our darkness, assurance for our doubts, and peace for our souls. As we seek this light, give us the courage and faith to be Your people who we profess to be, and help us to find that light.... We bow our hearts and our lives before You now that we may rise to praise You. Coming to us is food. May this food nourish our bodies and may this occasion strengthen our lives. These are our prayers. It is!

Dr. John Q. Taylor King was a president extraordinaire. His love for Huston-Tillotson College was demonstrated throughout his twenty-three years as the CEO and president of the college from 1965 to 1988. He grew the institution by growing its faculty and making HT home for its students. He knew when it was time to pass the mantle of the office of presidency to the next president who could build on his legacy.

In 1988, King decided to step down, realizing that his time was up and wanting to spend more time with his family. In that same year, King and his wife Marcet received an honorary doctorate from HT. King was appointed chancellor and president emeritus of Huston-Tillotson. Later he continued his service to the college when he was named director and chairman of the Center for the Advancement of Science, Engineering, and Technology, a research branch of the college.[93] King was hailed by future presidents as one of the greatest presidents of Huston-Tillotson College/University. President Pierce Burnette had his picture in her office, along with that of President Mary Branch. His dedication to HT continued until his death in 2011.

His Story: Lessons from Dr. King's Presidency
Understanding HT as HBCU

HT is an HBCU, which fact alone has tremendous historical significance. King understood the powerful role that HBCUs have in educating Black students within a historical context.

> The private Black College has been one of the most, if not the most, important single factor in the progress of Black Americans since the Civil War. They have produced education where, at least at the beginning, there was none. In fact,

in the early days it was illegal in some Southern states to educate Black People. There is irony in the fact that this is recognition of the power of education and the fact that Black People could and would, if given the opportunity, seek the power that comes with the knowledge that education brings.[94]

King knew HBCUs and HT's story well. King knew that without HBCUs, the fate of Negroes/Colored/Blacks/African Americans would be vastly different and dismal.[95] Despite demeaning names given to Blacks over time, HBCUs gave students positive identity and regard, letting them know that in a family environment, they are valued and can succeed. During segregated America, African Americans could only attend HBCUs as they were institutionally denied entrance into predominantly White institutions (PWI). During the Jim Crow era, enrollment at HBCUs was not jeopardized by PWIs' enticing them to cross over. However, as more PWIs opened their doors to the best and brighter African American students, HBCUs had to change their mission, policies, and resources to attract those very students.

Transitioning: Segregation to Desegregation
King assumed presidency during an era when Jim Crow Laws were alive and well even though the Supreme Court struck down the separate but equal doctrine[96] in its 1954 *Brown v. Board of Education of Topeka*[97] decision, and President Lyndon Johnson signed the Civil Rights Act of 1964[98] which made discrimination against Blacks illegal. It is the "with all deliberate speed" of the Supreme Court decision that gave state and local school boards the ability to desegregate schools on their own timeline. This same principle operated for the implementation of the Civil Rights Act of 1964. Simply stated, states and cities felt no sense of urgency to enforce either desegregation edicts or nondiscrimination laws. Suits against Austin Independent School district in the 1970s and 1980s, in consequence, alleged failure to comply with desegregation guidelines.[99] In the center of these social forces for change, King had to guide HT through a maze of uncertainty and continuous discriminatory policies within the City of Austin. During King's presidency, segregation impacted where HT students could do their student teaching and be placed as certified teachers. Ambivalence about integration also existed during King's presidency as many believed that segregated schools better prepared Black students for their careers. Black schools were believed to be more nurturing, as mentioned by King about his education in all segregated schools.

King described his experience in Austin segregated Anderson High School in an interview with David Williams.[100] King graduated from the Old Anderson High School in Austin which eventually closed in 1971 as part of Austin's desegregation plan. He said he had great teachers who not only taught him academics but through their personal relationship kept them focused on goal setting and character building. He believed integration provided students with academic knowledge but often eroded students' self-esteem resulting in poor performance. The communities surrounding the Black public schools were extensions of the schools and our families. Teachers lived in our community; they knew our parents and went to our churches. Parents and teachers worked together to ensure student success. That condition did not exist when students were bused.

King's interview also provided insight as to why students who lived during segregation responded to education and educational opportunities differently from students who lived during desegregation. According to King,

> Parents then did not let their students go out as much as parents nowadays do, and there were not as many places to go then as there are places to go now. Parents were not well-traveled at that time, nor were the students well-traveled. Now, many of the students who begin high school have been places other than Austin or Travis County or even other than Texas. But so many of the students in my class, my first-year class of high school, had not been out of Austin, certainly had not been out of Travis County, to say nothing about going outside of the State of Texas. It's vastly different now. So the social atmosphere then is vastly different from the social atmosphere now.[101]

Like so many L. C. Anderson High School alumni, King felt unhappy about its closure in 1971. He believed that the school could have remained open if the desegregation plan included making it a magnet school which would have drawn people from across the city to want to participate in the programs at the school. Instead, they closed the school and sent students elsewhere; in many cases they were not welcomed nor wanted and were grossly mistreated.

Emergence of HIV Epidemic
Not limited to Austin, Texas, United States, but globally, HIV/AIDS came to the forefront shattering lives, families, communities, and nations. This infectious disease became conspicuous towards the latter part of King's presidency. It had to be addressed because the college was not an isolated entity but a micro community

reflecting its host community. One of the institution's music professors died from AIDS but due to stigma and shame the cause of death was not publicized. HIV was found disproportionately in the Black community among men who had sex with men and women who had sex with bisexual men. King supported a partnership with UT Austin to engage in HIV Education in the Austin community. It was during King's presidency that I began my journey as an HIV campus and community educator. His recognition of the severity of this problem was passed on to the next president to create policies, to provide resources, and to give support towards the reduction of HIV.

Chapter 2

Dr. Joseph T. McMillan Jr.

The Dash Between "I Love HT"

"I BEGAN MY REMARKS AT MY INAUGURAL CONVOCATION IN October of 1988 with the acclamation 'I love it!' I end my administration at Huston-Tillotson College (June 30, 2000) with the same acclamation: 'I love it!' Indeed, I do love Huston-Tillotson College," asserted Dr. Joseph T. McMillan in his final report to the Board of Trustees.[1] The dash in between the beginning and ending "I love it" reveals the personal and presidential Dr. Joseph T. McMillan's time at HT.[2] His dash at Huston-Tillotson contained an ebb and flow of ups and downs—at times steeped in divisions and conflicts and other times bursting with hope and expectations. He was endearing to some while held in low esteem by others, as if two men resided in a single body. I present the story of McMillan's dash with candidness and facts, sometimes from my personal perspective as I was both a recipient and a key player in forming part of McMillan's dash.

CHAPTER 2

Who Is Dr. Joseph T. McMillan Jr.?

The fourth president of Huston-Tillotson University, McMillan was born in Valdosta, Georgia, on July 19, 1944, the son of Rev. Joseph T. McMillan Sr., a minister in the African Methodist Episcopal Church (AME), and Olivia Cooper McMillan, a former teacher. Reverend McMillan Sr. moved his family every two to three years to assume new pastorates. As a result, the family lived in Georgia, Arkansas, and Florida. In reference to his family, McMillan said,

> I have never married, and I have no children. However, I am an active member of a rich tradition extended family of which I am very proud. I am the oldest of three children and the only son. My family is distinguished by its commitments, over several generations, to education and community service. My paternal grandfather was also a minister in the African Methodist Episcopal Church; my maternal grandfather was a farmer and active deacon in the local Baptist church. My paternal grandmother was a nurse and seamstress; my maternal grandmother was a homemaker. Most of my aunts and uncles, on both sides of the family, were teachers, businesspeople, and community leaders. I am very close to my family, playing the roles concurrently of a devoted son, brother, uncle, nephew, cousin, and heir-apparent to the patriarchy of the extended McMillan family. Additionally, I am a youth advisor at my church; and the Godfather, counselor, or confidant to the sons and daughters of many friends, neighbors, and members of our congregation, and to others.[3]

McMillan lived in and attended public schools throughout the South and graduated from New Stanton Senior High School of Jacksonville, Florida, in 1961. He received his bachelor of science degree from Howard University in 1965, with a major in psychology; his master of arts degree in Student Personnel Administration from Howard University in 1970; and the doctor of education degree in Higher Education Administration from Teachers College, Columbia University, in 1986. He also earned the Certificate in Educational Management from Harvard University during the summer of 1990.[4]

In the years between his BS and master's degree (1967 to 1970), McMillan worked as a residence hall counselor at Howard, at the time the youngest such employee at the institution. His involvement at Howard University, one of the best known and largest HBCUs, gave him the backdrop for his career moving forward. He left Howard to work in the denomination that became his faith tradition, the United Church of Christ (UCC). He worked at the United Church

Board for Homeland Ministries, holding the position of Secretary for Higher Education Relationships and Executive Secretary of the Council for Higher Education, from 1970 to 1988. In those capacities he directed the church's ministry in church-related higher education. He convened meetings of the presidents of all the thirty colleges related to UCC, of which six were HBCUs. It was in that position that McMillan became familiar with Huston-Tillotson as Tillotson was founded by the American Missionary Association, a precursor of the United Church of Christ.[5] Having both the United Methodist and the United Church of Christ connection, Huston-Tillotson had Board of Trustees members from both traditions. McMillan became a consultant to HT's board, representing UCC under the presidency of John Q. Taylor King. In fact, King worked closely with McMillan to secure additional funds from UCC.

During his time at HT, McMillan was the recipient of many honors. He received two honorary degrees: the Doctor of Letters degree, awarded by Yankton College in 1978, and the Doctor of Laws degree, awarded by Huston-Tillotson College in 1984 under King's presidency. He also received honors as the 1993 Outstanding Texan Award in Education from the Texas Legislative Black Caucus and the 1995 Whitney M. Young Jr. Award of the Austin Area Urban League.[6]

McMillan was active in civic, cultural, religious, and educational organizations throughout the nation. He was a trustee of the Pension Boards of the United Church of Christ, a member of the Board of Directors of the United Negro College Fund (UNCF) and of the Independent Colleges and Universities of Texas (ICUT), Secretary of the Council of Presidents of the United Methodist Church, and Chair of the Council for Higher Education of the United Church of Christ (1996–1999) and of the Board of Directors of the Texas Association of Developing Colleges (1993–1997). In Austin, he was a member of the Austin Regional Advisory Board of Chase Bank of Texas; a member of the Certification Advisory Council of the Texas Higher Education Coordinating Board; and a member of the Board of Directors of the Greater Austin Chamber of Commerce (1990–1993). He was a member of the Congregational Church of Austin and a Life Member of Alpha Phi Alpha Fraternity, Incorporated. In 1999 he served on the Mayor's Blue Ribbon Task Force to advise the Austin Independent School District in the election of its Superintendent of Schools.[7]

Dr. McMillan's Appointment

Dr. McMillan was nominated to be the fourth president of Huston-Tillotson College by Dr. John Q. Taylor King, with whom he had a good working relationship as an HT board member and a personal friend. According to King:

I could not be more delighted at this choice. In his current position, Joe McMillan has a deep familiarity with Huston-Tillotson College and has a historic linkage with Huston-Tillotson's roots and its traditional church sponsors. His experience as an advisor to the board uniquely equips him to understand the college, to lead and plan for its future.

Dr. McMillan has worked closely with all of the educational institutions related to the United Church of Christ and especially with the six Historically Black Colleges related to that denomination—Fisk University, LeMoyne-Owens College, Talladega College, Tougaloo College, Dillard University, and Huston-Tillotson College. I have the deepest respect for Dr. McMillan's intelligence, professionalism, and commitment.

Dr. McMillan brings to this office many important professional attributes. Some of these are: Significant administrative experience, dedication to the philosophy and mission of Historically Black Colleges, broad knowledge of the issues and trends in higher education, a commitment to the responsibilities of a small college of quality, the ability and commitment to communicate and work effectively with Huston-Tillotson College's constituencies, including a diverse student body, faculty, staff, trustees, alumni, as well as the local community, the general public, governmental agencies, accrediting agencies, foundations, corporations, and many other friends.

Finally, it is interesting to note that Dr. McMillan is the same age that I was when I was elected president of Huston-Tillotson College. He is the same age as our older son. His youth, his vitality, and his enthusiasm will be of utmost importance to the college as it continues to move forward![8]

McMillan's election by the board was unanimous, as were the recommendations of the Presidential Search Committee. His appointment might have been influenced by the fact that he was an HT board member, knew the fellow board members, and was the first United Church of Christ president. Commenting on the announcement, Board Chairman Edward B. Adams said:

Joe McMillan was selected because of his deep involvement with higher education, his familiarity with the history and challenges of the Historically Black College, his special familiarity with Huston-Tillotson College, his youth, his dynamism, and his personality.

We have found the person who can be the appropriate successor to John King. We feel confident Dr. McMillan will not only lead Huston-Tillotson College but will also take a leadership role in all aspects of Austin community life. I look forward to working with him for many years to come. Dr. McMillan's vision will shape the future of Huston-Tillotson into the twenty-first century and beyond.

King's children, Marjon Christopher and Stuart King, recalled their father's and McMillan's relationship.[9] "My dad and Dr. McMillan were close. When he came to Austin for board meetings, I would pick [Dr. McMillan] up from the airport," said Stuart King. "He would have meals with us and even occasionally spend the night with us," Stuart continued. "His sister and I were roommates at Fisk University even before I knew him," stated Marjon Christopher. "My dad felt good passing the reins of the college over to him," they both chimed in. "But things changed after [McMillan] became president." Those changes will be illustrated later in this chapter.

McMillan accepted the position of fourth president of HT and sent out a press release which is included here in its entirety:

> I am honored that the Board of Trustees of Huston-Tillotson College has elected me to succeed Dr. John Q. Taylor King as the next President of the College. I thank the Board of Trustees, individually and corporately, for the confidence and trust that you have bestowed upon me; and I ask your continued support and prayers for me and for Huston-Tillotson College.
>
> I express special appreciation to the Presidential Search Committee for their kind and efficient services throughout the process which culminates in my election today, notably: Mr. Edward B. Adams, Chairman of the Board of Trustees; Dr. Connie Yearwood Conner; and Dr. Frank H. Dietz. I also express special appreciation to Dr. and Mrs. John Q. Taylor King and family for their gracious and abiding hospitality and friendship.
>
> I am challenged by the opportunity to serve as President of Huston-Tillotson College, an institution related to the United Church of Christ and one with which I have worked closely during the past seventeen years of my service with the United Church Board for Homeland Ministries. I am doubly challenged by the fact that Huston-Tillotson College is also related to The United Methodist Church. As President of Huston-Tillotson College, I shall seek to continue and build upon the institution's commitments as a church related college which is affiliated with two historic Protestant churches, each with a long and proud tradition of support for quality higher education.

CHAPTER 2

I am challenged by the opportunity to serve as president of a Historically Black College at a time when the future of Historically Black Colleges is bleak and the challenges to their survival are great. Indeed, the challenges confronting Historically Black Colleges, including Huston-Tillotson College, are not significantly different than those which confront all small, independent colleges and universities in the United States. However, the special circumstances related to communicating the continuing mission and service of Historically Black Colleges, in general, and Huston-Tillotson College, in particular, are especially challenging during the modern, post–civil rights era, when many segments of our society believe that Historically Black Colleges are anachronisms of a past era or are inferior institutions which do not warrant public, church, corporate, or foundation support. As President of Huston-Tillotson College, I shall seek to build upon the Huston-Tillotson legacy to further establish an exciting and efficient model of a Historically Black College, in Texas, which instills continued pride and new appreciation for its mission and services, among the College family, the alumni, the Austin community and its civic leaders, the constituencies of The United Methodist Church and of the United Church of Christ, and among the friends of higher education, everywhere.

I am also challenged by the opportunity to provide new leadership for Huston-Tillotson College at a time when the College faces that fragile moment which many organizations, businesses, and institutions face at some point in their corporate life—the retirement of the chief executive officer. Indeed, the retirement of President John Q. Taylor King provides an appropriate moment for the institution to acknowledge and celebrate his great contributions to, and personal sacrifices for, Huston-Tillotson College. It is also a timely opportunity for the College to assess, to plan, and to renew for the future. I look forward to enabling Huston-Tillotson College to aspire to a renewed and new vision of its mission and purpose for the late twentieth century and for the rapidly approaching twenty-first century.

I invite the College and the broader community to review the President-Elect's outline of initial priorities and goals for the College, entitled, "A Renewed and New Vision for the Future of Huston-Tillotson College." ... Moreover, I invite comments, questions, and support for this vision and for the survival and growth of Huston-Tillotson College, with a renewed commitment to institutional integrity, sound fiscal operation, educational innovation, quality student development, and recommitment to its historic mission in ways that are appropriate for the new and coming day.

I accept these awesome challenges and responsibilities with excitement, with humility, and with abiding faith in God's purposes in my life. Again, I thank the Board of Trustees for the opportunity to serve Huston-Tillotson College in the capacity of President, effective July 1, 1988. I thank you each—members of the press, representatives of the Austin community, representatives of The United Methodist Church and of the United Church of Christ, members of the Huston-Tillotson College family, and friends of the College—for sharing this high moment in the history of Huston-Tillotson College and this most humbling moment in my personal life. May God bless you and Huston-Tillotson College and empower me for greater service to this venerable institution, to the Austin community, to our nation, to our global world.[10]

McMillan was thrilled to become the fourth president of Huston-Tillotson College. The presidency brought him power and prestige not experienced in his previous positions. He loved being in the spotlight, and as an excellent orator he was able to woo his audience. During the spring of 1988, between the announcement of his selection as president-elect and his assuming that position, McMillan commissioned a presidential chain and a college mace, the two formal pieces of academic regalia. The Presidential Chain of Office was dedicated to Dr. John Q. Taylor King Sr. on Saturday, October 22, 1988, at the Service of Investiture of Dr. McMillan; King placed the Presidential Chain of Office on McMillan. The mace was dedicated at the same time. McMillan provided this information in his inaugural program.

> The College Mace and Presidential Chain of Office continue a tradition in academia which has roots in ancient medieval universities. It is practiced today by most of the colleges and universities in America. The Mace symbolizes the heritage of the College and reaffirms the institution's commitments. It is carried in academic processions by the senior ranking member of the faculty and displayed throughout all formal programs of the College. The Chain of Office symbolizes the high office of the President and reaffirms the community's commitment to support the leader of the academic community. It is worn over the academic robe of the President of the College.
>
> Funds for the Mace and Chain came from fundraising specifically for that purpose. Both Dr. King and Dr. McMillan made contributions to it. Both the Mace and the Chain are made of sterling silver, partly gold plated and blue acrylic. Both symbolize disciplines of the academy, against two Texas Bluebonnets.[11]

CHAPTER 2

Having the most senior professor lead him into the investiture and being adorned with the Presidential Chain of Office gave McMillan pride at his perceived power and acclaim. Others, however, felt it represented arrogance. But after the pomp and circumstance, work must begin. He took his mandate to be a change agent. He came with ideas of where he wanted to take the college. Those ideas were noted in his inaugural address which was full of rhetoric, dreams, and commitment. Below is an excerpt from his address:

> Today we renew a covenant—a covenant with generations yet unborn—to spread knowledge, to seek truth, to build character, to teach skills, to instill a sense of wonder, and to encourage commitments of service to humankind. I reaffirm the covenant, an educational mission which was inherent in the founding of Samuel Huston College by the precursors of The United Methodist Church and of Tillotson College which was founded by the American Missionary Association of the Congregational Churches, one of the forerunners of the United Church of Christ.
>
> Today we dream a new vision—a vision of "a prophetic cutting edge" of educational distinctiveness for Huston-Tillotson College as we seek—with commitment to even greater effectiveness—to prepare leaders for the 1990s and the 21st century. I pledge to keep on dreaming; I pledge to continue trying to make dreams reality. And I pledge to seek and to accept your help in implementing the mandate of our history and promise.
>
> The "cutting edge" which I envision for Huston-Tillotson College is one which reaffirms the College's commitment to the liberal arts tradition, with dynamic institutional commitments to the teaching of the foundations of truth, the fundamentals of knowledge, as well as career education and skills involvement in the life of the East Austin community; and sensitivity to the issue of justice in our local, state, national, and global communities.
>
> I have dreams. I have many dreams for Huston-Tillotson College. I want us to fly—to take off and soar to new heights of academic excellence in community service for the 1990s and the 21st century. Without the help, commitment, and support of each of you, all I will have done today is to raise the issues and point the way. But, with the partnerships of the friends of higher education in general and of Huston-Tillotson College in particular, we can soar to new heights. Won't you join me on this flight?[12]

McMillan drew in HT's constituents with his moving address, giving them hope and the desire to move into the future under his leadership. At the beginning of his administration, his inheritance of students, dedicated faculty, and staff were his greatest gifts. They wanted to be part of McMillan' successful administration, but unforeseen challenges, including distrust, shaped their complicated relationship.

Dr. Joseph McMillan's HT Inheritance
Inherited Alumni
McMillan inherited existing students and leader-alumni; both groups are the true measurement of HT's success. HT's rich history was a beacon of hope for hundreds of thousands of students who might not have been able to get a college education elsewhere. These students, and their spheres of influence, benefited greatly from having Huston-Tillotson College as their alma mater. Some even returned to teach or work as staff. In addition to the alumni highlighted under King, McMillan inherited HT's alumni with their brilliant picture of achievements in diverse careers, advanced education, and civic engagements. Many give HT credit for their educational foundation and life successes.[13] A few alumni are cited below:

- Dr. Merle Miles-Adams (Sociology) was both an alumna and an HT sociology professor.[14] She taught sociology at HT from 1973 to 2000 and directed the SACS accrediting process carryover from King to McMillan. Miles-Adams came from the Austin community and was deeply involved in her community as she was elected chair of the City of Austin Human Relations Commission in 1979 and was a charter member of the Austin Metroplex Chapter of National Women of Achievement, Inc. Miles-Adams was the niece of the renowned J. Mason Brewer, a scholar, folklorist, oral historian, and author.[15]
- Three generations of the Harden family: Ada Harden (mother '78), Billy Harden (son '77), Marilyn (daughter '77), Anita (daughter '78), and Camisha (granddaughter '12). HT had many instances in which multiple members of a family were students, but to have a mother, three children, and a grandchild in one family as alumni is unique in the history of the institution. Ada Harden was a teenage parent who dropped out of school, having four children by the age of 21. Her children grew up with John Q. Taylor King's children. After Ada's children were grown, she decided to go back to college to study business administration, remarkably graduating the same year as her daughter Anita. Ada recalls being

in the same Human Sexuality class as her daughter—sometimes embarrassing. After graduation, Ada Harden worked for Austin Independent School District (AISD) as a volunteer coordinator and hosted AISD educational programs including *It's Your Future*, a talk show centered on successful entrepreneurs. This program aired on PBS and more than ten other channels. Ada Harden performed in more than eleven movies and television shows and five stage performances and commercials. Billy Harden, a retired high school principal, was a musician, actor, and director and regularly worked with his mother, who is CEO of A Harden Production, a talent and entertainment company, in Austin. As a transfer student from UT, Billy was drawn to HT's nurturing environment for all students, regardless of race. He knew all of his teachers, who cared for him as a person. Billy Harden majored in sociology but later got a master's in education because, as he said, "I wanted to positively influence the life of young people."

- Bishop Robert E. Hayes Jr. ('69, English) also obtained other degrees: M.Th. degree from Perkins School of Theology, Southern Methodist University, Dallas (1972) and a DMin degree from Drew University, Madison, New Jersey (1997). Hayes was ordained in the Texas Annual Conference of the United Methodist Church. Before his election to the episcopacy, he served the following appointments: McCabe UMC, Longview, Texas, as well as chaplain and instructor of Religion and Philosophy at Wiley College (1972–75); Blueridge UMC, Houston, Texas (1975–86); Riverside UMC, Houston (1986–94); superintendent of the Houston Southwest District (1994–2001); and treasurer, Texas Annual Conference (2002–04). He was named an Outstanding Alumnus by the Houston Chapter, Huston-Tillotson College (1989–90). His daughter, Joya Hayes, also attended HT, where she became student body president.
- Nelson Linder ('84, Government) had rich life experiences after graduating from HT.[16] He became a Licensed Insurance Agent in 1985. He worked for Allstate from 1986 to 1992, and in 2006 he became the founder and owner of Linder Insurance which is still operating under his ownership. Carrying out his civic duties, Mr. Linder has served as the president of the Austin Chapter of the NAACP from 2000 to the present. He is outspoken on matters related to people of color, including police brutality and other national and global incidents. Reflecting on

his time at HT, Mr. Linder said that his business and civic endeavors were grounded in how he was taught and the leadership of President King. Thinking about HT under President Pierce Burnette, he liked how HT became more visible and valued but did not want the original historically Black mission to be lost in the rush for diversity.

- Patrick B. Love ('88, Mass Communication) began his career with the Department of Justice (DOJ) in February 1988 as a federal officer in Bastrop, Texas, and was named Rookie of the Year. In August 1996, he was promoted to Deputy Chief, Office of Emergency Preparedness (OEP), BOP/DOJ Headquarters, Washington, DC. Love was also assigned as the Officer-in-Charge while assisting the former Immigration and Naturalization Service (INS).
- Volma Robert Overton Sr. ('50, Chemistry) was a celebrated civil rights leader who advocated for equality in Austin schools. He was the president of the NAACP from 1962 to 1983. In that capacity he joined Martin Luther King in the 1963 March on Washington and participated in the 1965 Selma to Montgomery march. Overton's most important accomplishment was his work leading to the desegregation of Austin public schools during the 1970s in which he made his daughter, DeDra, the lead plaintiff in a 1970 lawsuit. The matter was resolved ten years later when a federal court finally declared that the Austin school district be desegregated.[17]
- Tammy Terry ('84, Sociology) came to HT from Gary Job Corps, a governmental program to help troubled teens become contributing adults. In 1980, Job Corps contracted with HT to accept more than twenty students with tuition fully paid by the program. As one of those students, Terry majored in sociology and later graduated from a law school in Detroit. After strict screening for federal security clearance, Attorney Terry was selected as one of a small group of bankruptcy attorneys and has been in that position for decades. Bankruptcy Attorney Terry employs over thirty individuals, including an HT alum. She told me that she was well taken care of at HT. In 2019 she sent her son to HT to get the same great education as she did. Her son graduated in 2023.

Alumni stories give insight into the quality of education they received from gifted teachers inherited by McMillan. These alumni were community leaders, teachers, government workers, lawyers, actors, civil rights leaders, and business owners: just a small representation of the large pool of alumni.

Inherited Faculty

McMillan inherited many committed professors and staff, persons who understood the role of Historically Black Colleges in the advancement of African Americans and others. McMillan's initial twenty-nine stellar faculty members executed sound curricula for their students. He later added faculty, some of whom will be highlighted in Pierce Burnette's chapter. By educating liberal arts majors, professors have prepared thousands of students to meet personal, professional, and community challenges. Many of McMillan's inherited faculty members were HT alumni, indicating their commitment to excellence by giving students the skills and tools needed for success. Listed below are other inherited faculty members not mentioned in the alumni section.

- Dr. Marion Curry, Chair, Department of Education, and wife, Mrs. Martha Curry, professor of Business Administration (mid '60s to early '90s). Both Marion and Martha Curry began their tenure at HT under the presidency of Dr. Seabrook and were peers to King, prior to his promotion to presidency. Not only were they professionals in their discipline, but they also brought history to McMillan's early presidency.
- Dr. General Marshall (Mathematics) came to HT in 1966 and retired in 2001, after thirty-five years of service.[18] He served under King and McMillan and retired after the first year of Earvin's administration. His commitment and dedication to HT were evident in all that he did on behalf of students and the institution. He became chair of the Division of Natural Sciences in 1980 and maintained that position until he retired. He was the first director of AusPREP, a pre-freshman science, technology, engineering, mathematics (STEM) program that continues today. Additionally, Marshall, an avid golfer, turned his love for golf into many opportunities to provide students with academic scholarships through winnings from golf tournaments. Marshall was one of McMillan's advocates during faculty unrest, although he agreed with faculty that McMillan didn't handle conflicts well, escalating them due to poor communication. Marshall was the first College Marshal, carrying the presidential mace that was commissioned by McMillan. Austin named a school the Dr. General Garwood Marshall Middle School, which opened in fall 2023.[19]

- Dr. Beulah Agnes Curry-Jones (Music) was HT's choir director and vocalist for thirty-one years (1969–2000).[20] She worked under both King and McMillan and was called on regularly to take the choir to sing at various venues to promote visibility and encourage donations to HT. She described her time at HT as fulfilling her destiny. "Even before becoming full-time, I was an adjunct. I moved from instructor to assistant, to associate and to full professor and throughout that time I felt that I was carrying out God's calling on my life." Curry-Jones knew the importance of mentoring and being a role model for her students in order to help them grow mentally and emotionally. She believed that when students grow, real change can occur. Likewise, she felt that HT allowed her own growth and professional accomplishments. She has great pride in HT, especially when it became an All-Steinway campus in 2017. Her mother graduated from HT with honors in the 1950s, and her aunt and husband also graduated from HT. Curry-Jones went to HT but graduated from Prairie View A&M, receiving her MA from Texas Southern and her doctorate from UT Austin while also teaching at HT. Curry-Jones, born in 1927, continues to be active in the Austin community and to mentor others in music. Her music contributions can be found in the Texas Music Museum, Austin, Texas.[21]
- Dr. Lenora Waters (Vice President of Academics Affairs) taught in public schools prior to coming to HT in 1972, under the presidency of King.[22] For the next twenty-eight years Waters held many positions, beginning as a counselor (1973–1981). She was Director of Basic Study for a short time and in 1985 became the chair of the Education Division. From 1986 to 1999, Waters served as the Vice President of Academic Affairs and from 1999 to 2000 was appointed director of Self-Study. Her final year was as Senior VP, Dean of the College, a newly created position, given by McMillan after the faculty protested her sudden removal from VPAA without her knowledge and without faculty input. Waters was a consensus and team-builder who demonstrated, through her deeds, that students' and faculty's best interests were paramount in all that she did. She sometimes felt she had to resist directives from President McMillan when she believed they were not for the good of the college.
- Mrs. Harriet Buxkemper (Physical Education) was a Physical Education professor who inspired her students on many levels.[23] As an avid swimmer, she encouraged her students to engage in healthy lifelong strategies,

including exercise routine habits. Her love for HT was demonstrated in her roles as a committed professor and a mentor for students; later she was one of the founding members of an underground organization known as Save HT. Her daughter, Alexa ('00), spent most of her youthful years on the HT campus, later as a student. Alexa was an honors alumna who actively participated in the Save HT organization, like her mother.

- Dr. Judith Loredo (Chair, Division of Education) came to HT in 1986 and left as Professor Emerita in 2008. She continues to be connected to HT as an adjunct professor in the Adult Program. Serving under Presidents King, McMillan, and Earvin, Dr. Loredo came to HT having been the superintendent of a small school district in Texas. Deeply entrenched in teacher education state requirements, she brought that knowledge to HT, and through her committee work, aligned HT's curricula with those of the state. Through building a relationship between the Texas Higher Education Coordinating Board and HT, Loredo secured major grants to strengthen HT's education program. A remarkable professor, her education students excelled, and many won awards such as First-year Teacher of the Year and Teacher of the Year and/or became principals and top administrators. Loredo told me that when she taught students, she was privileged to see them move from "a caterpillar to a butterfly." She had the respect of professors, as evidenced by those who, in 1999, petitioned McMillan to appoint her as dean. Loredo left HT to become the Assistant Commission of P-16 Initiatives with the Texas Higher Education Coordinating Board.
- Ms. Jennifer Davies (Education) worked at HT for twenty-seven years, leaving only after feeling disrespected by her dean. She and Loredo were a powerful duo, teaching, mentoring, and guiding students through the teacher education process and preparation for the teacher exam. A hands-on, student-centered teacher, Dr. Davies was critical to the success of HT's Teacher Education program. Here's what she said about her time at HT: "I jumped at the opportunity to teach at HT and to mentor students, assuring thoroughness of training so they can become effective classroom teachers. I taught loyally for years, always received outstanding faculty evaluations, never received a student complaint, never been involved in a colleague tangle, served as chairperson for nine committees, written large sections of the SACS reports, and hosted visitors to the campus, etc."[24]

Knowing some of the faculty members who traversed from King to McMillan is critical to understanding McMillan's relationship with them. Other faculty members, including myself, Dr. Kathy Schwab, Dr. Paul Anaejionu, and Dr. Horacio Peña, will be highlighted under President Pierce Burnette's administration. I believe one could not have found professors more committed and more in tune with the needs of HT and its students. Unfortunately, as McMillan's presidency progressed, he valued faculty less and less, as will be discussed later.

McMillan also took over the reins of HT under the cloud of many difficulties, which required constituents' support and decisive leadership intervention.

Dr. McMillan's Immediate Challenges

Under a new administration of the 113-year-old institution, Huston-Tillotson's vibrant legacy rested in the leadership of McMillan. His presidency began with numerous challenges, including the following: 1) whether HT should merge with Texas and Wiley Colleges, 2) how to continue with the Southern Association of Colleges and Schools (SACS)[25] reaffirmation process that began under King, 3) how to increase low student enrollment/retention, 4) what to do with the old administration building that had been condemned, 5) how to raise sufficient funds to advance the college and to pay for ongoing expenses, 6) and how to increase the low salary being paid to faculty. These were the same six areas that King faced with a positive, collaborative and mutually respectful relationship with faculty and staff who were engaged in every aspect of institutional development and implementation. How McMillan addressed these challenges would determine the successful outcomes of HT under his administration. It is his "dash."

Merger with Wiley and Texas College

The recommendation for merger by King to HT's board was still on the table when McMillan became president. However, the final decision by the Wiley and Texas Colleges' Boards of Trustees to merge with HT was "no." McMillan said that he didn't know whether the vote ever came up for HT's board since the other two colleges rejected the proposal.[26]

Institutional Self-Studies

By 1988, King had already set into motion a process for conducting an in-depth self-study, a requirement of HT's 1990 reaffirmation application. King appointed Professor Merle Miles-Adams as director of the SACS Committee, and McMillan kept her in that position. Under McMillan's leadership an Institutional Self-Study

1988–1990 Manual was developed. With full press from HT faculty and staff, consultation from an accrediting specialist, and input from SACS, the HT reaffirmation report was sent to SACS in June 1990. A SACS visiting team visited the campus to interview various constituents as well as review primary documents. SACS microscopically examined HT's finances. The team addressed complaints from students and faculty as well as examined faculty credentials. The two major foci for reaffirmation were whether HT was financially solvent to carry out its mission and whether HT met educational objectives as stated in published documents such as its bulletin, handbooks, and catalogues. The college received the report of the reaffirmation committee, containing twenty-seven recommendations. The institutional response was due on October 15, 1990. On January 22, 1991, McMillan received the following letter from the Executive Director of SACS, James T. Rogers.

> It is a pleasure to inform you that your institution has satisfactorily completed the Institutional Self-Study Program and its accreditation was reaffirmed by the Commission on Colleges at its meeting on December 10, 1990. We congratulate you, your faculty, and staff on this attainment.
>
> Your institution is requested to submit a First Follow-Up Report, by October 15, 1991, which details progress in addressing Criteria Section 6.3.1 (Financial Resources). The report should detail plans to reduce the cumulative deficit and institutional indebtedness. The financial audit and management letter for the 1990–1991 fiscal year should be included as part of the report.[27]

This was great news for the institution but, as shown, HT was required to send periodic follow-ups specifically focusing on the cumulative deficit and institutional indebtedness. Since the required financial audit was not sent to SACS by the date requested, HT was required to send it by the end of May 1992. In July 1992, the college was placed on notice for not submitting the 1991 financial audit and was required to submit a third follow-up by October 15, 1992, containing the audit for 1990–1991 and 1991–1992. The college was placed on notice in December 1992 for continued deficiencies in financial resources. In April 1993, the college sent its fourth follow-up report and three months later was removed from notice. However, a special committee visited the college in the fall of 1993. Follow-up reports were required. HT complied with required follow-up reports and in January 1995 the final report was accepted; the college was notified that no further reports were due.[28]

Financial Instability

Fiscal tenuousness was an ongoing problem for McMillan and was the underlying reason that HT was placed on notice by SACS three times for the 1990 reaccreditation. As described previously, this problem was not unique to his presidency but also challenged the presidents who preceded him. However, as the president and CEO of HT, one of his primary functions was to raise funds for the operation of the institution. He inherited long-standing, ongoing grantor relationships with numerous organizations and funding sources, such as Title III, UNCF, UMC, UCC, Upward Bound, Ford Foundation, and others. These established relationships needed to be rekindled and nurtured under McMillan; proposals have to be generated and submitted on time. Upward Bound was lost under his presidency. HT continued to be negatively affected by White institutions competing for African Americans' best and brightest, resulting in their pool for HBCUs dwindling. Additionally, the federal government and other organizations had reduced their contribution to HT, decreasing scholarship monies and student services.

In order to increase the financial resources of HT, McMillan insisted that faculty and staff intentionally engage in fundraising activities. He stated that all should be seeking grants and writing proposals to support academic programs. But grant production and implementation were problematic, as it was difficult to secure grant money from HT's business unit for designated funded programs. This often resulted in reduced incentives for writing grants. Nevertheless, many faculty members wrote grants to strengthen their majors, which was used as a recruitment tool. As the primary fundraiser, with the assistance of his Institutional Development Officer, McMillan was still ineffective, spending more money than was raised. Mr. Terry Smith, Executive Vice President to McMillan, told me that McMillan didn't like to fundraise; that's why he pressed others to do so.[29]

Alumni data I collected for this document indicated that among the twenty-two respondents who matriculated under McMillan, one-third believed that HT was financially stable at that time and two-thirds felt it was unstable. Below are some sample comments from this respondent group.

- Must develop fundraising strategic plan.
- Academic support programs needed for student support have been cut because the grant money for those programs ceased to exist. This is true of academic programs such as Hotel and Restaurant Management and Gerontology that once existed on grant money but ended when external

funding ended. These programs, if continued could have brought in more students within our current demographic and tourism environment.

Faculty and staff salaries have been at a plateau for years with increases being infrequent and not an administrative priority. This has resulted in the loss of very qualified professors who received their worth in pay elsewhere. The same can be said for highly qualified staff.

Often restricted grant money is not available for grant use because the money might have been used to pay other outstanding bills. If this financial instability increases, then accreditation under McMillan might be jeopardized.

- At the time there was [*sic*] some issues with the funding and how [tuition] was being utilized. It was hard to pay for my education; very limited scholarships or financial assistance offered to me as a student. Extremely high tuition fees; at times it felt I was "nickeled and dimed."
- Many times there were cash flow problems.
- I am guessing HT is financially stable. I do not really know HT's financial status and have not reviewed any financial reports.
- [Stable finances] Always a struggle, true for most Historically Black institutions . . . few w/deep endowments, etc., dependent on church, other and Department of Education grants.
- It appears that there aren't enough unrestricted funds to properly support the needs in student housing, academic and support programs.
- While we are able to sustain ourselves, I believe that sometimes it calls for creative accounting. There is extremely guarded use of even restricted funds.
- There was never enough money for Alumni Affairs.

I believe that these comments indicate that students were keenly aware of the financial difficulties their college was experiencing. There was a strong negative relationship between HT's financial instability and the next challenge: low student enrollment and retention.

Student Enrollment/Retention
Another critical and ongoing challenge facing McMillan's new administration was student enrollment and retention. HT was/is a student tuition–driven institution; therefore, enrollment and retention had a significant impact on HT's income. The twelve years of McMillan's presidency found student enrollment fluctuating

from 539 (1988) to 543 (2000) students, with a high of 701 in 1996. With this fluctuation of student enrollment, and with a low level of endowment and low annual revenue, HT continued on a "hand-to-mouth" trajectory.[30]

In April 1989 McMillan established the President's Task Force on Student Retention. The theme for the task force was "We can fix it." The group's purpose was to identify problems at Huston-Tillotson College that caused students to withdraw or not to return and to propose immediate solutions to positively impact retention for the next semester. There were four work groups: Academic Affairs, Fiscal Affairs, Student Affairs, and Community Relations and Public Image. Among the many findings were these:

- Class size was too large
- Computer labs were not open long enough
- Lines are too long at Financial Aid and Business Offices
- Student refunds took too long
- The need to develop, strengthen, and enhance the operation of mentor programs
- To provide greater opportunities for students to participate in research on scholarly activities with faculty and staff
- The need to review the judicial policy for handling discipline referrals in the residence hall
- The need to advertise pre- and post-athletic event information
- The need to resurrect videos and make more videos to promote positive images of Huston-Tillotson.

The Student Affairs Office conducted a survey with students in 1989 and found their concerns included fighting; drugs/alcohol; loud music and noise; prohibited weapons on campus; vandalism; and abuse of class attendance. Respondents to the survey also believed that students who committed infractions of college regulations seldom, if ever, were disciplined.[31]

There was no indication that the findings from the committee or survey resulted in any policy changes or policy implementation. However, in a February 1991 memo on the "Prophetic Cutting Edge," McMillan shared with Dr. Lenora Waters, VPAA, his vision for academic affairs' involvement in improving retention. McMillan stated, "I affirm the role of the faculty, to include as primary responsibilities to: 1) recruit majors, 2) market departmental courses, 3) counsel and advise students, 4) mentor and solicit undeclared majors, and 5) advise and assist various administrative offices on strategies of student recruitment and retention."[32] Faculty members recognized their role in advising and even in mentoring but also believed that the primary function of recruitment was that of paid staff.

McMillan stated in the Spring/Summer 1995 edition of HT's magazine *The Ram* that the college's "greatest deterrent to our growth is the lack of sufficient scholarships and grants for promising students. We *must* reduce the amount of loans that we must require our students to take each semester in order to cover the costs of their education."[33] These difficulties plagued McMillan's presidency.

Old Administration Building

King had numerous conversations about what should be done with the old Administration Building. He also engaged in fundraising efforts specifically for the restoration of that building. The towering, even majestic building was a cornerstone of the Tillotson campus. In 1913 the old Administration Building was built with cinder brick made by students who learned their skills in industrial arts classes. It served as a stately memorial to generations' commitment to educate, to encourage self-help, and to empower African American youth. That building, made with students' sweat and blood, had substantially deteriorated over time, resulting in the city's order for its demolition if renovations were not done. King got an extension from the City of Austin and sought various grants and loans for its renovation, but to no avail.

McMillan inherited the condemned building. In 1988, during the first months of his administration, the Board of Trustees pledged their support for the renovation of the building, contingent on whether sufficient funds could be raised for the project. In 1993, the chairman of the board, Dr. Prenza L. Woods, appointed a task force of alumni and trustees to review the options concerning the building and to submit a recommendation to the board. The task force's decision was to postpone further deliberations until 1998—ten years into McMillan's administration. In his paper, "The Fate of the Old Administration Building," McMillan wrote:

> The Huston-Tillotson College Board of Trustees received the report and recommendations of a special Task Force, last fall, and voted to defer a final decision on whether to renovate or demolish the Old Administration Building until 1998. In the meantime the administration was directed to maintain the security of the building, to continue exploring grants and private gifts to underwrite the renovation, and to consider improving the building's appearance. Renewed interest in the building has surfaced among alumni, ex-students, and community

leaders, which complements the offers of assistance from the University of Texas at Austin (UT) and the Texas Historical Commission. Nevertheless, the fate of the building remains uncertain.[34]

The old Administration Building had not been used since 1969. The structure was abandoned but not forgotten: several architectural and engineering studies were made on the building. It was nominated by the Texas Historical Commission for listing in the National Register of Historic places. Still, twelve years after McMillan's inauguration, the fate of the old Administration Building was left to the new president, Larry Earvin.

Faculty Salary Increases
Another ongoing problem faced by McMillan was pay for HT faculty. In his first report to the board, McMillan emphasized the importance of paying faculty a salary comparable to that of other small liberal arts colleges. Throughout his presidency there was a request by faculty and staff to be more fairly compensated for their work. The need was especially great because faculty were expected to increase enrollment, to raise funds, and to serve on numerous committees in addition to their main function of teaching. Although a faculty senate was initially organized in 1975 it became inactive two years later. It was reactivated in 1989, during McMillan's first year, and compensation was one of its initial faculty concerns. This ongoing concern was linked both to HT's poor financial status and the low priority salary increases had for the administration. Despite low salaries and often no raises, most faculty members continued to be committed to HT and its mission to provide an excellent education to its students.

Financial Aid Fraud
A unique challenge for the McMillan administration was a Department of Education (ED) finding of HT's financial aid fraud. A student I interviewed indicated that one or two financial aid personnel involved some students in fraudulent activities by having them take out loans beyond their need and give part of the money to the financial aid personnel. Additionally, she stated, financial aid personnel, with the help of a business staff member, took out loans in the names of persons not at HT, deceased individuals, and other fraudulent names. As a result of this fraud, the student believed, many of her classmates left, and those who graduated swore not to look back.[35] This student's account was verified by McMillan's executive vice president, Terry Smith, and by Dr. Bronté Jones, an individual hired to "fix" the problem.

In a phone interview, Bronté Jones indicated that McMillan created a position for her to resolve HT's financial aid fraud problem.[36] Jones believed that McMillan had the foresight to hire her to work with the Department of Education. Jones indicated that HT had twenty-nine ED findings worth four million dollars. After reviewing and organizing students' financial aid files, she had to take all files to Dallas for ED's review. As a result of the negative Program Review, the college was placed on "reimbursement" status. Once proof of eligibility for each student was accepted and approved, ED disbursed financial aid to HT. As a result of Jones's work with ED, HT's debt obligation was reduced to $400,000. Additionally, in the process of her work, Jones wrote a default plan used by other HBCUs.[37]

Jones believed that the problem emerged because the wrong people were hired, probably because of inadequate resources to hire competent people. She also believed that a lack of presidential oversight of the Financial Aid Office accounted for some of the problem.

Dr. McMillan: A Different Kind of President

Regardless of the problems he inherited from his predecessor, or what his own administration set into motion, McMillan loved being the president of HT. In his inaugural address, McMillan provided insight into what was to follow. His repetition of the phrase "cutting edge" was well received by most; the HT community was ready for his new leadership. The HT community expected a leader who would unite and include the entire HT family. Many sat in awe as he spoke and were excited by how the community received him. But once he became president, it became clear that McMillan's inaugural address had stipulations: he required loyalty, not to HT but to him. Those who robustly "followed" him were seen as loyal, often rewarded with promotions, greater opportunities for securing funds, or other benefits.[38] Those who "disagreed or interjected constructive criticism" either were ignored or, worse, experienced revengeful treatment.[39] Some were fired without cause or belittled in the presence of others. While King valued teamwork and consensus as a result of an inclusive process, McMillan's actions indicated a top-down philosophy (especially when it came to certain people), despite his rhetoric of consensus. One of his favorite clichés was "Come go with me; but if you don't, don't hinder me." Another motto was: "We can do this, but if you don't want to work with me, let go of my leg." These mottos set the stage for his twelve-year presidency. His vision for HT was grand, not different from that of his predecessors, but I believe his personal characteristics sometimes got in the way of his implementing that vision.

Compared to his predecessor, McMillan was a different kind of president: unmarried, high energy, passionate, driven by the desire to "not leave any rock left unturned." Although his rhetoric was one of building on the past, he acted as if nothing right or good happened before he became the leader of HT. He was quick to criticize and ready to change policy without consulting with major constituents. His articulateness and abilities to sway an audience to his side were his initial gifts to HT, but his later actions often left many supporters wondering about his real agenda, or in fact disillusioned about his actions not being aligned with institutional objectives. Many students, however, did not see this side of McMillan and gladly embraced the person who called himself the "students' president."

"The Students' President"

It was clear that McMillan had an affinity for young people, as his master's degree was in Student Personnel Administration. At age 44, he was only 22–26 years older than most HT students and, in some cases, younger than some. Throughout his presidency he embraced certain students; they were his main concern. He pushed faculty members to accommodate students' needs. This is not a bad thing in and of itself but was sometimes misused by students, as if they were "pitting one parent against the other." At times McMillan blurred the line as he wanted to be one of them (students). Self-identified as the "students' president," McMillan reached out to students in numerous ways: he knew all of his students by name; he "gave" scholarships to some students and not others; he rented a bus at the last minute to take HT students to a basketball game; he had students drive him around; students were invited to his house, even for parties; and on occasion he hung out with students in their dorms.

He had an open-door policy and, according to McMillan, "that may have been a reason why other presidential things were left undone."[40] His favorite students were Alphas, members of his Greek fraternity.[41] His desire to be liked by his students sometimes resulted in his relating with some inappropriately and in non-presidential ways. In looking back at their time at HT, most student participants of the online survey (2017–18) had positive things to say about McMillan. This was also true of those who wrote memorial statements about him on King-Tears Mortuary website.[42] However, mixed reviews came from students who participated in a 1989 protest and others who participated in a similar protest in 1994. Written reports on the president and his administration during 1999 were also mixed. The following comments came from alumni who participated in my online survey:

CHAPTER 2

- [He was] very pleasant, always smiling and would greet you in the yard.
- He was okay with me, and my impressions did not change over time.
- My first encounter with Dr. McMillan is a lifetime memory. He was being very boisterous and laughing in a huddle with other students. He seemed at that moment to be down to earth and passionate with a strong love for the school. My opinion of him never changed.
- At first Dr. McMillan was excited about the needs of the students and the school but that changed over time. He became more about the business of how to make himself look good, not about the school's legacy and future.
- Great guy—presented himself well.
- He was a very flashy and confident individual.
- Open and caring. A deeply student-oriented president.
- Cool orator.
- Dr. Mac was intelligent and interested in knowing me personally. My impression of him never changed.
- Very friendly and outgoing.
- Eccentric, sociable, man of taste.
- Messy and rude.
- Flamboyant.
- Kind and caring.
- Intelligent; involved; progressive; sharp; it did not change, as he was about to retire at the end of my 1st year at HT.
- I thought he was a great man.
- I thought overall he had the interest of the students at the core of his mission as president.
- Open and warm.
- He was great!
- The first time I met him personally, he took the time to have an in-depth conversation with me. That conversation impacted my involvement in leadership activities on campus. He was always approachable, engaging, and professional.
- All about the students.
- Very visible; student-centric and very involved with campus activities and campus growth, enrollment, and trying to get HT to the next level as a staple in the Austin community.
- I loved him.
- Hard working and positive.

- He was tenacious. It didn't change.
- Standoffish.
- [He was] easygoing, very approachable, active on campus.

From this study's findings, most students concurred with McMillan's view of himself as a students' president. Students believed that he had an open-door policy, encouraged student governance, and enhanced students' academic programs; conversely, most students did not believe that McMillan appeared to be more concerned about his personal growth than the growth of others. Although international enrollment under McMillan was only about 7 percent throughout his presidency (down from King's high of 31 percent), there were as many as twenty-four students from one country: Jamaica. These were non-paying students who were provided with scholarships, tuition, full or partial room, and board primarily from the United Methodist Church. McMillan really treated these students well. He called a Jamaican student, Ms. Devan Spence, the "matriarch" of the group. Ms. Spence, in an interview, spoke highly of him, recalling that when the Caribbean students complained about the food, specifically rice not being served often enough, McMillan told the chef to cook rice every night, in addition to other dishes. The Jamaican students was a tight-knit group, and members held each other accountable for producing excellent academic work. Faculty loved them, often preferring them to American students because of their work ethic. American students complained that they (Jamaican students) got scholarships while they (American students) got loans. This caused some tension between the two groups.

The president's message in the 1994 *Ram Magazine* showed how important students were to him:

> We began the 1994–95 academic year with a tree planting ceremony. Symbolic of our commitment to the future, in collaboration of the lives of our students of the entering class of fall 1994, and in honor of Congressman Jake Pickle, the entering class planted fifty live oaks on campus on our opening day this fall. These tree seedlings were a gift to the College from the Honorable J. J. Pickle... we planted these trees with the fervent hope that our students will grow in love and loyalty to Huston-Tillotson College as each tree grows. We planted these trees with the expectation that our students will care for and nurture each tree, as we care for and nurture them in their growth and development. We planted these trees with the challenge that together we will all grow in appreciation and respect for the dignity of life, for protection of the environment, and in love and

CHAPTER 2

respect for each other. This is what the mission of Huston-Tillotson College means symbiotically. We care. We nurture. We grow together.

During that academic year McMillan wanted to improve students' academic performance via better advising, strengthening the developmental enrichment program, and launching a distance-learning program. Many students benefited from these improvements, which were created and supported by faculty and staff.

Still, some of McMillan's actions seemed to indicate that he didn't have the best interests of *all* students at heart. In at least one instance he used his presidential power in a way that emotionally devastated some students. Below is a statement, made in 1989, by a student who attended HT from 1988 to 1992.

> In 1989, I wanted to show my love for the college by running for Miss UNCF [United Negro College Fund]. In the past, the young lady crowned Miss UNCF had ALWAYS been the person who raised the most money. In fact, it is stated on the bottom of the Miss UNCF application that: "*The candidates for the 1989-90 Miss UNCF will be judged on their fundraising skills alone.*" With the help of my mother and friends I was able to raise $2,691.00. **That sum was greater than the combined TOTAL** of the other three candidates. Despite that, I did not win but came in last. The person who raised the second highest came in third. Why? Because the president [McMillan], along with the Vice President for Student Affairs, Dr. Clarence Bibby, changed the UNCF rules during the middle of the contest to include *a student oral presentation and a panel of student voters*. It was clear to me that I could have brought in one million dollars but would not have won based upon the judging scale which gave more points to the oral presentation than to the amount of money raised. The person who raised $571.00 was crowned Miss UNCF, a communication major and an intern to a local radio station.
>
> I gave up becoming a debutante so that I could raise money for Huston-Tillotson College (my mother gave a large contribution to my UNCF candidacy and could not have supported me in both). My family protested over how this contest was carried out. We wrote Dr. McMillan, the Board of Trustees, the National UNCF, and the president of HT UNCF Advisory Board. I also got petitions signed by alumni and community persons; but I was never crowned Miss UNCF. Instead, Dr. McMillan, through his then Vice President for Institutional Advancement, Mr. Walter Stafford, wrote me a letter stating, "Because of your misunderstanding of the procedure, and because you feel that

you solicited money under false pretenses, I am, by copy of this letter directing Mr. Paul Bailey in the Business Office to return to you the $2,691.00 which you submitted to the college. Please feel free to dispose of these funds in any way that you feel will maintain your credibility and integrity." In this letter Dr. McMillan and his appointed officers blamed me for the mix-up that came about because **they changed the rules**. Because they were unwilling to admit that they caused the problem, they were willing to give me back the money. Crazy, because they always complain of not having enough money! . . .

The next year there was not a Miss UNCF contest because of the mix-up of the previous year. The years after that, the Miss UNCF contest guidelines reverted back to the original ones: it was based on money raised ALONE. When I think of Dr. McMillan, that incident is in the forefront. I left Huston-Tillotson with a bad feeling. That's unfortunate because Dr. McMillan is not the college. I got an excellent education from caring, professional, and knowledgeable professors. It has been difficult for me to think about supporting Huston-Tillotson College as an alumna. I said many times that I will give back to my college when Dr. McMillan is no longer the president. I have not encouraged friends and family to go to Huston-Tillotson because of the president and NOT because of the teachers. This incident occurred in 1989. He has not changed. He will not change. I am not the only alumna who had bad experiences with Dr. McMillan. He had favorite students who were given special treatment. He had students to drive him around. Some students had greater access to him in his office. He hung out with his "frat brothers" who were students. This was common knowledge.[43]

This was not the entire statement from that student; however, she raised many important points about how the "students' president" did not treat all students equally or fairly. This example shows:

- The president changed his mind and changed rules without considering the consequences.[44]
- He did not recognize and take responsibility for poor judgment and behavior.
- He accused the student of wrongdoing.
- Money that could be used by the institution was returned to the student to do with as she would. Her donors told the student to apply the money to her education.
- This student gave up being a debutante to run for Miss UNCF.

- The winner did not enjoy the prestige of being crowned Miss UNCF due to the disruption and crisis that emerged around her crowning.
- The president did not have the best interests of all the students in mind.
- The president did not treat all students with respect, failing to take the legitimate protests seriously.
- The president did not recognize the long-term negative implications of emotionally hurt alumni: e.g., discontinued financial support, no longer recommending future students, in fact discouraging potential students from attending HT.
- This student and many in her cohort made an intentional and permanent decision not to participate in the HT Alumni Association.
- The perception of student mistreatment is damaging to an institution that really needs alumni testimony as a recruitment and fundraising tool.

A 1999 graduating student who strongly disagreed with McMillan's administrative appointments and who participated in the Save HT Committee said this about her final experience at HT:[45]

> I, Alexa Buxkemper, was given a printed transcript at the conclusion of the fall 1999 semester outlining all work undertaken at the college and my GPA at the conclusion of that semester. My GPA at that time was above a 3.75, which is required by the College Bulletin to graduate as summa cum laude. Since I received all "A" grades during spring 2000, my GPA should have risen. I had not checked on my GPA since the conclusion of the fall semester as I was satisfied that I had attained a GPA high enough to graduate summa cum laude. During rehearsal, the day before the commencement ceremony, my name was called out followed by magna cum laude. My heart sank. How could this be? I immediately went to the registrar after practice and told her that I thought something was wrong. A review of my transcript indicated that someone had changed grades on my transcript since the previous semester. Who and why? Not only was it too late to have my correct honor printed in the program, but the names of three sociology majors were totally omitted from the official college program. College graduation is a once in a lifetime event and after all the hard work all of us put in, we were severely disappointed that our names and honors were not correctly recorded.[46]

This student believed that these intentional discrepancies against her were because she was part of the Save HT Committee protest and spoke in front of the City

Council on behalf of the committee concerning a request for a zone change.

No matter how much many students liked McMillan, others were taken back by what they deemed as non-presidential behavior, which they perceived made HT look bad. Some student respondents even participated with McMillan engaging in those behaviors.

Being a "students' president" requires a president who is open and receptive to the entire student body and who treats students based upon respect, trust, and need. McMillan's having favorites, and treating them differently, was noticed, although not always voiced. In the online survey, some students expressed a belief that McMillan had favorites at the expense of other students. However, as noted, most students who responded to this survey largely viewed McMillan positively. More students supported him than did those who challenged his authority and decisions.

Core and Major Curriculum Emphasis
In his inaugural address, McMillan gave his vision for curriculum for each of the academic divisions. He said:

> In particular, in the humanities, we shall seek to reclaim a "cutting edge" in the study of religion and philosophy and the development of certificate programs for area ministers who may not have completed the baccalaureate degree in literature and history of the African American experiences, from the African diaspora to today; a mass communication, radio broadcasting, and television production; and in the joyous performance of a diverse repertoire of music. And, perhaps, one day, we might even expand our program to include painting, ceramics, and dramatic arts.
>
> In the natural sciences, we will seek to reclaim a "cutting edge" in the preparation of pre-professional degrees in science, engineering, and technology; and the development of early intervention programs to encourage more African American and Hispanic youth to pursue careers in mathematics, biology, chemistry, and technological research; and to reclaim an academic reputation for our work with artificial intelligence, innovative computer applications and research, and new computer languages and analysis.
>
> In the social sciences, we shall study the issues and implications of gerontology, juvenile delinquency, and urban crime. We will also consider the interdisciplinary possibilities for the college in the areas of health care administration, family counseling, physical therapy, and convalescent care.

In the field of education, we shall seek to build upon the college's cutting edge in teacher preparation and kindergarten certificate; and surely, we might want to establish a model preschool and daycare program for the children of single-parent students, and for the other families and single parents in the community.

In the area of business, we shall seek to establish an incubator complex and a nonresident incubator program to enable the revitalization of the East Austin community; to assist small developing businesses—especially Austin minority businesses; provide technical expertise, services, products, and training programs for employees of high-tech industries and telecommunication companies; and to train young entrepreneurs to find their own cutting edge in the marketplace.[47]

In a September 2017 interview, McMillan remembered being dissatisfied with the general education offerings. "I wanted new curriculum for the core curriculum. I worked hard on bringing that about during my administration. The quality of education was reflected in students' success once they left HT." He acknowledged that our diverse student population—academically and racially/ethnically—was the greatest challenge. "How do you take students with raw potential and make them competitive?"[48] His answer would be: through curriculum and teaching.

Three years into his administration McMillan provided an in-depth letter to the faculty, staff, and selected students that contained minute details on his "prophetic cutting edge in Academic Affairs." This was only one of many to follow. According to him, academic affairs is the foundation of the college's mission, and effective teaching/learning are at the core of Academic Affairs.[49] Furthermore, "significant progress has been achieved in each of the units of the College, and significant work remains in each area; however, Academic Affairs remains the 'Last Horizon' of challenge for institutional renewal at HT to achieve its mission of quality." In that 1991 letter, McMillan assessed the academic program and provided directives for changes, taking the form of asking "What if" proposals.

1. What if the College will fundamentally revise the General Studies curriculum:
    a. to define specific knowledge, competency skills, and minimum performance proficiency;
    b. to strengthen the developmental studies programs by effective coordination of the functions of testing, placement, advisement, counseling, and tutoring;
    c. to establish an Honors program in the general studies curriculum and in each academic division/or department; and to establish a required

core curriculum which emphasizes reading, writing, critical thinking, verbal communication, computation, and the interdisciplinary nature of all knowledge and truth. [McMillan provide more, very specific ways to do these things.]
2. What if the College will fundamentally revise its curriculum of majors:
   a. To reduce the number of majors;
   b. To establish a required capstone course in each discipline;
   c. To explore the establishment of new interdisciplinary majors, e.g.,
      i. Allied health
      ii. Gerontology [was established with funding; when funding ended it ceased to exist due to inadequate funds for faculty salary]
      iii. Sports medicine and sports management
      iv. Music industry management
      v. Psychology [established in 1996]
      vi. African American Studies [established as minor and then major and back to a minor]
3. What if the College will revise its administrative policies in the area of Academic Affairs to establish minimum standards of fiscal accountability and economy of resources. [McMillan described in detail how this was to be accomplished.]
4. What if the College will revise its administrative policies and practices to enhance academic support services? [Under this section he recommended changes in the registration process and improved library services. He also recommended that students under academic probation be under regular supervision and that the policy of "no pass no play" be rigorously applied. He wanted to strengthen the relationship between Academic Affairs and Student Affairs, to change how students received their grades, and to revise the policy on transfer credit.]

McMillan's nine-page letter ended with a request that the Committee on General Studies Competency (a committee he created) and the Educational Policy Council (the standing committee that reviews recommendations for academic program revision and new programs) work on changes.[50] Additionally, he asked for input from the faculty at large and other interested persons. Many of his recommendations did materialize, while others didn't.

Academic Affairs responded to McMillan's "What if" proposals in numerous ways. VPAA Lenora Waters distributed a document titled "Vision for Academic

Affairs."[51] That document contained unit goals that aligned with institutional goals.[52] Below are those goals that relate to McMillan's "What if" directives.

1. Institutional Goal: to advance the institution to a level which sets it apart as a dynamic, model, Historically Black, church-related college.
    a. Unit Goal 1: to maintain a curriculum that reflects emphasis on mastery of skills and concepts, common base of values, and a sense of responsibility for involvement in a global environment.
    b. Unit Goal 2: to coordinate activities and accommodate different learning styles and require students to engage in a variety of problem-solving learning experiences.
    c. Unit Goal 3: to strengthen the General Studies Program and keep it focused on student performance outcomes and changing needs of society.
    d. Unit Goal 4: to provide a competitive curriculum based on outcomes oriented and assessments supported by well-defined developmental honors programs.
    e. Unit Goal 5: to integrate a service-learning component into the curriculum.
    f. Unit Goal 6: to strengthen institutional-wide programs that develop cross discipline skills in speaking, reading, writing, and mathematics.
2. Institutional Goal 3: to attract and retain a diverse student enrollment.
    a. Unit Goal 1: to introduce learning enrichment activities which consistently emphasize value-added learning, cultural diversity, and a variety of leadership opportunities.
3. Institutional Goal 4: to develop and maximize the human potential of each student.
    a. Unit Goal 1: to utilize assessment data of student needs and expectations in preparation schedules, support services, and other activities.
4. Institutional Goal 5: to strengthen the human resources of the institution.
    a. Unit Goal 1: to provide faculty with ongoing opportunities for professional growth focused on teaching effectiveness.
5. Institutional Goal 6: to ensure the financial stability and viability of the institution.
    a. Unit Goal 1: to encourage faculty members to write proposals and to help nurture potential donors to annual and capital funds projects of the College.

A timeline for new academic unit goals with responsible parties for achieving strategies and activities was identified. Academic departments attempted to accomplish the many academic goals that came from our VP for Academic Affairs in response to McMillan's directives. In the Social Science Division 1991–1992 summary report, I, as division chairperson, stated, "In an attempt to secure additional funds for International and African American Studies, faculty wrote and submitted two proposals. Neither was funded. Additionally, my department hoped to be included in HT's Title III proposal but were not selected. The department did get an IBM loan professor who helped develop a major in psychology."[53]

Still, many faculty members felt that McMillan intruded into the business of faculty far too much and that he should have directed some of that energy overseeing the offices of business and financial aid, both of which were problematic. A 1992 response to McMillan's "what if, prophetic cutting-edge" challenge came from a faculty member's letter to him:

> You promote the concept of a core curriculum that fundamentally differs from the General Studies Committee's notion that the "core" should provide choice to students and to the faculty members who will actually develop the courses. There is a difference of perspective on what should be in the core. . . . It is my belief that we cannot, nor should we attempt to try, to devise a required set of courses that will make our students "literate" by virtue of having successfully passed those courses.

Her reasons for not devising a list of required courses include:

> . . . the issue at hand is motivation of our students, not covering specific set of materials that will guarantee their literacy; literacy in today's world deals more with knowing how to learn—the knowledge base is changing so rapidly that students need to learn how to access information and how to use it, rather than just to learn a body of knowledge, much of which will be forgotten after the test; self-esteem comes from knowing _how_ to do something with what you know; this insight relates to the differences between what a student's grade _is_ and what the grade _means_ (percentage in relation to others vs. insight); . . . this autonomy of teacher and student is what guarantees pluralism in the curriculum and emphasizes diversity rather than narrows the curriculum.[54]

McMillan did not respond to this professor's letter. Pushing forward with his agenda of core curriculum revision, the president included the Core Curriculum

Competency Program in the 1992 Title III program. The program was devised to support institutional goals and academic goals outlined previously. Under the leadership of the Dean of General Studies, Mrs. Teresia Lewis, the program's implementation was in seven major categories:

1. Creating a challenging learning environment which promotes a new enthusiastic spirit for liberal learning;
2. Maintaining a comprehensive basic skills mastery program to include reading, writing, speaking, listening, and computation;
3. Redesigning the College Orientation course to promote: (a) intense intellectual interaction between students and their instructors; (b) enriched out of class interactions driven by introductions of, but not limited to, an issue, a book, an article, or a case study, which requires a group decision prior to class discussion and/or delivery;
4. Developing and implementing a strong core curriculum to emphasize and build competencies, institution wide, in the following areas: (a) effective communication, (b) problem-solving, (c) values and self-knowledge, (d) critical thoughts, (e) historical and global awareness, (f) individual and social behavior, (g) understanding and applying sciences, (h) arts and aesthetics, and (i) wellness.
5. Implementing an intensive advising system as a part of the ongoing services of this program;
6. Implementing a collaborative support system for faculty and students;
7. Revising and implementing a stronger tutorial/counseling support system.

Each of these areas had in-depth discussion on their rationales and proposed implementation strategies. Although some professors might have had some differences in how they viewed general studies curriculum, many made varying attempts to implement parts of it by using the common syllabus format placed online. Nine core competencies that identified outcomes for all students, regardless of major, were included in all syllabi.[55] Those competencies were to be specifically aligned with course activities. Some professors embraced and emphasized the core competencies in their courses by including them in assignments and/or course lectures. I had students in my senior seminar course survey HT students' awareness of institutional core competencies and, if aware, how teachers accessed their awareness. The results indicated that few students even knew what the core competencies were and/or how they were addressed in classes, indicating that some professors only gave lip service to integrating the competencies into their courses.

McMillan's focus included other academic programs at different times of his presidency. He called Teacher Education his stellar program, after it recovered from many difficulties during his presidency. HT's education program had to adapt to societal changes and Texas regulations in order to continue to fulfill its mission of providing excellent education to African American students, and others, so they could meet teaching needs in Austin, the state, and the nation. Emphasis was on improving students' results on state teacher education exams. Too many of HT students failed the test. In a 1999 newspaper article titled "Teacher Training Is Under Scrutiny," Mary Ann Roser stated, "Program at Huston-Tillotson may be in jeopardy if more students don't pass state test."[56] For the second consecutive year HT's Teacher Education program was accredited but placed under review because students failed to perform at the state's passing standard in the prior year. At that time ten schools were under review, four of which were HBCUs.

To address teacher education concerns, McMillan, with the help of the chairperson of the Division of Education, Dr. Judith Loredo, received matching funds to create a Center of Excellence in Teacher Education.[57] In his report to the Board in May 1998 McMillan stated:

> The Lilly Endowment/UNCF HBCU Grant created The Center of Excellence: A Vision of Teaching and Learning for the Twenty-first Century. The grant will: 1) establish an endowed professorship in Teacher Education with an initial corpus of $500,000; 2) upgrade the College's Local Area Network with expenditures of $100,000; and 3) set aside $112,500 from the grant for scholarships to be awarded to students majoring in Teacher Education. Additionally, HT applied to the Black College Fund of The United Methodist Church for a matching grant of $250,000. This money, if received, will be used as the matching funds for the Lilly Endowment Grant. Black College Fund has historically provided Huston-Tillotson College with both annual and special funding. When our matching requirement to the Lilly Endowment/UNCF HBCU Grant is satisfied, the College will have established an Endowed Professorship in Teacher Education with a corpus of $700,000 and will restrict the final distribution of $237,500 to fund student scholarships in Teacher Education.
>
> The College has received more than $735,000 during fiscal year in funds for the Centers of Teacher Excellence initiative which was authorized by the 75th and 76th Texas Legislative Sessions. We will receive a similar appropriation of $735,000 in the 2000–2001 Fiscal Year to continue our professional development of faculty, enhancement of technology, curriculum revision and

alignment, student recruitment in Teacher Education, and distance learning, in collaboration with the four other HBCUs of Texas.[58]

The monies received in 1998 provided funding for technology infrastructure for distance learning and faculty training in the use of that technology. Teacher Education had substantial scholarships for students and was in a much stronger position to be selective in admitting students. Money was also made available to support post-baccalaureate individuals interested in becoming teachers through its fast-track Teacher Certification Program. According to McMillan:

> Under Dr. Loredo's leadership we awarded course completion certificates to twenty-five (25) post-baccalaureate students in the Alternative Teacher Certification Program on Saturday, May 6, 2000. All of these persons will be teaching in the Austin Independent School District this fall, several in the critical shortage fields of math, science, and special education. These 25 students, along with the 97 graduates in the Class of 2000, represent the largest graduating class at Huston-Tillotson College in more than twenty years, with only three exceptions in 1980, 1981, and 1983. Moreover, the data from the Department of Admission and Financial Services indicate that we have every expectation of achieving our projected enrollment of not less than 600 students this fall.[59]

Whereas Teacher Education was able to rebound, other academic disciplines were not as they lacked similar institutional and grant support. Despite demographics that showed increases in the proportion of older Central Texans, HT was not able to sustain a grant program on gerontology. That program existed for about two years, providing students with both classroom and experiential learning, valuable for a career in aging programs.

The major in hotel and restaurant management, with expected longevity and success, ended abruptly. With special funding, professors were hired, and a full restaurant kitchen and dining room were created in the lower level of Evans Hall. Students practiced their skills by offering meals for faculty and staff in a simulated restaurant environment, and some students were hired to provide catering for special faculty functions. Doing this, and completing internships in tourist industries, students were provided broad experiences. This major had tremendous attraction for both US and international students. In 1999, interim VPAA MT[60] recruited Jamaican students, who were studying in Canada, to complete their final fourteen months at HT majoring in hotel and restaurant management. While still in its seedling state, growth was evident, goals were established, students were successful. However, after only three years, the hotel and restaurant management program abruptly ended due to MT's inappropriate treatment of the lead professor. MT's harassment of said professor was met with an instant resignation by that professor. This is what that professor told me: "MT entered my office, unannounced, and authoritatively told me how to use my office hours. The individual said, 'You need to cease what you are doing,' referencing the fact I was looking at my checkbook. I responded: 'You never liked me. I quit!'"[61] Without a leader for the program and lacking adequate funding to hire another competent person, the program was eventually dismantled.[62]

A program developed for faculty by faculty was the Institute for Research Training (IRT), a brainchild of Dr. Paul Anaejionu, political science professor in the Division of Social Sciences. The program had an advisory board that assisted with the implementation of its primary goals of securing funds for faculty to do research and to implement creative programs to enhance student learning. This institute was viable, received many grants for faculty research, and secured Dell computers for a student lab. McMillan applauded this program in 1998 but in 1999 dismantled it as an act of retaliation against Anaejionu for his participation in efforts to remove him from his presidency.

As noted in chapter 1, in 1988, HT was asked to partner with UT Austin, City of Austin, and Planned Parenthood to develop a response to the HIV outbreak. Through HT's Office of Cooperative Education, Project REACH (Regional Education for AIDS in Community Health) was created under Dr. King's administration but implemented during McMillan's administration. I was the contact person and the outreach educator for the project. It was through Project REACH that the first set of Huston-Tillotson's HIV peer educators came into being. Students were trained to share information about HIV and sexually transmitted infections (STI) with their peers and in the community. Some completed internships in HIV-serving local agencies. As Project REACH's outreach educator, I conducted workshops for professionals, at churches, and at schools, and engaged HT students in most of these activities. In conjunction with a United Negro College Fund consortium (UNC/HOPE), I worked with faculty to incorporate HIV-related content across the discipline, recognizing that the HIV epidemic and its consequences impacted many social institutions. An HIV nondiscriminatory policy for HT was developed during this time. Had HT's HIV projects and community involvement been allowed to grow and expand, I believe HT was poised to become an HBCU HIV education and research center of Central Texas. However, in 1990, without explanation, McMillan placed a halt to any talk about developing a center. I later continued my HIV work not under the auspices of HT but under Planned Parenthood of Austin.

It was during McMillan's administration that AusPREP (Austin STEM Pre-freshman Enrichment Program) started. This pre-engineer program for high school students began under the leadership of the natural sciences chairperson, Dr. General Marshall, who raised money through golf tournaments and supporters. The chosen students in the program have access to professional engineers while being taught math and sciences during the summer residential program. Many of the participants enrolled in HT became successful in STEM programs. AusPREP has continued and thrived through three HT presidencies.

Like McMillan, HT faculty wanted Huston-Tillotson to become a first-class institution. However, there were differences of opinion on how to get the college to that level. Faculty looked to the VPAA, Dr. Lenora Waters, for leadership. Waters was beloved by the majority of the professors as they knew that she had their best interests in mind. Waters was steadfast in moving faculty issues to the president as well as moving faculty towards fulfilling McMillan's vision. McMillan was not always receptive to Waters and might even have been jealous of the relationship she had with faculty. That might account for his 1999 decision to abruptly remove her from the position of VPAA. That presidential decision derailed academic programming that might have moved HT closer to McMillan's vision of what the institution could be.

Question of Austin Community College (ACC) on HT's Campus

Nineteen ninety-nine brought a new concern around HT's health and survival. Alumni heard that the administration was considering leasing some of HT's property to Austin Community College (ACC). These alums feared that ACC on HT campus might result in the end of HT as they knew it. Some of the questions they asked the president and board were: Where would HT end and ACC begin? How would HT students be distinguished from ACC students? Would HT become a two-year college? In response to the dissension, McMillan clarified the events that had taken place. He wrote his response in the *Ram* newsletter on February 28, 1996:

> Early in 1995, I was approached by representatives from Austin Community College to discuss the possibility of HT and ACC collaborating on various academic programs on the HT campus which would advance our respective

missions. At the March 1995 meeting of the HT Board of Trustees, the administration presented this idea to the Board, which adopted the following resolution:

To approved in principle: 1. The development of collaborative relationships with ACC for the purpose of implementing articulation agreements for cooperative academic programs on the HT campus, and 2. For the administration to proceed with dialogue regarding the development of a lease of a sufficient parcel of land that the college owns for construction of a building by ACC, and to further explore mutually beneficial program possibilities.

In turn, the Board of Trustees of both institutions authorize their top respective administrative officials to meet and talk about a potential collaborative academic relationship. Since that time, teams of faculty and staff from both colleges have met to discuss academic programs which complement our respective missions and to explore the viable terms of the proposed partnership. . . . We have not discussed a merger, a change of name, nor any alteration in our respective legal and governance structures or bylaws. Most of our conversations have been about academic programs.

Yes, we have talked about ACC constructing an academic building on a portion of HT's undeveloped land, not on existing campus. We have discussed leased arrangements to include payments that would provide valuable cash flow for HTC; right now, we do not have a written agreement to discuss. If and when we do, those facts will become public. Both Dr. [William] Segura [at ACC] and I have proceeded with the understanding and encouragement of both of our Boards of Trustees. Please be mindful that the HT Board of Trustees includes several alumni of the college. Your specific concerns have and will be adequately addressed.

The academic areas identified for development or expansion in collaboration on the campus of HT include the following:
1. Early childhood education, teacher education, and operation of a daycare center;
2. Gerontology, applied health care, certification, and perhaps the development of the upper levels of the nursing program;
3. Business administration, hospitality management program;
4. Criminal justice program; and
5. Computer science and technology program.

I am encouraged that so many people want to know the facts about this issue. I'm ever mindful of the passion of those who do not want HT to change, nor be manipulated by others. I'm also pleased that several individuals have written to me and shared their opinions, both pro and con.

In conclusion, I should assure you that the two schools are in the talking stage. No decisions have been made at this time, and no formal proposals has been developed or submitted to our boards for discussion. Should a proposal be developed, it will be debated by our respective boards.[63]

Some older alumni interviewed for this research remembered the rumors on campus about HT "merging with ACC." They remembered being alarmed that their beloved alma mater might lose its uniqueness as an HBCU. Having some alumni on the HT board resulted in their squelching the possibility of such a merger with ACC. Terry Smith, assistant to McMillan, recalls that ACC wanted to lease HT property off-campus, build a building on it and, in thirty years, the land and building would be part of HT.[64] Had that happened, according to him, HT would have had total access to that building in December 2027. He described the alumni dissatisfaction and believes that they stopped a project that he saw as beneficial to HT in the long term.

Relationship with Faculty

Dr. Lenora Waters, as chief academic officer at HT, is my starting point for my discussion of the relationship of Dr. McMillan and the faculty. She spoke candidly in my interview with her as she compared her relationship with Dr. King to that of Dr. McMillan. She said that Dr. King appreciated her and the faculty, recognizing that we (faculty) could have gone anywhere but were committed to HT, especially to students' success. "He [Dr. King] let employees do their job." About Dr. King, Dr. Waters said, "He had confidence in us: he didn't micromanage." She indicated that she felt Dr. McMillan was verbally dynamic, sharp, and intelligent, but he didn't have academic experience as a faculty member or as a college administrator, and that hindered his ability to relate deeply to faculty.[65]

While McMillan had ideas about what constituted a quality institution, he didn't understand, or appreciate, the vision and role of the faculty. It appeared he lacked an understanding that a college cannot operate without a well-trained professional faculty who felt valued by the administration. Some faculty members were demeaned by him, resulting in very qualified and previously committed faculty leaving HT under his presidency. Many alumni disconnected from HT both financially and personally by not participating in alumni activities and/or contributing financially to the university. Although his door were open to students, it was less open to faculty, and especially to our VPAA, Waters. According to Waters, McMillan created a "different environment," *when compared to King* (emphasis is mine).

Initially and throughout his presidency, faculty embraced McMillan's vision for creating a world-class institution; as stated before, they had very different ideas on how to achieve that vision. Faculty had mixed views of McMillan, as indicated by survey responses. Some were strong supporters, others were neutral, and others critical. Outward expression of thoughts and feelings related to McMillan (positive and/or negative) depended largely on tenure status. Those more openly outspoken were tenured, while many junior and/or nontenured professors were critical only behind closed doors for fear of losing their jobs.[66] A few professors who actively sought to hold McMillan accountable became easy scapegoats for his anger and his dismissal, the reason why most faculty members backed away from the conflict. But backing away from the conflict didn't protect some from McMillan's ill-treatment. Many faculty members stayed but still felt belittled and dispensable; morale was low, and unity was absent. One professor said, "McMillan would run the college without teachers if he could."

Throughout his presidency, McMillan was frustrated at what he considered "the slow pace of change in academics." His frustrations sometimes became conflicts with the leaders responsible for the content area. In the midst of low faculty morale, concerns about McMillan's personal behavior, and major divisions between constituents, some faculty began to question his fitness for the role of president. Others continued to hold him in high esteem. This schism created an unhealthy and hostile environment: "a war zone," as noted by one professor.

Faculty Senate, Sometimes Called Faculty Forum
During the fall of 1973, under King, members of HT faculty saw the need for a faculty organization to provide a forum for free expression and discussions on a broad range of matters of importance to the faculty. The faculty met and agreed to organize a faculty senate. A task force was appointed to outline its major goals and submit recommendations to the entire faculty for discussion and a vote. This senate met formally over several years, with the latest available minutes those of February 1975. Without written documents, I was unable to determine what happened with any faculty organization in subsequent years. Yet, I remember that the existence of the Faculty Senate or Forum was on and off.

In the fall of 1989, during the first year of McMillan's administration, members of the HT faculty proposed to reactivate the Faculty Forum and to reconstitute it as a Faculty Senate. A constitution was developed. During the 1989–1990 academic year, faculty used the Faculty Senate to express concerns on a wide range of topics along with recommendations for improvement.

The Faculty Senate sent a fifteen-page document to McMillan, covering the following areas: faculty contracts, pay inequities, work overload, academic freedom, arbitrary decisions, communication, research support, grants, faculty evaluations, hiring of new faculty, maintaining the integrity of departments, endowed chairs, support, and committee membership responsibilities.[67] McMillan provided a fifteen-page response to faculty concerns and recommendations. Below are some examples of concerns expressed by faculty and McMillan's responses.

1. CONCERN/RECOMMENDATION: Make a commitment to meet state averages for faculty salary within five years.
   McMillan's RESPONSE: Need to review the data on HBCUs in Texas.
2. CONCERN/RECOMMENDTION: Workload recommendation to reduce faculty course load per semester from 15 [hours] to 12, with no more than 3 preparations; department heads to 9 hours and division heads to 6 hours over the next two years.
   RESPONSE: The first sentence of this recommendation has merit, in that it implies that reducing the course load for all faculty members to twelve hours will increase the quality of instruction, faculty-student advisement, and participation by faculty in student activities, community outreach, proposal writing and planning and evaluation of curriculum, syllabi, and instructional effectiveness. Additionally, however, this sentence implies that faculty members are overloaded with committee assignments. The irony of this recommendation is that many faculty members, if not virtually all, have asked to be involved more—not less—in the decision-making processes of the College. Most important decisions are based on the input and recommendations of various committees, and this is likely to increase in the coming year. Moreover, it is the requirement of the Southern Association that faculty, as well as staff and students, have been involved extensively in the various Self-Study Committees, which occurs only once every ten years. As the College seeks to redefine and implement its Strategic Plan, and to involve faculty more actively in various levels of decision-making, committee participation and perhaps more, not less—is essential. We will evaluate the implication of this recommendation.... [I]t is significant to note here that many of our faculty members only work about the equivalent of a half-year, when you eliminate the College's

generous holidays, breaks, and short class days.⁶⁸

3. CONCERN/RECOMMENDATION: (a) Faculty should be involved in any proposals that directly affect curriculum and course content; (b) if faculty is not involved, they should not be expected to implement it.
RESPONSE: (a) This is already the policy and practice at the College [this response came during his second year as president; however, his practice over the years did not prove that his statement was true]; b. I agree!

4. CONCERN/RECOMMENDATION: Have a faculty representative at Cabinet meetings in order to give the faculty a voice in decisions related directly to faculty.
RESPONSE: No thank you! The Cabinet is the President's advisory group of senior administrators. Other means and processes "to give the faculty a voice" are affirmed and some are already in operation.

Members of the Faculty Senate felt responses such as these were inadequate or inappropriate and they responded with their additional concerns. During the middle of McMillan's administration, he stopped acknowledging the Faculty Senate as a viable institutional organization. Without his acceptance, some professors felt uneasy continuing their participation in the senate. Those faculty members who still saw a need for a faculty organization pushed faculty to organize an American Association of University Professors (AAUP) chapter. The chapter had low participation and existed for only one year. Later, though loosely organized, a few professors continued to meet infrequently to address specific matters, one being tenure. McMillan refused to offer tenure to a seasoned, qualified faculty member who was a department chairperson. Some professors challenged McMillan, and he reluctantly granted tenure to her. Still dissatisfied with McMillan's not affirming a faculty senate, some faculty shared that information with the 1999 SACS reaffirmation visiting team. The SACS team addressed this faculty concern with McMillan, who then affirmed the reorganization of the Faculty Senate.

A President's Dash Plagued with Crisis and Dissension
Dissension occurred early in McMillan's presidency. He began his presidency stating that he would not let "any rock be left unturned." McMillan said this often throughout his presidency, meaning that every aspect of HT's academics and culture should be reviewed and changed if he deemed necessary. He would make decisions without first studying and understanding the consequences of

those decisions. There were three major periods when internal dissension became public due to decisions he made. The first was the fiasco around changing the rules for Miss UNCF in 1989. The outrage associated with the change in the rules resulted in strong community intervention including signed petitions, newspaper editorials, alumni expression of dissatisfaction, and parental involvement.[69]

McMillan's Fourth Year

The second period of internal dissension came between September and November of 1992, during his fourth year of presidency. McMillan received a lot of negative press written in local Black newspapers *The Villager* and *NOKOA* about his leadership at HT. Dr. Reginald Christopher ('60), a retired dentist, penned the first three articles in three successive weeks. In his editorial article in *NOKOA*, September 1992, he discussed reasons for HT's low enrollment and why he resigned as Director of Alumni Affairs, a job he loved. According to Christopher:

> I resigned out of pure frustration with its current administration. I have had a relationship with the College for over 35 years and have seen it grow to its current physical statute [*sic*]. Through the years, I have listened to harbingers of doom deny the need for and predict the death of Huston-Tillotson College and other small, predominantly Black institutions. My belief in historical mission and purpose of these institutions has been sufficient to overcome such negativism and racism up to the past several years. For the first time, I am seriously concerned about the future of Huston-Tillotson College.
>
> There have been many outrageous incidences contributing to the College's current predicament, some of which I fully intend to deal with publicly. But the single most damning problem at the College is the lack of real, dedicated, moral, Christian leadership at the very top of its administration . . . rather, there is a system marked by duplicity. How long will alumni, faculty, staff, and students continue to endure the snickering in the community and the negative image that the College has fallen prey to the past several years? We must face this crisis that confronts us. Harsher statements are going to have to be made, and more direct action must be taken by alumni, staff, faculty and student body or our college is going to drift deeper into a hole from which the recovery time is directly proportional to the tenure of the current administration. . . .
>
> There is no corporation in the world with a budget the size of Huston-Tillotson College that would allow such incompetence from its top administration and governing board.[70]

That initial newspaper article resulted in Christopher's receiving negative calls from alumni who believed that HT's dirty laundry should not be aired. He responded to those attacks in his second article a week later. In that article he stated, "The attempts to stifle [his] first amendment rights by administration sycophants is not to be totally unexpected.... I challenge those upset alumni to describe one element of the article that we have not privately discussed and expressed dismay about.... I love Huston-Tillotson College, won't do anything to hurt it and don't apologize for anything I've said about the current leadership. I take a moral stand. I've taken my chance that the harsh glare of public exposure will somehow flush, purge and get it back to HT historical mission."[71]

Christopher wrote three additional articles in October and November 1992, confirming his belief that McMillan was incompetent and that a vote of no confidence was in order. According to him, "A four-year honeymoon ought to be over at Huston-Tillotson College. I think the current administration has not lived up to its expectations."[72]

Christopher's articles resulted in other voices appearing in the papers. Mrs. Nancy Crayton-Jones ('53), recipient of a 1994 HT honorary doctorate and the president of the International Alumni Association, wrote in *NOKOA*:

> Mr. Christopher in no way shape, form or fashion spoke for the alumni of Huston-Tillotson College, but as a non-supporting alumnus. If he was loyal, he would not have degraded the institution which helped him obtain an undergraduate education, [as well as for] his daughter, and is continuing to provide a well-rounded education for students in Austin. The alumni of the school are very supportive of Dr. McMillan, and make it very evident by their dedication, devotion, loyalty, and financial support. I agree many alumni are not doing their fair share to support the College as they should. How do we change or correct problems? Certainly not by sitting or by complaining. If you don't have a solution, don't be part of the problem. This Alumni Association wishes to go on record by stating we support Huston-Tillotson College, its administration, staff; will continue recruitment efforts, contributing financially to its needs and projecting a positive image of our beloved alma mater.[73]

An anonymous student responded in an article in the local newspaper, *The Villager*.

> I'm a student attending Huston-Tillotson College and have come to finally agree

with Dr. Christopher. What Dr. Reginald Christopher has discussed by revealing the extreme faults about the administration of Huston-Tillotson College. So I decide to voice my own opinion about the College that I attend. . . . This past weekend I saw even more; it made me dissatisfied. This administration and the people that work for it attempted to block out the opinion of Dr. Reginald Christopher from the entire student body. They told students during classes not to discuss the opinions of a former graduate of Huston-Tillotson College. Why would you do this? Dr. Christopher felt a need to expose the truth of your wicked behavior, now you try to hide it from us. On Friday, October 9, 1992, at about 4 o'clock several faculty and administration employees felt it their privilege to walk into the Student Union, and as they were leaving for home, grabbed large stacks of the new issue of *NOKOA*. I watched it take place and knew then it was well planned and well thought-out. The administration, under Dr. McMillan, our so-called president, would come in and keep truth from fellow students yearning to read about the recent views expressed by our former graduate Dr. Reginald Christopher. . . . Don't hide the truth from us.[74]

I chimed in, writing an article in *NOKOA*:

This is probably the most difficult editorial I've ever written, and yet it is one that I must write. It is difficult because of how it might be misinterpreted by those who want to keep the problem about our beloved institution in-house. It is necessary because I know that the way to keep a family, church, or educational institution dysfunctional is to keep its members silent. Breaking the conspiracy of silence is the first step towards recovery. . . . I am standing with Dr. Christopher by saying that I acknowledge that there are problems at our beloved institution. I believe that once we get beyond the defensive and denial stage, we can address the real issues that plague our institution and get on the road to recovery. . . . Vindictiveness has no place in the recovery, and the redirection of this very important family! The future of our institution depends on it! There are still hundreds of thousands of people who need us to educate them.[75]

The *Austin American-Statesman* picked up the story with an investigative article:

In the midst of the fortieth anniversary celebration, Huston-Tillotson College has forsaken nostalgia for a hard look at its future and its finances. Gone are scholarships funded by the College's operating fund, part-time teachers, and the track team. In the works is a revamped curriculum with insufficient majors scrapped and more marketable ones introduced. . . . Austin's oldest College is embarking on a far-reaching overhaul, striving to survive a future financial uncertainty. Pres. Joseph T. McMillan, Junior says the restructuring is not a desperate gambit, but shrewd planning for the future. "We made severe financial decisions over the summer," he said, "tough decisions! But we wanted to get ahead of the game, not behind. We are in good shape." But not everyone is happy with the new direction of the Historically Black liberal arts college. Among the concerns: a drop in enrollment, poor accounting practices, a low student return rate and low faculty morale. And some say McMillan, named college president four years ago, has provided poor leadership.

A more hard-nosed approach to business was adopted. Students could no longer register for classes if they owed money from the previous semester. About $500,000 in college-financed scholarships was diverted to high-priority campus repairs and acquisitions. Enrollment plunged. Almost 40 percent, or 208, of the previous semester's students didn't return in August, according to college statistics. Though new students and transfer students brought overall enrollment to 536 full-time students, that was still 117 fewer than the previous year: the lowest in three years. . . . "We made a long-term one-time-only investment in the future—the College rather than in students," McMillan said. The money was used for infrastructure and to improve the computer system.

Notice of the scholarship cuts was mailed by the end of June, but several students say they learned of the change only after arriving for school. It was another frustrating indication of the inefficient manner in which the College is run, they said. "I understand you have to cut back here and there, but my God, why do you wait until the students get to school to tell them you have 36 hours to come up with the money?" asked Junior, Tracy Reed, Sec. of the school's student Government Association.

Students made additional complaints about lost or late financial aid paperwork, inaccurate tuition statements. and difficulty in getting refunds. "God practically has to come down and get them to release the check to you," said Junior Kimberly Wilson, who said she waited four months for last semester's refund. McMillan said the school made its best efforts to spread the news of scholarship cuts, acknowledged the complaints, and blamed the ancient computer for most of the problems. He believes a new computer system will vastly improve services at the College.

Such behind-the-scenes grumbling is mild in comparison to the public debates that occur during much of fall '92 on the editorial pages of *NOKOA – The Observer*, a weekly newspaper. Articles by Reginald Christopher, a local dentist and former Huston-Tillotson College director of alumni affairs, blasted his alma mater's direction and leadership.

The *NOKOA* fracas continued with Rosalee Martin Wingate, Chairperson of the Social Science Division, who wrote her own editorial supporting Christopher's opinion and adding concerns about the low teacher morale. "Relations between McMillan and many of the faculty generally have not been good. I don't know if he knows what we do," Wingate said in an interview, pointing out that McMillan has never taught at a college. "Teacher morale has further been eroded," Wingate said, "by budget cuts for equipment, travel, and professional education opportunities such as seminars."

General Marshall, head of the Natural Sciences Division, disagrees. He says faculty members he knows enjoy their work. The school has teachers who "are genuinely concerned about students and who will care about them as people, not just as students."

McMillan simply dismissed Wingate's claims. "I talked to faculty. I visit faculty. I visit classrooms," he said. "I am proud of my sensitivity to what faculty members go through."[76]

In the *Austin American-Statesman* article McMillan stated that he sent letters to students in June 1992, but the actual letter was not sent until December 3, 1992.

December 1992
To Huston-Tillotson College Students and Students' Families Greetings:
The 1992–93 fall semester has come to an end. By every measure, it has been an extremely productive time in the life of the College. The purpose of this letter is to follow up on a letter which I sent to all students who have an outstanding balance to the College, dated December 3, 1992. In the spirit of open communications, I feel strongly that all members of the extended College family should be kept informed about what's going on.
Very simply, our Business Office was most generous and flexible, during the fall registration period, to work with all students who had an outstanding balance, to facilitate their registration. Many students signed Repayment Agreements and many of these students and others signed Deferred Payment Plans for the 1992–93 fall semester. Surely, the College recognizes the harsh impact of the national economy on the lives of our students and their families.

However, the College is first and foremost a business whose primary product is education. We—like any other business—cannot operate without sufficient revenue for our services. We—like all businesses—must pay our bills each month in order to remain in operation.

The harsh reality is that a significant number of our students have not fulfilled their financial obligations to the College. If you are not among that number, I hasten to express the College's appreciation for your faithful discharge of your responsibilities. We value you very much as a cherished customer; and we look forward to seeing you on campus in January of 1993. Regrettably, several of your classmates will not be with us!

If you, or your family member, on the other hand, happen to be one who has not fulfilled *all* financial obligations to the College, I must admit my serious disappointment. The College has made its best efforts to be cooperative and reasonable. However, you have not done your fair share. Therefore, in compliance with the policies established by our Board of Trustees, I regret that the College has no other alternative but the following:

1. To expect that you will fulfill all of your financial obligations to the College, immediately;
2. To withhold your grades for the current semester and your transcript, until all financial obligations to the College have been fulfilled;
3. To deny you the opportunity to enroll for the Spring Semester or for any subsequent semester, until all financial obligations have been fulfilled;
4. To deny you the opportunity to move back or camp out in the residence hall, if you are a campus student, or to participate in any way in the practices or games of the athletic program, until all financial obligations have been fulfilled;
5. To refer your account to our external collection agency and legal counsel to assist the College to collect from you and your assets, and any expenses incurred in the process, if you do not make full payment or acceptable repayment arrangements with the Business Office, by January 15, 1993.

During the past semester, the College has issued at least three statements of student accounts to students with an outstanding balance. If, for any reason, you think that our records are in error, in any way, please call our Business Office, immediately, and ask to speak with our Student Accounts Officer, Ms. Pasty Flake. Effective, December 21, 1992. I assure you that Ms. Flake or her supervisor will work with you patiently and courteously to resolve any dispute or error on our part.

In closing, I want to share the Good News about the College. The administration, faculty, and staff move forward with plans to implement a Total Quality Management initiative in 1993. We seek to establish a World Class institution, which affirms the College's commitments to quality attitudes, quality communications, quality campus community, and quality educational programs and services. You will be hearing more about this plan soon and the role which we will be asking you to play, as we review our Mission, clarify our Vision, and strengthen our Strategic Plan for the future. Under separate cover, you will also be receiving a Season's Greetings letter soon, which will outline our significant accomplishments during 1992.

I close with a personal expression of appreciation for your support for Huston-Tillotson College.

Sincerely,
Joseph T. McMillan, Jr.
President

P.S. We are still reviewing applications and admitting new and returning students for the Spring Semester. If you know of interested students, please ask them to call Dean Charles Dubra . . . immediately!

To be sure, students must meet their financial obligations, and the financial security of HT rests in part on students paying their bills. As the students' president, Dr. McMillan gave institutional scholarships even when money and financial aid was not available, conveying to students a false sense that education is free. Not informing students on a timely basis that expected scholarships would be cut resulted in many students not having the funds to return to school. A consequence was that fewer students returned the next semester due to lack of money. McMillan's actions contributed to a cycle of student dropouts that resulted in a financial shortfall.

These private and public utterings in 1992 resulted in little change at the institution. For the next seven years conflicts were either squelched or people kept personal feelings to themselves. The well-being of students continued to be paramount for teachers and most staff, but students not paying their bills continued to be a problem, as were recruitment and retention. The academic work, handled mainly at the division level, was mainly in curriculum review, program assessment, student advising, and overall academic success. McMillan continued being nontransparent in many ways, imposing less than best practice expectations on professors, sometimes punishing those who wouldn't comply. Despite the fact that there was little outward expression of group dissatisfaction, there was an often-unspoken belief held by many faculty and staff that McMillan valued himself more than he did students and professors.

1999—Dr. McMillan's Final Crisis
McMillan's final crisis came in July 1999, following his appointment of MT as Vice President for Academic Affairs. Faculty believed MT was not qualified to hold that position. MT's appointment caused the most intense dissent against McMillan's presidency, as it was intertwined with the 1998 self-study difficulties, the financial aid reimbursement scandal, and extremely low faculty morale. These various episodes of dissatisfaction and unrest caught fire and could not be suppressed, hidden, denied, or silenced.

Although she felt faculty outrage may have negatively impacted the outcome of HT's 1999 reaccreditation, senior administrator Bronté Jones described McMillan this way:

> Dr. McMillan was unqualified and led with his heart and not with his head. He made rash decisions not in the best interest of the College. Once he made a decision, he would not change it even if his administrative team counseled against it. He was a dictator who relished in chaos and drama. He could be punitive and messy. He did not do things that were in good practice. A major problem was that the leadership team went through a revolving door; frequent changes impede stability.[77]

Faculty unrest was evident on many fronts; some quit and filed grievances. Some were mistreated but stood firm. A former faculty member sent this email to me:

> November 3, 1999
> I spent seven years being very outspoken at HTC about the needs of the students, faculty, and the curriculum. Some of what I fought for was received, but most of what I said fell on deaf ears. Many times we worked very hard on proposals which only required the support of the executive administration in order to succeed. We usually did not ever receive a response. Four years ago, when I took steps to exercise staff discipline in my department, the departmental headship was taken from me. At the same time the Rank and Tenure committee was so

pleased with my academic and administrative performance, they recommend promotion to Associate Professor.

Last year I was promised a well-deserved raise and signed a contract promising such, which was violated by the administration's default. The worst thing to happen, in my opinion, to my department was the administration's failure to dismiss an inept department head who in two years drove away over half of our students and greatly discouraged the rest. I made the facts known at every opportunity. When I could not take it any longer, I left as quickly as possible.

I have a lot of great memories of my associates and students, but I have a lot of disappointments over what great things we might have accomplished if we had been empowered to do so. My best wishes in your efforts to affect [*sic*] meaningful change and to create a new HTC which can finally fulfill the mission to which we were called and assembled.

Appointment of MT, the Beginning of the End of Dr. McMillan's Presidency
In 1999 Dr. McMillan removed Dr. Lenora Waters from her position of Vice President of Academic Affairs. He did this without informing her, as she heard it when the internal letter was sent to all faculty and staff. President McMillan gave the Acting VPAA position to an Upward Bound director. Upward Bound is a high school program held on college campuses; that was the appointee's only college connection. MT had no college teaching or college administrative experience. Appointing MT in that position was seen as disrespectful, a betrayal of the faculty, and extremely deceitful. His appointment was made during the summer when the majority of faculty members were away from campus. However, some faculty were on campus and received the announcement of MT's "promotion."

In a July 14, 1999, letter to McMillan, fourteen faculty members called for a meeting with him. They strongly felt that by promoting MT to Acting Vice President of Academic Affairs the president clearly demonstrated an inability to make appropriate appointment decisions that would strengthen the college. The faculty met in a spirit of compromise, hoping that McMillan would understand their position related to MT's appointment, and would reconsider it. Being in the middle of our self-study, an important faculty question was "How will the Self-Study team evaluate our institution's Academic Affairs unit with the appointment of MT?" This and other critical questions were included in a prepared letter given to Dr. McMillan prior to the meeting. Early in the meeting it became clear that he would not budge as he became very defensive about his power to make the appointment. McMillan responded to the faculty in writing on July 16, 1999.[78] His introductory statements included:

> ... while I hear your dismay, I believe that your concerns are unduly reactionary.... I appeal to you to give MT a chance to do his job. I am confident that MT can serve effectively in this interim position if you will work with him cooperatively and with an open mind and heart. You have listed two recommendations: 1) that MT will not be offered the position of Vice President for Academic Affairs and that 2) Dr. Judith Loredo be offered that position.... I am confident that the self-study team will evaluate our Academic Affairs unit based upon our responses to the SACS criteria regarding academic instruction, curriculum, teaching effectiveness and the credentials of faculty.... I believe the self-study team will affirm the qualification of MT's credentials as an "ABD" [all but dissertation] candidate for PhD. I believe that the team will muse and perhaps comment about the morale of the faculty and your lack of support for your President and my decision to appoint MT, if you express this concern.[79] However, I believe that most members of the Self-Study team will affirm the President's right to choose whoever the President believes can do the job effectively.... Furthermore, MT's appointment is a win-win for HT as follows: a win for Dr. Waters[80] in that it recognizes her distinguished career in higher education and crowns it with the singular, focused challenge to lead the College through the critical final stages of the Self-Study process; a win for faculty in that it provides a timely process of transition in leadership, a wonderful "window of opportunity" to help create a "change in the culture of faculty self-governance, assessment, and accountability," and an invitation to help choose a worthy successor to the VPAA; it's a win for the College in that it takes advantage of interim enthusiastic leadership in Academic Affairs, with a fresh perspective, while we complete our Self-Study under the seasoned leadership of Dr. Waters.

Many faculty members didn't accept this argument in person or in writing. I believe McMillan's incompetence was glaring. Insight came from his description of MT as being an enthusiastic leader. Another word for "enthusiastic leader" was a pawn that would carry out his wishes. Without saying it, he evaluated Dr. Waters as not being enthusiastic in the VPAA position; she often questioned his decisions and supported the faculty too much. Placing her over the self-study was not a way of honoring her but rather replacing her with someone he could control. She knew this and retired at the end of the academic year.

CHAPTER 2

Since McMillan did not remove MT from the position of Acting VPAA, many professors asked to speak to the board to share their concerns. McMillan was not fazed by this request as he had offered an amendment to the board's bylaws in November 1990: "to clarify that the Vice Presidents of the College are staff of the corporation and senior administrative officers of the College, who serve under the supervision of the Presidents, and as such, are not officers of the Corporation and may not obligate the corporation in any way, except by the delegation of specific duties and responsibilities by the President, who maintains the authority and accepts full responsibility for their actions and decisions."[81] This amendment precludes the board from reversing his decision or intervening on behalf of the faculty. The board approved the change, indicating that they would not intervene on behalf of the faculty.

The faculty members weren't aware that McMillan had the decision sewn up, so a meeting between faculty and trustees was set to coincide with a semiannual board meeting. The time and date were agreed upon, but the time was suddenly changed to three hours earlier. I believe that this change was intended to guarantee no or limited faculty participation. However, twenty-three of the approximate forty-four full-time faculty members were present. This occurred because a point person was assigned in each building to notify persons in that building if a time change occurred. Once I was informed of the time change, I called them. Faculty members met with the remaining few trustees in the president's dining room, still dirtied with lunch dishes not yet removed. These faculty members requested that McMillan and other administrators be asked to leave but were denied. Faculty members spontaneously described their experiences with MT and McMillan. After each professor shared, the five or six remaining trustees were not moved, and in fact some said disrespectful things to the faculty. The faculty left demoralized, not only by the time change and the unclean dining room but by the dismissive attitude of Board members. One faculty member quit. The reason she gave was this: HT was a "war zone" and she "did not sign up for war."

Three faculty members—Dr. Paul Anaejionu, Mrs. Harriet Buxkemper, and I—felt so strongly about MT's appointment and the overall treatment of faculty that we engaged in an all-out campaign for the removal of MT. Letter writing, meetings, and verbal attempts to bring about change were the initial strategies. On July 21, 1999, Mrs. Buxkemper sent a letter to MT asking him to give up his internship as VPAA. On the same date she sent a letter to Dr. John Rouche, MT's UT professor/advisor.

Dear MT

Senior faculty at Huston-Tillotson College met with Dr. Joseph T. McMillan, Jr. regarding the recent personnel changes he has made on our campus. We welcome the opportunity for you to serve in an academic internship on campus to fulfill the requirements of your doctoral program at the University of Texas at Austin. At the same time, we have stated to Dr. McMillan and wish to inform you directly, that we request that any appointment of a new Vice President for Academic Affairs be made with input from faculty.

We do not concur with Dr. McMillan's decision to appoint you Acting Vice President for Academic Affairs for a one-year period in order to fulfill your internship requirement. We have requested that he reconsider this decision since we believe strongly that the senior academic officer of the College should have several key qualifications. These include extensive teaching experience at the postsecondary level, an earned doctoral degree, a clear vision for academics at the College, and academic administrative experience.... Further, we have stated our objection to such a major decision relating to academics at the College being made without any input from senior faculty.

We want Dr. Judith Loredo to be appointed for a one-year term as Acting Vice President for Academic Affairs. She has agreed to serve in this capacity and to supervise your internship in the area of Academic Affairs. We believe this offers a solution both for faculty desire for input in decisions relating to academics, and your need to serve an internship in this area.

We are sending a copy of this letter to your adviser at the University of Texas at Austin. We would like for him to know our position on this matter.

Mrs. Buxkemper included a copy of her letter to MT with one that was sent to Dr. Rouche: "We, the faculty of Huston-Tillotson College, are disturbed by the appointment of MT as Acting Vice President for Academic Affairs. We will not support him in this position. We recommend that you advise MT to seek an alternate internship that would help him achieve his educational goals." The letter was sent with the hope that Dr. Rouche would remove him as an intern. Dr. Rouche responded that he did not want to interfere with HT's operations.

Other correspondences were sent to the HT board and to its president. In response to letters written to Jim George, attorney at law and the president of the Board of Trustees, Mr. George wrote to Anaejionu, Buxkemper, and me as follows.[82]

CHAPTER 2

July 27, 1999
Dear Dr. Anaejionu, Ms. Buxkemper and Dr. Martin:
Thank you for your letter of July 20, 1999, and the accompanying observations. Your letter and the observations raise many serious concerns. However, the specific catalyst for those concerns seems to have been the decision by the Board of Trustees to approve retaining MT as the Acting Vice President for Academic Affairs to accomplish specific numerated tasks during the school year.

The Board of Trustees has determined that it is imperative that the administration of the College and all of the College family be evaluated against specific measurable objectives. MT has been assigned five very distinct tasks which we believed were important and that needed to be handled by someone on an interim basis until a permanent Vice President for Academic Affairs could be selected. Given Dr. Waters's announcement of her impending retirement and given the need to concentrate as much time as possible on the accreditation process for which she is responsible, it was our judgment that the specific tasks assigned to Dr. MT[83] could be best performed by someone who was not on the faculty and who would not remain with the College after those tasks had been completed.

As I told Dr. Anaejionu, it was our judgment that we are too thinly staffed with faculty to divert our outstanding leaders to these five tasks. We wanted the faculty to teach, as opposed to determining the schedules for the Spring and Summer sessions of the year 2000, or implementing articulation agreements with various other institutions. It was also our judgment that someone needed to take on the day-to-day responsibility of finding potential candidates to be reviewed by the faculty and the Board of Trustees, as well as the administration, for acting as the permanent Vice President of Academic Affairs. It is my personal desire that we bring in a new person to take on this responsibility, not try to promote from within.

Obviously, I am one vote on the Board of Trustees and do not speak for the Board, but I hope that we can select a whole group of outstanding people who are interested in the job and would be willing to make a change and come to Huston-Tillotson College. As I see it, and as I believe most of the Board of Trustees sees it, there is one central problem facing Huston Tillotson College and that is that we have been unable to attract an adequate number of qualified, motivated, responsible students. This situation has existed since 1987 when I first joined the Board and has not improved significantly since then. There are many reasons and excuses for our failure to attract an adequate student body.

We have had very difficult financial circumstances that are continually aggravated by problems that we have encountered. We have had inadequate equipment and facilities, from computers to buildings, and we have had mismanagement in some of our fiscal affairs that have resulted in criminal prosecution of some of our staff. However, it is my personal view that we have reached a point where we cannot accept any more excuses.

Frankly, it's irrelevant to me whose fault it is. Ultimately, it is the Board's responsibility to hire a president, an administration, and a faculty who can recruit and retain students who want to take advantage of the special education they can receive at Huston-Tillotson College. As far as I am personally concerned, it is everyone's fault that the College has not succeeded in recruiting and retaining students. We need an emphasis on accountability and success for everyone on that campus. It has been my hope that we are making progress in that area.

Thank you again for your candid comments. All of your views are seriously considered by the Board of Trustees of Huston-Tillotson College. However, it is my judgment that MT's nine-month assignment to achieve five specific tasks is a relatively minor decision in the grand scheme of the College's success. There are very important decisions that have to be made in the next year and if we do not recruit and retain students in adequate numbers to justify the College's existence, the choices that the Board of Trustees have about Huston-Tillotson's future will be significantly reduced.

If any of you would like to visit with me in person, please call my office and set up a time to come in and I will be happy to talk with you.

On August 10, 1999, Anaejionu and Buxkemper responded almost word by word to Mr. George's letter, correcting factual errors and sharing their understanding of the problem, with an emphasis on the fact that the major problem was not just HT's problem with recruitment and retention but with administrative decisions about personnel. They also mentioned that "fault" did matter and that persons should be held accountable. Mr. George responded on August 13, 1999.[84]

Dear Dr. Anaejionu, Dr. Buxkemper:
I was disappointed that you cancelled our meeting scheduled for August 12th to review the contents of your letter of August 10th. I believe that we will have an opportunity to discuss your concerns in the near future. Prior to my conversation, however, I would like to respond to your letter of August 10. First, as Chairman of the Board of Trustees, I am disappointed and concerned about all aspects of Huston-Tillotson College. That disappointment and concern does not exclude

the administration, the faculty, the financial aid office, or any other part of the College. It is my personal view that every aspect of Huston-Tillotson College needs dramatic improvement. We need better and more effective maintenance, security, and grounds operations. We need more effective fundraising, more effective faculty, and we need a more committed and responsible student body.

It has been my personal goal to move Huston-Tillotson College forward and improve each aspect of the campus and the campus community while I had the opportunity and privilege of being Chairman of the Board of Trustees. We are in the midst of an elaborate, well thought-out, long-range planning process in which we are, as a Board and as a community, reexamining every aspect of the College so that by the school year 2001–2002 we are implementing the change in all aspects of Huston-Tillotson's life that are necessary to make it a viable, effective institution for the 21st century. I believe every aspect of Huston-Tillotson will change as a result of this process.

It has been *my impression that there has been an attitude at Huston-Tillotson that is present in the administration, the faculty, the grounds and security department, and in the students that "it's not my job,"* and that personal pride, personal status and personal interest have taken priority over the interest of the College. You and your group are correct in your assumption that there is a "hidden agenda" in the selection of MT for the interim position of Acting Vice-President of Academic Affairs. That agenda is that I, as Chairman of the Board, have determined that the status quo at Huston-Tillotson College must change. While I do not speak for the Board, I believe others agree with me. [Italics are mine.]

The College is not retaining an adequate number of the students who enroll at the freshman and transfer level. For some reason, those students do not believe that it is in their best interest to return to finish their Baccalaureate degree at Huston-Tillotson College. That must change. For some reason, Huston-Tillotson has found it very difficult to recruit responsible, committed new students in adequate numbers who will pay their bills, make their grades and act responsibly on campus. If I have anything to do with it, we are going to change those facts so that we retain the students.

Huston-Tillotson will retain the students by convincing them that the quality of the education they receive and the quality of the campus is so good that it would be foolish to transfer to another institution. Huston-Tillotson College will get responsible, committed new students by convincing the public that the best education and the quality of the campus experience offered, and the quality of the spiritual and religious life on this campus is such that families cannot afford not to send their children to Huston-Tillotson College. I am not sure how this change can be accomplished, but it must occur even if the administration, faculty, staff, maintenance staff, student aid office, and Board of Trustees must all be replaced. Of course this will not happen but change and improvement are necessary.

I do not question the sincerity of your group's concerns. As a practical matter, I am not willing to change the decision about MT because I want someone in that position that absolutely have [sic] no loyalty to anyone on that campus and who will bring new vigor to the position for a period of time and help the administration, the faculty, and the Board of Trustees select a permanent Vice-President of Academic Affairs that will continue the reinvigoration of Huston-Tillotson College. Your expressions of concern are healthy. Your concern about the President is healthy. Your concern about the staffing of Vice Presidents is healthy and I believe you are truly committed to the welfare of Huston-Tillotson College and not to your personal agenda.

Disagreement is healthy. However, disagreement that gets in the way of commitment is destructive. Hopefully, everyone associated with Huston-Tillotson College can disagree with each other but remain committed to invigorating Huston-Tillotson College to such an extent that the great tradition of Huston-Tillotson College will be fully restored and there will be a waiting list of students clamoring to attend.

I look forward to having our meeting in the near future.

Yours sincerely,
Jim George
cc: Board of Trustees

The correspondence above from Mr. George as the board president clearly indicated his dissatisfaction with every aspect of Huston-Tillotson, believing strongly that each constituent of the college failed to attract and retain motivated, responsible students. Low enrollment and low retention plagued McMillan's administration, but Anaejionu, Buxkemper, and I felt the crisis at hand was about a poor administrative appointment, resulting in faculty unrest. Attorney George's letter also stated why he and board members approved MT's appointment indicating five core functions MT was to fulfill. But faculty experienced disrespect and mistreatment that were not included in the stated functions. Moreover, those working with MT saw his arrogance and authoritative actions demeaning and clearly falling outside the board-given parameters most of the time. Attorney George's explanation added fuel to the fire, and the three dissentient professors took their case to the newspapers.

When none of our efforts worked, we went to the *NOKOA*, *The Villager*, and *Austin American-Statesman* newspapers. Three articles appeared, including one in *NOKOA* written September 9, 1999, by me; one in the *Austin American-Statesman* written by Mary Ann Roser and published September 10, 1999; and one in *The Villager* on September 24, 1999, again written by me. In the *NOKOA* article, "HT Rebellion," I opposed McMillan's dictatorial leadership which was further intensified when McMillan justified his appointment of intern MT with the following statement: "I meditated, and God directed me to do it."[85] "What?!" was the general faculty response.

The *Austin American-Statesman* investigative article by Ms. Roser on September 10, 1999, was titled, "Huston-Tillotson's Crisis of Confidence: Fight Against President Divides the Campus." Ms. Roser contacted McMillan, George, and board members, as well as Anaejionu, Buxkemper, and me. In her article, Roser stated:

> "Three outspoken professors, an irrepressible college president and a prominent attorney are at the center of an increasingly bitter dispute at Austin's oldest institution. 'I'm concerned about the image this is creating in the wider community,' said Board of Trustees member Wilhelmina Delco, a former state legislator, who defended McMillan and was reluctant to discuss the dispute. 'It's like scabs breaking a union shop.'
>
> "Board Chairman, First Amendment–free speech Attorney, Jim George, threatened one of the three faculty members with a defamation lawsuit and was angered by the *Austin American-Statesman* inquiries. 'What are you trying to do, close the college?' asked George, who has given time and money to the school. He said the faculty should calm down and accept Dr. McMillan's appointee, MT.
>
> "Twenty-three faculty members, more than half of the full-time faculty, signed a resolution on Aug 17, 1999, urging McMillan to appoint "someone with the necessary experiences, credentials and leadership qualities." Eight faculty members signed a statement of no-confidence in McMillan, who has weathered several high-profile controversies in recent years, including high rates of default on student loans and embezzling by former financial aid office employees.
>
> 'This school was here before we came, and we need to leave it better for future generations,' said Anaejionu (14 years at HT), Political Science professor.... 'If we fail to do that, then we have failed in our missions.'
>
> Dr. McMillan entered this conflict with faculty in the middle of low student

enrollment and financial problems including inadequate funds for basic supplies. Dr. McMillan said in the article that his faculty resists change, and he is trying to make them more accountable . . .' some faculty do not keep regular office hours, provide syllabuses to their students or show up on time for class. Part of MT's job is to monitor that. . . . I feel I am called to lead HT into the 21st century,' he said. 'What we are doing is rattling the cages of complacency."

Impulsive behavior was evident when he became angry when a student criticized a mission statement he had written as "fabricated." The president responded by shooting his middle finger into the air. McMillan said he was sorry as soon as he did it . . . he wrote a letter apologizing for his "angry finger."

Student Government President Jason Campbell indicated that he thought that MT will do a good job, and that President McMillan is a good president to a degree. 'Sometimes he's too involved with the students, and sometimes students take advantage of that.' Another student, Rosa Nichols, circulated a petition supporting faculty and quickly got fifty signatures. According to Nichols, 'I know for a fact these professors are not getting credit for what they do. The harassment these guys are taking is ridiculous'"[86]

Roser further said that "Dr. McMillan had proposed putting the college up for collateral. 'As it turns out,' he said, 'the potential lenders were right.'"

McMillan's executive vice president, Terry Smith, stated in a December 2017 interview that he felt, in hindsight, that the institution's crisis was primarily because "we [top administration] should have done a better job letting people know what we were trying to do with the college. We were not using our internal communication mechanism to share with each other; being transparent should have been done showing that what we are doing would be in the best interest of the body [HT constituents]. If the body is not involved, they will find reasons to object."[87] In my 2017 interview with former board president Attorney George, he revealed that "in hindsight, I realized that Dr. McMillan was not the right person for the presidency." That was an admission, however, that he didn't make in 1999. George also said that board members never have a complete picture of what goes on at the college. In fact, they see "as through a straw, only what the president presents." His 1999 letters were very different from his 2017 acknowledgments. George's relationship with me was different in 2017 than in 1999, when he threatened to sue me. In 2017 he contributed $5,000 towards this research.

There were more than twenty letters and memos exchanged among McMillan, Board President George, Anaejionu, Buxkemper, the faculty, and me between

June and October 1999, with no change in anyone's position. Although the battle seemed to be between the three outspoken persons and the administration, faculty as a whole were impacted and weighed in, as shown in the memo below.

> To: Dr. Joseph T. McMillan, President
> From: The Faculty
> Date: August 17, 1999
> Dear Dr. McMillan:
> The following resolution has been voted by an overwhelming majority of the faculty of this college:
>
> During the coming academic year Huston-Tillotson College faces formidable challenges. We must complete the accreditation process, develop a strategic plan for the future, implement a new core curriculum, increase enrollment, and raise academic standards. To accomplish these tasks, which affect the health, vitality, and survival of this institution, we need strong leadership in the office of Vice President of Academic Affairs—someone with appropriate credentials and extensive experience in college teaching and administration. In view of these facts we, the faculty of Huston-Tillotson College, urge you to appoint someone with the necessary experience, credentials, and leadership qualities as Vice President of Academic Affairs, and to appoint MT as an intern to assist the Vice President for Academic Affairs.
>
> We sincerely hope that you will comply with the wishes of the faculty as expressed in the above resolution.
>
> Respectfully,
> Signatures of 20 faculty members[88]

Although the full list of correspondences highlighting the severity of the conflicts between June 1999 and June 2000 are held in HT Archives, I include here part of a memo I sent to McMillan on September 13, 1999:

> MEMO
> To: Dr. Joseph T. McMillan, Jr., President
> From: Dr. Rosalee Martin, Sociology Professor
> Re: Many Concerns
> Date: September 13, 1999
>
> 1. Although I am no longer chairperson of the Social Science Division, I am concerned about what is happening to the division. It appears

that it is being dismantled, step by step. This is in relation to MT making schedule changes without consulting faculty, hiring professors without consulting faculty and not ordering textbooks requested by some faculty.

2. Six weeks have gone by since Intern MT, Acting VPAA, has taken over the academic affairs' unit. During those six weeks he overly monitored faculty in their office for no apparent reason. MT didn't attend required meetings while insisting that faculty does. He was very aggressive and unprofessional in how he treated professors, resulting in one professor quitting on the spot. He was offended when memos addressed him as Intern MT, rather than MT, VPAA, believing that the memos were not addressed to him. He showed poor interpersonal skills; and he was a bully. It became clear during these six weeks that his mandate was to prune the faculty, causing persons to leave due to harassment or stress. It actually worked in three cases. At a time when HT had limited financial resources, MT had the computer science teacher fired, and hired a firm to teach Computer Science rather than hire a full-time professor even though the cheapest would be the latter: at least $60,000 cheaper.

3. Where does Mr. Terry Smith fit within the Academic Affairs Unit? He sent faculty a memo requesting copies of our syllabi. I thought that this was MT's job! Is there anyone at HT who does not have the authority to give us orders? We get orders from the Business Office, Recruitment Office, Registrar's Office, and others. Yet, we ask none of these persons to teach for us!

4. I am glad that you "respect the faculty's right to speak out and will not retaliate." . . . But non-tenured faculty don't believe that. They ask tenured professors to be their voice. They know of others who experienced your wrath.

5. MT said that you asked him to be Acting Vice President for Academic Affairs. You said that he asked you. Both of you cannot be right. Someone is not telling the truth. Yet, you ask us to trust you! Trust is earned!

6. Attorney James George wrote the following statement in his September 2, 1999, letter to me. I'm not sure what he meant by it. Perhaps you can interpret it for me. "It is certainly possible that you are absolutely correct that Dr. McMillan is the wrong person to lead

Huston-Tillotson College. If you are correct, and ultimately the Board of Trustees agrees with you, your current *gorilla* [my italics] warfare against Dr. McMillan, the Board, and the College will not have the effect of causing the Board to remove Dr. McMillan but will have the effect of destroying the College."

7. MT said that you assigned him the responsibility of overseeing some of the existing grants. I asked him if this is a sixth area of measurable objectives as outlined by the President. He said "no," that it falls under *Number 4* which speaks about establishing and implementing viable articulation agreements and programs with ACC and others. I read that area many times and cannot see how grant management falls within that category. Can you explain that to me? If he can just walk in and take over existing grants, what incentive is it for anyone to write a grant?

I am expecting a response to many of my concerns. Thanks.

cc: Mr. James George[89]
Faculty

McMillan did not respond to this email. The faculty and staff decided to gather information among themselves about perceptions of MT's performance and interpersonal interactions. They created a survey and made it available to all faculty and a few staff (since staff was not the primary focus). About one-half of the 1999 faculty anonymously completed it. It was hoped that the results of the survey would precipitate a change of heart from administration and the board. Faculty feelings about MT are presented below.

1. Every interaction I have had with MT since August has been negative. He has behaved in an aggressive, unreasonable, and just plain nasty manner in every instance. I believe MT is in serious need of psychological counseling or in-depth therapy. Every experience has the same theme—he tries to set up a situation to make it appear that you have been incompetent, dishonest, disrespectful, or something else negative—then he pounces, threatens, bullies, demeans, etc. He is totally lacking in professionalism and honesty. He has proved himself incompetent—as a leader, as an academic, as an administrator, in fact, he lacks basic written and oral communication skills. His grammar in written materials is an embarrassment to the College.

2. I have had several negative experiences with MT. A couple did not directly

involve me, but I ended up in the middle of them because MT does not take the time to meet in private with staff he is about to reprimand. Several times in my presence he confronted a colleague and harassed her. He was downright abusive and intimidating. I felt bad for my colleague and also for myself for being caught in such a demeaning situation but most of all I felt embarrassed for MT for carrying on in such an immature manner. He showed no respect for my colleague, for me and especially not himself. MT comports himself in a very unprofessional manner and we are supposed to think of this man as professional, capable and our leader. I don't think so! He lost my respect when he involved me in his degrading behavior.

Staff opinions about MT's conduct were as follows:

1. I would decide MT should go because the faculty obviously does not want him here. Any good results of his efforts here are outweighed by his demoralizing effect on faculty and staff members.
2. He can stay as an intern under the directions of the chief Academic Officer.
3. He is not an asset to the College.
4. I really believe that MT has no business being VP for Academic Affairs. Aside from not having the credentials to serve in such a position, I think he is not capable of being a good leader because of his arrogance and his lack of social skills. MT has created nothing but discord among faculty and staff. He is one of those persons who thrive on creating animosity between others. He has been disruptive, abusive and dictatorial. He knows most of the faculty and staff are opposed to his serving as VPAA, yet he continues to remain at this post. What is MT hoping for? That everyone will resign before he does! *If that isn't arrogance, what is?* A true professional would acknowledge his inabilities.

Four faculty members gave the following examples of negative behavior:

1. After an interaction I had with MT, I left feeling I had been dealing with a robot, not a man. His cold, distant manner casts a shadow wherever he goes. It is such a contrast to the warm, friendly feeling that has been one of HT's biggest assets.
2. One of the many negative experiences has to do with when he wrote to me claiming that a student had been looking for me in my office during office

hours, and that the student informed him that she had left work to come to see me. I later found out that MT made up or "manufactured" those facts.
3. Every time that I have had the displeasure of talking to him and I have told him a positive about my department, he brought up something else that had not been accomplished yet. He told me exactly where I must recruit; yet my experience had proven these are not the best places. His ego would not let him consider that someone knows more than him.
4. MT pushes his weight around because he has the support of the Board of Trustees and the President. He has no knowledge on how to effectively supervise senior PhD professors. He has no manners, is often disrespectful, has angry outbursts, harasses others and is a bully. Having poor interpersonal skills, he imposes his views and wishes on others. He has confused arbitrary change with genuine progress. Although much change has occurred, they are not for the good. MT refused to respond to a memo I sent because it was addressed to MT, Intern to the President. He stated that he was the Acting VP for Academic Affairs. If I did not believe him, I can look on his door (his name and position was on it). He threatened to have security throw me out if I taped a faculty meeting. He has pressured his appointed Chairperson of the Social Science Division to intimidate and harass me. She refused to. She was fired before the semester was over.

Furthermore, five professors gave the following reasons why MT needed to go:

1. His attitude is destroying the College. The students think he is a joke, and he is driving many students and faculty from the college.
2. He is a divisive, negative, debilitating, and demoralizing influence on campus.
3. MT's leaving HT now is the only prayer HT has. The morale of the faculty is at an all-time low.
4. MT is an intern and needs to be supervised by someone who has experience in academic affairs. He is not being supervised by someone with the appropriate experience. He is not being guided and cannot learn enough to do the job effectively.
5. Any minimum wage worker can do what he does!

After MT changed course schedules without professors' approval, a student sent this letter to him:

There has recently been some unrest amongst the students regarding the proposed class schedule for the spring semester of 2000. I, too, have strong concerns in this matter. I recently found out via my academic advisor that a number of classes that I needed to graduate in the spring were not going to be offered. This puts me, and a number of other students, in an uncompromising [sic] predicament. Upon my advisement for my fall 1999 course schedule, my advisor and I specifically designed my schedule according to what was to be offered in the spring. Without warning the classes that were originally to be offered in the spring are now dropped and no substitute courses are provided as a replacement. I believe that a decision with ramifications such as these should be brought to the attention of the students before it is made, as it affects us greatly.

It was said at Charter Day this fall by Attorney James George, Chairperson of the Board of Trustees, that the Board and the rest of the faculty at Huston-Tillotson are here for the students. The decision to amend the class schedules in the manner that it was done does not reflect this ideal. I sincerely hope that this letter does not fall upon deaf ears and some reasonable change comes about.

Another student sent this letter to McMillan and MT:

I am writing to you in regard to the spring 2000 schedule. I am a junior at Huston-Tillotson College majoring in sociology. The spring semester classes for sociology are very limited. There are only five classes to choose from, most of which I have already taken. The other classes such as biology, education, business, and accounting offer a wider variety of classes as well as times available to take them. . . . If the scheduling does not improve it will force me, as well as many other students, to leave Huston-Tillotson College.

Another student wrote MT, "I did not learn anything in my field placement course because my adjunct teacher was not qualified to supervise me in my placement." The student complained that he was not getting the education he paid for and expected; he wanted his money back. MT told him, "You got the minimum from the course and therefore do not deserve to get your money back. [He can get the refund only if he drops the course and took it at a later date.]" As a potential May 2000 graduate the student could not drop the course and in fact got an "A" in that course even without learning anything. He felt cheated. This type of student is not likely to be a good alum, and like all alumni, he has the potential either to recommend HT or to discourage others from attending HT.

One student in the field placement course didn't start his placement until after midterm.[90] Since the student didn't perceive the teacher as qualified or knowledgeable of potential supervisors, he asked me (I was the usual teacher of the course) to find him a placement. Students were caught in the middle, and the very mission of the college was derailed. If how they were treated during the semester was not bad enough, sociology graduates were not listed in the official graduating program. Their names were listed on a plain white, 20-weight paper that was inserted in the program. No apology was given. The damage was done. How could an entire major be left out of a graduation program? It had never happened before. Why did it happen now?

One of the graduates took me out to lunch the next day to thank me for helping her get through and to voice her concern about the program. She had more than one hundred people attending her graduation. As an older student, completing college was one of her dreams. The dream was realized but was dampened by the fact that she was not officially listed. She wanted an official program with her name on it so that she could distribute them to her family and friends. HT owed them that. I cried at that graduation because of the trauma of the semester, for my students who were treated as outcasts and for a major that I built and was destroyed by persons who did not put the welfare of our students first. I cried because my students did not deserve to be left out on this important day!

Faculty and staff evaluations and students' letters, sent to the president and board members, were totally ignored. Faculty and staff responses to the survey and students' input clearly revealed that it was not just the three designated "troublemakers" who had problems with MT's appointment. Yet, the three faculty members were scapegoated; neither the administrators nor the board assumed any responsibility for the hostile environment created on campus.

Despite the loud unrest on HT's campus, and HT's receiving a warning from the Southern Association of Colleges and Schools (SACS), Joseph T. McMillan's message in the fall 1999 *Ram Magazine* was upbeat, without any evidence of the crisis on campus or problems with reaccreditation.[91] It was as if he were in total denial. Below is his editorial in that *Ram Magazine*:

> The culture is changing at Huston-Tillotson College. Following 10 years of "ebb and flow" in the life of the College, I am excited to report that Huston-Tillotson College is on the crest of the wave of change and renewal. No longer tolerant of this status, no longer patient with the snail's pace of change that is typical

of the academy, I am proud to report that Huston-Tillotson College is finally sharpening its future. Although the future is unknown, I am confident that it is a future of which you can be proud....

The culture which we seek to change is internal and external, formal and informal, that which is assumed and understood within the family and that which is perceived by others. Throughout the life and vision of Huston-Tillotson College, at the levels of the individual members of the College family, the academic and administrative departments, and organizational units of the institution, we must strengthen morale, improve efficiency, and enhance effectiveness. We must develop teams of cooperative spirit, consensus, and shared commitment. We must reaffirm or adopt new core values, make systemic change, as well as change the perception of the institution in the Austin community, the state of Texas, and the broader world.

From isolation to mainstream, from obscurity to prominence, from prospective perceptions of mediocrity to undisputed excellence—these are our goals. From uncertainty to confidence, from apathy and indifference to excitement and commitment, from feelings of being left out to assurance of each person being taken seriously as a valued, responsible, and contributing member of the Huston-Tillotson College family—these are our expectations. From opportunity to challenge, from the statement of mission and vision to the development of a comprehensive strategic plan, from the restoration of the foundation of the College to the positioning of the institution to shape its future—we seek nothing less than change and renewal for the best interests of Huston-Tillotson College.

This is the charge of the fourth president of Huston-Tillotson College, on the eve of the 21st century. To students, faculty, staff and administrators, trustees, and special friends, to alumni in the broader community, come! I seek your support, cooperation, and commitment to the College's new process of strategic planning. I close with the reaffirmation of the motto of Huston-Tillotson College, In Union, Strength.[92]

Save HT: An Underground Organization

McMillan's words did not match real events. There was fear among faculty and students that the board and the president had intentions to close the college. The perception that the president was incompetent precipitated the organization of an "underground group" named Save HT. Paul Anaejionu, Harriet Buxkemper, and I started this organization, consisting of former faculty, staff, and students who strongly felt that without intervention our beloved HT would close. The immediate goal was to place pressure on the board to fire McMillan so that HT would have a chance to survive. The organized group was kept secret; few people then, and even now, knew of its existence. The first meeting was held September 22, 1999. The minutes of meetings are provided in their entirety:[93]

> Persons present: Reginald Christopher,[94] Tex Moten, Paul Anaejionu, Jane Anaejionu, Harriet Buxkemper, Alexa Buxkemper, Teresia Lewis, Susan Williams, Beverly Silas, June Brewer, Fannie Lawless, Floyd Davis, Morene Douglas, Rosalee Martin, Tisha Christopher, Nannette Glenn, and Jocelyn Taylor
>
> The meeting was called to order by Reginald Christopher. Everyone introduced themselves and told their connection to Huston-Tillotson College. Several of the persons were alumni, others current or former employees and current students. Most of the meeting consisted of persons telling their stories about their relationship with the College and with McMillan. It was apparent that all persons had strong feelings about Huston-Tillotson College and wanted it to survive for present and future generations. It was also apparent that many of those present were directly hurt by the actions of McMillan. All have come to realize that McMillan was a destructive force and needed to resign or be asked to resign from his position as President of Huston-Tillotson College.
>
> Dr. June Brewer told her story about how she received a registered letter in the mail stating that she was fired. McMillan had problems with how she was administering a Lillie Foundation grant worth $300.000.00 over a three-year period. He actually tried to turn her grant program administrator against her, and when that didn't work, he tried to turn that administrator's boss against her, neither worked so he fired a tenured professor.
>
> Teresia Lewis told of how McMillan gave her a letter indicating that she was fired in front of two other persons. Her immediate boss didn't know that she was going to be released. McMillan boasted that he was the one who fired her. Teresia Lewis found out two years later why she was fired from an EEO officer who informed her that the reason given was poor performance. Mrs. Lewis has all of her evaluations which were excellent.
>
> Rosalee Martin, Paul Anaejionu, Jane Anaejionu, and Harriet Buxkemper provided information about the current climate at HT based upon reasons already discussed.
>
> Beverly Silas was on McMillan's inauguration committee and talked about

the extravagant expenses associated with that event (even with HT's inadequate financial resources).

Teresia Lewis, June Brewer, Reginald Christopher, and Tisha Christopher said that they would not recommend any relatives to attend their Alma Mater because of the current administration.

Tex Moten, Fannie Lawless, and Morene Douglas talked about life at Sam Huston and Tillotson before the merger and how the community really looked out for them.[95] They wanted to return to when students strived to do their best, when faculty gave much and set high standards for students, and when the administration was supportive, respectful, and strived to do the best for the College.

Although most of the time was used with the sharing of stories, it became apparent that there was a need for a formal organization that would identify its missions and goals. The first step was to elect a chairperson. After some discussion, Reginald Christopher was elected chairperson. Dr. Davis, Teresia Lewis's brother, was elected parliamentary. No secretary was elected at the time, although June Brewer agreed to serve as secretary until one is elected.

The second thing to do was to decide on a name. The suggested name was *Save Our College: Huston-Tillotson College;* and *Save Our College: Huston-Tillotson*. None was agreed upon. The group said that one would be decided upon at the next meeting.

The third thing was to decide upon a day and place for the next meetings. It will be held on Wednesday, September 29, 1999, at Oak Springs Library at 7–8:45 p.m.

The group agreed that the primary goal is to save the College from closing and believed that this can only be done if McMillan is removed as president.

The group agreed that the meetings were to be taped. Group members were also asked to bring documentation which support claims and concerns. Christopher stated that he would keep those documents in a safe he had at home.

The group thanked the three college professors who were brave and courageous enough to speak out publicly about the state of affairs at HT. The three professors are Paul Anaejionu, Harriet Buxkemper, and me [Rosalee Martin].

Members were asked to invite other supporters to the next meeting. Minutes of the second meeting follow.

CHAPTER 2

Second Meeting of Save HT: September 29, 1999

Minutes by Rosalee Martin

Present: Dr. Paul Anaejionu, professor; Mrs. Jane Anaejionu, HT Consultant; Mrs. Morene Douglas; Mrs. Teresia Lewis, terminated Dean of General Studies; Dr. Floyd Davis, alumni; Dr. Reginald Christopher, alumni and former Director of Alumni; Dr. June Brewer, Professor emeritus; Ms. Alexa Buxkemper, senior student and Harriet Buxkemper's daughter; Mrs. Harriet Buxkemper, Chair of Physical Education; myself, sociology professor; Mr. Robert McHaney, non-reappointed music professor; Ms. Tisha Christopher, inactive alumni; and Tex Moten, alumni. Not present were Mrs. Fannie Lawless, former staff; Ms. Susan Williams; Ms. Beverly Silas; Dr. Nannette Glenn, former staff; and Ms. Jocelyn Taylor

1. Each member was given the opportunity to express their feelings on a variety of issues. This time of sharing seems to be crucial for the bonding of members of this group.
2. The need for legal advice and representation were discussed. Dr. Davis would talk to two persons at the Bar Association about free legal service. NOTE: Dr. Davis was referred to Legal Aid.
3. Documents offered as evidence should be notarized. NOTE: Ms. Alexa Buxkemper was a notary and is willing to get her license renewed in order to be the group's notary.
4. The Mission, goals, and strategies need to be identified. NOTE: Mrs. Jane Anaejionu, Dr. Christopher, and I will bring a proposed draft to the next meeting.
5. Old business of adopting a name for the group was not done. Ms. Alexa Buxkemper has a name she would like to present at the next meeting. [Ultimately, Save HT was adopted.]
6. We ran out of time and decided to meet earlier for the next meeting which will be on October 6, 1999, at 6:30. NOTE: Many attendees talked to each other outside the library for over an hour. It is evident that much needs to be *done*.

While the Save HT Group was meeting, correspondence continued to flow between Attorney George and me; between Buxkemper and Anaejionu and George; between me and McMillan; between students and administrators; and between students and teachers. Reginald Christopher and an alumna highlighted, in separate articles, in the *Austin American-Statesman* what each thought was important. Pressure was coming from every quarter to do something; doing nothing was perceived by this group as no longer an option! On October 28, 1999, I sent yet another letter to George, copied to all board members, highlighting the groups' concerns. No board member could say that he or she did not know.

Bill of Particulars

As letters were going back and forth to Dr. McMillan and to Board President George, newspaper articles were written, alumni dissatisfaction and campus unrest continued, and the Save HT group moved forward with its investigation into the wrongdoings of McMillan. The Save HT group ultimately developed a document called Bill of Particulars that included several sections; references to this document have already been made. The bill contains well-researched and thought-out support for the request for removal of McMillan from his position of president of Huston-Tillotson College. The emphasis was on the president's accountability and stewardship. The fifteen-page document was written by Anaejionu, Jane Anaejionu, Buxkemper, and me. The Bill of Particulars was divided into five major headings, with case studies and documentations to support each premise. The headings were:

1. UNJUST AND INHUMANE PERSONNEL PRACTICES: Examples include a) abuse of the "At Will" firing policy, b) termination without grounds, c) failure to provide due process and appeal, and d) inhumane and shockingly reprehensible treatment of human beings.
2. MISTREATMENT OF STUDENTS: Case study cited represents an overwhelming number of instances of serious breach of the obligation a college has to its primary customers, the students.
3. GRANTS, GRANTS MANAGEMENT, FUNDRAISING: Often grant managers are subjected to constant undermining of authority and harassment when the administration refuses to comply with the terms of the grant. Often, the President and/or his appointees may redirect specific grant funds or delay releasing requested funds. Because of this and other related reasons, skilled faculty grant writers refuse to write grants.
4. FINANCIAL MISMANAGEMENT: Failure to implement checks and balances that led to FBI investigation. It is in the area of financial mismanagement that HT went on probation.
5. The ERRATIC AND INAPPROPRIATE BEHAVIOR OF THE PRESIDENT: The president has been known to drink alcoholic beverages

CHAPTER 2

with students in the dormitories; holler at people; take students' side without hearing from the faculty.⁹⁶

The specific cases highlighted in the Bill of Particulars covered a cross-section of faculty and staff concerns of both current and past employees of HT.

CASE OF MR. ROBERT MCHANEY

Mr. Robert McHaney was an assistant professor of music with nine and a half years of teaching at the college. In January 1999 he was given a letter of non-reappointment, despite having received exemplary performance evaluations for the previous several years and consistently exemplary ratings from students. At the time, McHaney had serious health problems, having suffered from a heart attack in August 1998. McMillan, in his letter to McHaney, cited "the urgent need to reorganize the Academic Affairs Unit of the college to address the decline in enrollment for the '98–99 fiscal year" as the reason for his non-reappointment. However, there was no instance of failure to fulfill his teaching and advising roles or to meet any other obligations to the students or the institution. Two part-time people were hired to teach classes formerly taught by McHaney. McHaney applied for one of those positions but was told the position was filled, even before it was.

Mr. McHaney was aggrieved and mystified by what he perceived as bizarre events that occurred in connection with May 1999 graduation exercises. Apparently, someone from Huston-Tillotson College called the Austin Police Department to report that McHaney had threatened to kill the president of the college. McHaney categorically denied that charge and was unable to find out who made that accusation against him. About two dozen APD officers showed up on campus. They were on various HT rooftops, armed and apparently prepared to shoot. McHaney stated that he removed himself from others at the graduation in order to protect them. He feared that if he made a sudden move he might be shot, and others would be in danger. McMillan knew of this report to APD the day before graduation. Hence, he could have prevented police coming to HT graduation by simply requesting that McHaney not attend it. Because of that incident and the unsubstantiated report, McHaney got a police record as a terrorist. He stated that consequently he was unable to find employment. Further, he believed that this traumatic incident was a threat to his well-being and, in fact, his life.

CASE OF MRS. TERESIA LEWIS ('65, FORMER DEAN OF GENERAL STUDIES)

Mrs. Teresia Lewis, with a BA in education and music, and an MA in Curriculum and Instruction, had twelve years of service to the college, serving both as a teacher and the Dean of General Studies. In 1995 she was summoned to McMillan's office regarding the grades of a student. The student had received two failing grades and McMillan requested that the grades be changed. The student was an athlete with a record of absenteeism. The student had never attended either of the classes for which he received failing grades. Lewis, after investigating the matter, refused to change the student's grades, the beginning of McMillan's looking for a reason to fire her.

On June 2, 1997, while in the midst of leading a workshop, Lewis was summoned to McMillan's office. She was given a letter of termination in front of her direct supervisor, Lenora Waters, VPAA, and Ms. Ethel Dilworth, Director of Human Resources. There was no advance warning that such an action was being contemplated. At no time was she advised of a need for changes or improvement in any area of her work. In fact, she had had excellent personnel evaluations throughout her tenure with the college. One month prior to this action, McMillan praised her proposal for the Developmental and Advisement Program. This action against Lewis was taken very shortly after the death of her spouse and her mother, leaving her even more devastated.

Case of Ms. Nancy Bandiera

Ms. Nancy Bandiera, with two master's degrees, and a PhD in progress, was an instructor in the Mass Communications Department. She refused to issue a grade for a student who was not in her course and not listed on the course schedule. Shortly thereafter, a campaign of harassment began against her. A Review Committee met, resulting in her being moved from the Mass Communications Department to the English Department. Bandiera reported that she had not received a raise since June 1995.

Case of Coach Carment Kiara

In my 2017 interview with Coach Kiara, he told me that immediately following spring break of 1997, two students wanted to submit a late term paper because they were delayed returning from a choir tour in New York. Coach Kiara informed his entire class on the first day of the course that no late papers would be accepted *for any reason*. During a delayed flight in Atlanta, Georgia, two students told Dr. McMillan that they were going to miss Mr. Kiara's deadline due to the late flight. The president told the students that he would declare a holiday for choir members and therefore the teacher would have to accept the paper. He also told the students that he signed the check for teachers. One student even said that McMillan told her not to turn her paper in on time, as it would look bad for other students. That student wrote and signed a statement to this effect. Kiara refused to accept the paper even after McMillan's intervention. McMillan instructed the VPSA, the VPAA, the Choir Director, and the Chairperson of Social Science (me), and others to intervene in order to pressure the professor. Kiara offered to resign because he would not accept students' late papers. McMillan called a meeting of Mr. Carment Kiara, sociology professor; VPAA Lenora Waters; president's administrative assistant Ethel Dilworth; and me. In this meeting he tried to pressure Kiara and said that the college was not big enough for Kiara and him. Kiara still refused to alter his policy. As a result of McMillan's interference, one student dropped the course (she received the $10 drop fee from McMillan) and the other student stayed in the class but had to accept a lower grade. McMillan's interference affected both students and faculty because the entire campus community became aware of the incident. I believe he tried to undermine the faculty but ended up hurting the students.

Case of Dr. Walter Redmond

Dr. Redmond was an internationally renowned scholar who was selected as the Distinguished AAUP Professor for 1998–99. He spoke and/or published in several languages, including English, German, Spanish, Latin, Greek, and French. He published frequently in a German philosophical journal and in numerous other academic journals. In January 1999, he was called in before his division chair, department head, and the Vice President for Academic Affairs and terminated with no advance warning and with no charge of incompetence or failure to perform his duties appropriately. Faculty members report that the college lost a scholar and a treasure. They believe this was an extreme example of excellence at the college being punished by the administration. This charge of being punished for excellence is one that was heard frequently by faculty and personnel in various positions.

Case of Dr. Charles Septowski

Septowski, chair of the Business Division, was physically removed from his office in the summer of 1997 by three security guards of the college. He was given no advance warning of this action. He was never given any reason for his dismissal, either in writing or orally. He did not receive due process. No hearing was ever held. Septowski had previously received an expressed promise of continued employment by McMillan.

Case of Dr. June Brewer

Brewer was a tenured professor of English (and holder of an endowed chair) prior to her retirement. She was both an alumna of the college and a professor emerita.

During her tenure at the college, Brewer was known for involving students in cultural and community activities—largely at her own expense. After retirement, she decided to give back to her college by writing and having many funded grants. Her problems with the administration began with the administration of the prestigious FIPSE grant which she had received.[97] McMillan, on numerous occasions, tried to influence her to use funds in ways that were inconsistent with grant requirements and program objectives. When she refused to allow him to control the funds, McMillan called her grant manager at her funding agency and attempted to undermine her authority and reputation. When the manager refused to comply, McMillan continued up FIPSE hierarchy in attempts to discredit Brewer. As soon as her three-year funding cycle was over, McMillan forced her second retirement and told her to clear her office and get off the campus. This is another instance in which the college lost the services of a distinguished scholar and humanitarian who continued her work under the auspices of other colleges and nonprofit community groups.

Faculty members interviewed for this project believed these incidents demonstrated several negative aspects of McMillan's leadership: 1) excessive use of power; 2) lack of respect for faculty; 3) lack of respect for academic freedom; 4) attempts to "use" faculty to accomplish his desires, frequently causing a wedge between community members; and 5) poor and erratic decisions that negatively impacted students. These are only a few cases of faculty members who reported abuse by McMillan, revealing the extent of his mistreatment of faculty. There were others who reported abuse—to include Anaejionu, Buxkemper, and me.

The Save HT Committee provided a second document, "Stewardship of Huston-Tillotson College Property," highlighting the shrinkage of HT's property under McMillan's watch. Of specific concern to the committee was the fact that in 1988, the Board of Trustees gave McMillan the right to buy and sell property under his signature alone.[98] This was especially troubling when a zone hearing sign appeared on HT campus during fall 1999, without any explanation by HT leadership to faculty and staff. Suspicion arose that McMillan wanted to sell the campus, which was intensified when a board member testified before the City Council that "we are not trying to sell the campus; we request this zoning change to make it easier to make changes on campus." Up to that time, no one had mentioned anything about closing the campus! It made the Save HT group wonder why he said that.

In October 1999, both the Bill of Particulars and the Stewardship of Huston-Tillotson College Property were given to Board President Jim George, with copies sent to each board member. Save HT requested a meeting with George, who initially refused. Most group members believed that he refused the meeting because we were primarily Black; he was White. Others thought it was a "power thing" since George was an attorney at a prestigious law firm. Regardless of the reason, Save HT sought assistance from two White attorneys who taught at UT Austin. One was the present president of American Association of University Professors (AAUP), and the other was a past president of AAUP. With them as part of Save HT, the group gained strength, prestige, and recognition. With the addition of the two White attorneys, George granted our request for a meeting. The committee met with Attorney George on November 23, 1999, in his affluent office board room. At the end of that meeting, in a private conversation with Anaejionu and his wife, Jane Anaejionu, George told them that the group's wish would be granted.[99] We met a second time with George. In December 1999, McMillan announced at a campus-wide meeting and in *Ram Magazine* that he was retiring, effective June 30, 2000—seven months hence.

With the end in sight, I believe Dr. McMillan set out to be vengeful towards those he perceived as the "troublemakers," specifically Anaejionu, Buxkemper, and me. He organized a team with the apparent sole goal of making the trio's work environment miserable so that they would quit.[100] An interim chairperson was appointed by MT to lead the Division of Social Sciences. The only problem was that the young woman was a recent alumna of HT who had served one semester as an unpaid sociology adjunct. She volunteered to teach as a way to give back since "HT teachers transformed my life." This young adjunct was a friend of MT's sister and had known him for a while. MT thought that, based on that friendship, she would take his side against me. That was not the case. She reluctantly accepted the position in order to protect me and Anaejionu from the administration's planned attacks. According to her, the administration wanted her to relocate me to a smaller office without a phone, make my course schedule without my input, gave me a poor evaluation, and act in other vengeful ways. The young adjunct refused to follow orders and was fired after only a semester. In her place, the only professor who didn't sign a letter submitted to McMillan on my behalf accepted the position of head of the Department of Behavioral Sciences.[101] This made her my immediate boss; I was the only one she supervised. It appeared that she wholeheartedly attempted to implement McMillan's and MT's orders to make me miserable. With any luck, she hoped I would become a former HT professor by forcing me to quit.

I wrote to my new supervisor on May 28, 2000, concerning a poor evaluation and unfair treatment. With the highest evaluation score being 40, my puppet supervisor gave me a score of 7, without citing any justification. A score of 7 means "Unsatisfactory below standard, without expectation of adequate improvement." The year before McMillan had given me the Teacher Excellence Award. I told my supervisor that with such a score, I should be fired. "If you do not fire me, then do not put the evaluation in my personnel file." She didn't do either. She would not give me a copy of this evaluation. I eventually filed a grievance against this supervisor, but nothing came of it. In fact, McMillan responded to my grievance request that my letters and actions could be construed as harassing him, my supervisor, my division chairperson, and MT. Certainly, I disagreed with him. As a person of integrity, I felt compelled to stand up for what I believed.

McMillan was busy on many fronts: working on self-study documents, reinforcing a hostile environment specifically for Anaejionu and me and, unintentionally, for the entire campus. He wrote his last Message from the President in the *Ram* Spring/Fall 2000 magazine.[102] This message was very different from his message of only six months before. He reflected on the highs and lows of his presidency—the hope, and even despair, he and others experienced. The following are quotes from his published message. Notice McMillan's first line.

> I was not forced out. I made this decision totally on my own.
>
> Greetings, I am pleased to share the report of the President on the State of the College. I assure you that Huston-Tillotson College is alive and well. The insidious email rumors of our "closing" which you may have received or heard about, represent a cruel hoax!
>
> Much has happened in the life of the College since the Board of Trustees met last on November 11–12, 1999. Following the Executive Session of the Board, Attorney Jim George, Chair of the Board, advise me of the continuing concerns among the members of the Board and Executive Board of Huston-Tillotson College International Alumni Association about the unrest among some persons within the campus community and the barrage of bad press and media attention to the College as result of my appointment of MT as Acting VP for Academic Affairs for the 1999–2000 academic year. The Chair of the Board directed me to do two things immediately: 1) to find a middle ground position that would bring peace and calm to the campus community; and 2) to confer with Dr. Gary H. Quehl, our consultant on Strategic Planning, regarding the immediate implementation of an aggressive, inclusive search for VP for Academic Affairs which includes the participation of disgruntled faculty members. I took the Board's

advice and Jim's directives to heart seriously: reflected and prayed over them for several weeks and then began to implement a strategy. Following consultation with a few personal friends, colleagues, and family members, including Dr. Tom Bergman, Associate Commissioner of the Southern Association of Colleges and Schools, and Attorney Jim George, I announced at a campus-wide meeting of the faculty, staff, and students held on Thursday, December 16, 1999, my decision to retire from the presidency of Huston-Tillotson College on June 30, 2000. Immediately following that meeting, I informed the members of the Board of Trustees of my decision and released an announcement to the rest and the community.

I reaffirmed today that decision to retire and again express my appreciation for the opportunity and honor and to have served in this position of distinction for the past 12 years. As we prepare for a new millennium and the release of the College's new strategic plan, it is indeed an appropriate time for new leadership to take the College into the 21st century.

In response to the challenge to find "middle ground" and to restore peace and calm within the institution, I am certain that those objectives have been achieved. I take this occasion to challenge all alumni and friends of Huston-Tillotson College to rally around our beloved alma mater, as we continue to renew the institution for greater service in the 21st century.

The state of the College is stable. The state of the College is also hopeful, optimistic, right, pregnant opportunity like an expectant mother, anticipate like a vulnerable old battleship, positioned employees eager to take the crest of the next wave of opportunity watching and waiting, change is in the air.

Despite these words, McMillan found out in June 2000 that HT had numerous SACS recommendations, serious enough for the institution to be officially placed on *warning* and then on *probation* under the next president due to McMillan's ineptness.

Losing Sight of What Matters—Reaffirmation Problem: On Warning
This internal crisis, along with financial mismanagement, hindered the college's focus on becoming reaccredited by the Southern Association of Colleges and Universities. Although the administrator was not named, Bronté Jones provided an excerpt from an interview she conducted for her dissertation. I believe this individual probably was McMillan. Jones quoted the administrator as saying, "I think that in the period in between the first and second time around [referring

to the 1990 and 2000 reaffirmation processes] I became jaded, I think I became haughty, I think that I became angry, and I think that I became tired. I think that I also grew impatient, and I wore that on my face and shoulders and people saw that and reacted to it and even said I can show you as well as you can show me. We just kind of 'dug in our heels,' and because of that, I don't think that I was an effective leader the second time around."[103]

The time that lapsed between McMillan's announcement of his retirement and his final day as president was seven months. He had sufficient time to intentionally discredit the two persons he held responsible for his retirement. In early 2000, McMillan held a faculty/staff meeting where he told them that there were "snakes among us; we need to rise up and kill them." I was not at that meeting but later was asked by a faculty member whether McMillan was referring to me. Additionally, McMillan talked to my pastor, asking him to encourage me to cease the campaign against him and his appointee, MT. Furthermore, Board President George asked me to stop alumni and others from voicing their opinions of McMillan on the ongoing crisis. I was accused of writing an anonymous letter critiquing the negative impact of McMillan, a ludicrous claim since I signed my name to everything I wrote. As a final act of vengeance, McMillan reduced Anaejionu's and my salary by $5,000 for the following academic year. Buxkemper had already announced her retirement and therefore had no upcoming contract.

All of this was going on as HT was on the verge of losing its reaccreditation. Its finances were awry, a financial aid scandal had recently been managed, and concerns of faculty, staff, and students were dismissed. McMillan knew all of this and called an emergency Board of Trustees meeting on April 28, 2000. HT was *on warning* from SACS at that time. The following is a report of the president to the board.[104]

> There is an urgency related to financial health. The institutional self-study was completed and submitted on schedule to the reaffirmation committee in February. Additionally, the administration completed and submitted to the commission on colleges in the reaffirmation committee the progress report required at the June 1999 meeting of the commission regarding the college's compliance with the condition of eligibility 13, section 6.3.1. There was a site visit March 26–29. On Wednesday, April 26, I received a draft copy of the 99-page committee report, which we are requested to review for errors and facts and make corrections and return it to Dr. Karen today [June 1999].
>
> The report from the visiting committee presented a total of 50 recommendations and eight suggestions, many of which were already identified by the

CHAPTER 2

College in its institutional self-study. The most significant finding submitted by the visiting team is that the College is not in compliance with two conditions of eligibility: *condition eight, planning and evaluation, and condition 13 administrative processes and financial resources....* It was imperative that HT successfully achieve compliance in order to avoid being placed on warning or probation or not reaffirmed.[105]

In his final message to the HT Board of Trustees, McMillan provided the following information regarding SACS:

> I will be leading the College's team to meet with the Criteria and Reports Committee of the Commission on Colleges in Savannah, Georgia, on next Tuesday, June 20, 2000. I will be accompanied by Mr. Dome, Chief Fiscal Officer, Ms. Bronté Jones, Dean of Admission and Financial Services, Mr. Bobo, Chair of the Board's Business Affairs Committee, and President-Elect Earvin. We will end our presentation with an appeal to the Criteria and Reports Committee to recognize the enormous continued progress of the College to restore its fiscal integrity and demonstrate compliance with Condition of Eligibility Thirteen: Criteria 6, Financial Resources and Administrative Process, and to give the College more time for a "fresh start" under a new Administration to demonstrate continued compliance with the criteria without additional sanction of public notice from the Commission at this time. But we *must* report that we will end the 1999–2000 Fiscal Year in the Black.[106]

McMillan ended his presidency dejected, tired, and overwhelmed with the campus unrest due to his administrative decisions, and because the institution was on warning by SACS. On September 19, 2017, seventeen years after his retirement, I asked McMillan when he decided to retire.[107] McMillan said it was at that SACS meeting (June 2000). According to him:

> I was at this association meeting, getting ready for my second accreditation. I had a cold then. The hotel was at the foot of the hill. I didn't make my reservations in time, so I was in a secondary hotel. I had to walk up the hill to get there. I couldn't find a cab. I've already spoken to my appointed person to talk about HT's accreditation. The rest of it was just a lot of speeches and different events. I said, "If I do not have to go to another meeting, and do not have to fly here, it would be so great. I think that I am so tired. I think I've done all that I could do.

I've had a great meeting with the accreditation. The process is already in place." I felt that it was time for me to take a break. Only if I could have gotten a sabbatical for about six months or even three months I would have been better; but I never had a vacation. I had legally thirty days. The phone rang and I was always in touch and never too far away. If I could have gotten more support from my board, and I didn't ask for it. They need to have done it on their own. They should have realized that Joe needs a vacation so he can retool himself for another five years. But I had a cold. I might have had pneumonia. I got tired. I need a break. And that was part of the decision. And I never looked back.

McMillan's recollection was not consistent with real-time information. As mentioned earlier, he announced his retirement in December 1999, seven months before that June SACS meeting. Still, it was his recollection, and with time memory alters and events change in their importance. What is salient in his memory is that he was tired, probably weary from the ongoing conflict that I believe was of his own making.

In May 2000, in my final letter to McMillan, I reflected on the past year as I recalled it, with objective evidence to support most of what I stated. The letter ended with me extending an olive branch to McMillan, wishing him a bright future. Here is part of the letter, focusing primarily on students.

> I have had time to reflect on spring 2000 semester and would like to share my reflections with you, being as objective as possible. Obviously, my objectivity is hindered by the fact that I was a major participant in many of the scenarios that played out this semester. Certainly, if you were writing about the same scenarios, your interpretation would be different. However, I can only write from my perception, my feelings, and my actions. I contemplated whether I should write this letter at all but decided that it was important for my own healing. This is not a "bash McMillan" letter, but an honest attempt to share. Clearly, I can be accused of many things, but not that I do things undercover. I am usually up front with my position, ideology, and actions.[108]

The body of the letter reiterated much of what had been stated earlier. I ended the letter by stating:

> So much has happened during fall 1999 and spring 2000. I am writing this letter as my way of letting go of the hurt I experienced, as I look forward to the future.

> As a professional counselor, I know what hurt, pain, and revenge can do to an individual. For my own mental health, I must move forward. I know that issues from this academic year MUST still be addressed. I expect the new President and his administration to review my concerns objectively, and to act in the best interest of this college. My grievances are real and will be addressed. As for you, I reach out to you as one human to another. I know that this was a rough year for you as you reaped the consequences of your decisions. Placing blame aside, I wish you the best as you move forward with your life.

McMillan didn't respond. I guess I didn't expect him to.

After his retirement, McMillan and I occasionally saw each other at HT. Both of us were cordial and never spoke of the year from June 1999 to June 2000. Then in 2016, McMillan did something quite unexpected: he nominated me for the African American Women's Profiles of Prominence in Education, sponsored by the National Women of Achievement, Inc., Austin Metroplex Chapter. Not only that, but he took out an ad on my behalf. I felt vindicated that he had come to appreciate the validity of my concerns sixteen years earlier.

To my 2017 question "What do you think your legacy should be?" McMillan's response was, "I am not the one to say; let history tell it." I told part of his history in this chapter. I described McMillan's presidency as I knew and researched it. To maintain objectivity, I shared this chapter with an individual who saw McMillan from a more positive perspective. We validated each other's perspectives and lived experience with McMillan. As is true with everyone, McMillan was multidimensional, having vastly different relationships with individuals. He interacted with individuals from dissimilar roles, perspectives, and levels of power. I encourage others to write their experiences with McMillan. A collection of those stories is also needed to give a fuller and more complete story of the "dash" of Dr. McMillan's presidency. However, regardless of who tells the story, I believe it must include his very words: "I began my remarks at my Inaugural Convocation in October of 1988, with the acclamation, 'I love it!' I end my administration at Huston-Tillotson College (June 30, 2000) with the same acclamation, 'I love it!'"[109] Although his "dash" was riddled with conflict, there is no doubt that he loved HT.

As a postscript, on December 7, 2017, I called McMillan to schedule a second interview. He informed me that he was in the hospital. He was coherent, though not well. He died on December 12, 2017, only five days later. We can therefore say that Dr. McMillan loved Huston-Tillotson until he died.

His Story: Lessons from Dr. McMillan's Presidency
A Top-Down President
Throughout McMillan's story a theme emerged—he was a top-down president. He said he would "not let any rock be left unturned." He urged everyone to follow him: "If you don't want to follow, don't hinder me." He came to HT with a well-developed plan that didn't have input from constituents who had to implement the plan. For example, he would not let academic departments do their job but frequently told those departments what to do by using "What if" questions or giving specific directives. He moved people around when what he wanted wasn't done and hired people who were "loyal to him" while firing people who stood up to him. He was easily agitated and aggravated, and at times made bad decisions when he couldn't control individuals. He made the decision to place MT in a position that brought extreme dissension among faculty but refused to listen to reason. I suspect McMillan found company with other presidents who allowed their presidential position to "go to his/her head." Being a top-down president made McMillan an ineffective president. According to Dianne Hayes, "Gone are the days of decades of top-down leadership, now replaced by a need for charismatic personalities who are well skilled at fundraising while navigating internal needs and external stakeholders, as well as politics and long-standing traditions."[110] Presidents who are unwilling to engage other constituents in good faith might find a similar fate to McMillan's: forced retirement—and even worse than that, forced retirement in the face of the institution's possibly losing its accreditation.

McMillan's Handling of Conflicts
Conflicts are inevitable, but combat is chosen. McMillan most often chose combat when conflicts arose, some of which were his own making. Under his administration, HT was riddled with conflicts, and he was unwilling to seek win-win solutions; this resulted in McMillan's downfall. It was not unusual for him to pit staff against faculty with such words to staff that faculty do not work all week or eight hours a day. He brought to staff attention that faculty have longer holidays and may travel more often. This created suspicion and distrust among constituents, resulting at times in a hostile environment. His leadership style reflected who he was. Had he entered his presidency with leadership qualities such as self-awareness, being consistent, rejecting favoritism, emphasizing building strong, positive relationships, being humble, empowering others, willingness to learn, and being committed to positive action, his management of conflicts would have led HT into positive terrain. Additionally, had McMillan been able to accept counsel and

responsibility for both his good and bad decisions, the morale of HT would have been healthier. McMillan lacked most of these characteristics, and consequently HT suffered.

Not all college/university presidents are a good match for the institutions they lead. Better search processes and fewer appointments of friends and colleagues may increase the success of HBCUs and other institutions. Presidents are appointed by boards; selection of appropriate board members is critical to who is selected as president.

Abdicating Presidential Duties
One of the primary roles of a college president is to intentionally raise funds to support university scholarships and programs. According to Terry Smith, McMillan did not like raising money. That very fact caused many institutional problems because of the lack of resources for students' programs, academic programs, unrestricted funds for institutional advancement, and earmarked funds for maintaining our mission. Just as important, HT was placed on *warning* and later *probation* primarily because of our financial difficulties.[111] HT was in the company of other HBCUs that also had reaccreditation problems. According to Crystal Keels, "Many Historically Black Colleges and Universities (HBCUs) have either teetered on the brink, suffered or closed entirely following the loss of accreditation from the Southern Association of Colleges and Schools (SACS)," due to financial insolvency.

Joseph McMillan talked about making HT an "HBCU Harvard" (that is, an Ivy League HBCU) but didn't put in the work. According to Reginald Stuart, HBCUs "are facing increasing pressure to reinvent themselves to stay alive and relevant as more and more Black students choose to attend majority institutions and private, for-profit colleges."[112] Had McMillan embraced the key presidential function of fundraising and spent less time fostering conflict, HT would have been further along in fulfilling institutional goals of increased enrollment and retention by providing more substantial scholarships and resources for student success. Being able to accomplish this will provide real options for students to come to HT and to remain here, despite offers from PWIs.

Chapter 3

Dr. Larry L. Earvin

Accomplishments vs. Absenteeism

Selecting our Next President During Institutional Crisis
Upon the announcement of McMillan's retirement in December 1999, HT's Board of Trustees established a search committee chaired by board member, former Texas Rep. Wilhelmina Delco. Unlike the selection of McMillan for which there was no extensive, rigorous vetting process, HT's Board of Trustees put into place a meticulous selection process to secure the best-qualified fifth president. The faculty selected two of its members to serve on the committee: Dr. Kathy Schwab and me. Other members included students, board members, community members, and representatives from United Methodist Church and United Church of Christ. After McMillan heard that I was the faculty pick, a colleague overheard him hollering on the phone, "I had no choice, she was chosen by the faculty!" It was clear that I was neither McMillan's nor the Board of Trustees' pick, and the Board Search Committee members placed numerous roadblocks to hinder my participation.[1] Even though the committee and its chair knew that faculty input was necessary in light of the existing HT environment of distrust, hostility, and uncertainty, many committee members treated me with disdain and accused me

of sharing information outside the committee after signing a confidential form. Information did get out, but not from me. The situation became so unpleasant that I wrote the chairperson a letter insisting that I be treated fairly and that accusations against me cease. Still, this treatment did not prevent Dr. Schwab and me from sharing faculty concerns and recommendations during the presidential selection process.

After the initial dissonance, and with Dr. Schwab and me remaining steadfast, the board recognized that faculty satisfaction with the presidential process and pick was essential. We were then allowed to actively participate in the process without further hindrances. The nationwide search resulted in about seventy applicants, narrowed down by the committee to twenty. These twenty were interviewed by phone using a consistent list of questions. Seven semifinalists were invited to campus, after which the field was narrowed down to three finalists. There were three criteria established by the committee:

- The individual must be an African American with experience at an HBCU;
- The individual must have appropriate academic credentials, i.e., a PhD or EdD; and
- The individual must be an expert in fundraising.

Earvin was ranked the top finalist because of his educational experience, knowledge of SACS requirement processes, and having met the above criteria. Earvin spent his twenty-six years of professional service at Clark Atlanta University in multiple positions, with his last as dean of the School of Arts and Sciences, overseeing numerous departments and hundreds of faculty members. Schwab and I embraced the selection of Earvin as he had a distinguished educational background and from the interview appeared to have a moral compass. Even without an on-campus interview, the Search Committee unanimously decided on Earvin as HT's fifth president.

Prior to his selection, Earvin and his wife were scheduled to come to Austin for a face-to-face interview with the Search Committee and other HT constituent groups. But that meeting didn't happen; his wife, Rev. Valerie Earvin, died in a car accident on the day the trip was to take place. For a couple of months, it was uncertain whether Earvin would accept the appointment. Even though it was a painful road to HT, Earvin decided to accept the position of President of Huston-Tillotson College effective August 2000, later than the initial intended start date. The loss of his wife of twenty-five years left him emotionally drained, but he gave himself permission to grieve in the presence of trusted friends. Many believed that the sudden loss of his wife may have changed the nature of his presidency, although they may not know how, or how much.

Inauguration usually occurs at Huston-Tillotson's Charter Day celebration in the same year as the presidential appointment. Because Earvin would only be on the job a few months prior to Charter Day, inauguration occurred fifteen months after his appointment. During those months Earvin engaged in tedious work on behalf of the college. According to him:

> My first two months have been spent both on and off campus in attendance at meetings of various national, state, and local higher education organizations with which the college is affiliated. Participation in a meeting such as the National Association of Schools and Colleges of the United Methodist Church, the United Negro College Fund, Independent Colleges and Universities of Texas, and many others, ensures that Huston-Tillotson College receives its fair share (finances) and is at the table when decisions are made that affect our future. As I travel, I will have the opportunity to get to know the alumni of Samuel Huston, Tillotson, and Huston-Tillotson Colleges, and share information about our college.[2]

Having fifteen months under his belt, Earvin had time to solidify his vision for the college as outlined in his inaugural address on October 26, 2001. It is included in its entirety as it certainly informed his fifteen-year presidency.

> Huston-Tillotson College, like its peer institutions founded to offer educational opportunity to disenfranchised African Americans, has had a rich but often stormy past. From the beginning, the peer institutions, Samuel Huston College and Tillotson College, struggled against many barriers to help countless young men and women reach for the American dream.
>
> Now on this day as we come to formally install the fifth president of the consolidated Huston-Tillotson College and celebrate the 49th anniversary of the merger, and 126 years of providing educational opportunity, we are given cause to pause. Pause in gratitude for God's grace that has allowed the institution to persevere and even sometimes prosper. But we also pause as we consider the immediate challenges for us.
>
> Our history has been one of celebration and intervening episodes of uncertainty. It is perhaps these intervening episodes that have given us the courage and strength to confront the challenges of today. And so it is with a renewed passion

and sense of purpose that we come this day ready for the battle. Armed with a renewed spirit, we are determined to keep the doors of educational opportunity at Huston-Tillotson College not only opened but inviting for the 21st century.

This inaugural celebration has been a deliberate display of what an institutional Huston-Tillotson College can bring to its community. But more importantly, it is a statement of what can be achieved if we plan and use abundant resources that are available to us and work together for the good of those whom we serve.

Thus, it is no accident that the Rev. Zan Holmes's penetrating message at our opening prayer breakfast implored us to make a certain investment in an uncertain time in this, his alma mater, and our beloved institution. It was no accident that during Wednesday's symposium, former United States Secretary of Labor Roy Marshall and Dr. Anthony Carnevale of the Educational Testing Service set forth the public policy imperatives that confront Huston-Tillotson College and its constituents. We must understand these imperatives in order to influence the public policy formulation process and address the issues that forced disproportionate numbers about constituents into the underclass and to the ranks of the underemployed.

And finally, it was no accident that this community was treated to the unparalleled brilliance of the Dance Theatre of Harlem, the stirring talents of our gospel choir and Austin's ProArts Collective, and the melodic presentations of James Polk and company at the Bob Bullock Texas State History Museum. As these artists speak to our very souls, they help us give expression to our appreciation for the culture that has been so vital to our survival.

All these activities were planned to show us that we have today a rich legacy to advance for our children and our children's children. And yes, brother Holmes, these activities were planned as part of this inauguration to press home the need for substantial investment from us now in these uncertain times, to sustained investments made over the years by those who have gone before us.

Inaugurations, then, are not really about the new presidents. Indeed, these events are about institutions, about the histories and their futures. This inauguration has, therefore, presented highlights of the College's vision of itself on the threshold of a new century. Over the last fifteen months, staff and faculty have worked untiringly to craft a strategic plan that we called an Agenda for Excellence. This Agenda for Excellence will position Huston-Tillotson as a premier academic institution; a lofty goal, indeed, but an attainable one.

We want to assure you that whatever our goals, Huston-Tillotson College will remain true to its roots. We will continue to embrace our responsibility to challenge the well-prepared student while offering the less-prepared student an opportunity to reach his or her potential. This sweeping commitment leads us to recruit across a wide spectrum of ability. If a young person has the aptitude to succeed, Huston-Tillotson College wants to be the vehicle for that success. We recognize the risk inherent in this philosophy, but we believe the risk to this nation would be far greater if we failed to meet students' education needs.

Huston-Tillotson College also invites students of varied ethnicity and personal circumstances to become part of our College family. *Inclusive* is what this notion is called today as institutions seek the whole of the mantra of diversity. We at Huston-Tillotson College simply call it tradition. And we teach our students that our doors are, and always have been, opened to any person desirous of an education.

We envision a student body that mirrors the diversity of race and social-economic class of American society. While African American students will continue to comprise the majority of our student population, Hispanic students and international students will approximate 30 percent of the College enrollment. Guided by faculty and administration dedicated to inclusiveness and ethical values, our students will study with, learn from, and interact comfortably with people of diverse heritage, religions, and life experiences. Whatever their differences, we will encourage our students to share a common sense of themselves as responsible people—responsible for their own lives, their families' lives, their communities and, ultimately, responsible for the integrity of our nation.

Much will be required of us to reach to make the vision into reality.

First, we must address the infrastructure of the campus. The task includes:
- Restoration of the old administration building to include a publicly accessible computer lab and African American Resource Center;
- Construction of a wellness center that will house our athletics, faculty, sports gymnasium, a personal fitness resources and community health program;
- Creation of a new science facility to house labs in biology, chemistry, physics, computer science;
- For consolidating the 23 acres of the developed campus with adjacent area acre of undeveloped land;
- Enhancing the library and student center to make them more accommodating to the needs of students in a technological society.

Second, we must build enrollment of the College to ensure intellectuals stimulating changes in all major fields. Over the next three to five years, we expect to double the size of our student population; stabilizing at about 1,200 will expand the College's recruitment beyond its current regional focus, with as many as 25 percent of our students coming from beyond Texas. We also target effective articulation agreements with community colleges.

Third, we will redouble our efforts to make our curricular offerings responsive to market forces while maintaining a liberal arts core. The envisioned curriculum will have a liberal arts nucleus featuring a redefined set of classics by writers and artists of varied ethnicity as well as a growing body of technological resources [that] must also produce an increasingly challenging, technological[ly] rich experience that responds to the complexities of the global marketplace. We will develop an honest program to attract more high performance that will enhance development of curricula in science, math, and technology prepared teachers and career professionals. We will motivate our best and brightest to set their sights on attending graduate school and on becoming College professors. We will create more student internships and other service-learning opportunities.

Fourth, no curriculums shine in a vacuum: our faculty—empowered to be creative in their fields and engage students in a personal way—will remain the heart and soul of Huston-Tillotson College. I am pleased with the growing trend among them to embrace activities that enhance effectiveness and management skills. The College will develop resources to vigorously support professional development. We expect our faculty to grow in number from 40 to about 60, and in experience, teaching in diverse ways.

Fifth, we will seek to create synergy between business and technology, business and arts, communications, and technology. In this vein we will bring together various segments of the industry.

Sixth, we must engage our community as partners with the College. Towards this end, we are developing programs that will expand internships and service-learning opportunities, serve as a resource for community development and concerns, and create and sustain partnerships with private industries, government agencies, other higher education institutions, and pre-collegiate.

Seventh, our goal for the next few years is, at a minimum, to double the College endowment and increase annual campaign giving to five million. This we must do in support of the far-ranging scope of our goals.

Finally, those of us who choose to work at schools such as Huston-Tillotson College must demonstrate a work ethic and respect for others and go beyond the superficial. At Huston-Tillotson, we rise to the challenge. We will aggressively recruit and retain in all areas of employment, men and women who value one another's contributions, support their work in ways that demonstrate concern for the best interest of the College and of our students, and will allow spiritual values to inform the way they treat others. Together we will be models of the citizens we want our students to become. Believing that it takes an entire campus to educate young persons, we also believe that the personal integrity of faculty, staff, and administration is a critical component in the success of our students. Therefore, we will create an environment that nurtures understanding personal development of not only students but of faculty and staff as well. Our focus on educating the total person challenges us to do far more than offer a series of courses leading to the degree. Instead, the Huston-Tillotson College experience must speak to the atmosphere on campus as the sum total of experiences and encounters that arise from respectful relationships among all members of the College.

These are the tenets that will guide us as we seek to redeem the promise of our leaders—Mary Branch, Matthew Simpson, John Jarvis Seabrook, John Q. Taylor King Sr., Joseph Turner McMillan Jr, and our founders.[3]

Inaugural activities including a prayer breakfast, symposium, evening gala, and worship service occurred over the course of two days. In light of HT's financial situation, Earvin was proud that those activities cost HT little financial outlay due to his professional contacts' contributions. Sunday worship service at Wesley United Methodist Church included songs by the HT choir, speeches by Dr. Thomas Cole, President of Clark Atlanta University, and a representative of the United Negro College Fund. MC Hammer, rap music entertainer and ordained minister, rounded out inaugural activities.[4] Wearing the Presidential Chain of Office, Earvin was ushered into his inauguration activities by me as the College Marshal, carrying the College Mace. In Earvin's thank you letter to the Huston-Tillotson family, he stated that:

> Each event was managed with a sense of professionalism that will be the trademark of our college. Your creativity, long hours, and purposeful spirit resulted in the best presentation of the college. I am particularly pleased with the services provided by our student ambassadors. Their calm demeanor, smiling faces, and helpful presence provided a special glimpse of our students. I know, too, you join me in expressing pride in the scope of talent displayed by our graduates ranging from Rev. Zan Holmes to James Polk to Melanie Wilkinson. While I was the beneficiary of many acts of kindness, I want to also acknowledge the thoughtfulness

with which you treated my family, visitors, and friends, and other guests of the college. I was grateful and gratified by their frequent comments on the warmth and hospitality they experienced throughout the College during their stay. In the end, inaugurations are not really about new presidents. Instead, they celebrate the hopes and aspirations of people for the colleges and universities we lead. We have cause for great expectations of Huston-Tillotson College as we move towards our sesquicentennial in 2025.[5]

Who Is Dr. Larry Earvin?

Hailing from Tennessee, Earvin's parents knew that education would bring their children upward mobility even though neither had a college degree. Earvin and his two sisters never had a choice—they were going to college. They were expected to achieve, and they did. Earvin and his wife had two children, son William Jarrett and younger daughter Allyson Valeria. Earvin's wife was a minister in the Atlanta area until her tragic death. After his wife's death Earvin came to Huston-Tillotson College with his daughter, while his son went to graduate school at Clark Atlanta University. Both of his children are now married with children of their own. His children and grandchildren give him great joy and are his priority. According to Earvin, they are important. If something should come up with them now, regardless of whatever it is—job, or anything else—I would put whatever I was doing on the back burner."[6]

Earvin described himself as shy and old-fashioned, tending to stick to traditional values. "There are times you really have to go deep within yourself to meditate, to think and pray to get through it. I think it's important for people who still have their loved ones to think about how they treat them. They should treat them like they are fragile human beings, who may not be here tomorrow or even later that day,"[7] said Earvin. He indicated that becoming president of HT when he did was good for him. "Given the needs of the College, it was kind of good to come at this time and have to immerse myself in the activities of the school, trying to get us on a firmer footing. Of course, I have to have balance in my life. I have to have time for relationships; time for myself. I try to do that but end up spending most of my time on the job."[8] In time, Earvin had a lady friend who lived in Atlanta. She attended special HT functions such as banquets, graduation, Charter Day, and other events with him. The HT family came to know her and to respect her relationship with Earvin. I saw Earvin at Dr. Melva Williams's HT presidential inauguration,[9] March 2023, and the lady friend mentioned above is now his wife.

Larry Earvin holds a bachelor's in business administration from Clark College, later Clark Atlanta University, a master's degree in urban administration and planning from Georgia State University, and a PhD in American Studies from Emory University. His vast professional service also includes membership on the Council of Independent Colleges Board of Directors and the Amistad Research Center Board of Directors. Within the United Methodist Church, Earvin has served as chair of the Commission on Black Colleges of the General Board of Higher Education and Ministry and was a board member of both the Committee on Planning and Implementation of the National Association of Schools and Colleges and the Educational and Institutional Insurance Administrators. He also served on the boards of the American Council on Education, the National Association for Equal Opportunity in Higher Education, the Council for Higher Education Accreditation, and the United Negro College Fund.[10] Earvin served on several state and national boards including the Executive Committee of the National Association of Independent Colleges and Universities (NAICU) and the Independent Colleges and Universities of Texas (ICUT).[11]

In 2009 Earvin was elected to serve on the board of the Southern Association of Colleges and Schools (SACS). On December 12, 2014, he was honored with the James T. Rogers Distinguished Leadership Award, the highest award presented by the Southern Association of Colleges and Schools Commission on Colleges (SACSCOC). This award recognized him for his exceptional leadership and distinguished service in the arena of higher education. His credentials and recognized leadership skills earned him the position of Chairman of the SACSCOC (formerly SACS) Board of Trustees for the 2013-2014 term, becoming the second African American to hold that top position. Earvin previously served on the Executive Council of SACSCOC as vice chair, responsible for the interpretation of commission policies and procedures.[12] He had these important positions with SACSCOC while still president at HT. Notice his extensive national appointments, and consequently meetings, providing evidence of his frequent time away from HT.

Dr. Earvin's Inheritance: Assets and Liabilities

Fully armed with a stellar background of knowledge, skills, and connections, Dr. Earvin was ready to roll up his sleeves and guide the institution into its future based on alignment between his personal vision and HT's mission. He reflected on the history of HT and was humbled by the legacy of HT's ancestors who created and kept HT alive for generations. He understood that the history of Sam Huston and Tillotson, as well as the merged Huston-Tillotson College, represented more than just educational institutions; they were both life-giving and life-breathing. By life-breathing I mean that Earvin understood that the historical, and more recent, alumni continue to breathe life into the institution by recruiting new prospective students and lending their success for others to emulate. More importantly, he understood the consequence of moving HT from probation to full standing with SACS.

To do what needed to be done, Earvin surveyed and embraced what he inherited from the previous administration. No person can be successful as president without having committed, professional faculty and staff. Earvin inherited *both* excellent resources, mainly HT people—alumni, current students, faculty, staff, and board members. Some alumni gave of their time, money, and other resources. Some brought potential HT students to special days on campus. Having pride for their undergraduate institution, some alumni always acknowledge HT on their resume and vita and in presentations. Others, through their alumni associations, provided scholarships, mentorships, encouragement, and professional role modeling. These were all greatly beneficial to the college. Earvin engaged alumni as assets, especially since change was needed.

Inherited Alumni
Some outstanding alumni were mentioned in the previous chapter. Here are others:

- Roger Adams ('90, Sociology) is employed by the US Department of Health and Human Services, Centers for Medicare & Medicaid Services as the Region Lead/Health Insurance specialist. Previously, he was the Marketplace State Leader for Texas, Marketplace Senior Caseworker, and a Beneficiary Services Representative. He was Director of the Texas State Health Insurance Assistance Program and Legal Services Developer for the Department of Aging and Disability Services. He met his wife at HT and had a son who attended HT. Adams gave back by sharing funding and grant information with appropriate units at HT. He also supervised HT sociology majors in paid internships in one of his positions.
- Kim Patton ('97, Sociology) received a master's degree from Prairie View A&M in 1999. A former counselor at Travis County Jail, Patton co-founded with her husband, Sherwynn Patton, a nonprofit consulting organization, Life Anew. Restorative Justice. This organization works with community partners using restorative practices for building healthier and lasting relationships with an ecosystem perspective. They

work with students and staff in local, state, and national public-school systems to reduce suspension of students and to improve internal and external relationships. They have trained the Austin Police Department to use restorative practices in their community engagement activities. Additionally, they trained HT students in restorative practices, allowing several HT students to complete their required internships in their organization. Both Pattons created a documentary on restorative practices with young people which caught the attention of President Barack Obama, who invited them to the White House to share their views.

- Joya Hayes Randle ('96, Communication) is the daughter of Bishop Hayes and has a master's in public administration. As an HT student, Hayes was the student body president for two consecutive terms and served on numerous community boards and committees. Hayes is a sought-after motivational speaker. She has received more than twenty-five community service awards for her volunteer work in Austin.[13] Joya Hayes is Austin's Human Resources Director who participates in all formal negotiations with the Austin Police Department, the Emergency Medical Services department, and the Austin Fire department.[14]

- Devan Spence ('99, Business Administration) was the first Jamaican student at HT in over twenty-three years. As an older student, she became the matriarch of younger Jamaican students who were actively recruited under McMillan's administration. While a student, she worked as the administrative assistant for both Social and Behavioral Sciences and Natural Sciences Departments. She was responsible for two academic changes at HT. Spence was a trained teacher in Jamaica and had her degree certified by an Austin specialist agency resulting in Huston-Tillotson College accepting her teacher degree to be equivalent to an associate degree. Based on the precedent set by Spence, the registrar accepted international students' teaching degrees as certified associate degrees. Second, as an honors student, Spence asked the registrar to stamp "honor" on her diploma. That was done for her and for all subsequent honors students.

- Candace Wicks ('89, Sociology) received an MEd in Early Childhood from Texas Women's University after matriculating from HT. A native of Dallas, Texas, she was an educator with the Dallas Independent School District for over thirty years and retired in 2019. In 2008, Ms. Wicks was given the ultimate honor as the Teacher of the Year for the Dallas

Independent School District 2007–2008. Ms. Wicks holds a certificate in Biblical Studies (Old & New Testament Survey) from Liberty University, Lynchburg, Virginia, and has online courses from Dallas Theological Seminary. She also has a certificate in Diamond Essentials from Gemological Institute of America in Carlsbad, California.

Distinguished Faculty Assets
According to Earvin, he inherited a faculty that had integrity and was the lifeline of HT. That same faculty was fed up with years of not being appreciated, and in many cases disrespected, by the previous president. Earvin came to HT at a time when faculty morale was low. Paul Anaejionu and I had our salaries cut due to retaliation for our campus activism. We wrote Earvin before he stepped foot on HT campus as president, requesting that he restore both of our salaries, and he did.

Earvin's distinguished faculty included many already mentioned, and others that will be highlighted in the chapter on President Pierce Burnette. It suffices to say that the faculty was ready for new leadership and willing to embrace the president's vision. Earvin also brought two professors with him from Clark Atlanta, Dr. Steven Edmond (Business Administration and Chair of the School of Business) and his wife Dr. Janice Sumler-Edmond, a lawyer with a PhD in history. The latter was hired to teach history and to organize HT's first established honors program, the DuBois Scholar. Earvin paid for HT to be a member of Faculty Resource Network (FRN), a faculty development consortium program at New York University, appointing Sumler-Edmond as its first liaison.

Liability: Financial Instability
Earvin inherited cash flow and financial instability that were called into question by HT's accrediting agency. Earvin immediately made friends who could help HT financially. In his first fourteen months, Earvin brought in $3.6 million in grants and donations. The largest donation, of $450,000, came from Dell Corporation to refurbish and update HT computer labs. In recognition of this gift, HT computer laboratories were named Dell Computer Labs. This gift was solicited by Earvin even before he was formally inaugurated. According to Terry Smith, Earvin's executive vice president, "Although these donations from Dell were greatly appreciated, Huston-Tillotson was negotiating with the Austin-based computer company to be awarded millions of dollars."[15] Instead, in September 2001, Dell gave UNCF $2.3 million to improve technology on member campuses. This award included

$1.3 million in financial and computers system contributions and $1 million to increase UNCF students' access to affordable notebook computers.[16]

Early in his presidency, Earvin crafted an annual black-tie gala, the President's MASKED Ball, to raise scholarship funds (MASKED: Mankind Assisting Students Kindle Educational Dreams). The event featured dinner, entertainment, student testimonials, and an auction. From 2004 to 2009 proceeds contributed more than $1 million to students' scholarships. During 2009, basketball Hall of Famer Magic Johnson was a celebrity guest. He unexpectedly auctioned off some courtside Los Angeles Lakers tickets that fetched winning bids of $7,000, $8,000, and $10,000. Additionally, he chipped in a $25,000 matching donation himself. Earvin attributed the ball's growth and success to the fact "we're emphasizing education."[17] Getting HT on solid financial footing was critical for the reaffirmation process. According to Board Chairwoman Wilhelmina Delco, the search committee was impressed with Earvin's philosophy of fundraising: "He told us that you don't raise money, you make friends."[18]

HT's Self-Study Process and Reaffirmation

In June 2000, under McMillan's presidency the Southern Association of Colleges and Universities (SACS) extensively reviewed HT's self-study documents and conducted a campus visit, resulting in HT being placed on warning. In 2001, SACS placed HT on probation, its most severe sanction, but removed it in January 2003. Although probation occurred during President Earvin's first year, it was caused by the actions of the previous president, McMillan. Long-term probation would have resulted in the closure of the institution, as its degrees would have been of no value. Earvin, very familiar with SACS requirements because of his long-term relationship with the organization, successfully guided HT through its reaffirmation process; HT was taken off probation and in fact was given no recommendations.[19] Reaffirmation with no recommendations is extremely rare. This was, in fact, Earvin's most important contribution to the college.

Low Student Enrollment

An institutional objective, throughout Earvin's entire presidency, was to recruit more students with a larger percentage of student diversity. The semester prior to the Earvin presidency, student enrollment was 536, almost as low as the enrollment of 506 inherited by McMillan. By 2008 Earvin had moved HT to its highest enrollment to date, followed by increases each additional year except his final semester. He did this in part by instituting the Adult Degree Program, which boosted enrollment to more than 1,000. However, because tuition for this program was lower than for regular students, the financial impact was less than would have occurred if these students had been regular paying students.

Old Administration Building
Earvin inherited the question of what to do with the old Administration Building. Both of his predecessors had a vision for renovating it. Earvin was able to fulfill that vision. After being vacant for thirty-seven years, in 2006 the 92-year-old, three-story structure that had been built by students was reopened with a new name, Anthony and Louise Viaer Alumni Hall. Viaer ('58, Sociology) came to HT as a track student from New York City. He said that HT saved his life and was determined to give back to his beloved alma mater if he ever made it big. His wealth grew through real estate, and he gave millions towards the renovation of the old Administration Building. Additionally, he gave $1 million for student scholarships and a gift of money to each of the 2006 graduating seniors as an incentive for them to "pay it forward."

Institutional Climate
Earvin inherited low institutional morale, a sense of brokenness, and a need for intra- and interdepartmental healing. Earvin was not blindsided by the internal turmoil, as he was informed of it by members of the Save HT underground organization prior to his first day on campus. That organization sent Earvin a letter with the sixteen-page detailed Bill of Particulars described in the previous chapter.[20] Below is the letter to Earvin, dated August 14, 2000.

> Dear Dr. Earvin:
> We write on behalf of community members—from both our college and the broader community—to welcome you to Austin and to our campus. We are members of *Save HT*. This community-based organization was established to address the major issues at the College and to facilitate bridging the chasm between the College and the larger community. We were concerned with the long-term survival of the College, and the serious grievances of several persons associated with the College. Membership of this organization includes the immediate past-president of the Huston-Tillotson College chapter of AAUP, HT alumni, some senior faculty, faculty Emeriti, HT staff, former HT faculty, along with two nationally renowned University of Texas attorneys with a long history of leadership in the National AAUP. One of these attorneys is the

current General Counsel of the National AAUP, the other is the former General Counsel and former president of national AAUP. The organization was formed in September 1999 and continues to meet periodically.

We are delighted that you have accepted the challenge to lead our institution to greatness. We hereby pledge our support to work with you in every way possible with the goal of rebuilding our College and strengthening the links of friendships within the larger community. Our group welcomes the changes taking place on our campus. We are delighted Dr. Sandra Vaughn joined us as a new VPAA. Many of the on-campus members have already met with her and appreciate her responsiveness to our concerns in her vison for the future.

Over the course of the last year, we developed a number of informational documents that we would like to share with you. Some of these documents have been shared with the Chairman of the Board of Trustees. We believe these documents will help you become aware of some key issues that, among other things, could establish the basis for crafting viable solutions in these areas where we can be of service to the College. The enclosed documents include:[21] 1) Faculty letter of "no-confidence," 2) observation presented by a group of faculty members, 3) Bill of Particulars, 4) interview with a former employee, and 5) Stewardship of HT property. Information for these documents came from committee members.[22]

As you may know, the catalyst for much of the upheaval that occurred on the campus in the last year was Dr. McMillan's appointment of [MT] as the Acting Vice President of Academic Affairs. He was a UT student intern and a former employee in the Upward Bound program on campus. That appointment was made without any input from, or prior knowledge of, the then current VP of Academic Affairs, Dr. Lenora Waters. Many campus members were deeply distressed at the apparent lack of regard for those who serve the institution with integrity and dedication. During the course of the past year, we had several useful conversations with Attorney George, the Chairman of the Board of Trustees. With your presence here, we can say that we have started to witness some of the positive changes he spoke to us about at those meetings. We were surprised, however, that contrary to Mr. George's assurance to us that [MT] would not be on campus after his internship, he returned to his pre-VPAA position, Upward Bound. Frankly, given the egregious treatment that he inflicted on faculty and staff over the past year and the compromise of the College's reputation within HT and in the community, we wondered why Board President George's commitment to this group was not met.

Additionally, several highly respected educators experienced personal and professional harm during the tenure of Dr. McMillan. Such persons as Ms. Teresia Lewis, alumna and former Dean of General Studies, Mr. Robert McHaney, former Professor of Music, Dr. June Brewer, alumna and Professor Emerita of English, and Miss Nancy Bandera, former Professor of Speech and Drama have unique and unbelievable stories which might have legal implications for Huston-Tillotson College. Their specific stories are highlighted in the Bill of Particulars. They need your urgent attention. We believe the integrity you bring to this campus will guide the much-needed changes in many areas. In addition to the grievance process that needs to be put into place, there's a need for healing of numerous riffs that have occurred in the past. We wish to be part of putting a healing process in place—it is very much needed in order to get on with the business of educating our students. With our collective skills and talents we know that we can restore greatness to our beloved institution.

The committee looks forward to our meeting with you. We will schedule a meeting with you through your secretary. On behalf of the committee, we respectfully submit this letter.[23]

Those who sent the letter and the Bill of Particulars wanted Earvin to be informed of the deep divide on campus and the pathway that led to that divide. Paul Anaejionu, his wife, Jane Anaejionu who was a consultant at HT, Harriet Buxkemper, and I authored the letter. Unfortunately, Earvin never responded to that letter. In fact, Earvin initially treated me and Anaejionu with suspicion, as the board fed him damaging information about us.

Each Huston-Tillotson president brings to the campus his/her unique characteristics, knowledge, gifts, and skills. These characteristics, along with board direction, interact in such a way as to inform how the president will move forward in his role. After years of controversial leadership by McMillan, Earvin's initial focus was to provide stability to HT's campus. According to him:

> Part of the challenge is the recent history of the College and to convince people that the corner has been turned.... Upon accepting the presidency of Huston-Tillotson College, I knew that many of the challenges would be the same as most Historically Black institutions; maintaining our historical constituents while appealing to a broader population, cultivating alumni support both financially and intellectually, improving the financial stability of the College (operating, scholarships, capital, and endowment funds), and enhancing community support and pride. [To do this required time away from the campus to

establish relationships and to cultivate those that already existed.] However, never had I seen an institution so well poised for prominence and greatness. Huston-Tillotson College is at a critical period in its 125-year existence.[24]

Earvin wanted to change Huston-Tillotson's image and to elevate it to be recognized as one of the best liberal arts colleges in the Southwest. He wanted to double enrollment by reaching out to Hispanics and Anglos, letting them know that HT could give them a great education. Texas's increasing Hispanic population offered great opportunities for enrollment growth. According to Earvin, "We are determined to keep the doors of education open, not only academically but also historically." His initial challenge was to create new directions and offer new academic opportunities for the students.

With little input from the faculty, and approved by the board, Earvin changed the mission of HT, effective March 27, 2015, that includes the emphasis on diversity.

- *Mission Statement:* HT nurtures a legacy of leadership and excellence in education, connecting knowledge, power, passion, and values.
- *Vision Statement:* A connected world where diversity of thought matters.

Faculty believed that this generic mission and vision of HT were void of our historical relationship with the two religious groups, United Methodist Church and United Church of Christ, and void of its historical purpose of educating African American students. Those who opposed both the mission and vision recognized that we must actively seek a diverse population of students but raised the question as to why we could not do that while being true to our historical mission.

Earvin's plans included holding staff and faculty to higher standards and expectations to provide excellent education for the diverse population. Academically, he wanted to develop and support stellar programs such as a master's in teacher education. He believed that while teacher education groomed students to teach K–12, it also prepared them to attend graduate school. He wanted to add a wellness center and a better equipped science building. He knew that better fundraising strategies were needed to accomplish these goals.

Dr. Earvin's Immediate Focus: Strategic Plans and Reaffirmation
HT Strategic Plan: An Agenda of Excellence (Under the Umbrella of Redeeming the Promise)

CHAPTER 3

Board members asked Earvin to change HT's climate. The emotional upheaval, along with the threat of HT probation from SACS, may have influenced Earvin's decision to "Redeem the Promise." This theme was outlined in his inaugural address and HT's 2001 Strategic Plan. It undergirded Earvin's first decade as president. In Earvin's 2003 President's Report,[25] he highlighted the Charter Day keynote address by Dr. King Davis who had first used the phrase "Redeeming the Promise."[26] King Davis began his remarks that day by defining the meaning of the words "redeeming" and "promise":

> Redeem has multiple definitions, but I think the definition that applies most here is "recover something that has been pledged or promised, but which may have been lost, ignored, denied, or not obtained in full."[27] A promise, on the other hand, is a "declaration that something will be done: an indication of what can be expected: or an indication of a person, in organizations, or a community's future potential for excellence or achievement." . . .
>
> When I integrate these two sets of definitions, it seems to me that we are saying that there is an historical commissary agreement between Huston-Tillotson's students, faculty, administration, churches, and the community about excellence and achievement that must be recovered. At the same time, there is a clear implication here that we may be at a point in history where there is a discrepancy between that early, lofty promise in the current reality.
>
> In the concept of "redeeming the promise" is an implied sense that our community has lost its way or lost sight of what is truly important in our lives and the lives of our community, our race, and our schools. Some have concluded that we had, in some materially important way, lost our moral or internal compass that guided us through difficult times. There's also the disquieting sense that the promise that once acted as a bond between faculty, students, parents, church, and the community is not as strong as it once was. Some believe that our community as a whole is now adrift without focus, commitment, or direction.
>
> Others would suggest that we have it made. All doors to our community and to our people are open and we just have to decide to exert the energy necessary to walk in and take advantage of the opportunities. In the generic sense, we must ask ourselves whether the historical promise that we have made to our communities has been broken, hidden, denied, or merely clouded by rhetoric. . . .
>
> In the final analysis, the critical promise that you have created here and that we must strive to maintain and redeem is a joint responsibility for *creativity, discovery, excellence, achievement, and integrity*. Everybody here must agree to

hold each other responsible for both the past and an uncertain future in which these values and characteristics are uppermost.

How we define promise determines how we recover this promise that we made to each other in the community seasons ago. It is this recovery process that is most important. How do we redeem the promise? I am requesting that you commit yourself to become promise-makers and promise-keepers. To do so requires individuals and organizations to take on responsibility for sustained and focused action over an extended period of time. Days instead of minutes; weeks instead of hours; years instead of months; centuries instead of decades. Promise keeping requires that we rededicate ourselves to the life principles and life values in both our personal and organizational charters. But how do we do this?

To redeem the promise, we must do some combination of the following things:
1. Build and pursue a shared vision.
2. Learn to be leaders and teach others.
3. Continuously renew knowledge and skills
4. Become involved in collective and political action.
5. Establish excellence as a continuous goal.
6. Take the risk to be wrong or fired.
7. Put the most important things first.
8. Think in systems and long-term ways.
9. Gain international experience.
10. Have a sense of passion for success.

HT's theme is designed to internalize a number of these characteristics and traits into the culture of the College. The theme is designed to force critical thinking about the purpose of life and what is required to render meaning in the lives of students while making an impact on the community. The College theme is like a wake-up call or an alarm clock that is designed to wake us up to our own potential for achievement. That is the promise![28]

Earvin's vision was in line with the college's mission:

Huston-Tillotson University is an Historically Black University affiliated with The United Methodist Church, the United Church of Christ, and the United Negro College Fund (UNCF). The mission of the College is to provide its increasingly diverse student body with an exemplary education that is grounded in the liberal arts and sciences, balanced with professional development, and directed to public service and leadership. The College prepares students with the integrity and civility to thrive in a diverse society, fosters spiritual development, preserves and promotes interest in the accomplishments and experiences of the College's stoic constituents and evolving population and creates and sustains supportive relationships which advance the Huston-Tillotson College community.[29]

Using the college's mission as his guide, Earvin, with select staff, faculty, and a consultant, developed the 2001 Strategic Plan: An Agenda for Excellence, carrying the same name as his inaugural address.[30] In this detailed 49-page document were institutional goals and goal alignments for every department of the institution. This plan established the blueprint for this administration. The strategic plan not only provided clear HT goals but contained an analysis of political, economic, social, and technological threats to and opportunities for the college. Implementation of the strategic plan was also a requirement of HT's reaffirmation process, thus constituting another reason to develop the plan based on research and best practices. Below are some excerpts from that document which was created by Earvin and his team even before his inauguration:

> With a proud history and a bright future, under the leadership of a new administration, the campus is experiencing a renewed spirit and sense of enthusiasm for the rebuilding to which it has committed itself in the new millennium. As a Historically Black College, Huston-Tillotson College has not been immune to the waning enrollments which have characterized the HBCUs since the latter part of the twentieth century. Now, on the heels of two consecutive years of declining enrollment, the College pauses to scan the educational landscape and position itself.
>
> In an attempt to Redeem the Promise, the purpose of this scanning report was to invoke thought, and inspire action, based on an intensive analysis of current market trends. Toward that end, we examined political, economic, social, societal, and technological issues that directly affect the future viability of the College. Following that examination, we present the College's response to the threats and opportunities it faces. Taken together, these two perspectives—the external and internal—form a strategic plan, which we believe sets forth an agenda of excellence for Huston-Tillotson College.

The strategic plan/environmental scan process yielded the following analysis of opportunities and threats to HT in 2000:

Political Environment: Effective July 1, 1999, the exemption that allowed Huston-Tillotson and other universities to have cohort default rates above 25 percent expired. Subsequently, each institution's ability to participate in the Federal Family Education Loan (FFEL), Direct Loan, and Federal Pell Grant Programs were placed in jeopardy. Over 86 percent of the students receive funding from the Title IV programs. This figure represented approximately $3 million in federal funds to support student tuition and fee charges at Huston-Tillotson College. HT was named as one of the 14 institutions in jeopardy of losing its Title IV eligibility. It was required to submit a satisfactory default management plan, hire an independent third party to help facilitate the default management process, and hire a default manager. Under Dr. Earvin, the College did hire a full-time default manager as part of its enrollment team.

Legislative change related to its TANF (Temporary Assistance to Needy Families) program can be both a threat and an opportunity. That program required recipients to go to work; but in some cases training was needed. An opportunity for the College is to establish a relationship with the Texas Workforce Commission in the Department of Human Services to explore job opportunities for TANF recipients. Another advantage could be that the College can develop articulation agreements with the Workforce Commission in the Department of Human Services and provide post-employment training opportunities for TANF recipients.

The *Hopwood* decision enacted by the Texas state legislature included a provision for a 10 percent plan which automatically qualifies top High School students for admission to all state-funded institutions, including the system's flagship campus in Austin.[31] The threat for HT is that inner-city high schools with high concentrations of minority students may find its brighter students going to state institutions, rather than coming to private institutions that have tuition not covered under the 10 percent plan. It is imperative that the College develop an aggressive marketing campaign to encourage minority students to consider attending a racially sensitive institution of higher education, preferably Austin's only Historically Black College, i.e. Huston-Tillotson College. HT should also market its programs to attract students who may not satisfy the admissions requirements at state-funded institutions but demonstrate the potential for success in a smaller, student-focused environment.

Economic Environment: In order to meet the changing job market requirements, HT needed to develop a curriculum that will address those requirements. In 2001, when this strategic plan was developed, the areas for high-paying jobs included various types of engineering, nursing, mathematics, and computer technology. HT already had mathematics and computer science degrees but needed to revise those curricula and include other majors that might meet those jobs forecast.

The strategic plan also recommended that HT create articulation agreements with Austin Community College and other local community colleges. These agreements would create a broad range of educational opportunities for students who wanted to transfer to a four-year College.

Huston-Tillotson College continued to secure grants from various sources, governmental and private. These grants would defray students' cost in the form of scholarships. Some of the grants have come from the United Negro College Fund, the National Science Foundation, as well as others. The college continues to strain its operating budget to cover expenditures that couldn't be covered by grant funds. If the college positioned itself to compete for additional grants, this strain would be reduced.

During the 2000–2001 academic year, in the State of Texas, African American high school students comprised 12 percent of high school graduates, while Latin Americans comprised 32 percent, and White students comprised 53 percent. The percentage of African American students is expected to decrease in years to come. Therefore, it is imperative that Huston-Tillotson College recruit and retain a more racially diverse population in order to remain viable in the coming years. Focusing solely on African American students will result in fewer students and a lower financial threshold. The recruitment team must broaden its territory and recruit not only locally but regionally and nationally targeting areas with a more diverse student body in mind.

<u>Technological Environment</u>: Technology was the hallmark of Earvin's new administration. Under King the first computers were introduced on campus. McMillan increased HT's technological capabilities by establishing an IT Department, securing funding and gifts of computers for labs and students. But Earvin was posed to move HT to the millennium technology needed to be successful in higher education. Institutions were competing against one another for students on the basis of their information technology facilities and resources. Not only was implementing information technology critical to the success of academic programs, but it was also equally vital to higher education administrative functions. Nationwide institutional websites were allowing students to not

only apply for admission and financial aid online, but also to register, apply for housing, and handle students' finances online. Colleges and universities, catalogs, degree curricula, and certification/special program courses were all available to prospective students at the touch of a button through the institution website. In 2001 Huston-Tillotson College had an institutional website, but it was limited in scope, reducing its competitive position to attract computer-savvy potential students who would prefer conducting administrative transactions over the Internet rather than standing in long lines and making numerous trips to campus.

State of the art administrative interactive database, when properly used, would allow for more efficient flow of information between departments. Unfortunately, even with the acquisition of new technology, HT did not have adequate training on the usage of that technology. Funding opportunities to secure technological training is needed.

Additionally, in 2001, the College library was antiquated, needing renovation to include computers and e-books. The residence hall was not fully Internet capable either. Under Earvin, funding was secured to renovate both the dormitories and the library.[32]

Education and Demographic Environment: Technology in the College academic arena was critical. With the increase of distance learning and online academic programs, it was critical for Huston-Tillotson to become part of the current and future trends. Having teachers available to hundreds and thousands of people simultaneously would provide Huston-Tillotson College with an additional viable financial base. It became important for Huston-Tillotson College to establish an incentive plan that would encourage faculty to learn and to offer online courses. Distance learning was a critical need on campus; staff and professors need to be hired. Collaboration with other institutions may help in this matter. In 1999 the College's Educational Policy Committee (EPC) approved distance learning policies and procedures which would allow the development of distance learning capabilities. Even though, in 2001, HT owned a cable channel that could have offered distance learning courses throughout Central Texas, it needed additional funding to enable its use for those purposes.[33]

As a result of this extensive environmental scan, the following institutional goals were established for HT to benefit its new millennium students. Each of these institutional goals included working objectives along with the responsible parties to establish implemental pathways for success.

1. The College will position itself as a premier academic institution by strengthening historical and new relationships.
2. The College will offer innovative academic programs in a learner-centered environment which provides challenging and exemplary educational experiences.
3. The College will increase enrollment by recruiting a diverse student population and retaining them through graduation.
4. The College will create and maintain innovative student programs to foster development of the whole person to prepare students for positions of leadership in the community, the workplace, and the world.
5. The College will operate under a participatory governance structure that involves and educates the entire College community while making use of the skills and talents of the Board of Trustees, faculty, staff, administration, and students.
6. The College administration will ensure fiscal stability and growth through annual formative assessments, sound financial management and stewardship, and enhanced external funding.

Earvin used research to inform his vision, which was reflected by both his educational and professorial background. Providing the framework for implementing his vision was not new to him, as his previous academic experiences gave him the skills he needed to be successful at HT. He provided clarification of the six institutional goals as needed, while engaging others to share in the goals' refinement and implementation throughout the process.[34] The Strategic Plan was directly related to a successful reaffirmation.

HT Reaffirmation Process (1998–January 2003)[35]
As briefly mentioned earlier, Earvin inherited HT's reaffirmation process from McMillan. The process had not gone well and in July 1999, under McMillan, the college received notification that it had been placed on *notice* for a twelve-month period for failure to comply with requirements for Administrative Processes and Financial Resources. The college was required to provide the following items at least four weeks prior to a Reaffirmation Committee visit scheduled for February 2000.[36]

1. Two most recent audit reports and management letters;
2. Most recent A133 or A128 financial aid audit;

3. Statement of financial activities;
4. Statement of indebtedness;
5. Full Time Equivalent (FTE) enrollment for FY 1998, 1999, and 2000 with projections for 2001;
6. Correspondence showing status with the United States Department of Education.

In May 2000, HT received recommendations from SACS; in June 2000 (and again in November 2000) institutional representatives were interviewed by the Committee on Criteria and Reports at the June SACS meeting. Several institutional representatives including President-Elect Larry Earvin, President McMillan, and Assistant Dean of Financial Services Bronté Jones attended that SACS meeting.[37]

In July, still under McMillan's presidency, the college received notification that it had been placed on *warning* status for failure to comply with several of the various criteria described above. The college was required to provide documentation of an appropriate plan, a planning and evaluation process, and an adequate financial base to accomplish the institution's purpose. Finally, the college was to provide copies of the last two financial audits and management letters and recent financial audit. All of the above was under McMillan's presidency.

Thus, in August 2000 Earvin stepped into a college that was in serious trouble with SACS. He needed to bring his knowledge and skills to the institution to comply with SACS requirements. Not having a magic wand, he had to quickly build an internal HT Self-Study team, made up primarily of administrators who would commit long hours each day—and night if needed. Their roles were to secure documents; write, revise, and rewrite reports; and indoctrinate the campus on the mission statement and short version of the strategic plan, so that if asked by the external SACS team, they could readily state them and their implementation process. Still with these early efforts, HT got into more serious jeopardy of being closed as was evident by a January 2001 *warning* for six months. In July 2001 HT was placed on *probation* for twelve months for failure to comply with criteria on Planning and Evaluation; Educational Programs, Planning and Evaluation; Administrative and Educational Support Services; Academic and Professional Preparation Baccalaureate; and Financial Resources.[38] In November 2001 the Fiscal and Strategic Technical Assistance Program team from UNCF visited HT to help ensure that the institution's processes followed SACS standards.

As a result of a site team visit in April 2002, the college received its recommendations that included one combined recommendation in Section VI–Administrative Processes. Specifically, by May 31, 2002, the college was required to provide evidence that the institution had sufficient resources to support all of its programs and that it had the financial stability essential to its successful operation. Because HT was not able to provide that evidence, in July 2002 the college received notification that it had been continued on *probation* for six months.[39] After the requested follow-up reports and documentation were provided, HT received notice in January 2003 that it had been reaffirmed and that the next follow-up report was due April 15, 2005. This date was the five-year mark of the ten-year reaffirmation requirement. The *reaffirmation had no recommendations*, a miraculous outcome.[40]

In light of the serious jeopardy facing the institution, this reaffirmation was Earvin's greatest contribution to HT. Without reaffirmation, HT would have quickly closed its doors. Without reaffirmation, credit from HT could not be transferred; students generally could not get state or federal aid; and other donor organizations and individuals would probably not make contributions to HT. In an institution where more than 85 percent of its students needed financial aid, HT would have not survived.

Earvin's second reaffirmation came up in 2010. He began the process in 2008 and with reports, visit from the teams, a stronger financial base, and meeting all criteria, HT was reaffirmed during that cycle.

Dr. Earvin and His HT Constituents
Relationship with Students
Although Earvin was extremely goal-oriented and faithful to his vison for the college, the old cliché that "I don't care how much you know until I know much you care" was reinterpreted by students as "I don't care what you do until I know how much you care." Earvin did a lot for the institution; however, his inability or unwillingness to relate to his many local constituents appeared to influence their perception of him. Many students, faculty, and staff who participated in surveys and interviews evaluated him in terms of his absence rather than his contributions to the college, which were many. Those who matriculated or served under both McMillan and Earvin saw a marked difference between the two. They felt McMillan's emphasis was on relationships (although often unhealthy) and Earvin's was on goal attainment (although often without input from key stakeholders). Actually, both relationships and goal attainment are needed, but leaning towards one while minimizing the other is problematic. What the both presidents had in

common was that they had a vision for institutional growth; however, neither did the hard work to really engage constituents on all levels of the hierarchy. Top-down was not an effective leadership style if the president wanted to "celebrate the hopes and aspirations of people for the colleges and universities we lead."[41]

The heartbeat of our institution was and is its students. In an effort to get students' valuable insights on the presidents under whom they matriculated, I asked students several open-ended questions in both surveys and interviews. Below are five of the questions.[42]

1. What were your initial impressions of the president(s)?
2. Did it change over time?
3. What did he or she do to create a family environment?
4. What was his or her leadership style?
5. What were his or her major strengths and weaknesses?

Below are comments from students who matriculated (entirely or partially) under Earvin.

- He was very personable when encountered, but there were concerns about his lack of presence on the actual campus.
- His major strengths were being well connected with individuals to help us with our accreditation, among others. Also, he was great with traveling and recruiting international students to attend HT. His weaknesses were taking away many of HT's traditions, rarely engaging the student body, hiring staff who were not great in their roles, especially in the business aspect of the school.
- He had a strong vision for the institution.
- I never really knew who he was and did not know what he did. I never really had the chance to get to know him or understood his role as our president.
- He was unapproachable. I saw him a handful of times and never truly shook his hand or interacted with him until the day of graduation. My impression never changed in the two years I attended there.
- He improved the look of the campus. It felt like an actual college and not "the hood."
- He obtained partnerships with various entities; business minded.
- I had very few, if any, interactions with him directly and/or indirectly.
- Weakness: students didn't know him or see him. I've never even had a

conversation with him
- Strengths: raised a lot of money for the campus. Weakness: not very friendly.
- Great with getting others to offer money.
- He had pull financially.
- His strength was that he was a great public speaker; his weakness was that he was too absent as a leader.
- Busy man with financial pull.
- I didn't really get the chance to know him because he was never around. He was very stand-offish from students, like he felt he was royal. His attitude never changed; instead it was worse.
- He showed A LOT of favoritism towards certain students.
- Support to staff and students; maintained HT involvement with local schools and churches.
- He created the MASKED Ball annual fundraising banquet, and it was wonderful to see students dress up and enjoy themselves amongst mentors and sponsors who gave to HT.
- I'm not sure what Dr. Earvin did to create a family environment. I felt he actually hindered it by taking away a lot of the student events and activities where we could relate to staff, faculty, and our peers.
- He wasn't a visible president during my tenure.

The most frequent themes among these responses were that Earvin was absent a lot; he was not approachable; students didn't have a relationship with him; he raised funds (e.g., the MASKED Ball); and he improved the campus.

Relationship with Faculty
Dealing with Faculty Unrest
As mentioned earlier, Earvin inherited many seasoned, highly regarded, highly honored professors who made substantial contributions in their respective fields and who made professional or personal sacrifices to remain at HT. These professors, ethnically and religiously diverse, add to the richness and intellectual distinctions that afford our students a great education. Fortunately, other qualified and passionate persons were also hired under his leadership. The mixture of long-term and newly employed professors brought both a link from the past and a road towards the future. Many newly employed professors deferred to their senior counterparts for leadership and voice on their behalf, while the seasoned professors benefited

from the freshness and new approach to knowledge that the junior professors brought. Professors zealously fulfilled their roles, recognizing their singular purpose of pouring both knowledge and values into the lives of students. In doing so, they forecasted their students' future of success and giving back.

The HT faculty were demoralized when Earvin came. The letter sent to him prior to his becoming president told him what he needed to know about faculty concerns regarding the former president and hinted at what the faculty needed from him moving forward. Faculty members were excited about ending the old and bringing in the new. However, much to their dismay, Earvin didn't embrace them or empower them in ways they had expected. I, along with Anaejionu and Buxkemper, personally reached out to him for three reasons: to inform him of campus life under McMillan; to have our salaries reinstated; and to welcome him and his daughter by offering them help as needed. I was truly ready for the new president and sent him the following letter:[43]

> June 20, 2000
> Dr. Larry Earvin, President Elect
> Re: Welcome
> Dear Dr. Earvin:
> I am so pleased that you will be our next President. As one of the faculty representatives on the Presidential Search Committee, I was privileged to cast my vote for you. What impressed me the most was your "quiet authority." I left feeling that you would be able to lead with integrity, compassion, and authority. I believe that our institution really needs someone like you to move us forward through periods of internal healing, reconciliation, and academic growth. Welcome to Huston-Tillotson College!
>
> I was impressed with your genuine love and appreciation for your wife. When the committee asked you what your greatest asset is, you said your wife. Thus, I feel deeply with you in the loss of your wife. I felt a tinge of guilt.[44] If the Search Committee did not send for you and your wife, maybe your wife would still be alive. Yet, some consolation comes knowing that your wife was a Christian who was not only saved but also a servant of the Lord. Upon returning from your wife's funeral, Dr. Wilhelmina Delco told us about the many tributes and honors that were given to your wife, and indirectly given to your entire family. I extend my sympathy to you and your family.
>
> I know that these are both difficult and challenging times for you and your family. I told Attorney Jim George, President of the Board, that I am willing

to assist you with your presidential transition in any way that I can. I wanted to tell you this myself. I am a Licensed Professional Counselor, and a Licensed Master Social Worker-Advanced Clinical Practitioner (these are the highest social work/counselor licenses given in the State of Texas). I am willing to provide therapeutic assistance to you and your children as you all go through the grieving process. Even as you take on the awesome responsibilities of being President of Huston-Tillotson College, you will need time to mourn, reflect, and examine what's really important in life.

Enclosed are two books of poetry that I wrote. *Sanctuary* is for you, and *Feelings* is for your son and daughter. Actually, please share them, as they may provide each of you some comfort.

Additionally, I have academic experiences and competencies which could be of great assistance to you as you transition into your position of President of the College. I have been at Huston-Tillotson College for twenty-seven years. As a tenured professor, I was the Chairperson of the Social Science Division from 1983 to 1999. I am well informed about the internal operations of the Social Science Division and have worked closely with other academic divisions. I am on the SACS Steering Committee and the Governance Design Team of the Strategic Planning Committee. My skills are numerous, and I have a good relationship with most of my colleagues. It is for these reasons that I can be of assistance to you.

I remember you saying (during your interview) that it is important that we (the College) "raise friends as well as raise funds and be good citizens." With your words in mind, I wrote Dr. Shilling (the consultant to the Presidential Search Committee) about an individual who would be good to have as a friend, and to whom we should extend our friendship. I am enclosing my e-mail to him and his response to me. Furthermore, I am offering myself as a friend and colleague.

I may be contacted at the above address, telephone number, e-mail address and fax number. I am currently scheduled to go to Jamaica, West Indies, from July 3, 2000–August 6, 2000. However, I am willing to leave a week later for Jamaica in order to be available to you. Please contact me if I need to delay my trip.

Again, welcome to Huston-Tillotson College.

Yours truly,
Rosalee Martin, PhD

Even with my reaching out to him and making myself available to him, Earvin accepted others' one-sided picture of me and never acknowledged the receipt of my letter. Three months into his presidency, I met with him, prompted by Dr. Sandra Vaughn, the new VP for Academic Affairs, who remained at HT less than a year. She told me that Earvin was told devastating things about me and that he needed to hear my side of the story. It was clear that Earvin bought the board's assessment; he had already denied me a promotion recommended by Vaughn. My conversation with Earvin went like this:[45]

> Martin: Thank you for seeing me. My condolences to you in the loss of your wife.
> Earvin: Thanks.
> Martin: Dr. Vaughn suggested that I talk to you due to your impression of me. I understand that some of the board members have told you negative things about me. I want to answer any questions you might have.
> Earvin: [silence]
> Martin: But you MUST know that if we [referring to involved faculty and Save HT] didn't do what we did that HT would have been closed due to inept leadership.
> Earvin: I don't know how the institution has survived this long. It is really in bad shape.
> Martin: Dr. Earvin, since you know that, then why are you treating me the way you are?[46]
> Earvin: There are consequences for what you did. There are some board members who want to know why you are still here! There are still residual effects of what you did.

The board hired Earvin; his first allegiance was to it. Even though Earvin didn't know me, he adopted the resentful feelings some board members had towards me. My efforts to reach out to him and his family were invalidated and rejected. I left that meeting knowing that as the "whistleblower" under the previous president I would suffer consequences under this president as well. And I did! I wasn't fired but was denied upward mobility at the college. I applied for several administrative positions and was denied either an interview or a serious consideration for those positions even though several people believed I was the best candidate. That initial meeting, in hindsight, gave me clear information on how Earvin would interact with those perceived as "troublemakers." My conclusions about Earvin were:

- He dismissed personal and professional concerns if they differed from those in power

- He would make decisions based not on objectivity but on personal bias
- He implemented others' grudges without wanting to know all sides of the matter
- He was close-minded when it came to certain faculty and faculty matters.

I continued to be the "face" of unrest, not because of anything I did during Earvin's administration but because of how I was viewed by McMillan's board and the chaos and discord Earvin inherited. It was early in his administration that most faculty perceived him as different from McMillan in a critical way: he was benign in how he treated them. They weren't degraded, nor were they held in high esteem. In fact many saw him as unavailable and even absent.

Faculty Perception of Dr. Earvin

Earvin's vision for HT was to "Redeem the Promise," but he depended on his administration and other constituents for the promise to be redeemed, and faculty were often left to strategize on their own. Throughout his presidency, Earvin had very high turnover in key positions, including the Vice President for Academic Affairs (about five of them). For a period of two years that position was vacant, and Earvin acted in that position as well. The critical position of Institutional Development Officer was often vacant, probably resulting in HT having fewer fundraising projects and funded grants.

Despite these limitations, faculty busied themselves with ongoing curriculum revisions. Professors used Title III funds to support Core Curriculum revisions, i.e., to develop core values and curriculum to support those core values.[47] Additionally, criteria and a process were developed for writing-intensive courses, diversity courses, and African/African American content courses, approved by faculty and submitted to EPC for approval. All students had to take at least fifteen hours of intensive-writing content courses other than the required English courses, a general diversity course, and an African/African American course. Having content courses deemed writing-intensive required a rigorous Core Curriculum Committee process; the same was true for diversity courses. Best practice guided both process and decisions.

Professors fulfilled their role to teach while Earvin fulfilled one of his primary roles, to raise funds, a real contrast to McMillan. Students, faculty, and staff recognized that Earvin delegated presidential responsibilities to his senior staff during his frequent absences from HT. He relied heavily on Terry Smith, Executive Vice President, and through Smith, Earvin fulfilled many of his presidential roles. Earvin surrounded himself with highly paid administrative staff but rarely sought input from others. However, faculty wanted more: They wanted a president who made them feel valuable both as a person and in the work they did. In fact, one professor commented that Earvin insisted that we "stay in our lane," which from that professor's perspective had squelched innovative activities. Here are some other faculty comments from surveys and interviews:[48]

- Initial impression was that he would be the change HT needed; later that he was an "absentee parent" traveling a lot and leaving HT to some unqualified persons.
- He was good at networking.
- Very nice man but very stressed; seemed to always be going someplace else, even when sitting in a meeting.
- Rather than invite multiple and variant [sic] perspectives, Dr. Earvin preferred his team to be like-minded. I regret that Dr. Earvin didn't walk the campus to chat with students and faculty. He seemed distant and shut off in his office.
- Remote - leadership through providing a vision.
- It was remarkable to me that I rarely saw him on campus interacting with students.
- He was gone so much that some students indicated even after 4 years, they did not know who the president was.
- He was a very kind, fair, and reasonable leader but often absent from day-to-day service.
- Disinterested.
- Only saw Dr. Earvin on campus about 2–3 times.
- Throughout his years, I observed him to be more corporate-minded than educational-minded. He operated with his own self-image and professional goals in mind.
- My first impressions were that with fresh ideas and a clean slate he can move HT forward. He came with HT on shaky ground, and he was knowledgeable about the SACS process. He did get us off of probation. However, my later impression was that he was gone from the campus too much.
- I don't believe he did anything to create a family environment. He was not accessible to students as much as he should have been, and he was not very supportive and encouraging to faculty and staff.
- Until the day I left HT, the most common complaint from students was

that he was never on campus and that they don't know him. The students did not find him to be a credible person.
- As a weakness, I would say he was an absentee president.

Dr. Terry Smith, Earvin's Executive Vice President, responded to my question: "If someone would ask you to take him/her to HT's leader, who would it be?"[49] Reluctantly Smith said it would be him. He actually ran the college when Earvin was absent, but emphatically emphasized that "Dr. Earvin knew everything that went on the campus in his absence." Smith added, "Our regular conversations were about things he heard, providing counsel on how to handle those matters." He was physically absent a lot, but very informed. As evidence of his (Smith's) leadership power at HT, Smith said that he signed all requisitions and often Earvin's correspondence, even Christmas cards to Earvin's constituents.

Supporting the impressions from his constituents, Dr. Earvin recognized that he spent a great percentage of his time traveling. Perhaps addressing what he sensed or even heard from students, faculty, and staff, Earvin noted in his 2005 President's Update newsletter:

> Throughout the course of an academic year, a college or university president will find travel consumes a large share of time commitments. Chief executives find that they are away from the campus anywhere from 40 percent to 75 percent of the time. The experience at Huston-Tillotson College is no different than at any other private institutions.
>
> Given fundraising initiatives, service to alumni groups and participation with constituent groups, the United Negro College Fund (UNCF), the United Methodist Church, the United Church of Christ, and others, the travel schedule is aggressive. However, the benefits to the College that result from such travel are critical to the advancement of students and faculty.
>
> As the programs at the College are strengthened, enrollment grows and more doors will be open for students to pursue graduate/professional school and meaningful careers. In my absence, the senior staff is available to address any issue needing immediate attention.[50]

Earvin's explanation was certainly plausible but was not often communicated to students, faculty, and staff. While they knew that Earvin was often away fundraising, they still expected more positive and frequent interaction with him and had questions about his frequent travels. Some questions were: 1) Was it more important to nurture external sources of potential funding than to nurture internal relationships? 2) Could both be done simultaneously? 3) Did his frequent trips also include establishing a pathway for his life after presidency? 4) How did his serving on so many national boards that took him away from HT actually help HT? 5) How could he engage his greatest assets—HT students, alumni, faculty, and staff—in fundraising efforts and goal attainments?

Faculty Voice: An Ongoing Struggle

Due to the turmoil that still affected many faculty members and the lack of faculty voice in critical decisions, fifteen faculty members revived the Faculty Senate on September 27, 2001. The Huston-Tillotson College Faculty Senate was established in order to support the mission of the college by:

> 1) Providing a forum for free expression and discussion of a broad range of matters of importance to the faculty in the College community, 2) Creating a direct line of communication to the president for the expression of the faculty's concern, 3) Establishing a vehicle for the exchange of ideas among the faculty, 4) Providing a focus for efforts to bring about change in those procedures and activities which undermine academic excellence, 5) Strengthening the resources of the institution, and 6) Working together to make Huston-Tillotson College the best small liberal arts college in the country.

It was believed that a collective voice would be better than individual requests. Nothing in the Faculty Senate constitution was intended to be against administration; rather it was about shared governance. At the initial Faculty Senate meeting, I was voted as interim president and later voted as president. Faculty also voted for me as their faculty representative to the President's Cabinet, a position that did not even exist. The senate engaged Dr. Vaughn, the VPAA, to inform President Earvin of our request for a board seat. Minutes from that initial senate meeting also included initial concerns:

1. The hierarchical nature of the new structure, with additional administrators at the top, leaving faculty input minimal, even those decisions that directly affect them.
2. There is a salary disparity between administrators and faculty, with faculty salaries being relatively low even when compared to similar size colleges. Faculty haven't received regular raises.

3. The role of faculty in strategic planning has been questioned. Who is editing the strategic documents? How can faculty become more involved?
4. Faculty representation in other HT governing boards such as the Cabinet and the Board of Trustees is absent.
5. A question was raised about the need to evaluate administrators and trustees, as faculty are evaluated annually.
6. Earvin's Board was to vote in November 2001 on tenure reinstatement. Would tenure be reinstated?[51]
7. Faculty recommendation was that they should have only three preparations, meaning teaching as least two of the same class.

These concerns were presented to Earvin and Vaughn. A three-member Faculty Senate ad hoc committee reviewed HT's tenure policies and those from three other higher education institutions. Since HT tenure policies was abolished by McMillan with board approval, no additional tenure was granted (accept once when McMillan caved to faculty protest on behalf of one of their colleagues). HT faculty totally disagreed with McMillan's tenure policy and wanted Earvin to change it. The Faculty Senate asked for a meeting with the president and was granted one on December 6, 2001. Not much came out of that meeting.

The faculty continued to meet and ask for greater voice in the creation of the academic calendar and revision of the faculty handbook to avoid arbitrary changes and inconsistencies, as well as to foster transparency. The Faculty Senate corresponded with the president on several occasions about these issues. A letter was sent to him along with an eight-page document containing faculty concerns and recommendations related to those concerns.[52]

> May 10, 2003
> Dear Dr. Earvin,
> The Faculty Senate has met and discussed some issues and concerns that we would like to share with you as this academic year comes to an end. Foremost, the faculty members of Huston-Tillotson College would like to express our gratitude for your leadership during the SACS reaccreditation process. The challenges the institution faced when you arrived at HT were daunting. We acknowledge that your guidance was instrumental in ensuring that we weathered a very difficult storm.
>
> In addition, we also acknowledge that during the past three years, there have been several positive changes for the College. In particular, we credit you for

improving HT's image in the community. Much of the College's improved image can be attributed to your networking both locally and nationally, the beautification of the campus grounds, and increased positive media exposure.

Although we have come a long way, there are still challenges we face. Attached is a document that details faculty members' concerns. Attention to these concerns is vital for the continual growth of the College. We respectfully request a written response to this document. We would also like to request a regular meeting between the Faculty Senate President and yourself so these challenges can be addressed collaboratively.

It is important that you know that the attached document is a result of faculty concerns expressed over the last academic year. Four persons wrote the concerns, and five persons edited the document. Several versions of the document were sent to the faculty over the last month for their input. Each faculty member had the opportunity to vote on the content of the document. Seventeen full-time faculty members responded. Ten of them agreed with all of the concerns; five persons agree with some of them; one person agree with a few of them; and one person did not agree with any of them. One part-time professor agreed with most of the concerns. Dr. [Horacio] Peña asked me to attach his personal letter to this document.[53]

Thank you for accepting this document in the spirit in which it is being sent to you. We look forward to working with you to ensure the continued improvement of Huston-Tillotson College.

Sincerely,
Rosalee Martin,
Faculty Senate President

Attached to the letter was the eight-page document that contained both faculty concerns and recommendations. Faculty tried to be respectful and to acknowledge success in all correspondence to the president. The introduction to that eight-page document was thoughtful and collaborative:

> The faculty of Huston-Tillotson College, in an effort to promote the stability of the institution and to provide an arena of creative teaching, is seeking informal dialogue with the administration in matters that pertains to the life work of the faculty.
>
> Any institution operates by the cooperation of its various components—faculty, administration, students, and staff. Each component is a separate entity

within the institution, yet each component will not exist and be successful without the work of the other components. Having this concept of how our college works, <u>the faculty would like to share some concerns that have hampered our cohesiveness and our sense of common mission</u>. In order to assume a unified front as we enter a very exciting and potential full semester, the concerns set forth here need to be addressed by the administration in collaboration with faculty.

The motto of our institution is "In Union, Strength," and it is in that spirit that the faculty presents its concerns. Furthermore, we are trying to model good communication skills and encourage an honest, open dialogue. We would like to have a written response to our concerns which include:

1. <u>Pay Inequities</u>: Concern about the historical low salaries while administrators are hired with substantially higher salaries.
2. <u>Arbitrary Decisions</u>: In an attempt to move HT forward, some decisions had to be made in a short period of time. Those that impact faculty should be made with input from faculty. An example of an arbitrary decision was not to promote any faculty during the 2002–2003 academic year.
3. <u>Hiring New Faculty</u>: Although the need for new faculty is known long in advance, too often faculty are hired within the week of school and even in some cases after the semester begins.
4. <u>Faculty Retention</u>: It is critical that highly qualified and well-prepared faculty with good/excellent teaching skills are hired and retained.
5. <u>Consistency of the Academic Programs</u>: It is important that majors have at least two full-time professors so that all of their major courses are not taught by one professor. Some majors have two full-time professors with fewer students while other majors with a higher percentage of students only have one full-time professor.
6. <u>Textbooks</u>: There are times when textbooks are either not ordered, ordered late, or experience reduction of order, resulting in students not being ready to start the course with an essential tool—the textbook.
7. <u>Physical Plant</u>: Although during the past year there has been considerable improvement in the College's physical plant, a major problem is the inability to control the temperature in some of the buildings. Some professors had to change classes when the room became unbearable—either too hot or too cold.
8. <u>Evening Classes</u>: During the last three years evening class has been kept to a minimum. This resulted in some students having to take

courses at other colleges.

9. <u>Institutional Mission and Direction of the College</u>: Currently the College stands at a crossroads with unique opportunities in front of it. With input from faculty, reflective questions must be raised as many of the questions are academic in nature.
10. <u>Academic Standards</u>: Although the College currently doesn't have an open-door mission policy in the books, it does, in fact, operate as if such a policy exists. Faculty may find themselves in the position of assisting students in developing basic skills as well as teaching them how to be students. Few faculties have the appropriate training in their graduate programs to meet such a need. A consequence of this may be student and faculty retention issues.
11. <u>Communications</u>: Although promises have been made to be more inclusive in decision-making, faculty members often remain outside of the discussion and decision-making process. Information continues to flow from the top down and is perceived by some as being highly restricted and censored.
12. <u>Work Overload</u>: Effective learning is greatly affected by teacher preparation. Adequate preparation time is greatly reduced when the professor must teach twelve hours with four different preparations; add committee and administrative requirements, and our students might suffer.
13. <u>Evaluations</u>: Evaluating teacher effectiveness is an essential element of assessment that assists in improved teaching and may be necessary when considering promotion and tenure. Faculty evaluations are rarely used as a basis for merit raises and promotion. Administrators should also be available to faculty and staff in order to improve open dialogue and constructive feedback.
14. <u>Student Retention</u>: It is important that the administration, admissions, and faculty work in unison to find highly motivated and prepared students to attend Huston-Tillotson College. There are two critical elements which go into making a first-rate institution of higher learning: excellent students and excellent faculty.[54]

A month after the letter and concerns were sent to Earvin, he responded with the following email:[55]

CHAPTER 3

June 10, 2003
To HTC Faculty and Executive Cabinet
Subject: Letter from the Faculty

Several weeks ago, I received a letter from a group of faculty members outlining concerns. While I share many of the concerns delineated, I have not issued a formal response for two principal reasons. First, I do not want to start an endless exchange of points and counterpoints.[56] I would much rather address these issues at a forum that would allow for questions and answers. Second, I believe they are streams of information both about college and higher education in general. They should inform our discussions. I write to you now so that you will not interpret silence as a lack of concern. Instead, I have not responded because the context of any substantive reply is shaped daily by local, state, and national legislative actions and by shifting priorities of private philanthropy. These are not easy times.

Therefore, I have chosen an approach that I feel would be productive and will engage each of us in thoughtful dialogue about the issues raised. Over the course of the summer, I will share various materials with you for your review. In return, I hope you will share articles and relevant research with me as well.[57] We will set aside time to discuss these issues during Open [Faculty] Institute for the fall semester. I will invite trustees to share in this activity as they are available. It is important to have open and frank communication about issues of concern to the College.[58]

Sincerely,
Larry L. Earvin, PhD
President

Many faculty members were alarmed by Earvin's response. Faculty concerns were real; to refer them to articles appeared to be a "cop out" and disingenuous. That letter didn't contain his real position, that he didn't want a Faculty Senate on the HT campus. However, that fact came out in an email he sent to two people, with a copy to me, *not to the faculty*.[59]

From: Earvin, Larry L.
Sent: Tuesday, August 26, 2003, 3:26 PM
To: Elbert, Marian M.; Loredo, Judith G.
CC: Martin, Rosalee R.
Subject: Faculty Senate Meeting
Dr. Martin has asked that I appear before the Faculty Senate to hear its concerns

on September 11. My existing schedule for September is so frantic that I cannot accommodate this request. For reasons that are delineated below, it would not be advisable for me to meet with a Senate at this time. I would be pleased, however, to identify an alternative time to meet with faculty later in the month.

The request to meet with the Senate poses a few concerns. As has been communicated before, the College has not recognized a Faculty Senate. While I personally endorse the concept, the structure has not been approved by the College Board of Trustees.[60] It is my expectation that the Board will address this matter when it acts on the governance doctrine in November. Given the lack of standing of a Senate, it is appropriate that I hear and converse with faculty in a meeting of the faculty. Faculty in such a setting are not precluded from broaching any issue that they may wish to raise. We should identify time for such a meeting, if needed.

A second concern centers on protocol. Faculty concerns are to be directed to the academic affairs officers in the first instance. The Dean and VP should be able to address the issues that faculty may have.[61] If using this route does not yield a satisfactory response, then an "issues meeting" [with the President] is in order.[62] Otherwise, a meeting with the President once or twice a year should suffice purposes. We already hold Institute meetings twice a year when questions are raised and answered: we just finished one such meeting.

Finally, if faculty have issues that they feel only the President can address, a determination must be made that this is the case. Therefore, the issue should be directed to the appropriate academic officer first. There would be increasingly difficult demands placed on the Office of the President in the current economic climate that restrict the amount of time that may be allocated to internal matters for which there are executive staff to manage. I hope the gravity of the present environment, as articulated in this year's faculty and staff Institute, is comprehended.

Larry L. Earvin, PhD
President
Huston-Tillotson College

Revealed in this letter were six critical things:

1. Earvin did not support a Faculty Senate. This was a surprise since he was a faculty member and a dean at Clark Atlanta University, an HBCU in Georgia.
2. He did not want to meet with a formal governance committee; rather, he preferred to talk to the faculty at an institute. Most professors at the faculty

institute do not open up to the president for fear of losing their job. It is not unusual for non-tenured faculty to ask tenured faculty to speak on their behalf.
3. He didn't have an open-door policy for faculty; rather, he adhered strictly to a bureaucratic structure—ruling from the top down.
4. He believed that a meeting with him once or twice a year was sufficient.
5. He had no intention of really addressing faculty concerns.
6. It appeared that his statement in his June 10, 2003, letter, "It is important to have open and frank communication about issues of concerns to the College," was not genuine.

Despite these earlier roadblocks, faculty continued to pursue shared governance. In 2003, after much consideration, some faculty established an AAUP chapter on campus. At least a minimum of seven paid members was required to establish a campus chapter. It was difficult to get a larger faculty membership because many were afraid of administrative backlash in an at-will state.[63] Some tenured faculty leaders listened intently to colleagues' concerns about not being heard at HT. Some professors even felt that in order to teach at HT they had to give up their First Amendment right of freedom of speech.

Recognizing that faculty's voice was not being silenced, Earvin agreed to accept a faculty group if it changed its name to Faculty Advisory Committee. This way faculty would know their place; being an advisory committee lowered their expectation of being equal partners in shared governance. Faculty members were reluctant to make that name change as it diluted the "power" that faculty would have in an organized senate—but they acquiesced. With the help of the Vice President of Academic Affairs and the President of the Faculty Senate, the following description for the Faculty Advisory Committee (FAC) was established:

> The Faculty Advisory Committee is a standing committee which serves as a representative of the faculty, and it is as an advisory board to the VP of Academic Affairs and Student Affairs/Provost and to the President. Faculty advisory committee shall be comprised of two representatives from each department and shall be elected by the faculty for two academic years. Initially, half of the elected members will be elected for a two-year period: the other half of the members shall be rotated out after one year. As the faculty voice, the Faculty Advisory Committee will be called upon to participate in major university decisions such as faculty hiring procedures, decisions which affect academic curriculum, faculty

development, and policies related to institutional and educational partnerships with the community.[64]

The faculty voted to accept the name change and had its first meeting on Thursday, October 25, 2007. I was voted as chairperson. On October 29, 2007, I sent an email to Dr. Earvin, copied to the faculty. The second and third paragraphs read as follows:

> In an effort to support our University mission of teaching/student excellence, the Faculty Advisory Committee (FAC) has raised concerns about two areas vital to faculty work – student tutoring and faculty development.[65] Current funding appears to have been cut substantially for both before new funding had been clearly identified. This situation has resulted in a serious lack of necessary support for student learning this semester (resulting in an increased percentage of student failure at midterm) and widening the gap in support for essential faculty development.
>
> We have noted significant shortage of necessary tutoring for all students this semester. It is our understanding that Title III, which has been funding the tutoring labs staffed by student peer tutors, is no longer funding learning support services. We understand that needed, but limited, tutoring in some areas has been made available through the grant from the Coordinating Board managed by Dr. Loredo. Those available funds for tutoring are inadequate, and tutoring has been redirected primarily, if not exclusively, to students having the greatest risk for failure. We also understand that some tutoring has been provided by volunteers and some by small pockets of funding in individual areas. We understand that the Writers' Studio has been short-staffed, in large part due to confusion over what budget was providing funds for peer writing tutors, and thus has not been able to offer tutoring hours to meet student demand. We believe that all students should have access to trained tutors in both the Writers' Studios and in the Center for Academic Excellence. Tutoring should be an institutional commitment.
>
> The FAC wants a voting member on the President's Advisory Committee (in addition to the academic deans). The committee would like a written response from you.

Earvin's response came on October 30, 2007, acknowledging the receipt of the email. He asked that a meeting with the faculty be arranged by his administrative assistant, Business Dean Steven Edmond, and College of Arts and Sciences (CAS)

Dean Joseph Jones. He sent a follow-up letter on November 9 to HT faculty, Ora Wilson (Director of Title III), Stephanie Bond-Huie (VP for Institutional Development), and the HT Executive Committee.

> Dear Colleagues:
>
> On October 29, I received an inquiry from Dr. Martin in her capacity as Chair of the Faculty Advisory Committee. She posed questions about Title III funding for faculty development and peer tutors and asked for a written response. My reply to her stated that I would prefer to meet with the faculty rather than send a written response. However, we have not been able to schedule a meeting in a timely fashion. Therefore, I am taking this opportunity to respond on an interim basis. I would still like to meet with the faculty to discuss any remaining concerns.
>
> First, you should know that Title III is a capacity building grant. As such, there is expectation that Title III funds will be used to launch initiatives, and that the institution's faculty and staff will seek other resources to sustain such initiatives after a reasonable period of time.[66] We have just begun a new five-year Title III grant which reflects this expectation. As you probably also know several activities at Huston-Tillotson University had sustained Title III support.[67] Therefore, some activities were continued but were either scaled back or altered to remain in compliance with Title III guidelines; others no longer receive support from Title III.
>
> Second, support for faculty development has not been ended. However, faculty development has a different focus than in the past. For the next several years these funds are being targeted towards faculty development to help satisfy requirements for reaffirmation of the University's accreditation (emphasis on student learning objectives: the QEP, etc.) which includes workshop activities for the faculty. Further, as some of you have indicated, our previous management of faculty development funds gave resources to a few individuals but had little impact on the broader faculty. The present focus will increase the benefits to large numbers of faculty members. Title III support for faculty travel must be tied to specific Title III activities.
>
> Third, given the need to modify long-standing programs, the number of peer-counselors supported by Title III was reduced. Every effort is being made to assist programs that use student peer-counselors through this period of transition. One option is to use work-study resources and funding from other grants to fill gaps this academic year.
>
> Finally, one shortcoming of email responses is that they sometimes generate

more questions. This may be the case here. However, I ask that you save such questions until we can meet. I just did not want more time to elapse before you got a reply.

Sincerely,
Larry L. Earvin, PhD
Pres. and CEO

These correspondences over the years provide evidence that Earvin's views on faculty governance did not change. Preferring to speak to the entire faculty at a Faculty Institute undermines the strength and influence of a faculty group that focused on faculty issues, in writing and verbally. A concern addressed by the Faculty Advisory Committee was faculty development. Earvin partially addressed this when he first came to Huston-Tillotson College by introducing the faculty to Faculty Resource Network (FRN), housed at New York University.

Earvin's Contribution
Faculty Development: FRN and Title III
No education can occur without faculty; the better prepared they are, the more successful students can be. Earvin supported faculty development to some professional conferences, including travel to FRN conferences and seminars at New York University. He was the liaison for FRN while he was a dean at Clark Atlanta and saw the value of FRN for Huston-Tillotson College. He provided faculty members with financial opportunities to network workshops and seminars giving evidence of the importance of FRN and what it provided for faculty. Below are FRN programs that benefited HT faculty.[68]

- *Network Summer* provided a variety of summer seminar topics that were presented through lectures, field trips, presentations, research, hands-on demonstrations, and interactive discussions. Participants are exposed to the most recent scholarship in their fields while being given the opportunity to develop teaching and curriculum strategies for direct classroom application.
- *Network Winter*: Similar to Network Summer, the winter network is held in various member institutions, including Greece and Puerto Rico. It had been held at Huston-Tillotson, requiring extensive planning and implementation by faculty and staff.
- *Summer and Semester Scholar-in-Residence* are scholar-in-residence

programs that allow Network faculty to complete either a summer or semester at NYU to engage in research, develop curricula, and/or produce manuscripts for publication during the residence semester. Throughout their residency at the university, Scholars confer periodically with NYU faculty who serve as Research Consultants and assist them with the process.
- *University Associate* (UA) is a program that enables full-time faculty members of Network institutions to come to New York University throughout the academic year to use some of NYU's academic facilities. Faculty can audit courses, conduct research in the university libraries, and participate in open departmental or interdisciplinary colloquia, lectures, symposia, and seminars. As a UA, report of use was required to be sent to the institutional liaison.
- *Symposia and Institutes* are a series of symposia and institutes designed to bring faculty and administrators together to examine the broader issues that are timely and important in academia. Based on the Network's mission to foster connection, collaboration, and collegiality, the institutes and symposia provide rare opportunities for communication across institutions, disciplines, and professions.

Having access to FRN's programs was invaluable to HT faculty in areas of professional research, networking, and overall faculty growth. Title III, federal funding, was also used for faculty development in the United States but couldn't be used internationally. Faculty apply for such funds through a specified process, and their requests may be awarded depending on the amount solicited and whether funds had been given to the faculty member during the current academic year.

Eventually, each faculty member could apply for up to $1,500 for approved faculty development opportunities, with funding coming primarily from Title III. That funding opportunity continued throughout Pierce Burnette's presidency.

Huston-Tillotson: New Name and New Structure (2005)
Part of Earvin's forward vision was to change the name Huston-Tillotson College to Huston-Tillotson University. It was no surprise then that in February 2005 the name change became a "fait accompli." With the pro bono services of GSD&M advertising company, a new RAM mascot and a new typestyle for the new university with the new tagline "Learn More" became HT's new media image. The name change was first announced at the March 2005 MASKED Ball. In September 2005, a major public announcement was placed in *Ebony* magazine's special college

and university issue. This magazine is the widest-read publication that highlights African Americans and has a reach of more than 12 million readers monthly.[69]

Under the new name of Huston-Tillotson University, Earvin restructured the institution into two main academic areas—College of Arts and Sciences and School of Business and Technology, with three deans in the academic arena, as required by the "status of university."[70] Even with these structural changes, faculty benefits did not change: i.e., no raise increase, no reduction in course load, and no additional funds for faculty research and development. Some recognized the future benefits of HT's being a university, but for the ten remaining years of Earvin's presidency, faculty benefits were not increased as a result of the name change.

COLLEGE OF ARTS AND SCIENCES (CAS)

Dr. Joseph Jones initially came to HT as an adjunct chemistry professor from the Graduate School at Texas Southern University. He was later appointed dean, above the then chairperson of the Division of Natural Sciences. The key word to faculty was that he was *appointed* without faculty input; this fact resulted in Joseph Jones starting his deanship under a cloud. The new CAS consisted of Departments of Humanities and Fine Arts (languages, music, history, and communication), Natural Sciences (biology and chemistry), Mathematics, Social and Behavioral Sciences (criminal justice, political science, psychology, and sociology), Teacher Education, and Kinesiology. Dean Jones's vision for CAS was consistent with the institutional vision. CAS's three goals are: interactive curriculum enhancement, faculty development, and the development of students' research potential. Faculty members were urged to look at the total curriculum and think in terms of where the demands are in American society. Jones wanted current curriculum to be synergized and linked to societal demands.

Related to faculty development, rather than always incurring the expense of traveling to other locations for professional meetings and conferences, Jones wanted to offer campus-based activities. Toward this end, he attempted to bring to campus outstanding speakers to explore new cutting-edge curriculum that could work at HT. Note that this follows the tradition of looking outside for experts rather than among HT's faculty. Dean Jones was also interested in stimulating students' ability to think critically and to communicate effectively. During 2005, the college implemented University Research Day, an opportunity for students from all departments to present their research to a university-wide audience. The result of the annual day was that students who participated gained confidence with increased communication and research skills. Research Day continues to this day with a new name, Dr. Jones Research Day, honoring retired Dean Jones, who gives financial support annually for student research.

Additionally, CAS faculty engaged in various research projects, and some faculty members published books and articles in peer-reviewed journals. Some students were co-researchers and co-writers with professors. Student research presented on Research Day was included in an HT Research Journal. Furthermore, the English Department annually publishes a magazine for creative works called *900 Chicon* (HT's mailing address).[71] Additionally, students participated in experiential learning in community internships and with research institutions. They were/are mentors at neighborhood schools and work in various capacities in community agencies. CAS activities are truly impressive; faculty routinely strengthen their disciplines by incorporating best practice content and reinforcement activities in their classes.

After Dean Jones retired, the position of dean of CAS was filled by five people in three years. Part of the reason might have been Earvin's decision not to promote from within, even though there were qualified professionals who had applied, including me. Two persons were fired and two were named interim (one being the acting provost who held both roles simultaneously). In February and effective March 1, 2014, Dr. Earvin asked me to become interim dean for six months, with the intention to complete a search. This interim position lasted fifteen months, until Earvin retired in July 2015. I continued in that position (as acting dean) for two additional years until 2017, under President Pierce Burnette. Earvin asked me to fill the vacant position because the provost couldn't handle being both CAS dean and provost. Earvin knew I could do the job—though I was still not his preference, as evident by conversations and email exchanges. I was chosen as a last resort, and besides, he was leaving. Needless to say, I was surprised by the request in light of prior refusal to consider me for that very same position.

School of Business and Technology (SBT)

Dr. Steven Edmond was brought to HT by Earvin to strengthen and later restructure the Business Department. He was instrumental in developing the structure of the School of Business and Technology, and then served as its first dean—appointed (again, no faculty input). This school consists of Business Administration, Computer Science, and an Engineering 3/2 program with Prairie View A&M and UT Austin.[72] Edmond placed considerable emphasis on "excellent teaching and attention to the academic, personal and professional development of our students." The School of Business and Technology is an innovative, enterprising, and forward-looking school committed to preparing students of diverse origins and backgrounds to follow their career paths in this global business environment. In 2013, the Department of Business Administration was accredited by the Accreditation Council for Business Schools and Programs (ACBSP). This was an impressive accreditation that recognized the quality of the programs offered. The school's unique relationship with the business community provided students the opportunity to meet potential future employers.[73]

Dean of Academic Support

In 2005 a new position was created, the Dean of Academic Support, given to Dr. Judith Loredo who was a twenty-year veteran at Huston-Tillotson with a strong history of developing educational programs and bringing to HT funds for education.[74] The purpose of the Academic Support Office was to provide oversight and coordination of campus-wide, cross-disciplinary initiatives. This meant providing support services to both SBT and CAS, through several different programs and services. These included academic support for the core curriculum, the DuBois Honors program, writing across the discipline strategies, academic advising, supplemental instruction, library and media services, instructional technology and distance learning, sponsored projects, and continuing education. Loredo was particularly pleased with the university's renewed commitment to continuing education, which had not been offered in approximately fifteen years. During the first year of operation, the Academic Support Office had several important accomplishments. All course offerings were renumbered to be consistent with the Texas Common Cause numbering system, for easier student transfers. The Academic Support Office also developed new faculty trainings and student advising material and advanced a student portfolio initiative.[75]

New Academic Programs
In addition to regular review of academic programs, including the general education curriculum, other academic changes were made during Earvin's administration. Several new initiatives are important to note.

Distinguished DuBois Honors Program, 2003

One of Earvin's visions for HT was to institute an honors program that would draw very successful students to the campus. Dr. Janice Sumler-Edmond, the first director of the program, described the DuBois Honors program.[76]

Together President Earvin and Dr. Sumler-Edmond envisioned an honors program dedicated to honors students in an organic learning community. Recruitment targeted high school seniors with well above average GPAs and high standardized tests scores with leadership potential through campus and community service. Five key goals were identified for the DuBois Honors Program:

1. to motivate academically talented students.
2. to foster intellectual independence and the pursuit of academic excellence.
3. to intensify the learning experience at Huston-Tillotson University.
4. to prepare students for graduate schools and professional careers.
5. to promote lifelong learning.

Moreover, a rigorous honors curriculum, fellowship among honors students, and character development undergirded the program goals. The program's written application and telephone interview sought to identify articulate young men and women who had given some thought to a career objective and had participated in a community service project.

The DuBois Scholars were expected to obtain an in-depth understanding about the life and legacy of the program's namesake Dr. W. E. B. DuBois. DuBois (1868–1963) was an African American intellectual, sociologist, civil rights activist, and co-founder of the NAACP. Following Dr. DuBois's tradition of civic and community engagement and leadership, the Scholars engage in many civic activities and tutor the newer scholars. As a group, they have the highest GPA of all campus organizations.

The DuBois Lecture and the Hackathon competition are two highly anticipated Honors Program events. The DuBois Lecture was launched during the spring semester of 2004 when John Bracey, a renowned scholar on the life and work of Dr. DuBois, gave a lecture to the HT community. Bracey also shared advice about careers with the Scholars during a luncheon event. Since that first guest in 2004, other distinguished guests have shared their talents with the DuBois Scholars and members of the HT community. Prominent history scholars, a nationally known photographer, and a popular romance novelist have presented at the DuBois Lecture.

Similarly, the annual Hackathon competition has become another favorite event on the Honors Program calendar. During the 2014 spring semester, Prof. Autumn Caviness, who was then the Assistant Director of the Honors Program, introduced the HT Hackathon Competition where HT students and local high school students formed teams tasked with creating a computer application.[77]

Teams collaborate over the course of the weekend followed by presentations of their creations to a panel of judges.

The Honors Program has experienced a great deal of success over the years and is poised to continue on that same positive track. Success came early to the Honors Program when three members of the 2007 inaugural graduating class of DuBois Scholars entered careers in the medical field. A pediatric dentist, a pharmacist, and an optometrist emerged from that initial group of Scholars. A partial career list for the DuBois Scholars alumni includes software engineers, civil engineers, social workers, public school teachers, attorneys, and others who have earned their MBA degrees and are employed in corporate America.

At the same time the honors program was established, a Student Ambassador program was created. These students were charged to be active in major HT functions by being ushers at Honors Day, Charter Day, Graduation, and other campus and off-campus HT events. The Ambassadors could be identified by their maroon jackets with HT emblem. Many of the students were honors students, but other students, exhibiting integrity and school spirit, were also included.

Adult Degree Program (ADP)[78]

The Adult Degree Program extends the university's educational offerings to full-time, working adults in need of college opportunities. The ADP degree program reflected the urgent demands of the changing times by providing the practical, relevant knowledge needed for success in today's global economy. While highly focused and accelerated, all ADP curricula retain the same high standards that have distinguished HT graduates. Student placement strategies are designed to meet the learning needs of individual students while nurturing group management skills through the program's emphasis on learning teams. Student cohorts are used to facilitate learning. Students take one course at a time for five weeks, giving them a different structure from semester courses. Full-time and adjunct faculty teach students in this evening program. The Adult Degree Program has its own director and financial aid specialist, but students are well integrated into the overall college experience.

Discover Law

In partnership with the University of Texas, Huston-Tillotson provided pre-law students from both universities the unique opportunity to interact with legal professionals in the community on either campus. These students also benefited from on-campus summer residential experiences to further their training for careers in law. HT students, upon graduation, can apply for admission to UT Law School. Despite its worthy goals, HT had problems implementing this program as HT administrators didn't always fulfill its contractual obligations to its dedicated staff responsible for HT's part of the program. Another problem was in recruiting the ten students to fulfill the HT slots; UT filled ten and sometimes was given some of HT's slots.

MASTER'S IN EDUCATIONAL LEADERSHIP WITH PRINCIPAL CERTIFICATION
Implemented in 2015, this master's program was the first postgraduate degree ever offered by Huston-Tillotson University. Students can complete the thirty-three credit-hour program in four semesters. The graduate program is designed primarily for working teachers seeking advancement to the administrative level. Applicants must have a bachelor's degree, a teacher certification, at least two years' teaching experience, letters of intent and references, pass a background check, and meet the minimum grade point average requirement.

Students were taught by experienced award-winning principals, superintendents, and administrators. Evening classes were scheduled to fit around working adults' schedules and were kept small to allow for individualized instruction.

The program prepared candidates for meaningful careers in educational leadership framed within a social justice perspective. Candidates developed knowledge, skills, and dispositions necessary to become effective and caring principals in an ever-changing society.

Huston-Tillotson University's educator preparation certification process operated under the auspices of several accrediting bodies. The Texas Education Agency assigned the "accredited" status to HT's Accountability System for Educator Preparation in 2015. The program is accredited by the Southern Association of Colleges and Schools Commission on Colleges and by the Texas State Board for Educator Certification.

HT Sustainability Efforts
HT sustainability efforts began under Earvin in 2008 when the first steps were taken to improve its environmental profile. Recycling throughout the campus was instituted with the placing of bins to collect recyclable material. HT joined the American College & University Presidents' Climate Commitment (ACUPCC), a signature program of Second Nature, now known as the Carbon Commitment.[79] Other sustainability efforts are described below.

CENTER FOR SUSTAINABILITY AND ENVIRONMENTAL JUSTICE, 2011
The Center for Sustainability and Environmental Justice is under the directorship of Dr. Karen Magid, who has worked tirelessly to make HT a sustainable campus, using both internal and external resources. A major accomplishment was securing funds for the installation of 240kW rooftop solar panels on several HT buildings. Based on the Association for the Advancement of Sustainability in Higher Education's database of university solar installations, HT had the largest rooftop solar installation of any private HBCU.[80] The center annually hosts a day-long Building Green Justice Forum with funds from community partners, with presentations from local and national experts, including HT faculty. The Sustainable Center is also the umbrella for other new sustainability initiatives.

ENVIRONMENTAL STUDIES MAJOR, 2012 (NAME LATER CHANGED TO ENVIRONMENTAL JUSTICE MAJOR)
The environmental studies major included sustainability issues such as environmental justice, climate change, conservation biology, renewable energy, air and water pollution, environmental law, and many other related topics. The primary focus of this major was teaching students how to reduce the effects of human activities on our planet through development of more sustainable lifestyles. This is an interdisciplinary major that include courses from other majors. Teaching methodologies include field trips, guest speakers, student projects, and community engagement.

THE DUMPSTER PROJECT, 2013–2014
Dr. Jeff Wilson was the founder of the Dumpster Project and CEO of Kasita (a modular home builder of Austin). In 2013 he applied for the position of dean of the College of Arts and Sciences at the university. Although he did not get that position, a new position was created for him, Dean of Freshman Studies.[81] Soon afterward he created the Dumpster Project with the assistance of Dr. Magid and Dr. Amanda Masino and the student group Green Is the New Black. A dumpster on HT campus was designed to become the home of Wilson, who lived in it for one year. The objective was to highlight the culture of accumulation and waste with an emphasis on downsizing. The Dumpster Project was "many things: a reimagining of home, a portable learning initiative, a sustainability conversation, a creative branch of a wider green campus initiative at HT, and, most importantly, an innovative STEM education platform that used the real-world challenge of transforming a trash dumpster into a tiny sustainable home to inspire learners of

all ages."[82] The project sparked interest in the way that fun and forward-thinking innovation can help address the challenges facing both current and future generations, as our world becomes increasingly complex. Five educators spent one night or a week in the Dumpster through the Home Residency Program. The project also hosted public school field trips to allow youth to experience the Dumpster home.[83] The Dumpster Project ended when Wilson accepted another position in industry furthering his interest in small homes. The Dumpster Project was short-lived on campus, but an emphasis on sustainability continues as a priority.

GREEN IS THE NEW BLACK (2013–2015)

Green Is the New Black (GITNB) was an active Huston-Tillotson University environmental student group. Its vision was to "foster new shades of green" on the HT campus and in the surrounding East Austin community to make environmentalism more just and more inclusive. GITNB projects include organic food gardens, both at HT and in partnership with Blackshear Elementary, campus recycling, and peer education. GITNB won first place in the Ford Corporation's HBCU Community Challenge in 2013 ($75,000 grant) with a plan to make HT the greenest HBCU in the country.[84] The group also received $10,000 from Office Depot to develop sustainable projects on campus. Monies were used to establish a solar charging station, place bicycle racks on campus, and for scholarships. GITNB was named among the 2014 "Best of Austin" by the *Austin Chronicle*.[85] Student delegates attended the United Nations Conference of Parties (COP) 21 Climate Convention in Paris, France, in December 2015, along with delegates from other HBCUs as part of the HBCUs' Student Climate Initiative. Magid and Masino were the advisors to Green Is the New Black and went to Paris with them, along with one other staff member. This group worked closely with Wilson in his Dumpster Project, which got much newspaper and TV coverage. The hope was that similar GITNB organizations would spring up at other HBCUs. This organization remained "in name only" during Pierce Burnette's presidency as the key leaders graduated.

The Tom Joyner Foundation Recognition (2014)

Tom Joyner is a TV and radio personality. He used his media network to give concrete support to HBCUs by providing scholarships and institutional financial support to HBCU institutions. His foundation selects twelve HBCUs annually and recognizes one HBCU each month; Huston-Tillotson University was recognized in July 2014 as School of the Month. As one of the Tom Joyner Foundation

Schools of the Month, HT was promoted by the *Tom Joyner Morning Show* and received funds raised from listeners, alumni, and other interested parties that month. The show, aired in 115 markets around the country, reaches nearly eight million listeners every week.[86] This was another way to promote visibility for HT as well as to secure funds for student programs.

Study Abroad to China
Although HT does not have a study abroad office, students, along with those in other HBCUs, travel to China to take two courses in country—Mandarin and Chinese culture. Federal funds specially earmarked for the China trip, along with students' regular tuition, were used for the experience. The program, under the leadership of Dean Edmond, continued through two HT presidencies. Additionally, with Fulbright funds, Edmond invited exchange faculty from China to come to HT to teach Mandarin and other courses in Chinese culture.

Institutional Goals
Higher Enrollment
Each year Earvin strived to increase student enrollment. His success can be seen in the table below showing those metrics in his final five years at Huston-Tillotson. Part of this progress may be due to his reorganization of the Admission and Recruitment Unit by providing additional resources and personnel in the area. Despite the additional staff and resources, this area also experienced considerable turnover, which hindered achievement of its outcomes. Throughout Earvin's presidency, he worked with alumni associations and with personnel in the Alumni Office to reach out to alumni. Many of the alumni who graduated under McMillan did not participate in HT Alumni Association; a goal was to increase their involvement. Alumni are important because they promote the institution, provide financial support, and bring students to the campus during Preview Day. Everyone on campus was encouraged to participate in recruiting and retention activities, and some faculty went on visits with recruiters. Many efforts were successful, but HT still did not reach its goal of 1,200 students. The 2014–2015 academic year had both the highest and the lowest enrollment due to serious problems with financial aid. The drop in enrollment from fall to spring semester is a normal pattern; the number of student drops reflects various policies, personal finances, and/or retention strategies.

CHAPTER 3

Table 1

| Student Enrollment (Regular and ADT), 2010–2015 ||||
| Board Report, November 2016 ||||
Academic Year	Fall (year)	Spring (year)	Difference
2010–11	901 ('10)	867 ('11)	-34
2011–12	904 ('11)	856 ('12)	-48
2012–13	917 ('12)	823 ('13)	-94
2013–14	973 ('13)	889 ('14)	-84
2014–15	1031 ('14)	768 ('15)	-263

Renovation of HT's Library and Dormitories
Under Dr. Earvin's leadership, the library became a more modern and multi-use facility with a mini snack bar, computer spaces, small group spaces, meeting rooms, and greater access to eBooks and digital media. The dormitory included modern communal living spaces and improved rooms. A computer room and a communal kitchen were also installed in the dorms. Both improved the infrastructure in the absence of new buildings.

The Sandra Joy Anderson Community Health and Wellness Center
Huston-Tillotson University, the Dell Medical School at The University of Texas at Austin, and the City of Austin CommUnityCare engaged in a landmark partnership dedicated to helping underserved residents of Austin get, and stay, healthy. The Sandra Joy Anderson Community Health and Wellness Center, opened in 2016, was named for the late daughter of HT alumna Mrs. Ada Cecilia Collins Anderson, then 92, who gave Huston-Tillotson University $3 million—the largest gift in the institution's history.[87] Although the Health Center was officially opened after Earvin retired, the facility was built prior to his leaving, fulfilling one of his goals for HT.

Missed Opportunities

Perhaps the greatest opportunities Earvin missed were giving encouragement and tangible support to the faculty's creative insights for cutting-edge programs. New and innovative majors were needed to fulfill a goal of the strategic plan. Professors Debra Murphy (Psychology) and Lorraine Samuels (Criminal Justice) developed a major in Forensic Psychology. Even with both faculty and Educational Policy

Committee (EPC) support, the president and Board of Trustees did not approve this proposed new major. Those professors continue to pursue approval of the option as both an undergraduate and a master's program. A second major offered for consideration, approved by the faculty and EPC, was Applied Sociology, supported by Dr. Mike Hirsch and me. This service major was not approved by Earvin or the board—a lost opportunity to bring in students interested in social work, which is an applied major. The social work major requires accreditation, but applied sociology would only require a few additional courses and thus be more cost-effective. Reinstating hotel and restaurant management and gerontology would have provided majors suited for demographic and societal needs. Earvin inherited a strong committed faculty; failing to engage them in true partnership kept HT from getting closer to reaching some strategic goals.

Financial Aid Problem: A Real Crisis

Earvin decided to retire from HT in 2014, giving HT's Board of Trustees fifteen months to find a new president. His many accomplishments, including the 2003 reaffirmation, were tarnished by the fact that during his last two years a poison festered in the Financial Aid Office, resulting in a threat that many students would not receive financial aid and thus be unable to return to HT.[88] This problem was all-consuming during his final months. Earvin reported to the board that the Financial Aid Office was undergoing restructuring.[89] The Director of Financial Aid was fired, and that position was replaced by consultants. The two highly paid consultants unearthed a number of financial aid issues. A financial aid assistant was also hired to effectively carry out the functions of the office. Additionally, a financial aid staff for traditional and ADP students was hired. Earvin charged them to address all outstanding financial aid issues before June 30, 2015, his last day at HT. Unfortunately, even with "cleaning up" the office by firing key personnel and hiring outside, not-so-qualified consultants, he left a real financial aid mess for the new president to deal with. This problem was evident in the major drop in student enrollment between fall 2014 and spring 2015, as noted in the previous table.

Earvin's Dilemma Never Resolved: Accomplishments vs. Absenteeism

A review of his presidency will reveal that Earvin fulfilled many of his promises and left HT better than how he found it, except for the financial aid crisis; he can be proud of that. He strengthened HT's financial structure by meeting most donors in other cities, causing his home base to deem him as an "absentee father." But he didn't leave HT unattended; he had people in his administration to implement his directives and to inform him of campus life. His numerous positive changes and contributions were sometimes overlooked because what students, faculty, and staff wanted most was a meaningful relationship with him. He was a bureaucratic leader, not fostering faculty innovation as is evident from survey responses and interviews. His constituents wanted more involvement with him and more inclusion with program development and processes. How he could have been more involved in the life of HT while bringing needed revenue to the campus was an ongoing dilemma that was never resolved. Clearly, his predecessors were more involved in HT's everyday life; however, Earvin's legacy contains many major contributions that added to HT's greatness. Still, more could have been done in the Austin community. Earvin admitted that the school had "not reached out as aggressively as we should to corporate and personal philanthropy in the Austin community, where more than 2,000 of our graduates live, work, pay taxes, and raise children."[90] On HT's front, his last two years were plagued with a financial aid crisis that threatened to tarnish the good that he did. The next president was not aware of the extent of this financial aid crisis when she arrived.

Upon leaving HT, Dr. Earvin returned to Atlanta, Georgia, and, one month after retiring, he joined the Southern Association of Colleges and Schools Commission on Colleges (SACSCOC) as vice president.[91] To my knowledge, he has not been involved in the life of HT since his retirement except for his attendance at Dr. Melva Williams's inauguration as HT's seventh president, but the history of the university cannot be written without him.

His Story: Lessons Learned from Dr. Earvin's Presidency
Selecting a President with Knowledge and Skills

Dr. Earvin was familiar with HT prior to becoming president. He was on a SACS visiting team for HT in the early 1990s, McMillan's first reaffirmation. HT was in reaccreditation trouble, being on "warning" when Earvin assumed the presidency in 2000. In my brief conversation with him, three months into his presidency, Earvin stated he didn't know how HT remained open given its current status. I believe that HT retained its accreditation because the board brought Earvin in as president. His extensive knowledge of how SACs works and building a self-study team mandated to focus on all areas for review resulted in HT's eventually being reaffirmed without recommendations. Reaffirmation is difficult for most HBCUs as well as PWIs, and losing it results in colleges either closing or starting anew; both outcomes are difficult for faculty, staff, students, and alumni.

The knowledge and skills that presidents brings to the institutions they serve can either enhance or weaken those institutions. Even with the best intentions, the Board of Trustees, when confronted with a presidential opening, must move forward, engaging the assistance of a search committee and sometimes a search firm that is given clear directives about what presidential characteristics are needed for the institution to achieve its stated mission. According to the American Council of Trustees and Alumni,

> The early stages of a presidential search require critical assessments of the institution's mission, the appropriate job description for the next leader, how the search committee will be constituted, and how important constituencies will be allowed to participate in the overall selection process. The manner in which these decisions are made sets the stage for the ultimate success or failure of a search.
>
> The selection of a new president is an ideal time for a board to review the institution's progress, problems, and potential. Before any presidential selection can occur, the board itself should be clear where the institution stands and where it wants the institution to go.[92]

Fortunately Earvin fulfilled the immediate need HT had, its reaffirmation, resulting in full accreditation in 2002 and in 2010, ensuring its viability for the next ten years.

Research Influencing Institutional Goals and Missions

During his first year, Earvin used research to inform his strategic plan. The environmental scan process yielded an analysis of opportunities and threats to HT in 2000. He used the findings to inform his goals. Consequently, many of his goals were aligned to the scan and his institutional activities were aligned with the findings. The lesson is that research should inform the strategic plan. A finding was that the demographic of Texas experienced a drop in the percentage of African Americans and an increase in Hispanics and Whites. Thus a goal was to increase diversity, specifically Hispanic and White populations. That research finding informed HT's changed mission statement that emphasized diverse population and omitted its Historically Black College connection. Other HBCUs have changed their mission statement to focus on diversity.[93] According to Sarah Butrymowicz,

> Many of them [HBCUs] are actively courting low-income students of all races. Their goal, they say, is unchanged: to help those who have few other college options.

HBCUs "are there to provide opportunity and avenues for education for people who were disenfranchised," says Michael Sorrell, president of Paul Quinn College, an HBCU in Dallas. "Slavery has been over for a long time, so you can't have such a narrow viewpoint on this."[94]

Will this change in racial populations in PWIs give ammunition to those who say there is no need for HBCUs?

Fulfilling the Fundraising Function vs. Being a More Present President
Dr. Earvin highlighted the tension between raising money and being a relational, residential president. Earvin, like King, was away from campus more often than on campus. They both attended and chaired meetings, solicited funding agencies and philanthropists, and sometimes engaged in non-college work. Unlike King, Earvin's frequent absence from campus was done by sacrificing nurturing HT constituents and local partnerships. King was part of the Austin community and became president as a promotion up the ranks. Earvin did not have this historical connection to Austin and to HT. Clearly a balance between fulfilling presidential functions that take presidents from campus with that of being on campus nurturing critical constituent relationships is necessary. Students really need to see their president, engaging with them in meaningful ways. Faculty and staff also want ongoing engagement with the president, either individually or collectively, and not navigating the chain of command, as was recommended by Earvin. The structure Earvin put in place to support his frequent time away from campus was a top-down leadership style. Both Earvin and McMillan selected this leadership style, but for different reasons. Either way, both lost the support of many constituents.

Chapter 4

Dr. Colette Pierce Burnette

President of Geniuses

A SELF-FULFILLING PROPHECY IS ANY POSITIVE OR NEGATIVE repeated expectation of an individual, internalized by that individual, resulting in behavior that fulfills those expectations. Dr. Pierce Burnette told her students that they are geniuses, expecting them to rise to that label. She first called her students "my Genius Generation" at the convocation for the 2015 freshman class that she graduated in 2019. She repeated that phrase frequently to all students both in person and in speeches on and off Huston-Tillotson University's campus. Not only did she want students to believe that for themselves, but also she wanted HT, Austin, Texas, and our nation to believe and act on that designation. According to Pierce Burnette, accepting students' genius influences the way her daily decisions would improve their life outcomes and how students would operate in their genius. She believed the best tool she had was to ensure that her geniuses have the best education possible. "I believe education is a weapon against poverty, racism, economic limitations, and ignorance. The more advanced you are educationally, the better off you would be."[1] Therefore, Pierce Burnette's creative, innovative genius generation would thrive in an environment where teachers spark their interest and passion using nontraditional teaching strategies that enhance both in-class and external experiential learning.

Flexibility in teaching is what she advocates. "The geniuses of some of our students have not been discovered yet; that's our job—to move them from where they are to the greatness they are to become. We can do this by instilling the meaning of 'IDEAL'—Integrity, Diversity, Excellence, Accountability, and Leadership—into their character. I expect students to do their best, since education is the great equalizer, especially for females. My great passion and satisfaction is to be in a space where I can give young people an education."[2] That space is safe for the students to engage in courageous conversations around difficult societal issues, allowing for diversity of thought and acceptance of differences. "I try to be a role model at HT because engineering was clearly my foundation. It taught me how to be an effective leader and a thinker. But I did not find my passion there. I wanted to do something more; serving individuals was more gratifying. I tell young people, you must find your passion, what brings you joy. You will spend most of your time on your job during your working life."[3]

These are the words and thoughts of Colette Pierce Burnette, the sixth president of Huston-Tillotson University. Only the second female president in Huston-Tillotson's history, Pierce Burnette was inspired by Miss Mary E. Branch, the first woman selected to serve as the president at Tillotson Collegiate, an all-female school, in 1930. The similarities between these two women are striking. Both served in many other capacities prior to becoming president; neither had an initial passion to become president of HT. Branch was in a job with upward mobility and the possibility of salary increase; Pierce Burnette wanted to become president of a much larger HBCU. Both sought God's direction prior to making the decision to come to HT. Both became president under a cloud of institutional difficulties. Branch was faced with decreasing enrollment and a college that became a junior college due to budgetary problems. Pierce Burnette came to HT when it faced serious financial aid difficulties, resulting in the university having to pay back millions to the government. Just as important, both made decisions with their minds and hearts, an approach that Pierce Burnette said is most often exhibited in women.

Once Branch (1930) and Pierce Burnette (2015) became president, their singular goal was to make HT the premier HBCU in the South, west of the Mississippi.

Each had a passion for her students' success and strived every day to make a real difference at HT and in the community. As female presidents, each had to demand respect for their leadership role even among male president colleagues. Colette Pierce Burnette realized she had an important seat at the table. "When I go to meetings with other presidents, I'm one in a sprinkling of women. And one in an even smaller sprinkling of people of color," she said. "We've gotten to a place where there is equality, but there is not equity. And there is a big difference between being treated equally and being treated equitably. People like me don't rest until we find that equitable place for all."[4]

Because of President Pierce Burnette's genuine respect for President Branch, the brief history of Mary Branch's presidency provided below will yield nuggets of insight about how Pierce Burnette's presidency might evolve.

> Though [Branch's] parents were former slaves and unlearned, they were forward-minded, insisting that their children become educated. With a BA and a master's degree, and a job with good salary and upward mobility, Miss Branch's reputation was known by the American Missionary Association. She was twice offered the opportunity to become president of Tillotson in Austin, Texas, but turned it down because of low pay and having to move from her previous employment. She prayed about it and in 1930 accepted and was appointed president of Tillotson College in Austin, Texas, which was at that time a two-year women's junior college.[5]

Branch became HT's president at a time when schools were segregated and discrimination against Blacks was the law, but her vision of what her students could achieve was not curtailed by that social reality.

> As president, Branch sought to make Tillotson a successful and respected four-year college once more. Under her direction the college's facilities were improved: the library expanded; old buildings renovated; and a men's dormitory and a gymnasium were constructed. For recruitment and retention, Branch doubled the size of the faculty and raised education requirements for instructors. She recruited students throughout the Southwest and offered scholarships to the neediest. She permitted the organization of fraternities and sororities and encouraged the formation of academic and athletic clubs. Miss Branch worked to improve the college's relationship with the community by participating in civic affairs and establishing contacts with faculty at the University of Texas and

Samuel Huston College, as well as with public school teachers and administrators. She also worked towards a merger with Samuel Huston College, although the two institutions did not join until after her tenure.

During the Branch administration enrollment steadily grew. In 1935, Tillotson became a coeducational, four-year institution. In 1936 the college was admitted to membership in the American Association of Colleges, and in 1943 it received an "A" rating from the Southern Association of Colleges and Secondary Schools. While in Austin, Mary Branch became active in the civil-rights movement. In 1943, she became president of the Austin chapter of the National Association for the Advancement of Colored People. She also served on the State Interracial Commission of Texas. During the Great Depression she devoted much time to the National Youth Administration. In 1935 Lyndon B. Johnson appointed her to the NYA Negro Advisory Board for Texas. In 1944 Branch helped to establish the United Negro College Fund. She died in Baltimore, Maryland, on July 6, 1944, at the height of her career.[6]

Who Is Dr. Pierce Burnette?

Following the directives of her parents and grandmother, Pierce Burnette earned her bachelor of science degree in industrial and systems engineering from Ohio State University in Columbus in 1980. Reflecting on her experience at Ohio State University, she said:

> Ohio State University gave me the courage to move through my engineering program. Returning to Ohio State was a safe space where they encouraged you by saying, "You can do this." Despite some of the bad experiences I had with sexism, it grew me up. I would do it all over again with the same pain and the same disappointments because when you wrap it all together it was an experience that taught me that you can be a woman in this male-dominated field and you're going to do a good job.[7]

In 1983 she completed her master of science degree in administration with honors from Georgia College in Milledgeville. In 2003, Pierce Burnette was accepted and graduated from the Harvard Graduate School's Education Management Development Program.

Pierce Burnette was a military wife who travelled around the world, making her appreciate being an American. Throughout her travels with her husband, Pierce

Burnette had many opportunities to find jobs within her engineering expertise, and she did. However, according to her, something was missing. A glimpse of what was missing came each time she and her husband returned to homecomings at Morehouse, an all-male HBCU in Atlanta. Morehouse instilled pride and loyalty in its male students. Not graduating from an HBCU herself, Pierce Burnette was drawn by the richness of the HBCU, specifically relationships made and nurtured over time. She began to think about how it would feel to work at an HBCU.

"My career is split in half," she explained. "During the first half, I was a briefcase-carrying corporate executive, but I always had a passion to do something that required heart and mind. Then I tried working with higher education."[8] Pierce Burnette spent the first fifteen years of her career as an engineer, managing technical people. Before transitioning into higher education, Pierce Burnette worked as a computer analyst at *The Washington Post*, was an operations support engineer at Procter & Gamble, held the position of Director of Information Systems at Neighborhood Reinvestment Corp., and ran her own computer consulting firm, CompuMent.[9] However, fulfilling her desire to cross over to education administration initially came when she taught information technology at Pierce College in Puyallup, Washington. Later, she became interim president there, growing the college to serve more than 30,000 students each year. Her chance to serve at an HBCU came when her husband, stationed in Ohio, heard about an opening at Central State University (CSU) in Wilberforce, Ohio. Pierce Burnette worked there in several capacities from 1999 to 2012. The first position she held was Vice President for Administration and Chief Financial Officer where she provided leadership in finance, physical plant, auxiliary services, capital construction, and human resources. She later served CSU as Vice President for Information Technology and Chief Information Officer.

She was met with a glass ceiling at Central State because she did not have the doctorate needed for presidential appointment. However, she was asked to act as interim president at Pierce Community College. Pierce Burnette recalls the time, while still at Pierce College, that she knew she must get a doctorate. She was in a meeting with community college presidents; they introduced themselves as "Doctor" while she had to refer to herself as "Ms." "Not only am I the only Black woman and one of two Black people at the table out of maybe thirty presidents, I introduced myself as Ms. Colette Pierce Burnette."[10] That moment was deflating but reaffirmed for her the need to get her doctorate. Pierce Burnette thought being over 50 rendered her too old to work on her doctorate degree. However, she made the decision to do so with the support of her family and friends.

CHAPTER 4

How did Pierce Burnette, an engineer in corporate America, end up as president of Huston-Tillotson University? It was not a straight road. Pierce Burnette said, "We learn backwards to live forward. Everything in my life prepared me for my journey in Austin and for my presidency at Huston-Tillotson."[11] Looking back on her life experiences, she felt that getting her doctorate later was better than getting it earlier, as her work experiences informed her choice to pursue education. Pierce Burnette believed that all of her experiences, training, and traveling prepared her for a college or university presidency.

The eighteen-member presidential search committee, comprised of representatives from the HT Board of Trustees, faculty, staff, students, alumni, and community and business leaders, organized a nationwide search for the replacement of Larry Earvin, who announced his retirement fifteen months prior to his retirement date. The search resulted in about seventy applications including that of Pierce Burnette. She, then Mrs. Pierce Burnette (she didn't get her EdD until after her appointment), responded to the presidential search upon the urging of a friend. Pierce Burnette agreed to go through the search process, not really wanting the presidential appointment but as practice for the bigger HBCU she desired. However, she was among the three finalists—two women and one man. Invited to HT, each was engaged in two days of intensive interviews with groups of constituents: students, faculty, administrators, President's Cabinet, Administrative Council, and Earvin.

Pierce Burnette stated that when she stepped on HT's campus for the first time, she knew that it was the place she was called to be. No more "practicing," as something changed inside her—she had reached her destiny. The fact that Pierce Burnette didn't yet have a doctorate was problematic for the faculty, who wanted their leader to have the terminal degree. Pierce Burnette was informed of that concern. Despite this lack, her presentation to the faculty was engaging, resulting in many faculty members changing from their previous skepticism to positivity. Faculty were also appeased by the fact that Mrs. Pierce Burnette would earn her EdD in Higher Education Administration from the University of Pennsylvania in August 2015. Students were deeply impressed, as were most staff members. Pierce Burnette was unanimously approved by the board at their March 2015 meeting. Her road to the presidency was not traditional. When she got her terminal degree, she already had a presidency—not the norm for your average doctorate recipient.

A press release went out on April 1, 2015, identifying Colette Pierce Burnette as HT's sixth president.[12]

(AUSTIN, Texas) 4.1.15—Huston-Tillotson University Board of Trustees today announced Colette Pierce Burnette as the institution's sixth President and Chief Executive Officer, effective July 1, 2015. Pierce Burnette becomes the first female president of the merged Huston-Tillotson University and only the second female president in the institution's 143-year history.

Pierce Burnette said, "I am deeply honored to serve as the sixth President of Huston-Tillotson University. When I stepped on the grounds of this campus and interacted with the distinguished faculty, administrators, alumnae, and bright and engaging students, I could see myself here. HT has a rich and remarkable history of preparing students for careers that enhance our society and world. The diverse student population, enhancement of STEM offerings, the future Community Health and Wellness Center, and this beautiful campus are just some of the reasons why I see Huston-Tillotson as a truly special place."

Larry L. Earvin, President and Chief Executive Officer, said, "Colette Pierce Burnette brings a set of experiences that help ensure the continued advancement of Huston-Tillotson University."

Albert Hawkins, Chair, HT Board of Trustees, said, "The leadership skills and abilities among the candidates were impressive. However, Colette Pierce Burnette's vision, experience and determination solidified the decision and will propel the university to higher levels. I extend my thanks to everyone involved in this process during the past few months as we prepare for the next phase of Huston-Tillotson."[13]

In addition to the press release sent to local newspapers and placed on HT's website, Mrs. Pierce Burnette was introduced in person to the HT family and the Austin community at large to a cheering audience. Board President Albert Hawkins welcomed her with Larry Earvin also in attendance. Pierce Burnette expressed her pleasure in her appointment, offered words of commitment, and shook people's hands. By then, Pierce Burnette was deeply in love with the university she would lead. Although later blindsided by the many difficulties she was to face, Pierce Burnette said in her interview with me, "Knowledge of them [the HT family] only made me more committed to become part of the change needed for growth and greatness. My becoming president was a family affair."[14]

A Product of Family and Family Values
The belief in the dynamic power of education was instilled in Pierce Burnette at a young age and confirmed again and again by her life experiences. Her father's large

family migrated to Cleveland, Ohio, from Mississippi after defending his mother against a White man who disrespected her. Her grandfather "quit the Kansas City Monarchs Negro League Baseball team and worked in Cleveland's factories because he refused to tolerate the humiliation of sleeping in cars and being spat on as they travelled from town to town to play."[15] Her paternal grandmother greatly influenced her by teaching her that education can improve one's quality of life. Pierce Burnette recalls that this grandmother would get extra pieces of butcher's paper from the meat market and then write multiplication tables and vocabulary words on the paper and place them around the kitchen. The grandmother would make toast and English tea for breakfast, but the girl couldn't have any until she knew all of that day's vocabulary words and math facts. This is how she first learned math skills, the precursor of her interest in STEM. Now, "I think young people should take as much math as they can," Pierce Burnette says. "Whether you're going to be a history major, a journalist, a philosopher ... math makes you think critically, and it stretches the brain in ways that other courses of study cannot."[16]

Her parents also pushed education even though neither went to college. Her father only completed the sixth grade, while her mother was a high school graduate. They were working-class parents, wanting a better future for their children. She and her sister knew that going to college was not optional. She got a scholarship to predominantly White Ohio State. Few women, and even fewer Black women, were in the engineering program; that fact alone changed how she matriculated there. "I am so proud of my parents who raised two daughters who now have doctorate degrees, even though neither parent attended college."[17] Her father collected articles announcing his daughter's presidential inauguration, knowing that the success of his daughter reflected well on him and his wife.

Her first post-college job was at Procter & Gamble in Cincinnati as an operations support engineer. Soon after she started there, she met and married her husband, Daarel Burnette, an officer in the Air Force. As a military wife, she spent twenty-one years in service, including eighteen years on international soil. Currently retired from the military, her husband was a proficient administrator and consultant in higher education finance and fiscal leadership. Not only did her husband support her as president but he also encouraged her throughout the process. They are parents of two children, who during their K–12 years changed schools more than ten times. Their beloved children are Daarel II, a journalist in Washington, DC, and Daana, a producer in Los Angeles, California.

Deeply religious, Pierce Burnette's parents and grandparents made God real to her; her connection to God has carried her through difficult times and helped her to make difficult decisions, such as accepting the presidency at HT. She celebrated her inaugural service at David Chapel Missionary Baptist Church in Austin, Texas, where HT's choir sang during worship service. Pierce Burnette started administrative meetings with a prayer from either the chaplain or a member. Whenever possible during her earlier years, she attended Thursday chapel and encouraged others to do the same. Usually, when you converse with Pierce Burnette you sense her deep spiritual convictions.

Inauguration weekend brought all her family members to Austin, a happy place for their beloved daughter, mother, wife, and sister. Their presence brought her joy. "I was at HT, late into the evening prior to my inauguration, when my daughter came to take me off campus. Once home my husband asked me if I had finished my very important speech; I didn't. I was too excited to have my family around me. I had writer's block. I went to HT early in the morning. That's when God gave me my message that centered on flying a plane while building it. That message is not written; it was spoken spontaneous and from my heart."[18]

Affiliations, Memberships, and Awards
During her presidency, Colette Pierce Burnette was affiliated with many organizations. She is a Delta sorority member, proudly wearing her red and white colors. Pierce Burnette was a member of Austin Area Research Organization (AARO), on the steering committee for My Brother's Keeper, and served on the advisory council of Big Brothers Big Sisters of Central Texas. She also sat on the Board of Directors of Girl Scouts of Central Texas, Leadership Austin, the Greater Austin Area African American Chamber of Commerce, and the Austin Urban League. Pierce Burnette was honored as a Hidden Figure (2017) by the Greater Austin Chamber of Commerce. After having seen the movie *Hidden Figures*, the story of segregation of and discrimination against African American women at NASA, Pierce Burnette recalls her own experience as a new engineer in the 1980s, having to get twenty references for a job.

Her membership affiliations and awards occurred throughout her presidency at HT. Pierce Burnette was an honoree of the Anti-Defamation League's 2017 Golden Door Gala, with the Community Hero Award. In 2019 she received the 2019 Top Diversity Champion of the Year Award of Central Texas. Pierce Burnette was an Honorary Chair for the Girls Empowerment Network's "We Are Girl" Conference. Additional awards she received were Austin Women's Hall of Fame and National Diversity Council Glass Ceiling Award. When I commented on all the awards that lined the hall near her office, she remarked, "The awards are not mine but really those of HT"; as the CEO, she felt she was just the recipient of them. Also noteworthy is that most of the awards are Austin-based, unlike those of her predecessor, Larry Earvin.

Nationally, Dr. Pierce Burnette serves on the Minority Engineering Advisory Board for The Ohio State University's College of Engineering and is a member of the National Society of Black Engineers, the National Council of Negro Women, and the Puyallup Area Aging in Place Coalition, Puyallup, Washington.

Many of her affiliations enhanced both her personal and HT's status during her presidency. Organizations and partners worked closely with Dr. Pierce Burnette to achieve the institutional mission of academic excellence. In a June 2018 Facebook posting, Dr. Pierce Burnette wrote this:

> All happening on Huston-Tillotson University's campus today! We are very grateful to our community partners such as Counter Balance: ATX, and Stephanie Hawley (Austin Community College District) for helping us to meet our mission as the intellectual heartbeat and anchor institution of East Austin home of the #geniusgeneration. #WeAreYOU #WeAreHT #educationisthegreatequalizer.

Her goal throughout her presidency was to make HT more visible to the Austin community; her participation in community activities and being on local boards did just that. Pierce Burnette took students with her to many community engagements, to show off their talents and knowledge. Admiration for her and her presidency is found on her many social media platforms. Her followers' comments support her belief that HT's visibility was greatly improved due to her leadership. Acknowledging the support she received from community partners, her October 19, 2018 Facebook entry read:

> When something much bigger than you is in control . . .
> When you serve the #geniusgeneration deserving nothing less than excellence . . .
> When opportunity and hard work collide . . .
> When the city of Austin wants you to be successful . . .
> When the people around you have a can-do attitude . . .
> When dreams are no longer deferred . . .
> When grit and resilience meet innovation . . .
> When your partners embrace and invest in your mission . . .
> Your wheels go way, way up . . .
> #blessingsabound at Huston-Tillotson University

Settling in as HT's Sixth President

In her inaugural address, Pierce Burnette used the analogy that we are building the plane as we fly it, a thought that was unscripted, triggered by the holiness of the moment and her call for shared governance. Moved by the motto that the leaders of Sam Huston College and Tillotson College crafted for the merged institutions, "In Union, Strength," Pierce Burnette saw those words as a testament to the hopefulness that former leaders envisioned. "HT flourishes as a result of the combined strength of those we hold dear, and I am proud to be a part of this great legacy."[19] Thus, on July 1, 2015, Pierce Burnette found herself on a campus that she would consider home—and not only that, but as the head of the house. She looked across the campus, feeling that this was where she should be. God answered her prayer to become president of an HBCU, though her initial request was for a larger one. She greeted students, excited to become a role model for them, especially the female students. She wanted them to know that they could excel in STEM careers and become leaders of universities. She wanted both male and female students to do well in everything they touched. She believed this is accomplished through both academics and relationships. "You could be a president and never get to know the student body. For me, in order to provide the necessary services, I decided to be knowledgeable about students individually and as a group. My vision is that every student adapts IDEAL [Integrity, Diversity, Excellence, Accountability, and Leadership] both inside and outside."[20]

On her first day, she walked into the historic three-story Anthony and Louise Viaer-Alumni Hall, built with bricks made by students at Tillotson in 1914, and entered the office formerly occupied by Larry Earvin.[21] A female touch changed its atmosphere, making it more nurturing and, yes, feminine. She sat behind her presidential desk while burning the midnight oil, then moved to a small round table, creating an intimate space for courageous conversations and critical thinking. In her office were two pictures of former presidents, Dr. John Q. Taylor King Sr., a man of integrity who brought stability to HT, and Ms. Mary E. Branch, Pierce Burnette's role model and source of inspiration. According to her:

> Wherever I am, in a meeting or if I'm just coming in the office, [Branch is] looking right at me and I just feel like she's saying, "You got to stay focused. You got to stay on task and keep your eyes on the mission because you'll have a lot of detractors. You have things that feel like setbacks. You have moments that are all glory, but if you stay focused on the mission and you stay true to your purpose, things always come together." And they are slowly coming together.

Those [referencing Branch] are huge shoes to fill.[22]

Due to her desire to become completely immersed in the life and culture of HT, Pierce Burnette rented a house in East Austin, only minutes away from campus, where she lived for a few years before moving to downtown Austin. This allowed her to be on campus for students' activities as well as to learn about the college, its strengths and weaknesses, and to reflect on how to implement the college's vision and mission. Traveling throughout Austin, she was shocked to learn that many people did not know that HT, the oldest university in Austin, even existed. She recalls going into a store and asking the cashier if he knew where HT was; his response was "no." Pierce Burnette told him she was the president and then invited him to come to campus. As another example, after she injured her feet at an airport, she took shared rides regularly. Most of the drivers did not know where HT was. These and other contacts fueled her decision to increase HT's visibility in Austin, one of the fastest-growing cities in Texas, although African Americans were leaving Austin, reducing their percentage of the population. This brain drain can be offset by bringing students to HT from across Texas and other states. According to Pierce Burnette, "Every day presented new opportunities to tell the world about this historic jewel in the heart of Austin, Huston-Tillotson University."[23]

> We market ourselves as a part of Austin—a destination city; that's an advantage to Huston-Tillotson University. When college graduates love the city they matriculated in, they tend to stay in that city because it's their comfort zone; it's where they "grew up." That's an advantage to being in Austin. The first thing I did was to launch a visibility campaign to get us out into the community as much as possible and to share the stories of Huston-Tillotson University. I wanted Austinites to know that we are unique and that we are in the community—that "We are Austin," and we are the "jewel and crown of Austin." That we have been successful, and we cannot sit, or stop. We want people to know who we are and the benefits we can provide them.[24]

In an interview with Kate McGee, Pierce Burnette stated, "We have to continue to insert ourselves in and close up on the community. So, we are truly facing outward. I hear people say about the lost culture in East Austin, et cetera, et cetera: 'It's only lost if we lose it. We are deeply rooted in the community. We are a cultural icon.' It's possible for a beautiful, thriving community of color, [with] all kinds of people, to grow up and thrive around a university."[25]

From day one, Pierce Burnette hailed the value of HT to its Austin community by participating in conferences, meetings, and seminars. She identified key brokers of political, economic, and educational power and introduced herself in an unforgettable way. She met them, not for herself, but to reconnect the community to the powerhouse located at 900 Chicon. She threw the net wide, letting the community know that HT was open for meetings, events, activities, and programs; viable space and programs are available to all. The message was that HT is an equal and valuable partner within the Austin community. There is reciprocity in what HT can do for the community and what the community can do for HT. Even more important than that is the message that students should come to HT because of its quality education, preparing them to contribute to the global economy and community. Pierce Burnette believes that when a university is recognized, its degree is more valuable.

Getting positive recognition requires that an institution be both known and appreciated. In current times, viability must be realized both physically and digitally. HT's visibility problem was not a new problem, as all four presidents included in this study struggled to eliminate invisibility. However, Pierce Burnette, from her STEM and technology background, used all means necessary to push HT to the forefront. Increasing HT's visibility took various forms, including using social media platforms. In her November 3, 2017, report to the Board of Trustees, Pierce Burnette referenced Director of Communications Julianne Hanckel's outlining of HT's social media engagement activities.

> Huston-Tillotson University has several existing social networking sites, but the University's strongest social presence is maintained between three sites: Facebook, Instagram, and Twitter. The goal is to consistently grow the University's presence on social media in addition to becoming a "go-to" resource for everything HT in the social media realm. We engage with users by responding directly to their comments/inquiries; incorporating video and/or live streaming into Facebook posts; utilizing the opportunity to include direct links, photos, videos, and GIFs in Twitter posts. The HT story is presented in the framework of I.D.E.A.L., taking analytics into consideration.
>
> Since October 2016 analytics and engagement for the University on social media have increased. Approaching a growth of almost 1,000 new "likes" (users), the University's Facebook account continues to lead the University's social media presence with a total of 5,700 "likes" (users following the page). In addition, the number of followers of the University's official Instagram page has reached more

than 1,300 followers (growth in a year from under 1,000 followers in October 2016). The university uses a combination of video, photos, hashtags, and links to continually increase engagement. Between November 1, 2016, and November 3, 2017, the university had 17,000 views of the videos posted on its Facebook page, totaling 5,600 minutes of the Huston-Tillotson University story delivered to users.[26]

Pierce Burnette was found on many YouTube videos and made numerous online and in-person presentations for different organizations. She was comfortable using social media to spread the HT story. She kept in touch with alumni on Facebook, Twitter, LinkedIn, and other social platforms, making those platforms personal by remembering birthdays and acknowledging alumni successes. Additionally, she shared information about herself and her family, believing that doing so highlighted her humanity and embraced her extended fRAMily (that is, RAM family). President Pierce Burnette instinctively knew that connecting with her community on a heart level and not just a head level created a genuine safe place for intellectual exchanges around tough institutional and community issues. An added benefit to being "the go-to place" in the Black community is that HT brought Austin's corporate community onboard. "We had over 100 events during year 2016 on our campus. Earth Day Austin (over 8,000 persons were on campus), Black Lives Matter, League of Women Voters, Organization of Black Engineers, Black Chamber of Commerce, among others used HT facilities. Small to large organizations meet on our beautifully manicured campus or in our community health center. That makes me feel good."[27] Each year after that, except during the pandemic, HT was open to community organizations.

As a sought-out speaker, Pierce Burnette accepted many invitations to represent her now beloved institution. During her keynote speech for Austin Community College's Center for Public Policy and Political Studies Building Tomorrow's Leaders annual fundraiser, Pierce Burnette acknowledged the fact that although ACC was holding its banquet at UT, featuring the keynote speaker from HT was a clear way of building relationships.[28] Throughout the address, she referred to her students as she encouraged their presence at all "tables." Pierce Burnette urged listeners to commit to change by building a blueprint for their lives, having a deep belief in their self-dignity and worth, determining to be excellent in everything, and opening doors they and others needed to enter. Word for word, Pierce Burnette repeated the lyrics of John Legend's cover of the song "Wake Up Everybody," highlighting the power of the first two lines: "Wake up everybody, no more sleepin' in bed / No more backward thinkin', time for thinkin' ahead." She said it was important "to wake up" because we live in a time when there is a "ball of confusion," as sung by the Temptations: "People movin' out, people movin' in.... Fear in the air, tension ev'rywhere." She acknowledged that hope comes from the words of Marting Luther King, who said that "we should be the best we can be regardless of the job we have." Addressing her mixed audience, Pierce Burnette made HT more alive and inviting with every word she spoke.

Pierce Burnette was noticed by Austin's mayor Steve Adler, and two years into her presidency (2017) she and Dr. Paul Cruz (then superintendent of Austin Independent School District) were asked to co-chair Mayor Adler's Institutional Racism and Systemic Inequities Task Force. They oversaw five working groups: Education; Real Estate and Housing; Health; Finance, Banking & Industry; and Civil and Criminal Justice. The 259-community-member task force (many members were HT faculty and staff) gave visibility to HT while researching the issues related to Austin's racism. The 69-page final report contained 237 recommendations that were placed on websites and discussed on TV programs by Mayor Adler, President Pierce Burnette, and Superintendent Cruz. According to Pierce Burnette and Cruz, the task force subcommittees' recommendations were for a commitment to collectively make personal investments to:

- Engage in personal soul searching.
- Commit to lifelong intensive training.
- Learn how to have courageous conversations about race.
- Develop a deeper consciousness and more expansive literacy about the impact of race in personal life.
- Commit to function as agent of change to de-institutionalize racism and eliminate racial disparities in Austin.
- Build on the work of previous and current courageous activists.[29]

Pierce Burnette stated, "Serving as the co-chair of Mayor Adler's task force was a growth moment for me in improving how I could be more effective in leading my institution. The reason I say that is because it really put me in a position to study the history of Austin, and the role that my institution played in that history, or how my institution was affected by that history. It helped to inform my leadership in how I want to advance my own university."[30] Being on that task force was also important: "Improving Austin's effectiveness at social equity helped her day job. She discovered that she could not recruit effectively for a Historically Black College if the city's reputation were not inclusive. Also, she could draft local leaders in her efforts to build up Huston-Tillotson. 'It put me in a position to meet more people and share the gifts of the institution in a more public way,' Pierce Burnette said. 'I met the movers and shakers and thought leaders in the city.'"[31]

HT's visibility campaign got the university into the community, providing HT with a platform to share its stories.

> I wanted them to know that we are unique and that we are in the community. Also, by letting the community see our students, many come to the same conclusion as I, that they are a genius generation. On many occasions I took students with me to encourage them to speak and to let others see the genius generation instead of just hearing about them; once community persons experience our students, their image of HT changes.[32]

Pierce Burnette strongly believed that "HT is the best kept secret in Austin; a shining jewel," and she shared her belief widely. Her firmly held tenet was that nurturing mutually satisfying relationships would bring the best dividends. She relentlessly attempted to build multiple partnerships not only within Austin but also nationally, as she participated in HBCU presidential-related activities in various places including Washington, DC. Many in Austin's corporate community got on board, as was evident by more paid student internship programs and deeper financial contributions to HT. Current partnerships are with Apple, Google Fiber, and other high-tech industries. Pierce Burnette's message to the Austin community was "HT is not a charity but an investment."

Pierce Burnette was successful in her visibility campaign, as is evidenced by the fact that she was named by the Austin Chamber of Commerce as Austinite of the Year, 2021. According to Laura Huffman, president and CEO of Austin Chamber of Commerce, "the Austinite of the Year Award is given to people for making outsize contributions to the community. Dr. Pierce Burnette helped turn longtime talk on issues such as social justice, economic opportunity, and affordability into action, especially by making Huston-Tillotson a locus of that action."[33] This honor was especially significant as it was given during the ongoing Covid-19 crisis, as people were coming out of isolation and the devastation of the pandemic.

The community was also invited to HT campus to experience cultural activities unavailable in other venues. In March 2016, Ron McCurdy, of the Langston Hughes Project, was brought to HT at its expense. Pierce Burnette provided the performance as a gift to the community by voting down recommendations to charge a fee. The project, *Ask Your Mama*,

> was a multimedia concert performance of Langston Hughes's kaleidoscopic jazz poem suite. It was an homage to the struggle for artistic and social freedom at home and abroad at the beginning of the 1960s. The twelve-part epic poem was scored with musical cues drawn from blues and Dixieland, gospel songs, boogie woogie, bebop and progressive jazz, Latin "cha cha," Afro-Cuban mambo music, German lieder, Jewish liturgy, West Indian calypso, and African drumming—a creative masterwork left unperformed at his death.[34]

Pierce Burnette turned the details of bringing McCurdy to HT's campus to her capable faculty and staff. In an email to them she said, "I am so excited about this production being on campus and love the responses I received when I pushed it out from my own social media accounts." On May 8, 2017, an audience participant sent this email regarding the performance:

> Dear Drs. Pierce Burnette, Krueger, and Nash,
> I learned about The Langston Hughes Project performance from my friend Rosalee Martin. I attended with my best friend, and we were both blown away. Every aspect of the performance—the poetry, the spoken word, the clever introductions, the music, Dr. McCurdy's delivery, the rest of the quartet, the video—all combined to powerfully move my heart, my mind, and my soul. I've raved about it to many friends and am very sorry that I hadn't invited many more of them to join me that night.
> Thank you so much for bringing this amazing, outstanding performance to Austin. It was, without a doubt, one of the very best artistic pieces I've seen in many years.
> With gratitude and delight,
Juli Fellows, PhD[35]

Dr. Pierce Burnette responded as follows:

> From: Pierce Burnette, Colette
> Date: March 9, 2017
> To: Juli Fellows
> Cc: Krueger, Jennine; Nash, Ashley L.

CHAPTER 4

> Subject: Re: Thank you
>
> Dr. Fellows,
>
> THANK YOU so much for coming out and supporting HT. I'm delighted to hear that you enjoyed the performance. Your feedback supports and encourages our ongoing efforts to serve our students and the community in this way. Please watch for more of the same.
>
> Once again, thank you!
>
> All the best, cpb

Appreciating the importance of making our students contributing citizens, there were regular registration and voting drives on campus, supported by NAACP, Urban League, The Links, sororities, and fraternities as well as student organizations. On October 7, 2016, Texas Secretary of State Carlos Cascos came to HT to learn about and support HT's voter education campaign. His staff invited Austin-area media to attend the event. This voter campaign served several purposes: students practiced civil duties and met political leaders and vice versa, and TV and print accounts provided visibility to HT.

Following the tradition of HBCUs' engaging in civil rights and justice activism, Pierce Burnette invited Black Lives Matter (BLM) on its campus for a peaceful protest after the murder of George Floyd (May 25, 2020) despite the fact that the institution was on pandemic lockdown. She said that it was a difficult decision to make but gave BLM permission to do so. Thousands of people met at HT on June 7, 2020, to listen to passionate speakers and to march to Austin's Capitol in a peaceful protest.[36] This protest was televised by Fox News, highlighting George Floyd's death as well as other economic, political, and criminal injustices faced by Black and Brown people. Pierce Burnette later faced criticism for making that courageous decision, but she knew she did the right thing. It also provided tremendous publicity for HT, as both the history of HT and the protest were highlighted.

On June 3, 2020, Dr. Pierce Burnette sent a moving email message to her campus community related to George Floyd's death. Highlighting her own experience with racism along with other issues, she stated:

> Yes, my heart is heavy, my mind is weary, my soul is restless, and I am an angry Black woman. These moments may chink my armor, but they do not hinder me—they do not stop my thirst for dismantling institutional racism. Instead, just the opposite. They fuel my warrior spirit and make me want to fight for civil

rights and social justice even more. There is a Mexican proverb that says, "They tried to bury us, but they didn't know we were seeds."

Students, I continue to believe with every ounce of my being that it is your generation—the #geniusgeneration—postured to use its genius to indeed bend "the arc of the moral universe ... toward justice." I saw that in how you embraced with passion Professor Krueger using Black superheroes and the beauty of the spoken word in your English class. It is your generation equipped to hold the judicial system and government accountable. I saw that in my discussions with you about what you learned in Professor Martin's Sociology class and Professor Samuels's Criminal Justice class. It is your generation proving that education is the great equalizer. I saw that in your research with Professor [Amanda] Masino and Professor [Abena] Primo to identify and eradicate health disparities. It is your generation attracting committed allies and accomplices. I saw that watching you build the brand of excellence while networking with corporate moguls at Capital Factory. You are the generation embracing the power of the right to vote. I saw that in your success at starting an award-winning student chapter of the National Association for the Advancement of Colored People. These are just a few of the numerous indicators I have personally experienced that you are postured and eager to make significant contributions to society with knowledge, resilience, and grace.

#BlackLivesMatter is so much more than a trending hashtag or words on a sign at a march. It is a movement. Be a part of a movement—not just a moment. Stay in the fight. Be a warrior for social justice—you matter. Social change comes from educating ourselves, knowing, and learning from our history, exercising our right to vote and our right to protest peacefully. Social change comes from choosing where to invest our dollars, using our education as leverage to be placed in positions of power to set policy, respecting our property and sacred spaces, honoring our elders, learning and understanding the history of our nation, maintaining self-control, using our collective voices, all the while uplifting our race and culture. Stay focused. Use this time to read voraciously and be engaged in your studies—your learning matters.[37]

On August 6, 2021, during Covid-19, political activist Rev. Jesse Jackson and media personality Roland Martin met on HT's campus to shine light on the voter suppression underway in Texas and other states. The engagement activities described above advanced to make HT a destination place, an important goal of Pierce Burnette's. However, many faculty members were concerned that they were not made aware of the visit of such renowned men, hindering their ability to engage their students with such greatness as these men represented.

Colette Pierce Burnette: A Students' President

We have seen Pierce Burnette's efforts toward increasing student success in what has already been written. Making HT visible is only a means to an end, the end being the creation of more avenues to ensure student success. She strongly believed HT to be in the business of educating young and older minds, preparing them for successful careers and a life of service. Motivated both by deep challenges and powerful opportunities of leading this historic institution, Pierce Burnette started her presidency at her first Administrative Council meeting asking, "Are we ready? Are we ready to receive our 2015–2016 students? Readiness is a team outcome; builders of the plane while flying it . . ."[38]

> To assure campus readiness for the arrival of our new first-time and returning students there will be an "Are We Ready?" meeting on August 11, 2015. The objectives of that meeting are to assess campus readiness, identify resolutions to known and perceived barriers, encourage communication, and build support among and between all functional units.
>
> We must remain mindful that our students choose to attend Huston-Tillotson University. To meet the expectations of our students the entire campus must operate as a unified entity . . . nothing less than a high-quality collegiate experience. There are many moving parts on campus all dependent on the efficiency of each other. . . .
>
> Many of you are already immersed in meticulous planning and thoughtful attentiveness to campus readiness—both necessary components for excellence. A meeting to verify that all of the moving parts are in sync is the next step.
>
> Each functional unit will present. An agenda and order of presentations will be distributed under separate cover. Each unit head should come prepared to present the following for their respective area(s) of responsibility:
>
> 1. Steps taken to date towards campus readiness.
> 2. An assessment of outstanding needs and concerns you have.
> 3. A description of the strategies and timelines for closing any gaps you may be experiencing.
>
> The start of the fall semester is one of the most exciting times of the academic year. Huston-Tillotson University is fortunate to have such exceptional students. It is our responsibility to be sure they have a positive start to the academic year. It

is our duty to create and foster a culture of student success. Therefore, campus readiness for the start of fall semester and beyond is paramount—our students and their success are the reason we are here.

I am looking forward to your presentations, learning about your creative and innovative approaches to providing excellent service to new and returning students, and working alongside you in a collaborative and supportive environment.

I appreciate you for being committed to the mission and for choosing to be a part of continuing to move Huston-Tillotson University forward. See you on August 11th,

Colette Pierce Burnette
President and Chief Executive Officer
Huston-Tillotson University
900 Chicon Street
DiscoverHT
In Union and Strength

An August 19 follow-up email to her Administrative Council stated:

Before this morning's wheels-up for our students' Academic Year 2015–2016, I wanted to share three things:
1. Thank you for all that you do to create a culture of success for our students. I count each of you in my *Gratefuls*.
2. Your hard work is important and "well worth it" as we labor on Bluebonnet Hill.
3. Let's do this at Huston-Tillotson University!

In Union we find our Strength,
President Pierce Burnette

Clearly, Pierce Burnette was establishing her own flavor of excellence, a goal that was held high by her predecessors as well. Most people at HT had the singular purpose of working as a team to make sure every student was successful! During her presidency, Pierce Burnette supported students in many ways. She wanted her students to experience expansive education including lessons learned outside the classroom. One professor, Shawanda Stewart, sent an email to her:

I am writing to solicit your help. We have several students (ranging from first year to graduating senior) who have been accepted to present at various national

CHAPTER 4

graduate/undergraduate level conferences to international professional level conferences. I am writing to find out if there is any money available to help pay for the costs of their participation in these conferences. I am very proud of the work each student has done, and these opportunities are both important to the profile of our institution and for students' recognition that they are receiving a competitive education at HT.[39]

Pierce Burnette's response was: "These are wonderful opportunities. I'm sure we can secure funding. Let's talk specifics." She sent a follow-up email to Professor Stewart after students returned: "Once again – thank you for being a champion of students having these opportunities. I would like the students' experiences to be shared in the next issue of our *Ram Magazine*."

Pierce Burnette, having a STEM background, created opportunities to expose students to science, technology, and other STEM areas. Under the leadership of biology professor Amanda Masino, HT STEM Research Scholars spent the summer (2017) performing lab experiments in the fields of biology, environmental science, dentistry, and more. One of these STEM scholars reflected on his experience researching cognitive impairment associated with androgen deprivation therapy: "When I was younger, I had a pediatrician who always made coming to the doctor less scary. He always made sure I was comfortable and kept a smile on my face whenever I had to get shots. So, I want to impact children's lives just like he did mine."[40] A sociology Research Scholar said that as a result of her summer experience her career plans were to be involved in public health, policy, community development, and sustainability.

According to Kate McGee, "Dr. Pierce Burnette worked to get to know her students and to know their stories—what they are up against; what their needs are. The students call it the 'fRAMily' or the 'ram fam,'" referring to Huston-Tillotson's mascot, the ram.[41] "So, we have our family stuff, and that's life. But I truly feel that I know, I have a finger on the pulse of the student that Huston-Tillotson attracts." McGee's comments are supported in the activities noted below.

In 2016, Pierce Burnette co-sponsored with Miss HT an inaugural presidential tea. She sent this email to select students, faculty, and staff:

> Subject: Inaugural Presidential Tea: Ladies First!
> Please join Miss Huston-Tillotson University CarShandra Hollins, Miss UNCF Taleah Moore, and me in celebrating the Ladies of the Class of 2020 at our Inaugural Presidential Tea.

Our theme is *Ladies First!*

As a part of Ram Training Camp this is an opportunity for our young ladies to get to know the women on campus serving as a part of their support system guiding them through their undergraduate journey.

I hope to see you on Sunday August 21st at 12:00 PM at the Davage-Durden Student Union.

In Union we find our Strength,
Cpb

Reinforcing her belief in her students and predicting their greatness were evident in her words at the event: "Let it be known that from this day forward you are students first and a queen who wears her crown in royalty."

Further evidence of being a students' president can be found in an email sent to her administrative assistant requesting placement of student events on her calendar:

From: Pierce Burnette, Colette
Sent: Saturday, August 13, 2016 2:47 PM
Subject: Choir Performance Schedule
Virgie,
I would like to avoid as many scheduling conflicts with student and faculty events and activities as possible for the entire academic year by planning ahead of time. Understanding that conflicts are unavoidable, my goal is to attend as many as possible. I want to avoid what happened last year when I missed most (and in many cases all) events for some groups.

Please obtain copies of schedules for AY 2016–2017 from the following and mark my calendar accordingly:

- College of Arts and Sciences
- School of Business and Technology
- Admissions/ Recruitment (to include on campus (ex. large tour groups visiting campus) and off campus (large scale recruitment events where my inclusion and attendance will be fruitful))
- Campus Life / Student Affairs
- Residence Life
- Downs-Jones Library
- Choir
- Jazz Ensemble
- Green Is the New Black

CHAPTER 4

- DuBois Scholars
- Student Ambassadors
- Basketball games
- Baseball games
- Softball games
- Volleyball games
- Track and field meets
- Soccer matches
- Campus life

Thank you,
Cpb

Entries from Pierce Burnette's Facebook posts give insight into the depth of her love for her students.

My blessing of the morning! Grace before grabbing breakfast at Mickey D's enroute to perform in Houston with my HT Choir led by the remarkable Dr. Gloria Quinlan!

Thank you Choir for being such wonderful ambassadors for Huston-Tillotson University.

#roadtrip #youngandgifted #WeAreIDEAL 9/30/18

Thank you State Representative Eric Johnson for hosting a forum with the former Attorney General of the United States, Holder, on our campus. The discussion on redistricting and the power of civic engagement was invaluable to our young voters! AND I got to meet one of my heroes – Mr. Eric Holder.

#blessedandhumbled

The heavy lifting doesn't feel so heavy anymore when you realize that within the span of the last 7 days your students got to meet Nancy Pelosi, interview Eric Holder, attend the Texas Tribune Festival, and roll out an impressive list of events for NAACP Week on your campus. The students at Huston-Tillotson University are my WHY. #ihavethebeststudentsintheuniverse #geniusgeneration

This is our 2nd year hosting a cohort of the UNCF Career Pathways Initiative – branded as HT's Ram Career Connections. The students in the first cohort are trailblazers on campus and I have great expectations for this year's cohort as well. With the guidance of our Math and English faculty (Professor Jennine Doc_Krueger) our push for academic excellence is what positions us to be the "Intellectual Heartbeat of East Austin!" Let's watch these scholars succeed and excel! #proudpresident 6/24/2018

It's here!!!!!
 Welcome Class of 2022!
 Ram Training Camp starts tonight!
 Your success is our priority! #WEAREYOU 8/15/2018

The following September 21, 2018, Facebook entry suggests how her students could become grounded: "Reading is therapeutic to me especially when my life gets big, my heart gets broken, or when I need to pump the brakes to catch up with myself. It's particularly therapeutic when you read a book in which you can see your own self."

Another post shares her takeaway from one of the books she read:

1. You can either be a Super Negro or a Forgotten Negro.
2. The world is only as small as you let it be.
3. You only remember what you remember. I am #blessedandhumbled by my journey.

To maintain their genius status, her students needed to take holistic approaches to their lifestyle. Feeding the mind, spirit, and soul frees up the ability to become one's best self. Teaching by example, Pierce Burnette posted her acceptance to a thirty-day challenge to share her favorite songs. Music is universal and is her "go-to place" at any time. Her first song was "Red Light Special" by TLC. But it is her second song that I believe reveals her heart for peeling back the layers of diversity and embracing what she sees. The song, written by India Arie and titled "One," goes like this.

 Billions live their lives

Now Muhammad, Krishna, or the Buddha are the way.
Still some believe it's right to say
In the name of Jesus when you pray.

CHORUS: We are a humankind of seven billion
So many different races and religions
And it all comes down to one.

Some say God's a Him
Still many believe that He is a Her
Does God live in our hearts
Or is She somewhere out there in the universe?
[CHORUS]
How far will we have to go before we learn the lesson?
Gandhi was a Hindu
Martin Luther King, a Christian
Regardless of religion, they knew love was the mission
And it all comes down to one.

Is there no God at all
Or a pantheon of gods up in the sky?
We can heal our broken hearts
If we give up the desire to be right.

We are a humankind of seven billion
So many different races and religions
And we all want the same things
Health, Love, Prosperity and Peace
Tolerance is the seed
And the gift of pure acceptance is the tree
[CHORUS]
Whether you are red, brown, yellow, Black, or white
Man with a husband, or a woman with a wife
We can debate until the end of time who is wrong or who is right
Or we can see ourselves as one
Cause it all comes down to love.

Pierce Burnette does not need any specific reason or accomplishment to praise her geniuses. On October 21, 2018, she posted the following to her Facebook page.

> These are my Lady Rams!
> My Scholars!
> My Lady's Basketball Team!
> My why! My purpose

Student-Centered Programs

Being a students' president meant that Pierce Burnette valued her students and provided them with educational curricula, services, and resources needed for academic success for future achievements. Since education is the racial and gender equalizer, Pierce Burnette both nurtured existing programs and created new ones, which had the singular goal of preparing our genius generations for future success. Many student-centered programs that enhance student growth and opportunities are highlighted below.

Discover Law (DL)
As previously discussed, the Discover Law program provided both HT and UT students with hands-on and academic learning experiences related to law. HT students who successfully complete the program have a greater opportunity to attend UT Law School. Under Pierce Burnette the relationship with the University of Texas School of Law expanded its work, now with HT's newly formed (2021) Institute for Justice and Equity. In this partnership, their first major program was a free legal clinic (2022) for the expunction of arrest records and suspended driver's licenses. Pierce Burnette indicated that after retirement she would serve on the advisory board of the Institute of Justice and Equity, as she has a passion for both.

Diversity/International Initiatives
Embracing diversity is a core value at HT and is inherent in its mission. Providing students with global educational experiences is one way to support this value, demonstrating that the world doesn't revolve around the cities they live in and that what happens in other parts of the world can affect them either directly or indirectly. Global education provides students with a bigger picture, supplying information and experiences on the layers of the human condition, both similar and different from themselves. Global education is also about developing global

competence: the attitudes, skills, and knowledge needed to understand and participate in a globally connected world.

One way HT works to embrace diversity and provide students with exposure to global experiences is through Memos of Understanding (MOUs) signed by HT and international universities. In July 2017, HT signed a 2+2 (two years each) MOU with École Supérieure des Affaires (ESA), an undergraduate university in Lomé, Togo, West Africa, to allow ten to fifteen students from ESA to earn undergraduate degrees in accounting or technology. HT is also reviewing an MOU from two Pakistani institutions, including Fatima Jinnah Women University. In December 2021, HT cohosted the First International Virtual Summit on Medical Sociology and Public Health, organized by the Department of Sociology, Fatima Jinnah Women University. Huston-Tillotson's CAS Dean Mike Hirsch, Chair of Natural Sciences Amanda Masino, and I (sociology professor) presented on a platform with participants primarily from the Middle East. Additionally, I was an online guest lecturer at Fatima for Ms. Sara Aziz's sociology course Community Development in April 2022. These current faculty engagements are the basis for future student exchanges.

Pierce Burnette championed a diversified, global institution. She recognized past students' global experiences and supported new ways for students to learn and practice global skills. Under the leadership of Dr. Alaine Hutson, HT created a global studies major effective fall 2022. With partnerships with the University of Texas's four international centers and Indiana State University, African Studies Center, faculty have gotten release time to create courses with at least 50 percent content in Latin American, European, African, and Caribbean nations including Cuba and Eastern Europe. These centers have also funded library holdings and international travel or domestic conferences with international seminars. Preparing faculty for this interdisciplinary major will contribute to students' becoming global citizens.

Global opportunities can occur in the classroom, in the community at global activities, and in other countries, such as when students were taken to Jamaica (1994 & 1995), Costa Rica (2014), Paris (2015), Belize (2017 & 2018), and South Africa (2023). Under Larry Earvin's administration, with the leadership of Steven Edmond, Dean of the School of Business and Technology (SBT), HT students, along with Spelman students, took summer courses in China (2014, 2019).[42] This study abroad program continued under Pierce Burnette's administration. Prior to going to China, students were required to take a course in Mandarin from an HT Fulbright Professor from China. Edmond created a cooperative agreement with a

Chinese university that will result in exchanges of both students and faculty. The SBT website describes the China study abroad program this way:

> Short-term Study Abroad Program is a four-week intensive learning program at Heilongjiang University in Harbin, China. . . . In addition to the course work, students are involved in cultural immersion events which include visiting popular sites in the cities of Harbin and Beijing. Weekend excursions to communities outside of Harbin, China, as well as home visits with local families are also a part of the program. All of the activities outside the classroom are designed for students to gain a better understanding and appreciation of the culture and customs of the host country.[43]

Additionally, with funding from Title III Future Act funds, the Office of International Programs (OIP) was established. Under that umbrella, Edmond advised HT's international students, who have their own web page.[44] These students are high achievers—such as the 2018 Mr. HT, a W. E. B. DuBois Scholar from Nigeria—who are often role models for US students. That same Nigerian student encouraged his brother to come to HT. International students, although they often socialize primarily among themselves, are willing to share their culture in various venues. A male student from Sierra Leone fled from terrorists and was separated from his parents for many years. His incredible story moved classmates to tears; they encouraged him and wanted to know more about his country. This engagement gave classmates a greater comprehension of global crises and appreciation for being US citizens.

As part of extracurricular activities, international students look forward to International Day on campus when they share their food, dress, and stories. HT's Student Union is decorated with international flags from students' home countries. With alumni around the world, HT is becoming a destination college for students who want a small liberal arts environment where they are treated as a person and not just a number. Many of them return to their home country using skills and knowledge they learn at HT while recommending others to go to their university.

On April 9, 2016, Pierce Burnette sent an article via email to select staff stating, "A mission accomplished moment—An example of why we do what we do." The article, from a Nigerian newspaper, highlighted a returning citizen, an HT graduate. Dikibujiri Diri (Diki) left Nigeria in 2009 for HT, where she developed a love for teaching and mentoring. "I found out who I was; I discovered my true self," she said. Diki was so involved as a tutor at the Learning Center that she became known as a go-to person when students needed help. "It stopped being a job and became my calling... people would come to my room anytime, at all hours to get help." She returned to Nigeria in October 2014 with a determination to pursue that calling and make a positive impact in the community that gave her the opportunity to grow.[45] Diki's story highlights the importance of recruiting students globally as their stories back home bring visibility and potentially full-tuition students to HT.

While Emeritus Professor and Dean Edmond indicated that though enrollment of international students fell for the 2020–2021 academic year due to the pandemic, the 2021–2022 academic year saw an increase to twenty-eight F-I international students.[46] They came from Australia, Cameroon, China, Costa Rica, Côte d'Ivoire, Kenya, Morocco, Nepal, Nigeria, Pakistan, Senegal, South Africa, and Spain. US students gain insight on how students from various countries think about solving problems.

With money from Title III, Part F, Future Act, the Office of International Programs (OIP) was established in 2020. Its main goal is to assist in coordinating the university's international programs. Initially under the leadership of Dean Edmond and now Dean Rohan Thompson the center provides a variety of key services including working with international students and Education Abroad. For academic year 2021–2022, the center was awarded two international scholars to teach at HT, one to teach Chinese (from Taiwan) and the other business (Nigeria).[47]

Center for Entrepreneurship Innovation (CEI)
In 2020, the School of Business and Technology launched the Center for Entrepreneurship and Innovation under Pierce Burnette's leadership. It offers entrepreneurial education, provides incubator services, and assists individuals in the local community, especially women and minorities, in launching new ventures through classroom instruction and experiential learning. It is anticipated that through this center the next generation of women and minority entrepreneurs will have the skills and tools necessary to energize the economies of East Austin, Central Texas, and the State of Texas.[48] The vision of CEI is to be a global player in entrepreneurship and research; its mission is to promote entrepreneurship within the university and the local community as well as to provide education to entrepreneurs and small business owners.

The center has received funds from many corporations and philanthropists. It is held at a satellite location, just two and a half miles away from HT. "It is located in historic East Austin and will provide space for nonprofits and for-profits," said President Pierce Burnette. "And, just like HT, each organization will be exploring solutions to social issues, including education, access to health care, and poverty," said Dean Steven Edmond.[49] "This institute provides numerous opportunities for the community to connect with HT. The focus of the center is on women and minorities, all are welcome, as we make them millionaires." Community partners have connected with SBT, providing funds for programs and partial scholarships. CEI houses the master's in business administration (MBA) program that began in 2019, with its first graduate class in 2020. Professor Hector Gomez Macfarland was named the first director of CEI.

UNCF Career Pathways Initiative
Having a deep commitment to students moving from college completion to career, HT was granted one of thirty United Negro College Fund/Pathway grants. The purpose of the UNCF Career Pathways Initiative (CPI) at Huston-Tillotson University is to provide a seamless path from college to career. Students who are considering majoring in business administration, communication, computer science, criminal justice, education, kinesiology, or mathematics can engage in a four-year individualized academic experience that will lead to a career upon graduation. Students have mentors throughout their four years. According to President Pierce Burnette, "Increasing professional opportunities for our students through this initiative opens doors to retain and attract more students, especially in science, engineering, technology, and mathematics fields." This is done by HT employing innovative strategies to improve career placement outcomes of graduates, including aligning curricula with local and national workforce needs, developing intentional career pathway options for students across their collegiate experience, and strengthening their overall career readiness. During the RAM Career Connections Summer Program Pathway, students:

- Participated in leadership development
- Were engaged in career workshops
- Toured major Austin corporations
- Were assigned a career coach
- Developed a career portfolio
- Participated in presentations and conferences.

In the first year of the Pathway grant (2016), forty students (twenty per semester) were recruited for this highly tailored program, much like the W. E. B. DuBois

Honor Scholars. Some students have expressed concern about the lack of parity between them and W. E. B. Scholars. For the sake of equity, some of the services available to W. E. B. DuBois Scholars became available to Pathway students.

The fifth class of Huston-Tillotson University's Ram Career Connections program (2021) opened with a virtual orientation as some of the newest members of the #GeniusGeneration began their HT journey. A total of twenty students from Texas to Nigeria participated in the program's opening, with the goal of providing a seamless path from college to career, the original goal upheld.

Center for Academic Excellence (CAE)
The various units in this center were taken from other academic areas. It includes academic support service and tutoring in the areas of English, mathematics, critical thinking, and writing. Quite often students are hired as tutors. Academic advising and first-year experience are also located in this center. Workshops and seminars are given as well as classroom presentations.

Center for Academic Innovation and Transformation (CAIT)
Pierce Burnette reorganized academic support programs and placed them under one umbrella. Sporting different names at different times, it was finally called the Center for Academic Innovation and Transformation. This center is responsible for providing information and training on Canvas, HT's operating system, to both students and faculty. The center oversees Apple initiatives, facilitates faculty training opportunities, and processes funding requisitions for external professional development, among other responsibilities.

IDEAL Academy (Formerly All-Star Academy)
IDEAL provides an intense preadmission six-week summer program for students seeking enrollment, preparing them for academic success. Program success depends on the collaboration of the Center for Academic Excellence, the Office of Academic Affairs, the Office of Student Affairs, and Enrollment Management. Students are introduced to life on HT campus from a holistic perspective by participating in this academy.

The DuBois Honors Program
This program is a carryover from Earvin's presidency and was discussed in depth in chapter 3. It continues to yield high-performing students, all of whom are on

the honor roll. Funds for its support are varied, including individual churches and major church organizations.

Apple and HT Partnerships for Teachers and Students' Success 2019–2022
Apple has generously partnered with HT on several programs.

1. *HT Golden Apple Teacher*: Teachers are trained to design and support innovation in teaching and learning using Apple products through hands-on and online training. This program is located in the CAIT center.
2. *100 African American Male Teacher Initiative*: Leadership from the Education Department. This initiative is designed to inspire more Black males to pursue teaching, as recent statistics indicate that only 2 percent of K–12 teachers are Black males.[50] Pierce Burnette worked with Apple administration to address that need. The Apple Pre-Ed Scholars Program was created in 2021 to support 100 African American Male Teachers, funded by Apple Inc.[51] According to Pierce Burnette: "HT's education department provided excellent education for students who taught in segregated schools; now diversity on all levels are intricate parts of education curriculum. HT continues in the legacy of creating excellent teachers by incorporating best practices in curriculum and with students' mentorship; supporting its education program continues a priority. However, teacher education, as a major, saw a decrease in its students; yet more teachers are needed throughout the US. A partial reason for this decline is the reduction of major funding sources during spring 2018. With Texas Education Agency (TEA) funding, students were given scholarships; now that those scholarships are no longer available potential students go where the scholarships are."[52] The 100 African American Male Teacher Initiative is one way to provide scholarships to promising male students. Pierce Burnette identified this program as one she is most proud of in her administration. During academic year 2018–2019, Huston-Tillotson University was awarded a Certificate of Commendation from the Texas Education Agency for Exemplary Performance in preparing African American teacher candidates. To increase the number of male teachers, the funding provides one year of scholarship support to high-achieving HT freshmen who intend to pursue a career in education, renewable for a maximum of three years based upon performance and need. Teaching career fields include the following majors: English, history, kinesiology, mathematics, music, and science with an education minor. Scholars are selected on the

basis of financial need, academic performance, and demonstration.[53] Pierce Burnette has witnessed the power of that relationship firsthand. Her son had a Black male teacher in the fifth grade, and it transformed his education. "It just really did something magical for him," says Pierce Burnette. "So this is personal for me because of my own experience raising an African American male. It's my mission to be able to get these young Black men in classrooms, so they can pour into other vessels like themselves because they have shared experiences. And there's nothing like being taught by someone who has a shared experience."[54]

3. *Green Apple Fellows Grant* includes scholarships and equipment for Green Apple Fellows to facilitate environmental teaching and learning. This program is located in the Natural Sciences Department.

STEM Programs

STEM programs are located in both the Department of Natural Sciences and the Department of Mathematics. Department chairpersons are Amanda Masino and Ahmad Kamalvand, respectively. Both departments have brought in numerous grants to support student learning, internships, and career development. The Kinesiology Department, under the leadership of Dr. Carlos Cervantes, also incorporated programs for students to pursue allied health careers, clinical career pathways, and graduate programs in STEM fields.

> According to Pierce Burnette, HT has a strong sustainability component on many levels, with environmental justice, a new major, as a key component. The Green Is the New Black student organization has had a profound impact on HT's campus, resulting in local and national recognition, increasing visibility and used as a recruitment tool especially with the newly created environmental studies major. More emphasis on STEM disciplines has resulted in HT getting large federal grants to strengthen these programs, resulting in a dramatic increase in retention rates, especially in STEM programs. HT has retooled itself and is training young people for the pipeline in STEM by addressing business, scientific, and social needs to push more young people into niches they have not been in before.[55]

Optimism Meets Challenges; Challenges Are Opportunities

As the sixth president of HT, Pierce Burnette inherited both amazing successes and multiple problems, not unlike the previous presidents. These successes and problems along with the institution's mission and strategic plan informed Pierce Burnette's main goals for Huston-Tillotson. These goals included but were not limited to creating strong academic and co-curricular programs for students, building an IDEAL team, improving HT's brand, increasing traditional enrollment, retention and scholarships, keeping tuition affordable, growing the endowment and alternative revenue streams, launching a capital campaign to fund building upgrades and new buildings, and keeping HT accredited. Fulfillment of these goals requires a level of financial stability that fosters not just maintenance but thriving. These goals also included relationship building and creating an atmosphere of collegiality, respect, and excellence. There is a correlation between strong positive relationships and financial stability; both are needed to maintain greatness at HT. Yet achieving these goals was riddled with challenges both great and small.

Building Her Team

Dr. Earvin left many critical top leadership positions unfilled. His last years found many people wearing multiple hats, resulting in burnout and inefficiency. Various people held interim positions; the title alone indicated the lack of stability. This fact provided Pierce Burnette with both opportunities and difficulties. An initial question during her earliest years at HT was how to build her team with people who held the same passion that she had for students and for HT. Learning the culture while also identifying the informal leaders and conveying a positive message to students were among the many balls she had to juggle. This work, along with a financial aid crisis, had the potential to either break her administration or make it stronger. For her, breaking her administration was not an option.

As the president and CEO, Pierce Burnette had to create an environment of respect for all constituents, making it clear that disrespect was not going to be tolerated. She wanted an intimate and collegial environment that fostered student learning and success. The environment must also be one where faculty and staff worked together, handling their business in the spirit of IDEAL: "I saw Norman Francis, the long-term president of Xavier, speak at a Black leadership forum. He said you cannot build excellent organization with mediocrity. That was profound to me."[56] Moving towards excellence, Pierce Burnette stated:

> As the president you need to get to know the people and the functions they have. Different constituents have different personalities; those who work in student affairs differ from those who work in athletics. Just like your friends, you have artistic friends; you do artistic things with them. You play golf with friends who enjoy golf. Therefore, friendships require different things. I sustain those relationships by setting an example, by respecting everyone and by setting an example for the community.[57]

Pierce Burnette stated in one of our interviews that she met extraordinary students, passionate faculty and staff, proud alumni, and supportive community leaders. Bringing these people under her administration with her unique vision was important. Building a team with those from both Earvin's administration and hers became a pressing priority. Such positions as Vice President of Institutional Advancement and Financial Aid were vacant. Also, all key administrative interim positions needed to be permanently filled, e.g., Interim Vice President of Academic Affairs (VPAA)-Provost, held by Dr. Archibald Vanderpuye; Interim Dean of College of Arts and Sciences (CAS), held by me,[58] and Interim Vice President of Student Affairs, held by the University Chaplain, Rev. Donald Brewington. Pierce Burnette demoted her inherited dean of the School of Business and Technology (SBT) and brought back the retired SBT dean, Steven Edmond, as interim dean, pending a search for a new dean. Through a search committee recommendation, Dr. Vanderpuye became the VPAA-Provost, and in 2017 I vacated my interim position to go on sabbatical to conduct this research. Dr. Mike Hirsch was appointed to the position of dean of CAS after a search committee recommendation. Mrs. Ericka Jones was appointed to the position of Dean of Student Affairs (2016) but left that position in December 2021.[59]

It is not unusual but rather expected that a new president would make employee changes or even bring in her own people. Pierce Burnette brought with her a former colleague and friend, Mr. Wayne Knox. He was initially placed in a newly created high-level position, Chief of Staff, and later his title changed to Vice President/Chief Operating Officer and Clerk of the Board. His elevation became a bone of contention for some. These mixed opinions about his appointment and promotion existed partially because of his inexperience and partially because of his age and later because of his micromanagement leadership style. Such differences of perspective are not unusual at institutions of higher education.

Pierce Burnette was challenged to bring best practices in her management of human capital resulting in the professional outcomes she desired. Her philosophy of management was, "I give people an assignment with deliverable outcomes. I step back, give a reasonable amount of time, and give them space to deliver outcomes to me. I respect my management team, allowing them to supervise their staff. If management, and consequently their staff, do not deliver, I will become intrusive."[60]

President Pierce Burnette wanted to move forward with a team that was guided by IDEAL (Integrity, Diversity, Excellence, Accountability, and Leadership). IDEAL consists of lofty values that when not met become the basis for criticism against the administration. Given that individuals respond to their perceptions and not to what is real, strategic team building must be intentional by using effective communications that convey transparency, inclusion, and shared values. Time was needed to build a strong team; turnover often occurs before the right people are found. All employees and faculty expect to be treated fairly by their immediate supervisors and by the top administrators. When this did not happen, problems often surfaced, and Pierce Burnette's IDEAL goals were not always met. During her presidency, some administrators and faculty complained that there was a lack of transparency and inclusion in decisions being made; key people needed for implementation were not being informed of those changes. Some administrative assistants also complained that the lack of transparency is not IDEAL.

Throughout Pierce Burnette's seven years at HT there seemed to be a revolving door in many critical offices such as Financial Aid, Institutional Development, Human Resources, and business staff. Many new staff members stayed a few months, some were fired, and others left for higher paying jobs. Her team was sometimes splintered by decisions she made and those made by her leadership team. Below are some of the faculty/staff management concerns expressed in interviews and emails; these concerns increased over time.

- A staff member who worked closely with students, monitoring their academic and attendance progress, was terminated. Faculty called a meeting with Pierce Burnette, inquiring about her decision to let that person go. She told them that she was moving the college in a different direction; the person in place did not have skills needed for the transition. Months later that person, with eighteen years at HT and only two years before retirement, was rehired and positioned in the business office, where she had worked previously.

- A staff member, hired under Earvin, indicated both in informal conversations with me and in an interview that she was hopeful when Pierce Burnette first came, However, her hope changed to dismay after numerous contacts with personnel in the business office. Many were repeatedly disrespectful towards her and others, not upholding the values found in IDEAL. Disrespect coupled with not following processes and/or changing processes without informing key personnel really dampened her enthusiasm. Her passion for HT had diminished, as it appeared that IDEAL was not manifested in actions. Even after reporting unprofessional interactions with staff in the business office, those people [staff] kept their jobs. The staff spoke of times when Pierce Burnette came down on the wrong person as she (Pierce Burnette) was misinformed or even just frustrated, and never apologizing.

- One person believed that Pierce Burnette's commitment to students sometimes colored her objectivity. That individual felt she should hear all sides before favoring students' accounts.
- Some faculty and staff told me that Pierce Burnette dazzled people in the community, resulting in many accolades for her, but inside HT she was seen very differently as she did not always take care of business at "home." Examples were given about the time that two legacy coaches were fired and escorted off campus. Pierce Burnette told two faculty members to leave immediately after she was informed of their intentions to leave at the end of the semester.

Despite her words of wanting faculty and staff to work as a team, showing respect to each other, some employees felt that Pierce Burnette had favorites who received preferential treatment.

- In online posts concerning HT, there is a lot of information about Pierce Burnette and not about HT and the incredible work that faculty, staff, and students do. Thus, another concern was whether the Austin community that embraced her would continue to support HT after she left.
- In an informal conversation, a staff member told me he was ready for a new president as Pierce Burnette was a different person on campus than she was out in the public. He felt he was singled out to receive her wrath.
- A staff member of only two months resigned after being placed on paid administration leave due to an accusation against her. She sent an email to select people to clear her reputation, as well as to "out" a staff member who she thought provided a disservice to HT. The email contained an allegation about less-than-IDEAL actions carried out by some people

in Pierce Burnette's administrative team. The individual, a former staff member of Institutional Advancement (the investment and fundraising department), said: "I was asking too many questions and unearthing too many shabby and flawed processes, stepping on too many toes, and bringing to light certain individuals that are simply not equipped to do their jobs.... I spoke to Pierce Burnette about HT's 50 (or so) investors, mainly scholarship-endowed investors, alumni investors, foundation investors, who are angry about the lack of financial reporting. She didn't respond."[61]

Below are Pierce Burnette's positions regarding conflicts, hiring, and termination.

When differences occur between staff and/or faculty, I believe that when they talk to each other they can resolve it. When people sit down and work through topics, although not all the time, they can get things done. I noticed sometimes people are talking at people, at each other and not to each other. We need to sit down and talk about what we want to accomplish. People cannot stay here if they intentionally refuse to engage in problem solving, if they are lazy and not conscientious on a repetitive basis. Then they are the ones who I let go. People should be given an opportunity, but if their behavior is repetitive, then you must be let go. I will let go of faculty or staff if they do not have high work ethics and who's not holding true to HT's mission to give our students their best and to work well with colleagues. They are not performing according to institutional standards; no desire to meet the needs of our students or fulfill our mission. That is grounds for termination! In some instances, we tolerated mediocrity. That won't be tolerated at another institution; nor at ours.

From my perspective I consider hiring an individual who I believe would be sympathetic towards and care for our students. I look for people who can see students for who they can become and can do whatever they put their mind to. It's important that the people I employ create a bond with students. I expect this of everyone I hire regardless of the position they hold at HT—whether accounting, counselor, faculty, staff, or admin assistant. Everyone interacts with students, and they must be kind to them. Also, people come on campus and the campus should be welcoming.[62]

Relationships and conflicts were seen differently by faculty, staff, and students. One of the questions on my online follow-up survey was "What types of behavior

CHAPTER 4

can fracture relationships at HT?" What we learn from these responses can inform how to build a stronger HT team. The kinds of behaviors the respondents mentioned were as follows:

- Resentment ("How come X department has money for Y when I need Z?"); foot-dragging ("I'll work on X's request later"); missing or lack of communication ("I don't know who to talk to about this" and "I don't need to tell anyone about this"); blaming ("It's all X's fault; X doesn't do what they're supposed to"); delay ("I'll cancel this meeting with X without rescheduling, whatever it was can probably wait").
- Limited communication from top down; and feelings of not being valued can erode relationships.
- Staff not communicating truthfully as to what's going on here at HT. "Behind the scenes," things are not transparent or fair.
- Lack of respect, lack of support, and lack of engagement and intrusive behavior.
- Poor salaries for quality faculty and staff, with no hope for salary increases; hiring a consultant to research whether faculty members deserve raises, and that report not being complete in time for the 2018–2019 academic year. The cost of that consultant was over $40,000. That money could have been used for salary increase. Lack of finances to support faculty work & research.
- Poor use of talent and skills within the institution, leading to high turnover.
- If the person responsible for the error or mismanagement left, perhaps we can give the department/unit a clean start.
- Being comfortable with mediocrity, lack of functional organization and processes, disconnect with faculty, staff, and administration; procedures that do not serve education mission; slow paper trails.
- Negative talk in the community and on social media, irresponsible behavior of our alumni, faculty/ staff and business operations.
- Acting like students aren't the reason the university is open; and professors not having a good relationship with their students.
- Changes in process without informing key persons of the changes, while expecting behavior related to those changes are sources of conflicts and bad attitudes.
- Too frequent staff changes without notification of those changes.

In late 2017, Pierce Burnette reflected on her three-year-old administration and concluded that she was skilled in creating a transparent administration, revealing the good, the bad, and the ugly. She knew that there were relational difficulties identified as less than IDEAL. Pierce Burnette concluded she was competent and shared comprehensive institutional information with the board:

> I am competent and can fix problems. I have no doubt that I can. . . . I am the right person for this institution. It's me, and I know me for a long time. I came from a state school where board reports are public. So I came with that, and I was trained with that transparency. Some private schools can keep information more private from the outside. There are a lot of pluses from being a private school; you can manage your stuff very differently. You don't have some of the restrictions that public schools have. As it relates to day-to-day operations, I would hope my board would not see the university as [through] a straw, i.e., that they only have a peephole of what is really happening at HT. We try to give in-depth information to board members, as well as a snapshot picture of what is happening at the time of the meeting.[63]

Pierce Burnette had a mixed audience: her students, faculty, staff, and the Board of Trustees. As president, she wanted to build strong relationships with each of those constituents, recognizing that strong, committed relationships were important to move her goals of recruiting new students, educating them, and graduating them within five years. Conversely, fractured relationships impede the fulfillment of institutional goals.

Growing HT's Enrollment and Retention
Enrollment and retention were not new challenges for HT; all previous presidents were driven by the need to increase its enrollment and to retain students. Pierce Burnette's vision was to grow the college, but she admitted that she had not reached her target goal and indicated that HT's next president should continue to pursue that goal. According to her, a comfortable level for Huston-Tillotson would be to double its current size—from 1,500 to 3,000 students. The retention rate for freshmen usually fell between fall and spring semester, but under Pierce Burnette the drop was less, even during Covid-19, as shown in Table 2.

Table 2

Student Enrollment (Regular and ADT), 2015–2022			
Board Report, November 2022			
Academic Year	**Fall (year)**	**Spring (year)**	**Difference**
2015–16	1016 ('15)	931 ('16)	-85
2016–17	1040 ('16)	960 ('17)	-80
2017–18	1103 ('17)	1022 ('18)	-81
2018–19	1119 ('18)	1033 ('19)	-86
2019–20	1121 ('19)	1012 ('20)	-109*
2020–21	1058 ('20)	929 ('21)	-129*
2021–22	1001 ('21)	936 ('22)	-65
* 2019–2020 and 2020–2021 were Covid-19 years, when classes were online.			

Table 2 shows a big semester drop in Earvin's last year of presidency. Under Pierce Burnette, student enrollment grew, with a high of 1,121 students during fall 2019, the highest in HT history. Despite this recent growth in enrollment, student numbers remained below Pierce Burnette's goal. Increasing student enrollment could come from broader underserved communities/groups such as rural areas, older populations, first-time college families, and areas with diverse populations. These groups were/are ready for HT's inclusive message of "We Are You."[64] HT provides an excellent education while welcoming everyone who meets its eligibility requirements.[65] Note that during academic year 2020–2021, HT's education was online due to Covid-19. During that academic year, 129 fall students did not return for the spring semester; that number is still not as high as Earvin's last year as president. Pierce Burnette's last academic year (2021–2022) found the lowest drop from fall to spring (65), even though the institution was still under the cloud of Covid-19, returning to face-to-face after online teaching/learning.

A primary recruitment strategy that has been successful is the Adult Degree Program, which tripled in size since its inception. Established under Earvin, it was ever changing, but what was constant was that cohorts of adult learners encouraged each other to succeed as they matriculated through a program designed specifically for them. The Adult Degree Program provides students hope and opportunities to get a degree that might have been unobtainable otherwise. A second recruitment strategy was a focus on entrepreneurship, as evidenced by the creation of the Center for Entrepreneurship Innovation within the School of Business and

Technology (SBT). Students are recruited to participate in SBT's various programs. Natural Science's sustainability programs are similarly used for recruitment. These programs have already been highlighted.

The biggest challenge in recruitment and retention was finding ways to help students pay tuition without straddling them with high debt. President Pierce Burnette was poised to meet the state goal of no more than six years' matriculation for students. The longer it took to complete a degree, the more money it cost the students. This fact was always uppermost in mind, driving many of Pierce Burnette's decisions.

Pierce Burnette's final retention assist came from the March 2022 Thurgood Marshall College Fund (TMCF) and UNCF and Partnerships for Education Transformation Project. One of twenty UNCF colleges and universities participants, HT shared in $60 million that provided tangible long-term progress and impact on its campus and the Black community. Pierce Burnette viewed the inaugural HBCU Transformation Project as a "historic initiative that will unequivocally transform the HBCU landscape, resulting in increased enrollment, higher retention and graduation rates, and capacity building for faculty and staff."[66]

Pierce Burnette supported students' voices on every aspect of university life, including recruitment and retention. She was frequently conversing with students in a variety of settings. In my research I received both students and alumni comments about retention.[67] One ADP student's comment was the sentiment of many respondents:

> I came in when Kismye Elder was the recruiter. She made me feel so important and like I could do it [complete my degree at HT] that I saw it when talking to her. I think that in the cohort that I began with, we had some great professors who did not play. That weaned out [separated] those who were committed from those who were not. They gave us HTs expectations at the beginning and it helped those who were committed to know what we were getting ready to deal with; we stayed, or we didn't. That helped. Also, getting our grades into the system on time will help; getting consistent instructors who were there to help us truly learn. Pay people on time! Many people I knew felt they came in with an associate degree and were forced to retake classes that they had taken with their degree was overkill, and they left. Sometimes, you could tell that some faculty were not there to teach us, but for a paycheck.[68]

Another student said that adult students should be intentionally integrated into HT by providing activities they could relate to. For nontraditional students,

HT must promote academics as well as a thriving extracurricular experience. Most adult students are pleased to matriculate at HT, but transparency, revisiting financial obligations, and rethinking majors offered could yield more students, especially with good public relations and promotional efforts.

Traditional students and alumni also reflected on recruitment and retention, which included both good experiences and those needing to be fixed. Below is a sample of the themes and comments from these respondents. Some of the comments are direct quotes, while others are summaries of what some students said.

- I think that HT is a brand for itself; the things that it represents recruit and retain students alone. Continuing this brand will continue the legacy. Others should learn about the real HBCU experience and go from there. HT is a family; you have the happy moments, sad moments, and questionable moments. As far as retaining students I think it really starts with the student body. We really make a huge difference in how new students feel about HT. They look up to us for support and how to feel about HT.
- Students are the best recruiters for HT.
- When it comes to recruiting, we need to recruit students who are more prepared.
- I understand HT gives students chances but there should be a higher GPA average [required].
- HT should stop advocating scholarships so heavily. Students come in with the expectation that they are going to get a full ride. Yes, you have very intelligent students who deserve this full ride but there are some students who don't have the GPA requirement and get upset at the Business Office because they can't make an "exception." This is not sustainable from a business standpoint. Students need to learn that they need to invest in their education. Another retaining point is student involvement.
- One student said that veterans constitute an underserved group. According to that veteran student, Huston-Tillotson "makes you feel like you are a part of the school." However, "The one thing I would like to have changed would be the process for Veterans using the Vocation Rehab program. They seem to drop the ball because of the lack of knowledge on how this works with schools."[69]

Videos made during Pierce Burnette's presidency contain student testimonies.[70] Among their positive comments was that HT is diverse, a small community that feels like home. Said one respondent, "I am a second-generation Ram, came because of what I saw and not because my dad came." Another student said that HT is awesome; education is good and is diverse. Being in Austin is also a plus. Having great internships led to a job after graduation.

Not all comments from students who completed the survey were positive reflections. Some noted things they did not like, believing that changes were needed to improve retention. Following is a partial list:

- Tell future students the truth. You do not have to be direct but don't sell them a fantasy and when they get here that's not what they get.
- Find more funding; too many students have come and gone from HT because they can't afford it.
- Be honest; step up efficiency in almost all departments.
- Students leave because they feel disconnected from the school, or they had a bad experience with the business office. There are hundreds of schools in the US; finances are always going to be a problem, but HT has more problems because of bad customer service. I will have spent more than $50,000 to go to school here. At my jewelry store job, we treat customers who spend a lot less than we do at HT much better [than HT treats students]. Students should be #1 priority, involving them more in decisions.
- Instructors should treat all with respect, not just the disruptive students.
- During my time as a peer counselor, I found that many freshmen left after their first semester because they could have a better academic experience for less money elsewhere. They would leave HT for ACC. I see this as a big statement for how some see this school. Paying more attention to retention techniques by paying attention to students that are failing before it gets out of hand.
- We need to recruit more Black students. We are so busy focused on making the school diverse that we forget why HBCUs were founded and who they are catered towards.

Surveying students' reasons for attending HT and possible reasons for leaving HT can inform recruitment and retention strategies. Many of the student recommendations aligned with Pierce Burnette's actions, as evidenced by HT's increased enrollment in fall 2017. That fall a total of 315 students (first-time freshmen, transfers, and returning students) were successfully enrolled at HT. This tremendous effort was accomplished through partnerships with high schools, TRIO programs, community colleges, alumni, and the HT campus community. Increases occurred throughout Pierce Burnette's presidency.

Financial Aid Crisis

As was the case under other administrations and continues to be the reality, about 85 percent of HT students require some form of financial aid. Pierce Burnette inherited a massive financial aid debt to the government—more than a million dollars. This debt was a result of many students being given scholarships (under the previous administration) for which they were not eligible, and that money had to be returned. Under Earvin the director of Financial Aid was fired, replaced by inept consultants who failed to understand the problem and therefore didn't know how to fix it. The original two consultants were let go and new ones hired. Having to clean up prior years' financial aid "mess" resulted in fall 2015 new and returning students' financial aid packages not being available in a timely fashion. Some potential students went elsewhere, and many students just did not return.

In 2017 I interviewed Mr. Albert Hawkins, HT Board President. He indicated that he was not aware of the severity of the financial aid problem at HT, so therefore Pierce Burnette was not informed. "If I knew the seriousness of the financial aid problem," said Pierce Burnette, "my initial priorities might have been different and in a different time frame." Further, she said, "I am still learning; and you don't know what you don't know!"

Pierce Burnette believed that students play a major part in having their education financed. Obtaining documents needed to secure financial aid (FAFSA) must be done on a timely basis. Even with numerous attempts, students often did not comply, resulting in delayed financial aid packages and consequently receiving fewer scholarships. Students were reminded throughout the campus on media platforms, on posters, and by word of mouth to "Do your business [that is, complete financial aid applications procedures]." HT often offered organizational scholarships that went unclaimed because no one applied for them. Usually, the application only called for an essay, but even that limited requirement turned some students off. Faculty, staff, and even HT volunteers were available to assist students with securing scholarships—but the request for help must come from the student.

Need for Financial Stability

Stable student enrollment and retention increase tuition revenue, which increases financial security. Financial security, in turn, affects enrollment and retention through more available scholarships, better paid faculty/staff, HT/community programming, and student/faculty national and international academic travels. Throughout her presidency, Pierce Burnette believed she must close the gap for students who could not afford to pay their tuition.

One of the president's primary functions is to seek new funding streams and to nurture existing ones. Pierce Burnette inherited some well-established funding sources but far fewer than needed for adequate student scholarships, faculty/staff raises, support for existing academic programs and the creation of new ones, improvement of infrastructure including new buildings, and funding for faculty development. As requested by previous administrations, each department, including faculty, was encouraged to write grants for their areas to supplement their institutional budgets. Biannually, each department had to submit a summary report showing their program and activity alignment with HT's strategic plan. After review by supervisors, these reports were submitted to the President's Office for inclusion in the Board Report. In fall 2017, the Office of Sponsored Programs submitted its report to the president, who included it in her Board of Trustees Report.[71] She summed up HT's processes to ensure continuous growth and compliance with financial aid procedures.

- Implement and train key personnel on grants management system
- Conduct grant writing workshops as scheduled
- Conduct quarterly time and effort reporting
- Conduct monthly budget reconciliations
- Conduct schedule of monthly activity internal audits
- Host regional liaison to conduct project audits twice a year
- Submit at least $15,000,000.00 in proposals during the 2017–2018 academic year.

Most of the above processes for financial growth could be actualized if faculty and staff were given the necessary tools. However, having staff wear multiple hats was problematic, not because they did not care but because they had too much on their plates. Unfilled positions increased the workload for staff, thus limiting the execution of best-practice processes. Clear and effective communication with staff and faculty is critical for successful implementation of policies and goals but was often lacking. The absence of financial transparency influenced constituents' perception of HT's financial health. In my 2018 online survey, I asked participants to rate their perceptions of HT's financially stability.[72] The majority of the 111 respondents indicated that they believed HT was financial

CHAPTER 4

unstable (67.89 percent), while 28.24 percent said they felt that HT was stable. The respondents were not broken down according to the president they served or matriculated under. Below are sample comments from the 74 who rated HT finances as unstable.

- At the time there were some issues with the funding and how it was being utilized. It was hard to pay for my education; very limited scholarships or financial assistance offered to me as a student. Extremely high tuition fees: at times it felt I was "nickeled and dimed."
- Seems like much is dependent on grants and programs. . . . That is what is being relayed . . . that there is great financial instability.
- Unstable: limited funds for nonrestrictive use; sometimes "rob Peter to pay Paul."
- HT does not have enough funds to attract or implement any events that are wanted by the students. Any events that held are restricted by how much is allocated.
- Many times there were cash flow problems.
- My department (library) has been cut to the bone and we must scrape and compromise and negotiate to get even the most basic needs, many of which we do not get at all.
- Had to work & play basketball to sustain my needs!!!!!!!!!!!!!
- Since faculty and staff have meager salaries, my assumption is that HT is barely getting by. Also, the business office taking forever to release funds for travel makes me think HT does not have adequate funds.
- I have just assumed that part of the reason for the generally poor conditions of desks, etc. is the lack of funds for desks that fit students, for computer labs that are up to date and readily accessible, and other such things.
- It appears that there aren't enough unrestricted funds to properly support the needs in student housing, academics, and support programs.
- I attended the business meeting last year during alumni weekend and I had concerns. I feel that the president is doing a great job. I am not sure of the financial health.
- There are significant upgrades needed, especially in computer and software resources that simply cannot be met. The result is that we are forced to make do with outdated software that is no longer supported by the supplier resulting in significant financial aid processing delays and mistakes. Similarly, I have been working since I was hired in 2014 on a borrowed computer.

- While we can sustain ourselves, I believe that sometimes it calls for creative accounting. There is extremely guarded use of even restricted funds.
- Funds are poorly managed. There is an administrative glut, and poor business office and financial aid practices.
- Although I am unable to see the "books," the revolving door that is in the back office, coupled with the institutional, systemic, and ongoing failures to meet financial deadlines either with students, vendors, or routine expenses makes it difficult to believe that the organization is stable.
- Academic support programs needed for student support have been cut because the grant money for those programs ceased to exist.
- Students were never provided refunds in a timely manner. Sometimes it was almost next semester before a refund was received. Students who were provided university scholarships would have them rescinded if they applied for a loan.
- Classroom I use for ADP needs new whiteboard; professors have several jobs; Chalmers parking lot is riddled with potholes. Just have not seen any use of funds besides the library.
- Several travel plans had to be either canceled or limited for faculty travel. Also, most staff members have never seen any promotion/raise opportunities in over 10 years.
- Faculty raises have been "talked" about too long. It is time for action.
- There was never enough money for Alumni Affairs.

The following comments came from some of the thirty-one respondents who rated HT finances as stable.

- There are a large percentage of nonrestrictive funds that can be used readily for programs, faculty development, and other needs.
- There are sufficient funds to sustain programs even when grants are over, and for other needs.
- Being that a lot of students are able to qualify for financial aid there is money coming into the institution. However, I feel that we are stable because we are a private institution that gets funds from different sources.
- I'm in the ADP program. I have had the opportunity to receive scholarships as well as my grant.
- The university is fiscally fragile yet tremendously resilient. Using the definitions provided in this survey the university is stable. The current push

to bring in alternative revenue sources, increased fundraising efforts, and increased grant activity are important and necessary to move to extreme sustainability.

Financial Stability: Increased Alumni Giving—A Goal

Students and alumni are, and have been, the primary benefactors of Huston-Tillotson University. Recognizing that students have many options to attend other HBCUs or White serving institutions, it is important that students feel valued while getting an excellent education at HT. How they are treated as students influences their relationship with HT as alumni, i.e., whether they will join an alumni association, have a desire to financially give back, recommend potential students to HT, bring students to HT, host fundraising activities for HT and/or volunteer at HT events. Seasoned alumni are more active than ever and continue to support the university and students' endeavors. The presence, engagement, and giving of younger alumni, however, are not at the level needed. Some have indicated that they do not feel welcome in local associations; their suggestions and recommendations are met with "That's not the way we do it." Experiencing frustration that their voices are not being heard may cause them to direct their time and money and elsewhere. Building cross-generational alumni is the lifeline for growth and success.

In August 2017, an alternative group for alumni ages 22–39 was organized by Asia Haney and Dionte McClendon. They call themselves HT Young Alumni (HTYA). This group was established to provide a support system for young alumni and to bridge the generational gap that existed in the local alumni chapter. HTYA's mission is to cultivate and enhance relationships among alums. An additional goal is to give back to the university in the form of a scholarship. HTYA wants to develop a culture of stewardship while offering alumni professional development opportunities that align with the mission of HT. The group seeks participation through their monthly newsletter, social media, and statewide events. They use social media heavily—Facebook and Instagram. They host events to engage and prepare juniors and seniors to develop a mindset of giving back to HT as alums. As this group grows in number and recognition, providing scholarships and other mentoring services will be a major contributor to the life and future of HT.

HT's Office of Alumni Affairs works closely with alumni who are honored on their fiftieth-year anniversary at that year's graduation weekend. That class often provides a substantial monetary contribution and is an inspiration to students and younger alumni. In 2017, Ms. Tishana Lands ('92) recommended that the

25th year should be honored as well. Doing that would be an incentive for the younger alumni to become active members of local chapters. Many are engaged in their communities and in the workforce and could be major contributors to HT if they were intentionally engaged. The then Alumni Affairs Director, Mrs. Lajuana Sanford, shared this recommendation with Pierce Burnette, who supported that idea; however, the 25th graduation class was not formally honored in 2018 but was asked to stand during HT's 2022 graduation.

Large, predominantly White universities often get large financial endowments from alumni, unlike those of much smaller institutions, including HBCUs. Pierce Burnette visited alumni chapters throughout Texas and US so that chapter members could get to know her and her expectations. She also "friended" alumni on Facebook, frequently responding to their comments, making them feel good about her online presence. The positive regard alumni held for Pierce Burnette evidently increased their affection for HT, but it isn't clear if that translates into greater financial contributions. Even with overwhelming enthusiasm about the value of HT to alumni life accomplishments, it's not known whether they give back at the rate commensurate with their means. Developing a way to encourage those with financial means to give back to HT, like alumni Ada Anderson and Anthony Viaer (both previously highlighted), is a real challenge. Increased fundraising efforts among alumni has the potential to result in exponential, rather than arithmetical, increases in alumni giving. Online survey responses from some students and alumni clearly highlighted benefits of attending HT, but not how they give back to HT. Below are some of their comments:

- For me to go back to college at the age of 42, and hearing nothing but words of encouragement from my professors and office staff and classmates, even traditional students, made me feel like they were pushing for me w/o knowing me. Things like this overwhelm me.
- HT let me explore my skills. I found God at HT, made great life friends, and figured out my gift of advocating for undeserved communities because of my education at HT.
- HT is a community of people working together to enhance your educational experience. Working together fosters a positive environment and creates a thriving experience for all involved. If you want an excellent support system, HTU is for you.
- It was a defining experience for my life. My experience at HT was memorable, it was all a part of growth, and it was the best time of my life.

– The leadership of the national and international and local alumni chapters is key to increasing financial support to HT. Sometimes leadership is not willing to allow younger alumni to fully participate in its programs as they fail to consider new and different ways of doing things. The same people are elected to offices; younger alumni do not feel like their voices matter. Many leave the organization with their money, sometimes dissuading others who might be considering coming to HT.

Grants Received and Funds Secured
It is clear that financial stability is a MUST in the life and health of HT as it is for all universities; without it, HT cannot survive. Because many students cannot afford full tuition, institutional prosperity hinges on funded grants and other sources of public and private income. Barriers to writing grants need to be reduced. Three reasons that hinder faculty participation are a lack of release time; a ceiling on financial benefits that faculty can receive from funded grants; and the faculty perception that it's too difficult to get program grant money even after the program is funded. These are longstanding concerns even under previous administrations. Pierce Burnette attempted to address these concerns, as she knew that the more grants received, the better students' outcomes would be. Her business approaches are critical to successful fundraising from businesses, government, philanthropists, and alumni. However, some of the process for securing funds remained cumbersome, requiring too many signatures from people who were often slow to sign off on requisitions. This sometimes resulted in vendors not wanting to do business with HT, faculty missing registration guidelines, airfare going up, and students not being paid on time from the grant, among other issues.

Alternative revenue streams were part of Pierce Burnette's fundraising strategy. Her approach was to brand HT not as a charity but as an investment for organizations' success. She saw HT as a pipeline for supplying first-rate personnel. To that end, Pierce Burnette welcomed external organizations and groups to HT's campus. A diverse collection of organizations and groups met on campus, resulting in a new, unrestricted funding stream. HT's indoor and outdoor facilities were rented by community theater, other school events, community meetings, organizations conferences, and youth camps. Positive interactions with HT, on and off campus, helped Pierce Burnette show the community that HT is a cultural icon, to be treasured. This revenue stream dried up for almost two years during the pandemic but was renewed during the 2021–2022 academic year. By the end of Pierce Burnette's presidency, HT was busting at the seams with summer camps,

IDEAL Academy, seminars and workshops, and parents with potential students.

Pierce Burnette tried to meet her goal of raising $15,000,000 each year but fell short of it. However, many new funding sources were secured; several successful restricted grants were awarded between July 1 and September 15, 2017. The partial breakdown of external funding included US Department of Education–Title III–Part B ($8 million for five years—its largest grant); US Department of Education–SAFRA (Later called Future Act); Hatton Sumners Grant; STEM Scholarships; Heritage Foundation Preservation Grant; and General Board of Higher Education & Ministry-Black College Board (GBHEM) Capital Fund. Additional External funding came from United Negro College Fund (UNCF); Kresge Institutional Capacity Building Grant (ICB); AusPREP; National Instruments; Applied Materials; and in-kind donations from Texas Department of Transportation and Equal Heart; Building Green Justice Forum, planning and implementation. Many funding sources were not new to Pierce Burnette, but she nurtured the relationship to receive ongoing funding. Collaborating with Natural Sciences faculty, Dr. Amanda Masino submitted several grants on transforming HT's Natural Sciences training program to emphasize undergraduate research.

In 2017, Pierce Burnette launched a $2.25 million Reach for a New Rhythm campaign. An initial anonymous contribution of $800,000, designated to purchase fifteen Steinway pianos, gave Huston-Tillotson University's music program the All-Steinway School distinction, just like esteemed music programs such as The Juilliard School, Yale University School of Music, and Oberlin College Conservatory. Huston-Tillotson University is the only institution of higher learning in Central Texas, the fourth HBCU in the country, and the 196th university in the world to earn the coveted title of an All-Steinway School.[73] Students practice and perform on the best instruments, allowing them to compete with the best musical artists.

Given a major grant, the Mary Branch gym was renovated, improving the internal and external facility, gym equipment, roof, gym floor, and other areas; still lacking, however, was the installation of central air conditioning and heating systems. Pierce Burnette's ultimate goal was to locate philanthropists to fund a multipurpose gym complex. Additionally, Pierce Burnette secured restricted funds to improve HT's security. The funds were used to build fences around the campus with big HT signage being located at two entrances. Cameras were placed in and around the men's and women's dormitories. Both gates are staffed with security.

Gala fundraisers for scholarships and unrestricted funds occurred in McMillan's, Earvin's and Pierce Burnette's administrations. The success of the galas depended

CHAPTER 4

on several factors: whether the honoree chairperson was a renowned individual with deep pockets; whether the theme of the gala appealed to many people; the gala location; the event planning and implementation by those dedicated to the project; and the personal/social capital of the president. Huston-Tillotson's April 15, 2017, gala featured members of the Negro Baseball League while honoring Jackie Robinson's connection to HT. Mr. Robinson was HT's basketball coach briefly and later served on HT's Board of Trustees. Basketball player Roland Harden, one of the members on Robinson's team, was interviewed by KLRU for a segment that ran during the week of the gala. HT coaches were honored at the gala as well. Honoring our history, while raising funds, was a good match.

Pierce Burnette's second scholarship gala, Blues in the Night, held on October 27, 2018, was sold out—the first time ever, demonstrating evidence of HT's renewed visibility and community outreach. The more than $800,000 raised for scholarships provided students with needed funds to complete their education at HT, and some funds for faculty development. Pierce Burnette wrote about the gala and behind-the-scenes activities on Facebook:

> It's the Sunday morning after Huston-Tillotson University's 2018 Scholarship Gala and I have a testimony. #htgala18 was a success in sooooo many ways and for sooooo many reasons.
>
> God built an unstoppable team that only He could have brought together.
>
> Coincidence after coincidence revealing that coincidences are God's way of remaining anonymous.
>
> An event put on by a mighty few operating under His grace.
>
> Doors opening that only He can open.
>
> Hearts and minds focused on the HBCU mission in divine ways that only He could have orchestrated.
>
> In my frail humanity I held onto my mustard seed size of faith and watched God work. My guardian angels are real.
>
> On behalf of the #geniusgeneration I say thank you AUSTIN, TX for showing up and showing out.
>
> Everything in Texas is big – especially my gratitude for my friends, colleagues, supporters, allies, and accomplices. God is good! Emcees hold the success of an event in the palm of their hands! #htgala18 was a success – thank you to the witty, brilliant, first class, undeniable, and epic Joya Hayes and Jeffrey Pierce II. I am eternally #gratefulforyouboth.

This entry reveals not only the financial success of the gala but also the importance of teamwork in its production, both of which were Pierce Burnette's goals. It is because of relationships that the financial component of the gala was successful. Pierce Burnette's Facebook lit up with congratulatory posts and offers to continue with partnerships. Below is one such Facebook entry from Teresa Granillo.

> Last night I had the distinct honor of attending the Huston-Tillotson University 2018 Gala; wow what an impressive institution and an inspiring event. I want to give a huge shout-out to the fundraising gangsta, Ms. Pamela Benson Owens, who helped HT raise close to $800K for scholarships last night . . . whoa!!!! I want to congratulate and commend Dr. Colette Pierce Burnette for her vision and leadership of this great institution. I want to thank Ms. Fayruz Benyousef for having me as her guest last night, which gave me the opportunity to meet two HT students, Lenora and Marvin, who are going to lead our country one day AND I met a fellow Michigan alum, Mr. Marty Washington, who wore #36 as he played as the linebacker for the Wolverines back in the Coach Elliott years! And to top it all off, we got to hear Gary Clark Jr. live!!! In light of all the bad news yesterday, this event, these students, this institution, this community gave me hope! Congratulations to all those who worked so hard to make this event a wild success and to all the students who will benefit from that hard work and generosity of our community! #RamFam #HTGala18 #ItTakesAFramily #youstepupandbringyourbestwhenyourecalled

The gala helped HT to gain friends. Nurturing these friends will assist HT in gaining funds for unrestricted use including scholarships, maintenance, faculty/staff salaries, and other institutional needs. While Pierce Burnette's goal of bringing in $15 million annually was never met, upon her leaving HT its endowment increased by 50 percent, and grants from various sources increased each year from 2019 to 2022.[74] Many of these grants came from UNCF, United Way E3 Alliance, GET-PHIT-Public Health Information Technology, St. David's Foundation, Bank of America, African American Cultural Center, Welch Foundation, NASA ULI, and many others.

Pierce Burnette's final scholarship effort was her retirement gala, Celebration of the Right University, Right Community and Right Assignment, held on June 4, 2022, with all proceeds to go to student scholarships in the name of her parents, Ruth and Colon Pierce. Friends of HT had the opportunity to purchase sponsorship packages ranging from $5,000 to $100,000. Individual tickets could be purchased as well. Pierce Burnette was the only president who used her retirement as an opportunity to continue to invest in HT students' education.

President Pierce Burnette wanted to be remembered for how she shored up HT's financial portfolio. She believed she did that and passed to the next president a much better place than the one she inherited. "That president's beginning place is my ending place," she said in an interview. In her 2022 graduation alumni luncheon address, Pierce Burnette reported that HT was "in the black," meaning there were no serious outstanding debts, with some money even available for raises for faculty and staff. If this is true, she is the only president in this study to give the next president financial stability and leaving no unpleasant surprises. She also gave that president full accreditation from SACSCOC, no small feat.

President Pierce Burnette Inherited Outstanding Faculty

I have shared my research about Pierce Burnette's team, her students, her goals and visions, and her financial endeavors. For the previous presidents I provided information on inherited faculty and alumni in the beginning of their story; I choose to provide Pierce Burnette's inherited faculty at the end to highlight our stories. In this area I will share in detail the faculty she inherited and the relationships Pierce Burnette built with her faculty. An institution gets its reputation from its faculty and its students/alumni. Stellar faculty, well-trained scholars who are enthusiastic about teaching, can motivate, inspire, and push students toward reaching their potential. Pierce Burnette's relationship with her faculty was critical to the success of HT's mission. Increased ability to participate and influence decisions regarding professional and student learning result in greater satisfaction and engagement in those efforts. When faculty and staff work in concert to achieve shared goals, their collective sense of accomplishment can foster a willingness to take on additional challenges.[75] Pierce Burnette inherited many faculty members who fit that bill. She had an intergenerational, interracial, and culturally diverse faculty who brought their knowledge and skills to their students in unique ways.

By her fifth year as president, Pierce Burnette had at least nine professors who retired or left for better pay. They include retired Dr. Horacio Peña (Spanish, 33 years, also returning for 2019–2020); retired, now deceased Dr. Ruth Kane (Education, 15 years); retired Dr. Carol Adams-Means (Communication, 8 years); retired Mr. Dean Keddy-Hector (biology); retired Dr. Katherine Oldmixon (Department Head, English, 20 years); let go, Dr. Stuppard (band director); left for better pay, Ashley Nash, alum (English); left for better pay, Mike Hart (English); and let go, Ryan Sharp (Writer's Studio). Ms. Betty Etier (Physical Education, over

30 years, d. 2016) and Dr. Kathy Schwab (Biology, 40 years, d. 2021) both died while still employed. Pierce Burnette replaced these professors and added others. Her inherited faculty members were deeply committed to students' success.

Professors Hired by King
President Pierce Burnette had four legacy faculty members who were hired under King's administration and therefore worked with McMillan, with Earvin, and with her. These are Dr. Schwab (hired 1981), Dr. Kamalvand (1982), Dr. Anaejionu (1985), and me (1973, the longest employed individual in the history of HT, retired May 2023).[76] Despite being often overworked and severely underpaid, these professors stayed at HT because they love what they do, knowing they have poured their hearts and minds into the lives of generations of students. In 2018 the highest salary among this group of long-serving faculty was less than $60,000 for a full professor with tenure. Their salaries were lower than their counterparts' who were employed fewer years. Among them are three with tenure and one who had been denied tenure but, due to longevity, did not fall under the "7-year rule" in which a professor must either obtain tenure or leave. These devoted professors began teaching at HT when there were no computers; transparencies and overhead projectors were the technology of the day. With professional development and a desire to learn innovative technology, the four now use the most recent teaching techniques. They bring experience, compassion, and nurturing to their students along with imposing high academic standards that result in facilitating learning, growth, and expanding students' minds. They are mentors who give motivation to students needing an extra push. Positive faculty-student and faculty-faculty relations are hallmarks of these dedicated professors. Their stories are powerful and instructive. Legacy stories are rich, and this book will add to stories already been written.[77] A closer look at these four legacy faculty members is below.

- Dr. Kathy Schwab held multiple roles and titles in the years from 1981 to 2021 (the year she died). She was instructor, professor, Chair of the Biology Department, Chair of Mathematics and Natural Sciences Department, Chair of Natural Sciences Department, and in 2020 returned to the faculty as a biology professor. When you entered her biology lab and watched students dissect animals, using the lab book she created, you saw students having "a ha" moments. During Schwab's forty years at HT, her joy resided in the fact that many students went on to graduate school with majors in pharmacy, medicine, public health, nursing, and biological research, having goals of becoming doctors, dental surgeons, lead pharmacists, and environmentalists. Schwab beamed with pride when she spoke about her students, as if they were her children. Students knew she had an open-door policy, and their needs superseded administrative work.

Her relationship with faculty was strong as well. She recalled getting tenure even when there was a freeze on it: "Faculty rallied for me, insisting that I get tenure after the committee recommended me for it. McMillan gave in, reluctantly."[78] She also recalled her first days at HT: "I was raised in a White community, went to White universities, but landed at HT, an HBCU, first as an adjunct." With a smile on her face, she said she met me, "Who welcomed me with a hug. I pushed back, as that was unfamiliar territory. We later became close friends—students would mix us up as at that time both of our names started with 'W'—hers Wingate and mine Wiley. My response to them would be 'No, I'm not her; she's taller than I am.'"[79] This is an incredible response from a White professor about a Black one. She recalls getting sick at HT and my taking her to the emergency room, waiting with her until her husband came. "You were so attentive to me that the nurse thought that we were—you know what I mean." For Schwab and me race was irrelevant. "Our bond grew through our genuine love for each other and because of our desire to see our students fly." Her memory of HT, however, was not always pleasant. She recalls when McMillan was so angry in an all-campus meeting that he told those in the audience that there were "snakes among us; we need to rise up and kill them." Her voice changed as she told that story, feeling the pain that those words inflicted not only on Anaejionu, Buxkemper, and me—the three who started the Save HT movement[80]—but also those who were our friends. Another time Schwab lost a promising professor during the crisis under McMillan. That professor said, "'HT was like a war zone; I didn't sign up to fight a war.'"

Under Schwab's leadership, biology became one of the fastest growing majors at HT. The remarkable increase in this department over her last six years was partially a result of hiring Amanda Masino, a young, energetic, visionary, biology professor who had written large, successful STEM grants. Those monies became available to support student researchers, amazing internships, travel to conferences to present research findings, and updated equipment. Despite being only a two-professor shop, with adjuncts as needed, the Biology Department thrived. Schwab advocated for a third biology faculty position. This third position was once filled but was frozen when the new hire left for another university offering a living wage commensurate with job expectations. Schwab recalls that losing that professor was a real blow to HT as he was student-centered, high tech, high energy, and an expert networker—creating partnerships with University of Texas and others. As chair of the Department of Natural Sciences for over thirty years, Schwab was also a faculty representative on the search committee to hire Earvin. Reflecting on President Pierce Burnette, Schwab said, "One of her weaknesses was that she might not be listening to the right people; but as a new president this might change." Despites the ups and downs, Schwab said, "If I had to do it over again, I would still choose to teach at HT as I have spent over half of my life at HT, an institution that had a profound impact on me." Although she was of retirement age, and her husband was retired, Schwab stated, "It is still difficult seeing me not at HT." Death took her away in 2021; she was posthumously named Professor Emerita at HT's 2022 graduation.

- Dr. Ahmad Kamalvand started his career at HT in 1982 as a tutor in Upward Bound; later that year he was hired as a math professor. He has been at HT these 42 years because he feels like he belongs there. Kamalvand is of Iranian heritage; when he came to HT there were a lot of Iranian students enrolled. He recalled each of the four presidents under whom he served, indicating that he got along with all of them, mostly by doing his job and not causing waves: "Although they exercised their presidency differently, each president struggled with low enrollment." He saw King as being an approachable gentleman; McMillan as friendly but having difficulties with some of his appointments; although he was not on campus often, he saw Earvin as bringing HT to a better place and changing the college to university, and Pierce Burnette as approachable, having increased enrollment.

As the department Chair of Mathematics since 2012, Kamalvand oversees core math courses and the former QEP (Quality Enhancement Plan).[81] The University's QEP was a program established to work with students who have a fear of math by providing them with mentorship and targeted strategies.[82] Data show that many students drop out of school because of failing math. This program was under the leadership of

Dr. Aimee Tennant (2012–2019), who is now retired. Other math professors supervised by Kamalvand are Engin Topkara (2011) and Yusuf Yildirim (2011). Kamalvand also advises math and pre-engineering students. Always wanting to become a better professor, he seeks faculty development opportunities to retool with new techniques and strategies to help students get over their math fright. In our interview, Kamalvand said, "We still need HBCUs because we can help those who can't be successful at other institutions. We care for our students; they are more than just a number. We are more like a family; we are available to our students; they know they can talk to us."[83]

- Dr. Paul Anaejionu, affectionately called "Dr. Paul" by faculty and students, is truly a Renaissance man, with expertise in political science, law, computers, statistics, research methodology, urban transportation, business development and incubation. Originally from Nigeria, he came to HT in 1985 from the University of Texas after having taught there a few years. Dr. Paul is currently writing a book on one of his passions: research methodology. He trains students to identify the research problem—a prerequisite to determining the solutions, whether on a macro or micro level. He asks the questions, "What is the problem? How can the problem be reduced to its smallest denomination? What are the contributing factors to the problem? Who are the players who need to address the problem?" Dr. Paul's office is always full of students from his political science and statistics courses, as well as his pre-law students. He teaches Technology for the Social Sciences, a course designed to equip majors in political science, sociology, criminal justice, and psychology with specialized occupational computer skills. Dr. Paul has successful alumni in many professions. One of his advisees, a lawyer, made a substantial donation to the pre-law society in 2018 and was the commencement speaker for 2023.

    During McMillan's administration, Dr. Paul wrote numerous successful grants including a major Dell grant to create the Institute for Research Training (IRT), an umbrella training and research center. IRT sponsored both research and community engagement activities at HT and within community organizations such as Goodwill Industries. Despite its broad accolades, this institute was dissolved by McMillan; I and others believe this was an act of revenge against Dr. Paul, a co-founder of Save HT.[84] Dr. Paul's love for HT was unquestionable, placing his professionalism and job on the line to make sure that HT survived a very dark time.[85] Under Earvin, Dr. Paul worked closely with Texas Department of Transportation (TxDot) and Capital Metropolitan Transportation Authority in Austin to secure eight vans for HT. During 2021, Dr. Paul received funding to create a Center for Social Justice. The center's first activity was to bring to campus an expungement day when professionals worked on having select students' criminal records expunged.

- I, Dr. Rosalee Martin (a master teacher who loves teaching), was hired in 1973 during King's presidency and left after fifty years, in May 2023. I received a master's in social work in 1970 and a doctorate in sociology in 1979 with King's approval for a 1978 UNCF paid sabbatical. I was the liaison for many programs over the years and oversaw HT's international programs during McMillan's administration. I was the University Marshal from 2001 to 2023, under Earvin, Pierce Burnette, and Wallace, HT's newest president. This is an honor bestowed to the professor with the longest tenure at the university. At the 2023 graduation, I was awarded an honorary doctorate in Humane Letters and Professor Emerita for my extraordinary work and legacy at HT, a legacy that lives on through my daughter ('92) and a grandson, December 2024, as well as all the students I taught, counseled, and mentored.

  I was active in faculty governance under King, McMillan, and Earvin's presidency. Named Chair of the Division of Social Sciences in 1983 during King's administration, I remained in that position under McMillan until 1999, when I resigned in protest of McMillan's appointment of MT as VPAA. Additionally, in 1996, McMillan named me Head of the Department of Behavioral Sciences (being simultaneously division chairperson and head). During my time as chair, the psychology major was developed; internships were encouraged for all majors; and the Dell computer lab and the Institute for Research Training were established. I also brought HIV/AIDS awareness to HT campus as discussed previously. In 1998, the Social Science Division was given McMillan's Presidential Award for being the best division and department on HT's campus. The next year the division became the victim of McMillan's revenge, as described in his chapter.

  As CAS interim dean (2014–2017) I established an adjunct office space, created a newsletter, and encouraged fundraising to provide scholarships for senior students to prevent dropout for financial reasons. I created a streamlined method for processing adjunct hiring and encouraging faculty research. By the end of my tenure at HT, I taught children of my alumni, mentored students and alumni, worked with voter registration, nurtured community leaders for student internships, and contributed to HT's creative journal *900 Chicon* as a poet and artist.

As a social scientist, I sought ways to get students out of the classroom and become intimately involved with community individuals/partners, organizations, and/or agencies. Being aware of social phenomena and engaging in social justice matters requires a genuine interest and concern for human groups. I have this concern and taught social justice issues to students throughout my time at HT. I use my training in social work to assist students with nonacademic life issues; they know I care, and they trust me with their stories. Up to my retirement my passion has not diminished; students and I continue to learn from one another. Both an artist and a poet, I incorporated these gifts in my classes over the years, culminating in a course taught in spring 2023, Sociology and the Arts. (More than half of the sociology courses being taught at HT were created by me, my ongoing legacy.) I am deeply connected to HT's mission of educating students for a life of work and service; writing this book is an extension of that connection.

The four professors described above, having more than 170 combined years at HT, are legends and are highlighted because of what they have brought to, and continue to bring to, Huston-Tillotson University. However, no university can operate solely with its legacy faculty. HT's forty-five full-time faculty members rest not only on the legacy of these four but also on all those who taught throughout the last 149 years at HT.

Professors Hired by Dr. McMillan

- Dr. Ardavan E. Lotfalian, a 2020 retiree, was hired by McMillan twenty-eight years earlier as a kinesiology professor. He taught students to stay healthy through appropriate exercise, a healthful diet, and self-help activities. He worked well with our international students, praising them for their studiousness and acknowledging the honors students in particular. Many of our international students cannot get a comparable education in their home countries; they come to the US prepared to be successful. He encouraged these students to share with American students and vice versa, as each had experiences and knowledge from which the others could benefit. Sometimes criticized for not using modern technology to its fullest, Lotfalian compensated for that limitation by having deep relationships with students and colleagues. He had a quiet spirit strongly felt by others, making him easy to be around.

- Dr. Debra Murphy, a tenured psychologist, was hired in 1997. With a master's degree in public health and a PhD in psychology, Murphy continued the work on HIV on campus that I initiated. Murphy was held in esteem by some administrators because of her ability to get large health-related grants funded. Under Murphy's leadership, grants funded the creation of HIV and substance abuse programs, implemented in part by peer educators. HT became a smoke-free campus under Murphy's leadership. She was also instrumental in encouraging Pierce Burnette to endorse Sexual Assault Prevention Education. At the time of the writing of this book, only remnants of these programs remained on campus as the funding ran out. The psychology major, which I initiated when I was chairperson of the Social Science Division, is a sought-after major, in part because Murphy was assisted by Dr. Andrea Holman, a young psychologist, closer in age to that of HT students.[86] Many students gravitated to her because of her youthfulness, her relatability and knowledge, and her research aspirations. According to her, "Working at an HBCU is one of the ways I see myself connecting and giving back to younger individuals of my racial group and providing them with access to one of the most liberating tools they can have: education."[87] She sought opportunities to improve her knowledge and teaching methodology via faculty development and research. Holman worked with HT's Counseling Center and with UT on various research projects in the areas of race, White privilege, and their impact on interpersonal relations. She and her husband are licensed foster parents. She did not return to HT in fall 2021 because she was "offered a position in a major corporation that she could not resist," yet she robed up for HT's 2022 graduation, saying how much she missed HT.
- In the Fine Arts Department, Pierce Burnette inherited the singer and choral director extraordinaire, Dr. Gloria Quinlan (1998, McMillan) and pianist/organist maestro, Stephen Burnaman (2000, Earvin). Using their

expertise, they and Pierce Burnette went to New York to select fifteen Steinway pianos, purchased with the anonymous financial donation of $800,000. Stephen Burnaman received the Top Music Teacher award from Steinway & Sons in summer 2017.

Quinlan and Burnaman took the HT choir throughout Austin, Texas, the US, and the Caribbean. Their teaching schedules didn't reflect the enormous amount of time they spent on the road and interacting with students. Quinlan, a co-director for HBCUs at the Kennedy Center, took some of her students to Washington, DC, providing them with an extraordinary opportunity to perform at that internationally renowned facility. In April 2023, a month before her retirement, she took students to Carnegie Hall in New York City to perform with students from other HBCUs—an enriching experience for her and them. Some of her music students opened for Maya Angelou at UT Austin and for Carmen Bradford (a former HT student) and the Count Basie Orchestra. The choir has also sung in the Virgin Islands. Choir directors are always on call to take the choir on visibility and fundraising trips; each president was aware of the value of HT's choir for such efforts. Pierce Burnette frequently called on Quinlan, Burnaman, and the choir to perform. In 2016, the entire choir took a bus tour to four states, specifically meeting with alumni associations. Pierce Burnette caught up with them in Detroit and finished the tour with them. Exceptional gifts to HT, Quinlan and Burnaman brought visibility and money to HT through the work they did with music students. Burnaman is a scholar, a judge for music events, and a pianist who performs throughout Austin and Texas. His wife was an adjunct of music at HT as well. Quinlan and Burnaman worked with choir students in producing an online Christmas performance during Covid-19, not an easy feat. Quinlan retired from HT in May 2023. Her former students from the US and abroad gave her a musical tribute at HT. The musical event was directed by music alumni as well as Quinlan. The proceeds from the $100 tickets went towards music major scholarships.

Professors Hired by Dr. Larry Earvin
Approximately twenty-three faculty members who were hired under Earvin were inherited by Pierce Burnette; not all are highlighted here. Drs. Andrea Holman and Stephen Burnaman were mentioned above.

- Dr. Steven Edmond was brought to HT (2000) by Earvin, as both formerly worked at Clark Atlanta. Edmond's accomplishments as dean of SBT have already been discussed. He retired prior to Earvin's leaving but in 2015 was called from retirement by Pierce Burnette to serve as acting dean. He retired again at the end of the 2019–2020 academic year but returned in 2020–2021 part time to assist with administering HT's master of business administration degree program. Dr. Edmond in a brief interview said he loves HT and wishes his entire career in higher education would have been there. His love for the institution is evident in his frequent returns to HT to serve.
- Dr. Janice Sumler-Edmond, the wife of Dr. Edmond, was also brought to HT by Earvin. Both a historian and a lawyer, Sumler-Edmond was hired to teach history, to establish the W. E. B. DuBois Scholars Program, and to be the liaison for Faculty Resource Network, all of which have already been discussed. She retired in 2015 but returned as a history adjunct for one semester (spring 2020).
- Dr. Mike Hirsch was hired in 2003 to chair the Division of Liberal Studies and to teach sociology. In 2017 he was appointed dean of the College of Arts and Sciences (CAS) following my deanship. He brought and continues to foster critical relationships with sister universities and organizations, including UT Austin. Through the relationship with five UT global programs, he was able to secure funds for faculty international travel opportunities and other global-related activities. Hirsch is constantly on the lookout for groups and organizations that can provide students with intellectual stimulation. In conjunction with the honor society Pi Gamma Mu, he hosted the Baha'i Symposium on Race on campus. As former president of the Association of Applied and Clinical Sociology (AACS), he took several students to the annual conferences and prepared them to be successful in competitions at those association meetings. Hirsch received three awards from the AACS in 2017: the William Julius Wilson Award for proven efficacy in the eradication of poverty, the Alex Boros Award for service to AACS, and the Robert Ezra Park Award for sociological practice. His wide-ranging research interests include the career paths of Russian astronauts and how people make sense of what they believe to be encounters with ghosts.

As mentor to students, both current and former, Dr. Hirsch involves them as co-authors in professional articles and co-facilitators at conferences. He has published in both US and Pakistani professional journals. Prior to becoming dean of CAS, he was director of the Adult Degree Program, an enterprise that grew HT's enrollment. A former mayor, Hirsch also brought his political astuteness to students, along with other unique knowledge and experiences from his education and life history.

In 2018 Hirsch visited three Pakistani universities, as evaluator, curriculum developer, and workshop speaker. This visit resulted in Fatima Jinnah Women University, a nonprofit corporation located in Rawalpindi, Pakistan, and the National Academy of Performing Arts, a nonprofit corporation located in Karachi, Pakistan, wanting to establish a Memorandum of Understanding with HT. This MOU would seek to establish faculty and student exchanges and other intercultural experiences. Hirsch's contact with Pakistani universities resulted in return trips to Pakistan and HT's co-facilitating an online conference with Fatima Jinnah Women University during the pandemic. I was a presenter at that conference, resulting in an invitation to speak to an online class on community development.

Hirsch also seeks funds from friends and organizations to assist students with scholarships needed to pay off debts during their senior year. He doesn't want money to be a barrier for students who are shy of thirty hours to graduate. Many students are benefactors of his assistance, which is also a retention strategy.

- Dr. Katherine Oldmixon (2001–2021) is a renowned poet and creative writer who was HT's first chairperson of the Department of English. She brought visibility to HT through her participation in national professional and local organizations and artistic venues. Her poems have been published in both digital online and paper books. She advised students, coached them academically and artistically, collaborated with them on the student publication *900 Chicon*, and prepared them for graduate work by requiring a thesis for English majors. As an advocate for faculty within an environment where faculty were/are not always treated with dignity and respect, and their professionalism questioned, Oldmixon chaired the Faculty Advisory Council, a faculty-driven organization. In that capacity, and as department head, she was often the messenger for faculty members' frustrations resulting from "low salaries and demoralizing work environment, fraught with top-down decision-making and extremely poor communication practices."[88]

Driven by her desire to give her students an excellent education, Oldmixon hired an extraordinary English team and coordinated the core courses and assessment tools, while also supporting activities on campus. A blow to her team came when professor Ashley Nash left HT at the end of fall 2017 and Mike Hart at the end of summer 2018. Both were highly regarded by their students, and both left due to low salaries and perceived poor treatment by top administrators. The remaining excellent English professors described below were all hired under Earvin.

- Dr. Julie Hudson, an associate professor of English, began her career at Huston-Tillotson in August 2000. She specializes in African American literature with a concentration in African American Women's literary traditions of the seventeenth, eighteenth, and twentieth centuries. She is currently working on her first book, *Leading the Charge: African American Women Writers of the Late 19th Century and Early 20th Century*. Nominated by President Pierce Burnette, she and professors Jennine Krueger, Ashley Nash, and Shawanda Stewart were among the 2017 honorees in the inaugural edition of *Achievements in Black Austin*. The introduction of the book states, "*Achievements in Black Austin* not only presents a historical collection of positive images and inspiring stories of visionaries, business and community influencers throughout Central Texas history but it offers clear evidence of the magnitude African Americans have and continue to make on the Central Texas community, and beyond."[89] Hudson is one of the few faculty members who participates in many extracurricular activities, engaging with students and staff alike. She is an art lover, increasing her art collection regularly, even with some of my art pieces.[90]

- Dr. Shawanda Stewart became a professor at Huston-Tillotson University in 1999 (to 2004 and returning in 2009). As an associate professor of English, her primary research interests include African American rhetoric, language ideology and culture, writing transfer theory, and first-year composition pedagogy. Stewart received her PhD in rhetoric from New Mexico State University in 2023. Her dissertation, "Writing in the Workplace: Habits and Practices of African American Male Graduates of an HBCU," examines African American males' perspectives and the ways their personal and academic writing experiences affect workplace writing. Professor Stewart has a genuine passion for research and scholarship that examines and promotes voice and identity authenticity through language in the college composition classroom. For example, she co-authored an article with Brian Stone (a former HT faculty member), "HBCUs and Writing Programs Critical Hip Hop Language Pedagogy and First-Year Student Success," that was published in *Composition Studies Magazine*. She became chairperson of the Department of English in 2021, providing leadership to increase the number of English majors. She received a grant to furnish scholarships to incoming and transfer students. With those grants, the English Department offered scholarships to five new students for the 2022 fall semester.

- Professor Jennine Krueger is a 2006 HT graduate in English who began teaching English at HT in 2011. Professor Krueger has master's degrees in English and fine arts. She teaches in both the regular and adult programs and was named Teacher of the Year by the Adult Degree Program in 2016. Her scholarly activities primarily focus on writing, performing, and teaching poetry in the community. She is a nationally competitive spoken word artist and has published in *Imaniman: Poets Writing in the Anzaldúan Borderlands*. Professor Krueger is the co-executive director of the Speak Place Poetry Project whose goal is to bring slam poetry to local youth. Her current research is on marginalized heroes in comic books. Krueger is developing a new musical, *Green*, through Theatre Now in New York. Professor Krueger found favor with Pierce Burnette because of her engaging, funny, and outgoing personality that captivates students, both current HT and potential students who participate in recruitment days. She is called on to MC and to participate in various opportunities. In spring 2022, Pierce Burnette offered her a job to lead the student engagement unit that is funded by UNCF's Transformation Project. Professor Krueger, called "Doc" by Dr. Pierce Burnette, agreed as long she could still teach a creative writing course. She left HT in 2024.

- Mr. Tommy Mouton was hired to teach creative writing at Huston-Tillotson in 2018. Mouton is also a writing coach for up-and-coming writers, including his students. A former John Steinbeck Fellow for creative writers (2013–2014), his work appears in *Reed*, *Callaloo*, *Auburn Avenue*, and elsewhere. A dynamic dramatic reader, his work has been featured in venues hosted by KKUP 91.5 "Out of Our Minds" Poetry Radio, *Sacramento Stories on Stage*, *LitQuake*, Center for

Literary Arts, Poetry Center San José, ACC Literary Coffeehouse, open mic, and a host of others. Professor Mouton is now the editor of *900 Chicon* along with teaching his publishing class. He is currently working on a memoir and novel. He has helped to bring in more English majors by securing funding for scholarships.

HT has few English majors. However, "We have grown a strong English program serving students who are either underprepared or fully prepared. We serve students from every major on campus, not just in our core writing and literature courses but also in our upper-division classes. Teaching writing is labor intensive," stated former English Department head Katherine Oldmixon.[91] English professors work with students needing pre-college English courses while providing all students a solid understanding of the English language. Sociology and psychology majors are required to take two additional English courses, increasing the responsibility of English professors. The English Department offers a variety of courses that enrich students' lives, often providing global perspective.

- Dr. James Kraft (2001), a philosophical thinker proudly wearing Ghandi-style glasses, is often found engaging his students on topics of global religions and great thinkers. His engagements take the form of visits to mosques and temples and organizing panel presentations such as interfaith groups with diverse thinkers. An author of two books and a lifelong learner, he received a second PhD (2023) from the University of Edinburgh. He can frequently be found teaching students how to present their views in a logical way. A supporter of interfaith dialogue, Kraft worked with Reverend Donald Brewington (1992), campus chaplain and occasional adjunct, to try to create a minor in religious studies. This program is currently on hold by the administration. Securing a grant from the Arthur Vining Davis Foundations in 2020, Kraft used the funds to develop courses where interfaith experiences intersected with social and environmental justice issues. Student-centered activities were created both in the classroom and with faith-based and environmental organizations.

Kraft really wanted his story told, one that brought him from a White racist family in Spokane, Washington, to an HBCU in Austin, Texas.[92] In our interview, philosopher Kraft reflected on Blacks in a White world and his own place in that world. What he said demonstrates the quality of HT professors and their willingness to speak their truth on critical issues; for Kraft one such was race. "We still live in a time when a White police officer tells our African American student Breanna King, 'You are treated this way because Blacks are intrinsically violent.' This reminds me of my own childhood," he says.

> I first knew there were Black people from the *Star Trek* shows I watched when I was 6 in Spokane, Washington. I asked my kindergarten teacher how this happened, and she said their parents gave them too much chocolate milk. We didn't have African Americans in the Spokane valley. I am embarrassed to say it, but in the '70s, in my neighborhood, we used to sing with our parents' approval, "Eeny, meeny, miny, moe / catch a nigger by its toes / if he hollers let him pay, fifty dollars every day." Now we had a Black [US] president.
>
> What does it say that an African American professor, you [Dr. Martin], was instrumental in a White guy like me, from a neighborhood racist in the '70s, getting tenure five years ago, when I was told by the [HT] president that I must leave in a year? That signifies something significant. To me it signifies that we are trying to fulfill a higher purpose, cooperation among races for the betterment of all of us, despite racial difference, but also because of racial differences I personally don't believe there is anything as firm and static that the word "race" connotes.[93]

Kraft's story reminds me of my own childhood play with racism. In the 1950s, Black children in Harlem joyously engaged in internalized racism with the song they sang in unison while clapping hands:

If you are White you are all right
If you are brown stick around
If you are yellow, you are mellow
If you are Black get back.

Kraft, a White man, and I, a Black woman who experienced double oppression being both female and Black, were programmed to accept roles of superiority and inferiority throughout our childhood play—deadly scripts. The story could have ended there, but it didn't. Our paths crossed at HT: the person having the power was the Black woman; the person needing an intervention was the White male. Education is the equalizer, as Pierce Burnette often said. The truth is not only for students but also for the faculty who teach those students!

- Dr. Alaine Hutson, a professor of history, joined Huston-Tillotson University in 2008. She specializes in African and Middle East history with an emphasis on slavery and gender in Islamic societies. Hutson has won numerous awards and fellowships including an NEH Award for Faculty 2017, UNCF/Mellon Faculty Fellow International residency as the first visiting research fellow at the newly opened Qatar National Library in 2018, and the Sam Taylor Fellowship administered by the United Methodist Church. Hutson published articles on Muslim women's spiritual authority in Northern Nigeria and enslavement of Africans and Baluchis in twentieth-century Arabia. She maintains a database of freed slaves in Arabia called REMAP (Runaways Enslaved and Manumitted on the Arabian Peninsula) at remapdatabase.org. Hutson is the lead professor in developing HT's Global Studies Program and is the liaison for the HT/UT global partnership.

- Dr. Theodore Francis II, an assistant professor of history, joined Huston-Tillotson University in 2012 and left HT in 2022 for a better paying position with greater research opportunities at a PWI. He taught courses on US history, African American history, and Caribbean history. He is a graduate of Warwick Academy (Bermuda), Morehouse College, and the University of Chicago. His doctoral dissertation, "Fantasy Island: Race, Colonial Politics, and the Desegregation of Tourism in the British Colony of Bermuda, 1881–1961," charts the role of African American tourists as well as popular protests in the process of desegregation in Bermuda in the late 1950s and early 1960s. Francis's primary research and writing interests include the African diaspora in the Caribbean and Americas; historical and contemporary issues of tourism; anti-colonial movements in the Caribbean; and Atlantic world slavery, resistance, and post-emancipation societies. He has worked with the William Monroe Trotter Institute for the Study of Black Culture. He engaged students in oral history projects.

- Dr. Amanda Masino was hired in 2011 as a biologist in the Department of Natural Sciences. In fall 2019, she became the chairperson of that department. Her accomplishments have been discussed in several places throughout this book. Additionally, she is a strong grant writer, bringing hundreds of thousands of dollars to enhance students' STEM research and internships. Masino received funding from Apple, St. David's Foundation, Hogg Foundation, and others. She collaborates with faculty in other disciplines, demonstrating the importance of STEM and humanities to work together. Recently, she worked with the Austin Department of Parks and Recreation to understand the movements of coyotes in Austin, including appearances on local television explaining that work. Masino is HT's Faculty Advisory Council president and is the liaison between the university's president and the faculty.

- Dr. Carlos M. Cervantes was hired in 2012 as professor and chair of kinesiology. He earned his PhD in sports and exercise education from Ohio State University. He engages students in numerous volunteer opportunities such as hosting a field day on HT's campus for Blackshear Elementary School students, working with students at the School for the Blind, and working with baseball athletes at Downs Field. Cervantes accompanies his students to conferences at which they observe and present. Taking advantage of Cervantes's collaborative teaching environment, his students participate in the exercise physiological and movement analysis lab, which positions them for emerging careers in kinesiology where people of color are underrepresented.

  Cervantes's research interest focuses on identifying underlying mechanisms affecting physical activity among individuals with disabilities. Secondary research interests include obesity health disparities, accessibility, and physical activity opportunities for individuals with disabilities, and professional preparation of pre-service teachers regarding teaching and including children with disabilities in physical education, sport, and recreational settings. He has presented his work at local, state, national, and international conferences. He is a member of the Society of Health and Physical Educators (SHAPE), the National Association for Kinesiology in Higher Education (NAKHE), the National Consortium for Physical Education for Individuals with Disabilities (NCPEID), and the Texas Association for Health, Physical Education, Recreation and Dance (TAHPERD), among others. His instructional effectiveness has been recognized by a number of awards and student evaluations. In his undergraduate courses, he includes service-learning experiences in school and community settings as well as infused use of instructional technologies. Cervantes is deeply connected to his students and works closely with potential students by spending time with them and their families. Students have great affection for him.

- Dr. Lorraine Samuels (2005) is an assistant professor of criminal justice and is chair of the Department of Social and Behavioral Sciences. She holds a doctorate degree from Prairie View A&M University and was the first female in the country to earn a PhD in juvenile justice. In addition, Samuels has master's degrees in juvenile justice and business administration. She teaches a cross-section of criminal justice courses (both online and traditional format), with a specialty in juvenile justice and human trafficking. Her research included the ADAM Project (a drug research program of the National Institute of Justice), Tobacco Prevention Initiative Project (evaluation of law enforcement and judges' attitudes in enforcing tobacco laws), and immigration and deportation issues (as they relate to criminality and delinquency). Her research interests include the conditions of children of the incarcerated and children of deported criminal aliens. Samuels and English Department colleagues, Professor Julie Hudson and Professor Shawanda Stewart, received funding in 2021 to create digital and physical exhibits that display artifacts and information about labor trafficking on the Texas-Mexico border.

    Samuels's publications include "Sexually Offending Youth in a State Detention Facility," *International Journal of Academic Research* (2009); "Difference in Parenting Style between African American Alcoholic and Non-alcoholic Parent" (2002); and "Mentoring Programs" (2002). Additionally, Professor Samuels is a regular presenter at conferences. She works with Discover Law, a program that HT and UT School of Law conduct in partnership. Recently, she and Dr. Murphy, psychologist, created a master's in forensic psychology that is waiting for board approval.

- Dr. Robert Ceresa joined the HT faculty in 2013 as an assistant professor of political science. He received a PhD in international relations from Florida International University and a master's degree in public affairs from the University of Minnesota Hubert H. Humphrey Institute of Public Affairs. He is a political and international relations scholar with broad multidisciplinary training in political development and participation, the effectiveness of community/civil society groups and organizations, and urban and ethnic politics (including Cuban Miami diaspora politics). His research focuses on the role actors at the level of the local community or society play in shaping larger cultural environments. In 2018 he published *Cuban American Political Culture and Civic Organizing: Tocqueville in Miami* (Palgrave). Ceresa was one of the leaders who planned and executed the inaugural Texas HBCU Conference at HT, April 1–2, 2022. The event brought all but two of Texas's HBCUs to share perspectives on the theme: Community-Centered Public-Policy, Civically Engaged Higher Education and the HBCU. Texas lawmakers, faculty, and students from participating HBCUs were either keynote speakers or seminar presenters. The second Texas HBCU Conference was held on HT's campus in March 2023.

- Dr. Azubike Okpalaeze began his employment at HT in 2013, in the School of Business and Technology, Computer Science Department, and later became the department chairperson. He provides students with knowledge about computer hardware, software, and computer communication network management through direct hands-on training, research, and teaching. He serves as the director of the Robotics Center and facilitates ongoing research on physical human-robot interaction. He supervises collaboration between HT and UT at Austin and Apptronik Systems Inc. in actualizing robotics experiments, design, and implementation. His research efforts are in robotics exoskeleton design and fabrication and robots' communication. He co-authored, with Dr. Abena Primo, "Minority Student Learning in an Introductory Computer Science Course," *Journal for Computing Sciences in Colleges*.

- HT could not survive without adjuncts. Dr. Robert Kellogg came to Huston-Tillotson in 2001 as an adjunct instructor and continues to teach accounting. He participated on the Tenure Promotion Committee and freely shares his knowledge with both faculty and administration. Dr. Anne Cirella-Urrutia, an adjunct professor in French for over fifteen years, organized and hosted the American Association of Teachers of French (AATF) Central Texas Chapter at Huston-Tillotson in 2017. She has written two books and frequently participates in professional conferences. Dr. Carolyn Golden, HT computer science professor, retired in 2014 and came back later that year in a part-time role as chairperson of Computer Sciences, spending almost as much time as when she was full time. She retired again in May 2020 but returned in spring 2023.

Professors Hired by Dr. Pierce Burnette
Below is a partial list of professors hired by Dr. Pierce Burnette.

- Dr. Abena Primo, an associate professor of computer science, has a PhD in computational analysis and modeling from Louisiana Tech University. She was hired in 2016 to teach in the School of Business and Technology. She conducts research in cybersecurity, mobile computing, and machine learning. In her time at Huston-Tillotson University she received several awards including the IEEE CVPR Biometric Workshop's High Impact Award and the Huston-Tillotson Career Readiness Award. She is on the organizing committee of several conferences and journals in her field. She published several poems in the HT literary magazine *900 Chicon*. Dr. Primo is the editor of SBT's *HT Blockchain Bi-Weekly Newsletter*, first published in June 2021. This newsletter is aimed at making Blockchain concepts fun and easy to follow. It covers various topics such as FinTech, a term used to refer to technology built to support financial services.
- Dr. Rohan Thompson, associate professor of business administration, joined HT in 2016 as chair of the department. In July 2020, he became the interim dean of the School of Business and Technology and in summer 2021 became dean. Under his leadership the department maintained its accreditation by the Accreditation Council for Business Schools and Programs (ACBSP). He also ensured that the business programs, including the MBA, continue to be among the top enrollment programs at Huston-Tillotson University. Under his leadership, SBT established an integrated student success center, WeCare Center, that strengthens financial literacy and student persistence. Thompson is also a recipient of numerous awards including the Career Readiness Award for Students at Huston-Tillotson University in 2019 and Achievements in Black Austin in 2017. Thompson earned BBA and MBA degrees from Wayland Baptist University and a PhD in Global Leadership – Organizational Management from Indiana Institute of Technology.
- Other faculty members hired during Dr. Pierce Burnette's tenure were Dr. Alexandra Avila (2020, Communication), Kelene Blake-Fallon (2020, Kinesiology), Jason Carter (2017, Management), Jonathan Cosgrove (2017, Kinesiology), Cory Greathouse (2021, English), Deepti Gupta (2021, Computer Science), Dr. Farzana Hussain (2016, Mathematics), Rebecca Lawrence (2020, Mathematics), Hector

Macfarland (2017, Marketing, and Director of Entrepreneur and Innovative Center, off campus), Rosa Mino (2021, Biology), Dr. Yalan Ning (2015, Chemistry), Willian Oliver (2021, Music), Dr. Sarah Eileen Slaton (2019, Mathematics), Dr. Wenxian Tan (Biology), Rafael Vela (2017, Communication), and Alicia Zavala-Garcia (2020, Spanish).

Note that three of the recently hired faculty members were in education. Dr. Sarah Santillanes, chair of Education Preparation, came in 2020 and left in 2024; her colleagues Mr. Anthony Fairley and Dr. Jesse Rivers both came in 2021. The three of them worked to rebuild the education program which in earlier decades was an esteemed department. It is unclear how and why this department had to be totally rebuilt under Pierce Burnette's leadership, but faculty turnover was extremely high. The education master's program that started under Earvin's administration and with the leadership of Dr. Ruth Kane had no students after Kane left about six years earlier. Pierce Burnette could have done much more to build the Department of Education Preparation. This was a missed opportunity for student recruitment and retention for the graduate program and for female students. Male students are being supported in the Apple Male Teachers initiative.

Faculty Views of Dr. Pierce Burnette—Mixed Reviews

Having inherited an incredible faculty and hired others equally prepared in their field, Pierce Burnette could trust them to impart knowledge, wisdom, and compassion to students. Professors named above sought to implement Pierce Burnette's goal of "academic excellence as the great equalizer." Entrusted in faculty hands were the directives to make students know they are geniuses and to act accordingly. Yet, some professors believe they were not always valued for the work they do, the time they give, the knowledge they have, and the lives they educate. Substantial raises were not offered (with an emphasis on substantial), acknowledgments were few, retirees were not honored, and many administrative team members infrequently practiced IDEAL as part of their work ethic. These are concerns expressed by some professors surveyed. Another concern was about limited support services for students. Additionally, some faculty who were most knowledgeable about students' tutoring needs were not included in critical decisions about programs and personnel. The history of the Writers' Studio (WS) was a case in point, as described by one of my interviewees:

> I started the Writers' Studio in 2003, under a Title III activity for Writing Across the Curriculum. In those first years, I trained and supervised the Peer Writing Consultants myself, while teaching full-time. Gradually, we were able to hire part-time coordinators and sometimes to have full-time faculty serve some hours (as part of their teaching load) each week in the Writers' Studio. Finally, with the hire of Ryan Sharp, we were able to have a full-time coordinator to oversee all aspects of the Writers' Studio work. That work is more than a center for tutoring students with writing projects, although that is the core; the Writers' Studio also offered supplemental instruction, workshops, and assistance in classes, which met once a week in the Writers' Studio. It was the nexus of the writing in the disciplines program at HT. I also saw it move from a then unused classroom in A–L to a computer lab in J–M, which was outfitted with new Mac computers with writing and media production software funded by a 2010 Title III activity. So, for fifteen years the English faculty and I worked to develop a Writers' Studio that was a model for other small institutions. That department created the lab using best practices and initially staffed it with well-qualified individuals. When the director left, an administrator was given the responsibility of setting up the search committee to find a new director. The English department members were not key players in selecting the director nor do they work in the umbrella department where the lab is now located. There is the feeling that the Writers' Studio is no longer vibrant or meeting the needs of students. We are fighting to keep it from going dark under the new administration who made decisions without consulting us or knowing what work the Writers' Studio did.[94]

As a students' president, Pierce Burnette was sometimes perceived by faculty as either indiscriminately taking students' side or not being as responsive to faculty collective concerns. During our 2017 interview I shared this assessment with Pierce Burnette. Her response was, "I was not aware of that perception and if that perception does exist, it does not reflect what I want to convey. I need to do something about changing that perception." In 2022, some faculty members still held that view.

What are the collective thoughts of faculty towards Pierce Burnette? I created an online survey to collect faculty input on all four presidents. Thirty-one professors responded to the survey between November 2017 and March 2018 (during Pierce Burnette's third year of presidency).[95] The candid responses reveal that most faculty viewed her in a positive light, but others were clearly dissatisfied with some aspects of her presidency. Below are the questions asked and my summary of composite responses.

1. *What were your initial impressions of Dr. Pierce Burnette? Did that impression change over time?*

Statements from several respondents conveyed that Pierce Burnette's administration was still in the early days; however, she brought many skills to HT. She was seen as a visionary who was dynamic, charismatic, friendly, ambitious, positive, intelligent, passionate, detail-oriented, and dedicated to thoughtful change. She was perceived as having a business mind and that she believed HT was a calling on her life. Some felt connection with her and her goals. Contrary to these comments, one individual stated, "My initial impression was that Dr. Pierce Burnette is amiable, but unseasoned as the leader of an academic institution."

2. *What was her leadership style?*

Respondents believed that Pierce Burnette employed a corporate-based leadership style that was collaborative, engaging and business-minded. They believed she was inclusive and focused on people taking responsibility for their actions. They also saw her as reflective and organized and provided a model for what she expected of her team. One faculty member stated, "While I respect her and appreciate her, we have moved in different directions from where I think HT needs to focus on for growth." Another faculty member said, "I rarely see her, except at university events, so I assume Dr. Pierce Burnette preferred to lead through her circle."

3. *What did Dr. Pierce Burnette do to create a family environment at HT?*
    - A respondent stated that Dr. Pierce Burnette emphasized the fact that HT is a "fRAMily." "Dr. Pierce Burnette 's sensitivity to details lead to her ability to reflect care and concern. Both of these factors are important family values that translate into a family environment such as found at HT."
    - Family is her ongoing theme. She engages students in all types of activities.
    - She knows [students] personally. She calls them her genius generation. She has a positive attitude.
    - She is present with faculty and students: attending their activities and engaging in activities with them.
    - She is approachable and always willing to listen and to speak to faculty and

students directly; she knows us by name.
- "She promotes compassion and thoroughness and dedication of self to the cause.... Working together for higher ideals." Like in some families, she has favorite kids.

4. *Did Dr. Pierce Burnette give preferential treatment towards any individuals or groups? Please state who and how.*

My reading of the responses seemed to indicate that some faculty perceived that Pierce Burnette did not achieve her own standard of IDEAL and was partial to administrators, faculty, and staff who were "yes, ma'am" employees. They felt she did not advocate equally for all faculty and staff, and she elevated people whom she favored, some of whom did not seem to have credentials or expertise to merit their promotions. Many respondents believed she had high administrative turnovers in a short time—for example, five financial aid directors in six years of her administration.

5. *What are her major strengths/accomplishments and weaknesses?*
    - Many of Pierce Burnette's strengths and weaknesses were mentioned in answers to other survey questions. In a short amount of time, Pierce Burnette shifted the image of HT in Austin and reengaged with the Austin community including religious, business, and political entities. She took pride in showcasing her students, giving them opportunities to connect with various organizations. Her extensive community involvement also raised eyebrows with some constituents, deeming it might be more about her than HT and its students.
    - Pierce Burnette reorganized administrative structures, empowering academic departments and faculty-led entities such as Faculty Advisory Council to be more engaged in decision-making, although seen as insufficient by some.
    - Prior to the pandemic, she increased enrollment, retention, funding, and structural improvements. Dr. Pierce Burnette had an earnest desire to make the institution thrive. This was also true during the pandemic as she led in uncharted territory.

6. *How did Dr. Pierce Burnette handle conflicts, disagreement and/or dissension related to students, faculty and/or staff?*
    - During her tenure at HT, I've noticed that she tends to defend decisions rather than listen to concerns or make changes.

- She tries to meet with those in conflicts and work out differences.
- She is not as proactive as she could be in making sure that the core value of IDEAL is carried out by all entities.
- Dr. Pierce Burnette handled the firing of a CAE (Center for Academic Excellent) staff horribly. Students valued that staff member because they knew she cared. When the opportunity came for her to reconcile the situation, she didn't do it.

As HT's president, Pierce Burnette strived for excellence that can only occur through positive and wholesome relationships among all constituents. How she related to her faculty, either intentionally or unintentionally, influenced how faculty and students viewed her and each other. Education is the equalizer; student/faculty relationships are the vehicles through which education occurs.

Faculty Governance

Getting the approval to organize a faculty organization was problematic under McMillan and Earvin. However, Pierce Burnette embraced the Faculty Advisory Council (FAC) by engaging with them, meeting with the leadership, and encouraging faculty feedback on issues related to raises. Sometimes her responses were slower than would have been expected; still, she was approachable.

In 2017 Pierce Burnette responded to repeated faculty outcries over low salaries and a lack of pay raises for about eleven years (under previous presidents). Faculty were upset then (and continue to be) that she hired a consultant firm for $40,000 to review salary scales at HT compared to those other universities. The subsequent report to the Faculty Advisory Council left faculty feeling that the process was unclear and that money paid to the consultant firm could have been applied to salary inequalities. The findings of the consultants were just what faculty already knew: they were grossly underpaid. As a result of these findings, Pierce Burnette pledged to increase salaries but shared that realistically there was no way to close the salary gaps found in all academic ranks. She said that a minimal raise would be provided during the 2018–2019 academic year; it came during both the 2019–2020 and 2021–2022 academic years, those preceding her retirement. Those two raises increased a given salary from $59,000 to $62,000—a mere $3,000, which was still more than received in previous years. Pierce Burnette urged the FAC to come up with a formula for how salary increases should be implemented, e.g., by the lowest paid or according to rank or longevity. The first round of raises gave preference to those paid the least. While something was better than nothing, salary was only one of many faculty concerns.

In their monthly meetings with the president and provost, the FAC's chairperson and secretary informed them of the pulse of the faculty. Some faculty members were clearly hurting, and the source of that hurt was over how people were appointed without credible input from key stakeholders and how this approach flew in the face of shared faculty governance. Pierce Burnette asked to be invited to a FAC meeting during fall 2019 to address this concern.[96] She stated:

> The reason I want to come to you directly is that I just keep on hearing a repeated thread that is troubling me; I want you to hear directly from me as I want to hear from you. The continued thread is that faculty members do not feel valued. It bothers me because I do value my faculty. I want excellent education for our students and learning does not come without an excellent faculty; so clearly my faculty is valuable to me. The one thing I do not worry about is our academic program.... The second thread is that I did not believe in shared governance, but in token governance. That was really disconcerting to me, for that is neither who I am nor how I run my administration.... The perception of my engaging faculty in token governance came from my appointment of an individual to associate provost [*without going through a search committee*—implied but not stated by Pierce Burnette]. As president, I reserve the right to appoint persons I need with certain skill set.... I am not displeased with my decision. There have been several appointments since I've been on campus—the provost, the dean, the librarian—where I've involved and engaged faculty....
>
> That being said, I support shared governance. I believe without the support of every unit on campus our institution will not grow.... We have great opportunities to be "the jewel" in the city. We all have a role to play in getting our story told.[97]

The openness at that meeting clarified some of the faculty concerns. One professor gave the example of students being placed in a full class without the permission of the faculty member, or an instance of students being placed in classes a week into the semester without first notifying the professor. Another example given of token governance was the removal of the writing studio lab from under the English Department, not mentioned by the person most vocal about that issue; she was totally silent in that meeting. Later that person told me that there was a disconnect between what the president said and the actions she took: on the one hand she ostensibly valued faculty shared governance, but on the other hand she justified hiring an individual who did not go through a search process. The invested person told me she did not believe speaking up would have done any good.

While at the meeting, Pierce Burnette acknowledged that there were concerning areas at HT that she did not see and therefore depended on her team to inform and advise her. Owning some of HT's broken processes, she hoped that the few mishaps did not overshadow the good work being done at HT. Perceptions are real to those who perceive them; but owning them, examining them, and being transparent with each other will yield great dividends. Pierce Burnette, unlike McMillan and Earvin, was willing to engage in conversations with faculty around institutional issues and shared governance. Embracing visible changes in the infrastructure, some faculty members thanked Pierce Burnette for the work she did and her visibility in the community. Many left that meeting with the president feeling better or at least open to her perspective. Pierce Burnette gave faculty permission to call her as needed.

Pierce Burnette: The Covid-19 President

President Pierce Burnette will go down in Huston-Tillotson's history as moving the university through the worst pandemic in the US in 100 years. Her analogy for her presidency was flying the plane while building it. That analogy aptly applies to major on-the-spot decisions that had to be made when the pandemic was officially recognized in the US in March 2020. Her initial email response to the HT fRAMily on March 6, 2020 was her first step towards keeping all constituents safe:

> I wanted to ensure that you are aware of Huston-Tillotson's proactive and preventative stance towards the spread of the coronavirus (Covid-19). I have convened an HT Pandemic Preparedness team, specifically for monitoring the state of the coronavirus and for enacting best practices on our campus, as recommended by CDC, WHO, state and local agencies. HT serves a vital role in our greater Austin community, and I ask that you continue to remain vigilant in your daily efforts to prevent the spread of germs.

The letter listed standard precautions and provided important websites for review.

In Dr. Pierce Burnette's March 12 email, she stated:

> The health and safety of our entire campus community remain paramount. Thus, we have decided the following: 1) Spring break will be extended for students by an additional week to March 29th; 2) Beginning March 30th, ALL classes will move to online, until further notice; and 3) Residence halls will close

on Sunday, March 15, and remain closed, until further notice. (On-campus residents will receive further instruction from the Office of Residence life as developments unfold.)

Students, during this timeframe, you must do the following: 1) Remain in close contact with your respective faculty members; 2) Once online classes begin on March 30th, remotely connect to Canvas and Office 365 daily; 3) Sign up to receive campus alerts and notifications by text message at https://www.getrave.login/htu; and 4) Monitor frequently the university's web page dedicated to HT's Coronavirus Preparedness and our official university social media channels on Facebook, Instagram, and Twitter.

These are austere times and far from what any of us expected to be occurring during this spring semester. I appreciate greatly your continuing commitment to focusing on our collective efforts to remain vigilant, protecting ourselves and others from becoming ill.

In Union, Strength
Colette Pierce Burnette, Ed.D.[98]

Pierce Burnette sent another correspondence to the HT community. In that letter she reaffirmed HT's priority to keep the community safe. She positioned the postponement of spring break as an opportunity for students to prepare to engage in online learning by encouraging students to access the "Student Learning at a Distance" posting found on Canvas. This was also when faculty were asked to make the swift pivot from face-to-face teaching to interfacing with new online technology. This letter also announced that in accordance with Governor Greg Abbott's executive orders, HT would postpone its 2020 spring graduation. Pierce Burnette empathized with graduating seniors who would miss out on their special day. Finally, she informed resident students that they would receive a room and board credit applied to their balance. In the midst of the global pandemic, "We work through this together."

Between letters, Pierce Burnette had many things to figure out. HT was responsible for refunding students for unused room and board. This could have caused a financial disaster without the federal government's CARES Act, which provided funds for businesses, including colleges and universities affected by the pandemic.[99] HT signed and returned to the Department of Education a Certification and Agreement for Emergency Aid Grants to Students under the American Rescue Plan. HT's $2,467,276 was distributed to students in direct grants and by giving all enrolled students a notebook computer and a hotspot if needed. Many of the institution's students would not have been able to complete spring 2020 without both of these resources, since courses went online and they and family might not have had access to needed internet services. HT used students' FAFSA forms as one of the determining factors for how much each student got. For academic year 2020–2021, all students' debt was paid off by First United Methodist Church, bringing finances to HT while relieving student debt that might prevent them from returning to HT.[100]

On November 29, 2020, Pierce Burnette sent the email below to the Huston-Tillotson University campus community:

> The past nine months have been challenging, demanding, and wearisome for us all. Yet, step-by-step, hour-by-hour, day-by-day, despite a global pandemic, we have persisted. Students have remained steadfast in their pursuit of academic excellence. Faculty has remained tirelessly committed to finding and implementing innovative ways of teaching and cultivating the minds of the genius generation. Staff has continued to deploy support services and activities specifically designed to remove barriers to student success. Students, faculty, and staff, all working together, staying focused on our mission of education as the great equalizer. I appreciate you all.
>
> Based upon prevailing science, the advice of local and national health experts on stopping the spread of COVID-19, the current and expected surges of cases and deaths, and no vaccine expected for release to the general public until early spring—Huston-Tillotson University will remain online for the Spring Semester of the 2020–2021 academic year. The safety and health of the entire campus community remain paramount as our top priority. Please understand that the decision to be fully online was by no means an easy one. Unfortunately, the key factors leading to our decision for the fall term are still prevalent, and in some cases, even more daunting. Continuing with fully online teaching and learning is the best decision for our campus.
>
> In this temporary time of teaching and learning virtually, the University remains steadfastly committed to providing students with timely and engaging support. We continue to highly encourage students to utilize the many resources available to them. Students and their families can visit our Online Support site found here for a listing of resources designed to promote student success. In addition to the virtual Downs-Jones Library, a few examples of student resources found at our Online Support site are:
> - Automated Faculty Advising Scheduling
> - One-on-one Virtual Tutoring Options
> - Ram Connect: Personalized Technology Support

- Emergency Grant Funds
- Teletherapy and Disability Support
- Workshops & Training

Additionally, Huston-Tillotson University will be providing registered students with a persistence grant to assist with the costs of obtaining an education during such a tumultuous time. Please expect to receive more information about Huston-Tillotson University's persistence grant over the next few days.

Students, moment by moment you get closer to earning your degree. Stay encouraged. Stay focused. Please take advantage of every single resource available to you. These resources are all designed to remove barriers to your success—particularly during these unprecedented times. I encourage you to take a few moments to research all of the services and resources available to you—they are all just one click away. Our immense desire is for you to finish strong.

All updates regarding the coronavirus will continue to be communicated via HT email, the https://my.htu.edu/ics portal, the Coronavirus Preparedness campus link, and all official University social media channels on Facebook, Instagram, and Twitter. If you cannot locate a resource you need or have questions, please send an email to ht_covid-19@htu.edu.

Continuing with teaching and learning virtually for the spring semester is a crucial step in keeping us healthy, stopping the spread and defeating this virus so we can all be together soon. Please remain vigilant in protecting yourselves and your loved ones from the spread of COVID-19—wear your mask, wash your hands, avoid crowds, and maintain a safe distance.

Huston-Tillotson University is a much stronger university despite, or even perhaps because of, this global pandemic. We are all in this together. And together, we are getting through it.

On December 20, 2020, Pierce Burnette sent her holiday greeting to HT's Campus Community:

As 2020 winds down I wanted to express how grateful I am for each of you. It wasn't the year we envisioned. We sailed into a storm we did not see coming. I am very proud of how our campus came together as a community supporting each other with hope, resilience, intentionality, and compassion.

Please stay safe and have a joyful holiday break. Happy Holidays!

With Gratitude,
Colette Pierce Burnette, Ed.D.

CHAPTER 4

Dr. Pierce Burnette's priorities during Covid were for the university's safety and the students' receiving excellent education. She sent an email to her faculty and staff on February 4, 2021:

> In these extraordinary times, my appreciation for each of you is immense. Your commitment to student success is a gift to our mission and those we serve.
>
> The year 2020 will undoubtedly be recorded in the University's history as one when the entire campus community banded together and demonstrated the power of persistence. Moving into 2021, we continue to navigate situations we have never experienced before. We just keep building on what we learn from one day to the next, becoming a stronger university.
>
> Unfortunately, the fortitude and resilience of our campus does not isolate nor protect us from the tragedies and tribulations of a global pandemic. Please join me in extending love and prayers to members of the campus community who have battled the virus themselves and to those who have lost loved ones.
>
> For now, we are together apart. I look forward to the time when we can all be together again on campus. We will continue to follow the science and take proper measures to ensure the safety of our community. If you were unable to watch the University-hosted panel on dispelling myths / telling truths about the vaccines, please contact Ms. Linda Jackson for details on how to watch the recording. It was extremely informative.
>
> Finally, at this time we are planning to have an in-person highly modified socially distanced outdoor commencement ceremony honoring our 2020 and 2021 graduates. We are also planning for students to return to campus this upcoming Fall Semester. I emphasize that these are plans at this time—we will follow the same process with holding listening sessions, following the science, CDC guidelines, and all governmental policies. More details will be forthcoming.
>
> In preparation for whenever we are blessed to have our momentous in-person reunion, I am asking everyone to work together now to welcome students back to a vastly and positively different campus than the one they left in March of 2020.
>
> In Union we find our Strength,
> Colette Pierce Burnette, Ed.D.
> President and Chief Executive Officer

During these unprecedented times, many protocols were put into place. HT hired a Safe Healthy Rams coordinator to supervise Covid-19 efforts. The Covid-19 coordinator managed the newly created Covid app, called HT Ram

Check, which had to be shown upon entry on campus. The coordinator monitored those who had the virus or were quarantined on campus. Additionally, a 77-page Covid-19 document was posted on HT's website, with updates as needed.

Below are the guiding protocols for face-to-face campus reentry.

1. **Masks** are required for everyone in public indoor environments and recommended outdoors when unable to physically distance. For more information on masking requirements and other expectations, please review the full Reactivation document.
2. **Routine COVID-19 testing** will be required throughout the fall semester for any student, faculty, or staff member who is not fully vaccinated.
3. **Daily Health Screening** required for campus entry and participation in campus activities. Students, faculty and staff will complete the screening using the HT Ram Check mobile application.
4. **Vaccination or an approved exemption is required** for all students. Vaccination is highly encouraged for all students, faculty, and staff. We will have on-campus COVID-19 vaccination clinics that will be open to HT faculty, staff, students, alumni and their family members. More information on vaccine availability in the Austin area can be found here. Vaccination and testing services were also available to HT constituents at **Sandra Joy Anderson Community Health and Wellness Center. (NOTE: Incentives were given to students who had proof of vaccination.)**
5. When available, students and others were encouraged to get boosters that were administered on campus and at the care center.
6. **On HT's Canvas website**, Covid updates are regularly posted.

Pierce Burnette rose to the effort that overseeing a pandemic required. She made the right call to switch HT from face-to-face to virtual. With CARES Covid money, she was able to upgrade HT's technological system needed for successful all-campus online classes. Each department devised ways to be present and to serve students in different and unique ways. The campus was equipped with sanitizers and humidifiers in all offices and classrooms. Students and faculty were given either a notebook computer or a laptop. All critical, first responder employees such as IT staff, deans, and even the president stayed on campus.

Focusing on students' mental health and their ability to navigate classes at home was essential. Pierce Burnette did not expect her final two and a half years to be in crisis mode, yet her life experiences prepared her for "such a time as this." If a

CHAPTER 4

survey were given on her leadership skills during the pandemic, I believe that the results would have ranked her high. Through her leadership, the HT community was kept safe with relatively few Covid cases. Pierce Burnette described her feelings and actions during the Covid-19 pandemic in an interview with Jennifer Stayton.

> When you are a president of an institution that serves 70 percent Pell [grant] eligible [students], you're always in a crisis. You're always in a crisis. It can be expensive to serve excellence to the low income, especially when you're as determined as we are to give them excellence. So you're always in a crisis.
>
> But then a "real" crisis hits, and you jump in it and start leading your institution, making decisions, informed decisions through a lot of sleepless nights. Sleepless days, actually, I won't even say nights where you don't know what's next. I mean, we ran into a storm that we did not see coming with a ship that wasn't quite that stable. In higher education, we don't make hard right turns. We just don't. And it forced us to make hard right turns.
>
> We are not an online institution, but when you have a president who is a techie, an engineer, you invest a lot of time and effort into building out the physical and digital plant. We had the technology and the infrastructure in place to offer online [education]. My faculty were very malleable and asked for an extra week for them to be able to incorporate or change over their curriculum to be online. And they did it in a week. We extended spring break, and we lifted this 145-year-old institution fully online in a week. And we did it successfully.
>
> We had some bumps in the road, and we learned a lot. Like, for example, the internet is not a utility. Everybody doesn't have it. So we had to quickly pivot to accommodate that for our students. Many of our students didn't have computers at home so we had to quickly pivot to raise money—pre-CARES Act—to raise money for us to be able to offer the services to students, so we shipped them out to their house. So we almost became like a mini-Amazon where you're shipping; you're procuring; all the things that go on behind the scenes to get students what they needed for them to be successful.
>
> If you focus on student success, your decisions will be excellent decisions and then stay within the means of what you can do, but at the same time demand excellence. And then you really can't steer from that.
>
> So the crisis itself was very stressful. I have two vice presidents who came to campus with me every day because even though the campus was closed—we were online—the university was not closed. We still had to process mail. We still had to bring in a class. We still had to be recruiting students, and we lifted

everything virtually. So when I think about that, in hindsight, that was God. Because when you're in it, you're just doing it. And we did it. I'm very proud. We had no layoffs, no furloughs. We had some attrition in our enrollment but very minimal compared to some of our sister institutions. We were able to hold on to our students.[101]

Pierce Burnette led HT in other ways during her two and a half years of Covid. On February 14, 2021, all of Texas, including Austin, faced a severe ice storm, resulting in electricity being turned off at HT for many days. Classes closed February 14 to 22. Even when classes resumed online, many students were still affected from lack of internet service. Some students dealt with partially or completely destroyed homes.

Another crisis came on August 25, 2021, when an armed man was near HT, resulting in a lockdown. According to an email from Dr. Pierce Burnette:

> At approximately 12:25 PM today, we were made aware of an individual armed with a weapon in an area adjacent to campus.
>
> The Huston-Tillotson University Campus Safety Department was alerted, and local authorities were immediately contacted. At the same time, a university emergency alert system was activated, communicating directly to students, faculty, and staff to stay inside.
>
> Huston-Tillotson University sheltered in place, all gates were closed, and access on and off campus was restricted while authorities investigated and searched for the individual. Once the investigation was completed by the Austin Police Department, the campus was given an all clear to return to normal operations at approximately 3:45 PM.
>
> I am grateful to students, faculty, and staff for remaining patient and allowing our campus safety and local law enforcement authorities to resolve the situation while keeping our campus community safe.

Clearly, Pierce Burnette kept HT informed during crisis situations, exhibiting excellent leadership qualities particularly during the global pandemic, resulting in few HT fRAMily members getting Covid. In the midst of Covid, several unusual presidential tasks were required. Pierce Burnette led HT during the 2021 Valentine's Day Austin freeze that resulted in HT going offline for four days due to lack of electricity in many homes. Additionally, on January 31, 2022, and the first day of Black History Month, February 1, 2022, there were bomb threats at twenty-one HBCUs. Although Huston-Tillotson was not one of these, HT was placed on alert as a protection strategy. Fear that it would be next was calmed by HT's preparedness to deal with such attacks.

Concurrently with the pandemic, HT was in the midst of its 2020 reaffirmation. This is a difficult and intense process under any administration, as was described in previous chapters. With much of HT online, Pierce Burnette was able get the reports to SACSCOC, meet with the team online, and to successfully fulfill the requirements of reaccreditation. Pierce Burnette enthusiastically announced that HT was reaccredited at a reaffirmation party. Her March 4, 2021, letter to HT revealed her excitement.

> Dear Faculty and Staff,
> As we conclude our On-Site Virtual Visit of the Decennial Reaffirmation for SACSCOC, I write to thank the entire campus for your hard work and commitment throughout the process. I am very proud to share that the SACSCOC on-site committee will be recommending Huston-Tillotson University for reaffirmation to the SACSCOC Board, which convenes in December, for a final vote and decision.
>
> The process and the feedback received are invaluable to us on our quest for excellence and continuous improvement, in particular, for our Quality Enhancement Plan (QEP) RAMSS (Ready to Attain Maximum Student Success). We can now focus on further defining, assessing, and operationalizing the fusion of the selected three competencies into the student experience.
>
> We have a lot to be proud of, especially our students. As noted by the committee, our students are a clear reflection of the strength of the university. Moreover, the university's strength was demonstrated by our ability to navigate this process amid a global pandemic and one week after a climatic upheaval. We were able to deliver at a very high level of excellence. Many institutions would have crumbled under that type of pressure. Yet, we continued to meet our mission and move the campus forward.
>
> Thank you to all of the faculty, staff, and students who participated in the interviews. Thank you to all of the faculty and staff who worked behind the scenes to prepare our Focus Report, assembled additional information on request, and kept all of the other moving parts moving. Your dedication to the university and its mission shone through, even in a virtual setting. The teamwork exemplified during this process is a compliment to all and a standard I know we will continue to uphold. Our work is not done. We must keep pressing towards the mark.

I am grateful to serve with you and proud of our beloved 146-year-old institution – Huston-Tillotson University.

In Union, we find our Strength,
Colette Pierce Burnette, Ed.D.
President and CEO

HT reaffirmation is a major accomplishment, especially considering it was done during Covid, and there were *NO* recommendations. Pierce Burnette left her presidency bequeathing the new president without reaccreditation worries.

Dr. Colette Pierce Burnette: Her Final Decision

Pierce Burnette came to HT aware that her success depended largely on her developing a successful team while engaging all constituencies. A major educational goal was getting her "genius students" to their destination of being contributors as global citizens. The route of excellent education was couched in IDEAL, nurtured in a family environment where everyone counts. Pierce Burnette, the first female president of the merged institution—led by the spirit of Mary Branch, president of Tillotson (1933–1944), and her God—entered her presidency neither as a job nor as a career but as a calling from the Lord. Embracing the mission and vision of HT, she viewed her students as geniuses, expecting them to rise to that label. Not always perfect in her treatment of others and the outcomes reached, she was perfect in the vision she held for her students.

With HT's successful reaffirmation, a capable navigation of Covid challenges, and with substantial HT and community acclaim, HT's constituents and neighboring communities believed that Pierce Burnette's presidency would last for several more years. She told me in an interview that it would take at least ten years to complete her goals. In a later conversation, Pierce Burnette related that she had considered retiring from HT in her fifth year, but Covid happened; she knew she could not leave HT at that critical time. Then, on December 2, 2021, fewer than seven years into her tenure, Pierce Burnette sent this email to the HT fRAMily. Most were surprised, although there was a rumor that she had applied for presidencies elsewhere but was not selected.

> After considerable deliberation, thought, and reflection, I have decided that the time is right for me to pass the baton of leadership. I have informed the Board of Trustees of my intent to retire from my position as President and CEO of Huston-Tillotson University, effective June 30, 2022.

CHAPTER 4

Almost seven years ago, I began my journey at Huston-Tillotson University – Austin's oldest institution of higher learning and only Historically Black College and University, a beautiful albeit hidden jewel in Austin. From the first moment I stepped on this campus as the sixth President and CEO, I felt a sense of purpose. I was enveloped by a drive and commitment to strive tirelessly to foster a student-centered administration, a collegial and inclusive environment, and a culture of excellence – recognized and respected locally by the Austin community as well as on a national and global stage.

I have been blessed to serve our students with a supportive Board of Trustees and outstanding, deeply committed and mission-minded faculty and staff throughout my tenure. *Together* we have worked collaboratively, innovatively, and creatively to achieve several extraordinary successes. *Together*, we held true to our core values of IDEAL – integrity, diversity, excellence, accountability, and leadership. *Together*, we successfully launched our Career Pathways Initiative across our entire campus curriculum and a stellar MBA program at our expanded footprint, the Center for Entrepreneurship and Innovation. *Together*, we were selected as the only All-Steinway School in Central Texas. *Together* we launched a groundbreaking African American Male Teacher Initiative in partnership with Apple. *Together*, we forged sustainable and reciprocal relationships with Fortune 50 companies, Independent School Districts, and Non-Profits. *Together*, we welcomed our largest incoming freshman class with open arms and celebrated our largest graduating class in recent institutional history. *Together*, we lifted an entire 146-year-old brick and mortar institution entirely online – in two weeks – during an unprecedented global pandemic. *Together*, we witnessed an unparalleled increase in friend-raising and fundraising through grants, corporate sponsorships, donations, and community engagement. *Together*, all financial metrics reflecting the overall performance, fiscal health, efficiency, and sustainability are securely pointing in a positive direction. *Together*, we resoundingly showed persistence as our superpower. *Together*, we have achieved all of this and so much more. As I said during my inauguration in 2015, we have built this plane while flying it together.

Serving as the first woman president and CEO of Huston-Tillotson University since the merger of Tillotson College and Samuel Huston College will forever remain one of my most treasured and most valued life experiences. I have learned far more from my students (our genius generation), my esteemed faculty, and my amazing staff than they have learned from me. I am eternally grateful and humbled by the grace, love, commitment, encouragement, and willingness to embrace change and innovation you gave me during my tenure. My greatest hopes for the University's future are to maintain forward momentum, continue to radiate as a jewel in the violet crown of Austin, and continue transforming the lives of thousands of students and their families as they steadfastly persist towards the great equalizer – their education – earning their degree. The Board of Trustees is deeply committed to maintaining that momentum and assuring a smooth transition.

I love the HBCU mission in general and this University specifically. I look forward to seeing Huston-Tillotson University continue to prosper. I will be everlastingly proud to have played a role in the University's transformation, evolution to excellence, and growth. It has been my calling and an honor to serve. Huston-Tillotson University community, my fRAMily, thank you.

In Union, Strength,
Colette Pierce Burnette, Ed.D.
President & CEO

Compared to the previous three presidents (President King, twenty-three years; McMillan, twelve years; Earvin, fifteen years) Pierce Burnette had the fewest years under her belt. In her seven years, Dr. Pierce Burnette established numerous personal and institutional friends. Many of her constituents wrote to her on her Facebook page that they regretted her decision to leave but wished her well. Fellow presidents of HBCUs also sent their good wishes in a video to her. Many appreciation activities occurred, culminating in an Austin/HT gala in her honor, with proceeds going to a named scholarship on behalf of her parents, Colon and Ruth Pierce.

Perhaps Dr. Carol McDonald, chair of the Huston-Tillotson University Board of Trustees, best summarized in her news release how most community persons and many HT constituents viewed Pierce Burnette's presidency and her contributions.[102]

Huston-Tillotson University (HT) has been blessed to have Dr. Pierce Burnette's leadership for the past seven years. Her vision and perseverance have made HT a stronger, more vibrant, and more visible institution in Austin and beyond.

Since being named president in 2015, Dr. Pierce Burnette's tenure at HT has been one success after another. She has remained focused on HT's mission, serving students with excellence and compassion while carefully stewarding the University's resources and being active in the community. During this time, the HT endowment has increased by more than 55 percent. In 2021, she led

HT through its Southern Association of Colleges and Schools Commission on Colleges (SACSCOC) reaccreditation visit. The reaffirmation team reported no findings and fully recommended the SACSCOC's Board of Trustees for continuing HT's accreditation.

Under Dr. Pierce Burnette's leadership, HT initiated a series of new degree programs and innovations. In Fall 2018, HT expanded its footprint by opening the Center for Entrepreneurship and Innovation (CEI) on Springdale Road in East Austin. The following year, HT began a Master of Business Administration program designed for working individuals. At the same time, HT expanded the Center for Adult and Continuing Education and created the Center for Academic Innovation and Transformation (CAIT). Other degree programs planned and initiated during Dr. Pierce Burnette's tenure include undergraduate programs in Environmental Justice and Global Studies and the enhancement of the University's Science, Technology, Engineering, and Math (STEM) programs, with biology becoming the fastest-growing major at HT.

Dr. Pierce Burnette's historic tenure also included HT's collaboration with Tesla on a manufacturing engineering curriculum and a career progression internship for undergraduate students. She also solidified and expanded HT's partnership with Apple, resulting in the University receiving global exposure and recognition for her passion project, the African American Male Teachers Initiative.

From the beginning, Dr. Pierce Burnette has focused the University on building fiscal strength, forging strategic alliances, and achieving a culture of excellence in academics and student life while remaining student-centered, collegial, and inclusive. She guided HT to years of increased student enrollment, campus initiatives, and community partnerships. These include the largest recorded freshmen class, advancement in the University's listing in the National Register of Historic Places, adoption of the UNCF Career Pathways Initiative as the University's Quality Enhancement Plan, and HT's recognition as the only All-Steinway School in Central Texas. HT also reestablished its award-winning band program recently featured at the Council for Higher Education Accreditation's International Conference and the HT Jazz Collective's first-place finish at the Historically Black College and University (HBCU) C2 Spring Academy Battle of the Bands. In November 2020, the University launched the HT Center for Justice and Equity, dedicated to justice reform for all citizens.

Dr. Pierce Burnette completed numerous projects on the University's deferred maintenance list, making substantial improvements in many facilities.

Among the highlights are the construction of the Sandra Joy Anderson Health and Wellness Center (the first new building on campus since 1974), remodeling of King-Seabrook Chapel, installing new marquee signage on Bluebonnet Hill, new entryway signage and perimeter fencing to maximize the University's curb appeal, and new campus lighting.

Within two weeks in March 2020, Dr. Pierce Burnette oversaw the entire University's successful transition to online learning at the beginning of the COVID-19 pandemic, all while staying true to the University's core values (Integrity, Diversity, Excellence, Accountability, and Leadership), and maintaining a safe and healthy environment. This fall, campus reactivation took place as the University returned to in-person instruction for the first time since spring 2020.

Dr. Pierce Burnette's unwavering commitment to HT's mission has resulted in Huston-Tillotson University forging strong, sustainable, and reciprocal relationships with Fortune 50 companies, Austin tech companies and startups, independent school districts, and nonprofits. Her roots of community engagement for the City of Austin are profound and numerous. She has proudly served as the Co-Chair for the Mayor's Task Force on Institutional Racism and Systemic Inequities, Chair of the Leadership Austin Board, Chair of the Central Texas Collective for Racial Equity, Treasurer of the Independent Colleges and Universities of Texas. Dr. Pierce Burnette has also honorably served on several local and national boards: Austin Community Foundation, Greater Austin Black Chamber of Commerce, Austin Area Urban League, E3 Alliance, Austin Transit Partnership, Vision 2030, I-35 Cap and Stitch Project, Frontier Bank, DISCO, and Council for Higher Education Accreditation. Dr. Pierce Burnette credits the resounding success of her presidency at Huston-Tillotson University as the actual embodiment of the African proverb, "If you want to go fast, go alone; if you want to go far, go together."

We know Austin and the HT community love Dr. Pierce Burnette. She cannot be replaced. In the coming weeks, we will take steps to begin a national search to find a president who can succeed her and build on all Huston-Tillotson University has become.

Board President McDonald highlighted most of Pierce Burnette's accomplishments, but were there things not mentioned? Pertinently, how would Pierce Burnette's successor find HT? McMillan found the question of a second merger when he entered his presidency, Earvin found HT "on warning" by its

CHAPTER 4

reaccreditation agency (SACS), Pierce Burnette found financial aid in shambles. I asked Pierce Burnette, "What will the next president find undone from Pierce Burnette's presidency?" Her response to that question was, "The new president will find HT in good shape; it is in the black and fully accredited." In an interview with Jennifer Stayton, Pierce Burnette recommended that the next president continue to build:

> reciprocal and sustainable partnerships . . . because the partner benefits as does the university . . . to continue to advocate for the university in all circles. Have your seat at the table. Bring your own table. Bring your own seat. Make your own table, whatever it is. That's a cliché to keep the university upfront and present in people's minds and thoughts when they talk about the future and when they talk about next steps for all parties, all sectors of the university.[103]

After sharing that she was retiring from HT, Pierce Burnette sent a moving holiday video greeting to the HT fRAMily and her supporters in Austin and beyond. The transcript for that video follows.

> The past two years have demonstrated undoubtedly how precious human life is. Although we are living through never-before-known or experienced occurrences, we are also living through a time of potential renaissance, with hope and unbridled opportunities to build a beloved community for all. We are experiencing an emergence of servant leadership, openness to reflection, truth and having courageous conversations, a reawakening to doing the right thing, to do the heart work necessary to bend the moral arc towards justice. All we need is to continue having the courage, fueled by gratitude of hope and love swirling all around us in the air especially during this season, using the gifts of gratitude, hope and love. On behalf of the entire university community, we take this time to express gratitude for all of Huston-Tillotson's treasured supporters. We are bountifully grateful for you and your investment for our mission. Your faith in our campus demonstrates every single day that our persistence is our superpower. We thank you. Our greatest wish for this season and beyond is that [you have] the blessing of experiencing joy: joy in celebrating those you love; joy in spending time with those you love; joy in that you are one step closer in obtaining your degree; joy in pursuing that childhood dream you have deferred for far too long; and joy in having a blessed life. It is our students who give us all hope and joy. May their passion for life, the light in their smiles and the love in their heart

inspire us all during this season and beyond. From HT, Austin, Texas's oldest institution of higher learning and oldest HBCU, we wish you and yours a very merry Christmas, Happy Hanukkah, Feliz Navidad, and a joyous Kwanzaa. May God bless you all.[104]

Pierce Burnette stated often that "We learn backwards to live forwards. Everything in my life has prepared me for my journey in Austin and for my presidency of HT. I am praying and hopeful that my journey at HT will now prepare for my next chapter." Pierce Burnette's next chapter began on August 1, 2022, when she assumed the position of president and CEO of Newfields Museum in Indianapolis, Indiana. She would be the first African American woman in that role. According to Pierce Burnette, "I've seen the nurturing and transformative power of cherished institutions like Newfields. I am thrilled to become part of a team driven to meet Newfields' mission of enriching lives purposefully and intentionally through exceptional experiences with art and nature. . . . I believe strongly in service, and I am excited to lead Newfields at this unique moment to make it a place every person in Indianapolis and beyond is excited to visit, and every team member is proud to work." The chairperson of the Board of Newfields Museum indicated that Dr. Pierce Burnette was selected because "She is lauded by her staff, peers, and the communities she served for being a humble leader with an immense amount of respect and empathy for everyone she encounters. Her legacy has been to elevate the beloved institutions she's led into stronger, more inclusive organizations that others seek to emulate."

Her Story: Lessons from Dr. Pierce Burnette's Presidency
"I Don't Know What I Don't Know"
Sometimes confronted with a situation needing immediate attention, Pierce Burnette often responded with the statement "I don't know what I don't know" as she sought additional information. The intent of the statement differed depending on whether the information was critical to problem-solving or whether she believed someone kept vital information from her. A lesson learned is that no one person possesses all vital information; in fact, different information is needed from various team members. Communication is vital to share data needed to make informed decisions. Being open to learning more, not claiming to know everything, is a good quality for a leader.

Not only the president but also those responsible for implementing institutional goals need to know vital information to move the university forward. Often key players are left out of the loop even though goal achievement is expected. According to Gratz and Salem:[105]

> By and large, information processing in higher education is improvised, not planned. Although significant amounts of time are devoted to planning budgetary activities, personnel reviews, and other major activities, the majority of information disseminated within a college or university is communicated through telephone calls, [emails],[106] chance meetings, after-committee caucuses, memoranda, or other comparatively spontaneous methods. As a result, members who genuinely need information often do not receive it, specific roles and responsibilities remain unclear, and information frequently arrives in a distorted or an untimely manner. Because of this unmanaged flow of information, some organizational members become seriously overloaded while others suffer from inadequate information. An "information agenda" may help administrators plan communication more effectively.

Top-down leaders are less likely to want to hear from others or seek out what they don't know. Although Pierce Burnette did not always solicit opinions from all constituents, she frequently made the effort.

Visibility of Small HBCUs Is Critical
Dr. Pierce Burnette recognized the importance of HT's being visible in the Austin community. People in Austin often ask if HT is in Houston, even though the main highway has signs announcing the exit to HT. Thus, visibility was one of Pierce Burnette's initial goals, and by the time she left HT that goal was partially met. The relationship between visibility and funding, recruitment, retention, community engagement, and large donations is highly correlated. Philanthropists' gifts are usually given to institutions with name recognition. Even though HT is the oldest institution of higher education in Austin, UT Austin has the greatest recognition and receives regular large gifts from philanthropists and alumni.

This is also true with HBCUs, as evidenced in institutions like Spelman,[107] Morehouse,[108] and Howard[109] having greater name recognition than HT and receiving far more money from philanthropists, UNCF, and other funders. HT's largest gift of $3 million came from alumna Ada Anderson ('44). A question raised is how to make HT and other smaller HBCUs recipients of larger gifts; this question is even more salient given that Robert Smith, a Black billionaire with an office in Austin, gave Morehouse more than $34 million to pay off students' debts, bypassing the very HBCU in the city's backyard.[110] Why? Even after leaving HT, many Austinites ask about Pierce Burnette, commenting on how valuable she was to the community. A commensurate question is whether remembering Pierce Burnette will be translated into dollars for HT.

The Covid President

Being the president of a university during Covid-19 was a daunting task. Keeping everyone safe while providing excellent education in a financially prudent manner were the primary concerns—all other goals for the institution were placed on the back burner. HBCUs, like all universities, were expected to refund students for room and board and other expenses, while continuing to pay salaries and upgrade IT for effective online teaching. HT received philanthropic and CARES monies to make online teaching possible by strengthening IT, giving money directly to students, and hiring a person who monitored and implemented Covid responses.[111] According to Liz Schlemmer, "HBCUs have long been underfunded by federal and state governments. But this time, because of the way federal COVID relief money was allocated, these schools got a lot of it. For one thing, much of the funding targeted schools that serve more low-income students, which HBCUs do. And there was a whole other pot of money—$5.2 billion—just for HBCUs."[112] Pierce Burnette indicated that she left HT in the black. A possible contributing factor is that the funding HT received during Covid exceeded HT expenses.

Not simply an HBCU or PWI problem, Covid was a universal problem. All institutions of higher education experienced a period of institutional shutdown, relegating education to virtual learning. Online resources varied, depending on many variables including pre-Covid resources, private or public institution status, students' personal and parental resources, IT possibilities, and others. The important lesson is that HBCUs need to become more financially stable in order to successfully face unforeseen crises. It is unlikely that the federal government will make available such a windfall if a new universal crisis occurs.

CHAPTER 5

HISTORICALLY BLACK COLLEGES AND UNIVERSITIES (HBCUs) STILL NEEDED

JOHN Q. TAYLOR KING, JOSEPH MCMILLAN, LARRY EARVIN, AND Colette Pierce Burnette recognized that HT was and is connected to the other 100 HBCUs in many ways. HBCU presidents meet annually, have met with the US president as a group and lobby for government funds together, and are members of UNCF; some belong to the same religious associations. Most of these educational institutions were organized during the Reconstruction Era, a time when African American students were not allowed to attend predominantly White institutions (PWIs). HBCUs are important and vital institutions despite the fact that they were birthed into a racist country that devalued the newly freed slaves and their ancestors. HBCUs' birth did not define their destiny; millions of students since their inception, with no other educational opportunities, received their undergraduate foundation enrolled in one or more of the 101 HBCUs. Always open to diversity, HBCUs continue to shine light on how people of all races and cultures can live and learn together, focusing on excellence in all areas in their lives. They create environments where each student group is respected and included in the life of the campus. HT's former president, Dr. John King, stated:

> Our United Negro College Funds (UNCF) are all good colleges, striving to become excellent. If they fail to become excellent in the years ahead, they may then no longer even be good. And should this happen, the people to blame will

be those professed friends of the institutions who believe that just being good is good enough.... The liberal arts college is a genuinely American development in higher education—an institution where the student-faculty relationship is important, where homey virtues count highly, where young men and women live in an orderly existence that is designed to make them solid citizens if they pursue no further formal education, or prepare them equally well for the rigors of graduate or professional training.... *It is our philosophy that the church-related liberal arts college has a flavor and context that students can obtain nowhere else. This kind of institution stresses that the student's responsibility for knowing what he is, and is becoming, is just as important as what he knows.* It stresses the importance of "town-grown" relationship and seeks constantly to make this relationship most meaningful. They recognize the great value of being small and have no design on bigness. We would like to become big enough to provide the kind of education "no one can afford to miss" and a background sound enough for later life—and to provide this in an atmosphere that makes students and their parents interested and comfortable....We can be equal in the respect of the most munificent university in the country. We can exemplify in our own devotion to God and duty, in the living out of our own true, completest self, an ideal that will draw young people. We can bring to our faculty men and women whose very bearing is a rebuke to dull, meager and irrelevant living. We can insist that the curriculum of the college should teach not only the means, but the ultimate ends of life, by helping young people study those who have embodied it. And if we do these things, generations of students, and children unborn, shall feel our influence and will rise up to call us blessed, because we blessed them.... But these things can only be done if sufficient resources can be secured.[1]

King clearly believed in the importance of HBCUs, recognizing the similarity of their missions: their academic excellence, the emphasis they placed on character-building, and the importance of having sufficient resources to fulfill HBCUs' mission. Most HBCUs came into existence after the end of slavery. They were often created by White missionaries, philanthropists, or by state mandates for former slaves in times when it was illegal for people of color to attend White-serving institutions. Most HBCUs were organized before 1964. Twelve Black junior colleges were founded in Florida after the *Brown v. Board of Education* decision in 1954 in an attempt to show that separate but equal higher education facilities existed in Florida.[2] All were abruptly closed after passage of the 1964 Civil Rights Act. These HBCUs' history and missions varied in their location, public/private status, size of the institution, degrees conferred, levels of prestige and recognition, and other critical factors. The Higher Education Act of 1965, as amended, defines an HBCU as "... any Historically Black college or university that was established prior to 1964, whose principal mission was, and is, the education of Black Americans, and that is accredited by a nationally recognized accrediting agency or association determined by the Secretary [of Education] to be a reliable authority as to the quality of training offered or is, according to such an agency or association, making reasonable progress toward accreditation."[3]

While King's references were made to the private liberal arts institutions, public HBCUs have similar mandates despite their different origins. Their legacies also lie in the success of their students. Below is the 2022 summary information of HBCU institutions from the National Center for Educational Statistics:

> 99 HBCUs are located in 19 states, the District of Columbia, and the U.S. Virgin Islands. Of the 99 HBCUs, 50 are public institutions and 49 are private nonprofit institutions. The number of HBCU students increased 47 percent, from 223,000 to 327,000 students, between 1976 and 2010, then decreased 11 percent, to 292,000 students, between 2010 and 2022. However, the number of HBCU students was about the same in 2022 as it was just prior to the coronavirus pandemic in 2019. In comparison, the number of students in all degree-granting institutions increased 91 percent, from 11 million to 21 million students, between 1976 and 2010, then decreased 12 percent, between 2010 and 2022.[4]

These numbers show that hundreds of thousands of students prefer HBCUs to PWIs, as HBCUs are a better fit for them, perhaps because of racial discrimination and socioeconomic factors. Historically and now, "HBCUs offer all students, regardless of race, an opportunity to develop their skills and talents. These institutions train young people who go on to serve domestically and internationally in the professions as entrepreneurs and in the public and private sectors."[5] Many Black students go to HBCUs not because they can't be successful at PWIs but in part because of the inclusive, familial environment of HBCUs.[6] In fact, many students who grew up with a Black president and the Black Lives Matter movement are choosing HBCUs where they feel accepted and experience a sense of family.

The necessity for HBCUs is furthered highlighted in the reality that "controlled comparisons prove that HBCUs outperform non-HBCU institutions in retaining and graduating Black students, after accounting for the socioeconomic status and academic preparation of enrolled students."[7] The statistical evidence below supports this claim, especially since "these HBCUs make up only three percent of the country's colleges and universities, but 10 percent of all African American students and produce almost 20 percent of all African American graduates."[8] While HBCUs constitute only 3 percent of all US colleges and universities:

- HBCUs generated 25 percent of all bachelor's degrees in STEM fields for African Americans.
- HBCUs awarded 14 percent of all African American engineering degrees.
- HBCU students paid an average total cost of attendance that was 26 percent lower than four-year nonprofit colleges.
- Out of all US colleges and universities, HBCUs graduate the most African Americans seeking doctoral degrees in science and engineering.[9]

Additionally, "HBCUs actively work to address the financial obstacles Black students face. On average, the cost of attendance at an HBCU is 28 percent less than attending a comparable non-HBCU. Forty percent of HBCU students report feeling financially secure during college, as opposed to 29 percent of Black students at other schools."[10] Even with these impressive statistics, a high percentage of public and private HBCUs are on a slippery slope; many do not have enough revenue to avoid regular concerns about financial insolvency. Not all HBCUs face the same level of financial need. Like the hierarchical ordering of PWIs, there are some HBCUs with healthy endowments, philanthropists' contributions, and/or governmental subsidies such as Howard, Mahary, Morehouse, and Spelman.[11] These top-tier HBCUs do better during crisis situations such as the Covid-19 pandemic. But most private and some public institutions struggle to keep their doors open. Problems faced by HT such as financial instability, low student enrollment, and challenges with student retention also plague many HBCUs. These factors become a vicious cycle, resulting in HBCUs' closure, mergers, or loss of accreditation.

For my research I surveyed HBCU faculties in two ways. During a 2017 summer seminar I surveyed eighteen HBCU professors. In addition, in November 2018 I sent an online survey to HBCU professors I met over the years, as well as professors found on HBCUs websites. The list below contains the fifteen HBCUs represented by the thirty-nine respondents.

- Bennett College, Greensboro, North Carolina (3)
- Cheyney University, Cheyney, Pennsylvania (2)
- Clark Atlanta, Atlanta, Georgia (2)

- Dillard University, New Orleans, Louisiana (2)
- Florida A&M University, Tallahassee, Florida (1)
- Hampton University, Harrisburg, Virginia (1)
- Jackson State University, Jackson, Mississippi (1)
- Morehouse College, Atlanta, Georgia (1)
- Paine College, Augusta, Georgia, (2)
- Prairie View A&M University, Prairie View, Texas (1)
- Shaw University, Raleigh, North Carolina (5)
- Spelman College, Atlanta, Georgia (4)
- Tougaloo College, Tougaloo, Mississippi (9)
- Wiley College, Wiley, Texas (1)
- Xavier University, New Orleans, Louisiana (4)

The thirty-nine professor respondents were at their institutions from two to fifty years with an average of fifteen years. Their disciplines include the humanities, history, African diaspora, sociology, chemistry, communication, English, computer sciences, music, art, and women's studies. Questions on their survey sought to uncover whether there is a need for HBCUs; why they taught at their respective HBCUs; both negative and positive experiences; institutional strengths and weaknesses; family environment; and their risk of closing. The answers given by HBCU faculties are very similar to those of faculty at Huston-Tillotson University, discussed in previous chapters.

HBCU faculty members strongly believe that HBCUs are needed, even in the face of Black students' integration at PWIs. Table 3 provides a list of reasons why some of these faculty members believe HBCUs are still needed.

Table 3

Are HBCUs Still Needed? A Comparison of HBCU Professors and HT Professors (from HT faculty survey)		
	HBCUs	**HT**
Absolutely because HBCUs have the mission of helping underserved and underprepared students by mentoring and growing students so that they will graduate and become major contributors of society.	X	X

Absolutely. Laws may have opened doors for opportunities or afford civil rights, but it did not change attitudes. HBCUs are still fulfilling their mission of educating people of color in places they feel they belong and can thrive. It provides an educational experience that speaks to their unique experience. At White-serving institutions, students are a number; they are seen as individuals at the HBCU.	X	X
Yes, just as there is still a need for Hispanic-serving and Tribal colleges and women's colleges.	X	X
Every time a minority student is abused by a White police officer at a traffic stop, people reaffirm the purpose of an HBCU.		X
There is always a need (and increasingly a need) for small colleges as more and more students get mass produced in mega-public universities. And, there is currently an even greater need for small colleges that have the knack for working with first-generation college students of any so-called racial or ethnic group; i.e., they need places to learn where race and ethnicity is not the overriding issue, even though these institutions welcome students from diverse racial ethic groups.	X	X
Black students need to have models to whom they can aspire. HBCUs showcase the achievement of Black professionals and help motivate our students for success. The statistics on the number of doctors, engineers, nurses, and other professionals produced by HBCUs speak for themselves. People like to discount the relevance of HBCUs, but there are reasons why certain corporations, organizations, and institutions continuously come to HBCUs to recruit students of color.	X	X

We are a racist country and as long as that is true, African American students may want this type of environment where they can build confidence in their skills and knowledge before competing in wider "White" society. HBCUs help students understand their culture and history and provide a space to be unapologetically Black as they are central in their learning. It helps students learn about the diversity of "Blackness" as well. White institutions do not respond to the cultural needs of minority students and cannot give them a sense of who they are in a nation that has historically mistreated them.	X	X
Yes and YES and YES. I say this as a White person who grew up in PWIs. I think there are huge gaps in the education provided at PWI. Ethical gaps as well as purely factual and logical ones. It's not just that there need to be schools where Toni Morrison is not just a footnote. There should be schools where the purpose is not personal advancement but the critique of the predominant culture as well as the advancement of those who have been oppressed. White students at PWIs are plain ignorant about racism and social justice and large expanses of American history that are familiar territory to HBCU students.	X	X
HBCUs are critical to the ability of members of the Black community to build wealth—and not just financial wealth but also skills and knowledge. For the most part, HBCUs are the places where we can cultivate, promote, protect, and preserve our arts, culture, and heritage. My competency and expertise as a scholar was challenged more at the PWI than anything I have experienced at my present institution. I feel more respected and appreciated for my talents and abilities at my HBCU than when I taught at a major PWI.	X	X

A very difficult question. The loss of many of our best students gives students at HBCUs fewer positive role models. HBCUs do provide a major source of leadership development in a supportive environment, but it is always good to have the other "White" side to provide contrary perspectives. HBCUs are a strong voice to articulate the Black perspective, and for that purpose they are essential.	X	X
Absolutely! HBCUs prepare students in a manner that they are comfortable in their Blackness when they step out onto the world stage. Many HBCUs offer opportunities for students to broaden their personal and global perspectives, and these opportunities further prepare our students for the global marketplace. These experiences make it possible for African American students to escape developing an inferiority complex that can easily rise in spaces where there is no mentorship, no support system, or very few people who look like them.	X	X

Not mentioned by either HT or other HBCU faculties is the importance of HBCUs in civil rights struggles. The Civil Rights Movement of the twentieth century would not have happened or been as successful without the participation of HBCU students. HBCUs produced some of the great leaders of the movement, including Medgar Evers (Alcorn State); transportation desegregationist Rosa Parks (Alabama State University); Black Power leader Stokely Carmichael and Vice President Kamala Harris (Howard University); civil rights leader Dr. Martin Luther King Jr. (Morehouse College); Freedom rider Congressmen John Lewis (Fisk University); and Rainbow Coalition organizer Jesse Jackson (North Carolina A&T State University), among others.

HBCUs were also indispensable centers in the fight for equality.[12] Claflin University, South Carolina State, Knoxville College, Tougaloo College, Huston-Tillotson, and other HBCUs protested for voters' rights and desegregation of restaurants, department stores, and other institutions in the 1950s and 1960s. Campuses and churches became social networks for devising civil rights strategies and organizing student civil rights organizations. The Student Nonviolent

Coordinating Committee (SNCC) was formed at Shaw University. In recent history, Spelman students, in the face of #MeToo,[13] broadcast the names of alleged rapists and rape apologists on the campuses of Morehouse and Spelman, resulting in the creation of a task force to establish anti-assault and healthy relationships in the curriculum.[14] "Activism is an extremely important part of what your life here at Spelman should be," said one supporter. "I think of protest as a way of shining a light on things that perhaps need to be enlightened that we wouldn't know about."[15] A Kentucky State University commenter similarly said, "The campus activism, whether it targets big national issues or local administrative ones, shows that HBCUs are carrying forward their key missions of education and activism in a new era. Race relations are volatile, and the Trump administration has played a role in stoking the flames, but HBCUs have survived much throughout their 150-year history."[16]

In Texas, Volma Overton, HT class of 1950, was a tireless advocate for civil rights. He led the Austin NAACP from 1962 to 1983, participated in the Selma and Washington marches, and advised efforts to desegregate Austin's schools. HT alum Nelson Linder ('84) is president of Austin's NAACP, and HT's Derrick Lewis II (2018) revived HT's student chapter of the NAACP and led activities focused on police killings, voting, and economic empowerment. HBCU college campuses across the country participated in Black Lives Matter and police brutality protests.[17]

Since Blacks and other people of color continue to experience racism in all social systems of America, their collective strength, willpower, and passion for systemic changes are invaluable and their HBCUs prepare them to exercise strategic power directed towards change. Not working in a vacuum, students depend on faculty mentors and supporters for encouragement and guidance along with their education. Teachers/mentors help students in their HBCUs to grow holistically, training them in civic responsibilities and giving them a worldview. These attributes are common threads that knit all HBCUs.

Why Teach at an HBCU?

In part due to the value of HBCUs, respondents in my research made intentional decisions to work at an HBCU. Some had previously worked at PWIs and had a basis for comparison. Most continue to work at HBCUs despite poor wages, inadequate communication, problems with faculty governance, lack of trust, financial instability, and other administrative difficulties. They taught/teach at HBCUs for some of the following reasons. They include both third-person and first-person responses:

- To give back to their alma mater because of teachers who cared about their success; they stay to do the same for their students.
- To build Black institutions and to keep them strong.
- Their love for the rich culture and history of HBCUs.
- It is a calling on their lives to provide Black students a bright future that comes from having an excellent education.
- To see students blossom and grow, and as alumni making us proud.
- To provide an opportunity for Blacks who would otherwise not be admitted to college.
- Students need to see professionals who look like them.
- Watching students blossom as scholars.
- I love the opportunities to combine diaspora and music studies, and I enjoy the students.
- I stayed because it is profoundly gratifying.
- I found it fascinating; experience is full of chances for me to learn more.
- I really value the mission of HBCUs.
- I teach there because there are bright students; very interesting and engaged faculty, with common interest in promoting student success.
- I get personal satisfaction from helping students accomplish their educational goals.
- I was invited to teach at an HBCU and decided to stay there.
- As a White professor, I had to gain my comfort at an HBCU and to help other White students to do the same.
- I responded to job search; stayed because of mutual satisfaction . . . students and I.
- I knew that devoting myself to this student body would make a difference for my people and for my children.
- I wanted to aim my experience at an HBCU that was recognized for its legacy and history.

Most HT interviewed faculty members said they taught at HT because of students, even when their working environment was stressful, or they had opportunities to go to PWIs with higher salaries and with better benefits. In some ways, there is a mutual love relationship between faculty and students, with students being the greatest benefactors. Faculty members from other HBCUs agree.

Internal Difficulties

Although teaching at HBCUs is rewarding to most of my respondents, there are still multiple difficulties they described in their work environment. These difficulties are not unique to HBCUs but may be intensified when salaries and benefits are so low compared to those at public or private PWIs. The responses for the table below came from the following survey questions: "What are the weaknesses at your institutions?" and "What are some things that fracture relationships at your institution?" The HBCU column contains responses from the 39 HBCU professors already identified. The HT column came from the responses from the HT faculty survey. If most of the study participants answered yes, their collective response is placed as an "x" in the column.

Table 4

Internal Difficulties/Problems Needing to be Addressed		
	HBCUs	HT
Disrespect from my supervising administrators greatly disheartened me as administrators never walk the campus or visit classes. I felt unappreciated for the hard work I continued to give. The low salary was not nearly as important as feeling appreciated.	X	X
Students are disgruntled by some of the actions of the support staff. These issues vary from financial aid to registration and communication from the school about different steps in their programs.	X	X
When faculty and staff from majority White culture come and try to impose their values and standards on our learning and cultural environment.	X	
It has been hard work with a heavy teaching load, many administrative responsibilities, serving on several academic committees, and leadership in student-oriented teaching/learning designs. Everyone is overworked, leaving limited time to build relationships.	X	X
Staff and/or faculty shortage.	X	X
No or limited money for professional development.	X	X

Lack of trust and shared governance with limited faculty input and support.	X	X
Fractured communication from administration to other constituents.	X	X
Struggle for survival due to lack of financial support.	X	X
Competition vs. collaboration is a problem.	X	X
Don't accept institutional weaknesses.	X	X
There is a lack of properly functioning systems and procedures and a great deal of traditionalism that inhibits needed change. Processes in place are not always followed.	X	X
Some of our best professors prefer to teach upper division courses. I felt we needed strong professors for the freshmen and sophomores to give them adequate foundation and to assure retention		X
More student services are needed for those students who need extra help.	X	X
The only negative I have experienced lies in faculty-faculty relationships when junior faculty with an abundance of ambition seek to exploit the capacities of students for their personal benefit.	X	
Those who can fix problems often place blame on other units and individuals.	X	X
New president may not uphold institutional traditions because they are not in writing.		X

HBCUs: A Family Environment

Despite difficulties that emerge from working at HBCUs, most respondents viewed their institutions as family oriented. Historical reminiscence of HBCUs is that their colleges are families away from home. In fact, respondents spoke more about the strengths of their institutions than their weaknesses, which accounts in part for faculty longevity at their HBCUs. Branding HBCUs as a family began when PWIs were segregated and Black students could only go to an HBCU. With greater opportunities to matriculate at PWIs, many Blacks still find a home at HBCUs, and many faculties feel the same. Below are some of their responses to the prompt, "HBCUs are often described as providing a 'family' environment. If this is how you describe it, please discuss how that concept is manifested at your institution, both positive and negative."

- Caring and nurturing environment helps build students' confidence and accountability.
- It's a place where strong relationships are built between faculty and students; faculty and faculty and student with student. Lifelong friendships exist among each of those groups.
- Faculty and administration know students' names, treating them like persons and not numbers.
- Faculty and staff provide loving support to students, especially when they are experiencing personal and academic difficulties. They view students from a holistic perspective. This is usually not the case at PWIs.
- Faculty and staff work at HT and other HBCUs because they want to be there, although they could work elsewhere. They truly are committed to the mission of HBCUs.
- Faculty and staff provided a Thanksgiving meal for international students who did not travel for the holiday.
- Support of alumni and community.
- Students look up to me; I respect them and together we learn from each other
- At my institution, we care for students beyond the classroom. We invest considerable energy in advising students, creating career paths for students, funding opportunities for students, and being an ear and shoulder to listen to their needs and offer them the care they need when they doubt themselves.
- I can know my colleagues on a personal level. I appreciate the support and guidance they have provided throughout the years. They have been very encouraging of my personal and professional development.
- At my women's college, women are nurtured to be leaders, not allowing their gender to negatively impact their outcome.
- Like in families, my college is sometimes dysfunctional with poor communication and unclear policies.

HBCUs' emphasis on creating a family environment is consistent with an organizational systems model that states, "As the quality of relationships rises, the quality of thinking improves, leading to an increase in the quality of actions and results. Achieving high-quality results has a positive effect on the quality of relationships, creating a reinforcing engine of success."[18] If this model is accurate, the historical focus on building strong relationships with all constituencies, especially students, is one of the HBCUs' abiding strengths. Therefore, I believe, as HBCUs re-envision their future post-Covid, strong relationships continue to be central to their mission.

Future of HBCUs[19]
Are HBCUs at Risk of Closing?
As important as HBCUs are, many faculty respondents see them as being in jeopardy of closing because of financial instability, lack of relevant vision, reaccreditation difficulties, poor strategies for recruiting and retaining students, and external societal factors. However, respondents from the more privileged HBCUs, such as Spelman, Hampton, and Morehouse, indicated that they are not at risk for closing.[20] Professors at HT and less privileged HBCUs concurred that funding sources are inadequate, which causes stress and concern about institutional viability. Responses from participating faculty members indicated their concerns about possible institutional closures are due to some combination of the following institutional difficulties:

1. Poor endowment
2. Inadequate leadership, ineffective and inexperienced leadership; mismanagement
3. Lack of investment in institutional growth
4. Lack of external support, providing nonrestrictive sources
5. Failure to invest in faculty development and salaries
6. Need for rebranding in the current social, economic, and political dispensation
7. Increase diversity of student population
8. Improve infrastructure
9. Drastic reduction of financial aid
10. Need to upgrade the facility, educational materials
11. Recruitment/retention
12. Lack of progressive, economic agenda beyond state appropriations
13. If not progressive enough to stay relevant.

Note that numbers 1, 3, 4, 5, 8, 9, 10, 11 and 12 are directly or indirectly related to financial insecurities and instabilities. These answers from non-HT faculty members mirror those of HT respondents who were asked, "How financially stable is HT?"[21]

Table 5

How would you evaluate HT's financial stability? Data from 87 responses to a 2018 online survey of HT constituents			
Response Category	How Response Was Defined	Percentage of respondents	Number of respondents
Extremely Stable	There is a large percentage of nonrestrictive funds that can be used readily for programs, faculty development, and other needs.	2.35%	2
Stable	There are sufficient funds to sustain programs even when grants are over and for other needs.	28.24%	24
Unstable	Limited funds for nonrestrictive use; sometimes "rob Peter to pay Paul."	69.41%	59
Extremely Unstable	In jeopardy of losing accreditation if finances are not increased.	2.35%	2

Almost 72 percent (61) of the 87 HT respondents indicated that they believed HT was either unstable or extremely unstable. As one respondent said, it is "always a struggle, [which is] true for most historically Black institutions, few with deep endowments, and dependent on church, and Department of Education grants." Literature on HBCUs supports the above findings. Peter Jacob quotes the works of Marybeth Gasman below:[22]

> HBCUs often struggle because they have fewer resources than other colleges—typically due to lower endowments and less money coming in from alumni giving. Public HBCUs have even more problems, typically receiving inequitable government funding at both the federal and state level, compared with PWIs.
>
> "There are some of them that are quite strong, and have good enrollment, and

then there are some that are sort of in the middle, that have to really ramp up their fundraising, and make sure their students graduate," Gasman said. "And then there are some—probably about fifteen of them—that are having a really difficult time."

According to the Association of Governing Boards (AGB) of Universities and Colleges, HBCUs "remain bastions of opportunity for many low-income, first-generation Black college students [but] their futures are unsettled. As they grapple not only with the same challenges that all higher institutions are confronting today—declining enrollments, rising tuition, student loan debt, and public skepticism about the value proposition of higher education, among others—they are also struggling against long-standing patterns of underfunding and small endowments and new competition from other sectors of higher education that are seeking to diversify their student bodies."[23]

A new horrific event that might force the closing of some lesser-known HBCUs, that was not an issue when I surveyed participants, is the onset of Covid-19.[24] The disruptions of sending students home, closing dorms, losing revenue from food services, and interrupting normal streams of revenue reduced available resources, which intensified many HBCUs' struggle to keep their doors open.[25] Better-off elite HBCUs with financial security may not experience difficulties to that degree.

There were several emergency funding allocations by the federal government related to the coronavirus pandemic. $1 billion in emergency funds was given to HBCUs, tribal colleges and universities (TCUs), and other minority serving institutions (MSIs) to help them cope with the coronavirus pandemic. HBCUs collectively received $577 million out of that $1 billion. This amount was in addition to the $353 million given in 2020 by the Higher Education Emergency Relief Fund (HEERF) allocated by the Department of Education. The money given was to help HBCUs transition to online teaching, specifically investing in technology. This transition to virtual classes was especially costly for HBCUs because of the relatively high number of low-income students who returned to their homes without adequate hardware or internet access for online learning.[26]

Another funding source related to the pandemic is the CARES (Coronavirus Aid, Relief and Economic Security) Act. That act includes a provision for HBCUs on two levels: one for students and one for universities. The CARES Act Higher Education Emergency Relief Fund-IHE/Student Aid provides institutions with funding for emergency financial aid grants to students whose lives have been disrupted, many of whom are facing financial challenges and struggling to make ends meet. Institutions have the responsibility of determining how grants will be distributed to students, how the amount of each student grant is calculated, and the development of any instructions or directions that are provided to students about the grant.[27] The institutional funds included in this act cover the cost of technology associated with a transition to distance education, grants to cover the costs of attendance for eligible students, and faculty and staff training. Additionally, institutional funds may be used to cover operational costs such as lost revenue, reimbursements for prior expenses, and payroll.[28]

Amazingly, although the federal government provided some funds for HBCUs through these various measures, on July 8, 2020, it potentially took other funds away. The US Immigration and Customs Enforcement notified colleges that international students would be forced to leave the US or transfer to another college if their schools operated entirely online in fall 2020. New visas would not be issued to students at those schools, and others at universities offering a mix of online and in-person classes would be barred from taking all of their classes online. The guidance said international students wouldn't be exempt, even if an outbreak forced their schools online during the fall term.[29] International students usually pay full tuition, not expecting a handout. This mandate would have affected 1 million students nationwide who contribute $41 billion to the US economy. It would have further reduced the finances of HBCUs, institutions that cannot afford to lose the tuition paid by such international students. More prestigious and financially stable institutions such as Harvard and MIT have sued, while an online petition asked that this Donald Trump mandate be cancelled. The lawsuits and petition appeared to have worked, as President Trump rescinded his decision on foreign students studying online in the US on July 14, 2020.

An Uncertain but Hopeful Future

HBCUs have proven to be valuable on many levels, not just for educating students but also for being a pipeline for available personnel in the US and global marketplaces. Evidence of some outstanding leaders educated at HBCUs include the great scholar W. E. B DuBois (Fisk, 1888); Thurgood Marshall (Howard Law School, '33) who argued the *Brown v. Board of Education* case prior to becoming a Supreme Court Justice, 1967–1991; Azie Morton-Taylor (Huston-Tillotson,'57), a Black woman, the first and only female US treasurer for President Carter's administration; Charles M. Geschke (Zavier, BA, '62 and master's, '63), the co-founder of Adobe Systems; Marian Wright Edelman, (Spelman '60), founder of the Children's Defense Fund; Dr. Audrey F. Manley, (Spellman, '55) former Surgeon General of the USA; and Lionel Richie (Tuskegee '74), singer/songwriter. Equally important are those alumni who are not famous yet who make amazing contributions to society locally, nationally, and internationally.

The persistent question is, "How can we keep the doors of these important, but often fragile, institutions open?" These institutions need to create a specialty that brings attention to, and a great demand for, that training or skill set. Creative marketing of cutting-edge majors and specialties will bring students to these campuses. One cutting-edge specialty that HBCUs could highlight is STEM fields, as suggested by Matthew Lynch.

> HBCUs are important hubs for developing the greatest STEM minds in the nation, with 65 percent of all Black physicians and half of all Black engineers graduating from HBCUs. The Tuskegee University College of Engineering and Alabama A&M University of College Engineering, Technology and Physical Sciences are not just top engineering schools among HBCUs – they are among the best in the nation. Spelman College is the second largest school in the nation that sends Black undergraduates on to medical school. Jackson State University receives the highest amount of HBCU federal research funding every year, at $68 million, and is known for its "research intensive" programs. Claflin University students work alongside the South Carolina Center for Biotechnology and receive hands-on industry training and connections in the field long before graduation. Xavier University of Louisiana has a consistently top-ranked pharmacy program and is a sought-out school for those hoping to advance to medical school. Florida A&M University consistently ranks at the top of all colleges that graduate Black students with doctorates in natural sciences and engineering. In June, Fayetteville State was awarded a $718,000 government research grant that included plans to oversee STEM instruction to local high school students. The advancements these schools are contributing to STEM fields are not just relevant, they are groundbreaking and an asset to the industries the graduates eventually serve.[30]

With an engineering degree, HT's president Pierce Burnette both encouraged STEM programs and supported faculty who brought large, funded grants to support those programs. HBCUs receive grants from Title III, a federal government funding source. The federal government provided and still provides other funds to HBCUs as well. In December 2019, then–President Trump signed a bill to authorize permanent funding for HBCUs, tribal colleges or universities, and minority serving institutions. The bill, which replaced a former lapsed bill, provides HBCUs with $85 million in annual federal funding.[31] A distribution of $85 million among the HBCUs, however, is minimal and is unlikely to be enough to financially support colleges and universities with severe financial problems. During the Biden/Harris administration, HBCUs received additional funds because of the prominent position HBCUs hold, especially since Vice President Harris is a Howard (HBCU) graduate. The federal government also gave money to HBCUs that were affected by the 2022 bomb threats.[32]

Subject to societal, political, and pandemic uncertainties, HBCUs need funds from diversified sources other than the US government. Leadership development, capital campaigns, deep-pocketed board members, and alumni give-back are some potential sources of more diversified funding. According to the Association of Governing Boards of Universities and Colleges (ABG), HBCUs should intentionally engage in the following activities:[33]

1. Incorporate a business model that builds on HBCUs' historical vision/mission of being a nurturing family that fosters character building and relationship building. Having a clear business model makes HBCUs more competitive for philanthropic funding.
2. Engage in ongoing capital campaign that markets institutional strengths and alignment with community personnel needs. "Institutions must assess their capacity for undertaking such a campaign. Are institutional development staff able to tackle such an endeavor or should external consultants be engaged? And will enthusiastic leadership support the campaign? The president and board must be visible champions of the effort from inception to conclusion."
3. Expand academic infrastructure that scans need of corporations and businesses and develop programs that matches needs.
4. Foster a strong quality of student life so that students graduate with highly positive feelings about their experience and place a priority on donating as alumni on an annual basis.
5. Create a transparent model so that funds received and spending aligns with the institution's strategic plan.
6. Develop the ability to analyze finances, create reports, and develop budgetary forecasts—and it must also have adequate digital tools available to perform scrupulous fiscal oversight.
7. Intentionally increase the enrollment of non-African American students.
8. Practice the principles of good governance by:
    a. bolstering board leadership,
    b. bolstering board engagement,

c. bolstering board development, and
   d. bolstering the relationship between the board chair and the president.

As HBCUs seek to continue as viable higher educational institutions, they must engage predominantly White institutions in cooperative endeavors. Often, PWIs have the capabilities, contacts, and resources to secure large foundation and governmental grants that require participation from minority serving institutions. HBCUs should be poised to negotiate with those PWI institutions to secure funds consistent with their contribution to the success of the project. Too often in these PWI/HBCU partnerships, the PWIs maintain unmerited privilege in the management, implementation, and distribution of funds to the HBCUs, even when the HBCUs' contributions are critical. Often in such partnerships, HBCUs are paid much less than the PWI institution would pay another PWI.

Hope for HBCUs' survival also lies in their original mission of providing an education in a nurturing environment, where race is not a liability. In her article, "Why Students Are Choosing HBCUs: 4 Years Being Seen as Family," Erica Greene follows a Black student accepted to Yale but who chose Spelman because there she felt at home, didn't have to deal with racial hostility, and wouldn't feel isolated.[34] According to the student Greene interviewed, "College is the time when you're trying to figure out who you are. It's impossible to figure that out in a space where you not only feel like you have to assimilate to fit into that space, when they didn't invite you there or they tolerate you there, but you have to prove that your existence has value."[35] Greene further stated,

> In the past few years, the nation's HBCUs have experienced a boom. From 2018 to 2021, for example, applications for a cross section of Black schools increased nearly 30 percent, according to the Common App, a platform for students to submit one application to multiple colleges, outpacing the increases of many other schools. Submissions using the Common Black College Application, solely for HBCUs are projected to reach 40,000 this year, quadruple the total in 2016. And enrollment has soared at some of the schools, even as it declined nationally.
>
> Historically Black Colleges and Universities (HBCUs) have seen a surge in enrollment in recent years, indicating a rising demand for these institutions. According to a report by the National Center for Education Statistics, HBCUs witnessed a 6.9 percent increase in enrollment between 2020 and 2023, while overall college enrollment dropped by 5.5 percent during the same period. This is an exciting trend that is shaping the future of education and producing a new

generation of diverse and talented professionals.

The reasons behind this rise in HBCU enrollment are numerous. One significant factor is the increased awareness among students of the unique opportunities offered by these institutions. HBCUs offer an immersive academic and social environment that allows students to take advantage of mentorships, internships, and relationship-building opportunities. Additionally, HBCUs offer high-quality education in fields such as science, technology, engineering, and mathematics (STEM), which are in high demand in today's job market.

Another reason for the increase in HBCU enrollment is the growing emphasis on diversity and inclusion in higher education. HBCUs offer an inclusive environment where students can thrive academically and socially, regardless of their race or background. By embracing diversity, HBCUs provide a platform for students to exchange ideas and perspectives, prepare for global citizenship, and develop a deeper understanding of the world around them.[36]

As mentioned earlier, not all HBCUs are experiencing such growth, but if the trend continues, HT and smaller HBCUs may benefit as well.

The Bigger Picture

As HBCUs contemplate their future, excellence based on best practice must be required of their presidents, boards of trustees, faculty, staff, and students. HBCUs' successes have already been enumerated yet are often not suitably appreciated. Many even question HBCUs' inherent value to society. To throw light on why HBCUs are often devalued within our historically racist society, I will analyze HBCUs through the archetype of "Success to the Successful," one of eight systems archetypes developed by Peter Senge and others.[37] An archetype is a repeated pattern of behavior common in organizational and human systems. This archetype is captured by the well-known phrase, "The rich get richer, and the poor get poorer."

The environment in which this pattern emerges is one in which resources are limited (or believed to be limited) and two individuals, or groups, are seen as competing with one another. In this pattern *the two individuals or groups start out equally qualified or capable*. One of them, however, is more quickly successful than the other. This can happen through luck or chance, but most often it is because the rules or norms that govern the system favor one over the other. When that happens, the system or organization perceives that person or group as "better" than the other and rewards it with more resources. Over time, in an environment of limited resources (or perceived limited resources) this decreases the resources available to the other person or group. The pattern is self-reinforcing, meaning that it builds on itself, creating a "snowball" effect. As the "not favored" group gets fewer and fewer resources, their chances of success decrease. With less success, the "not favored" person or group is perceived as increasingly "less than" or "worse than" and over time their performance continues to get deeper and deeper into the hole, farther and farther behind.

This archetype suggests that *success may depend more on structural forces than innate ability or talent*.[38] Even if individuals or a group start at an equal point—e.g., in the case of higher education institutions, strong faculty and a desire to provide excellent education—the perceptions of those with power determine which group will succeed. If one group is initially given more resources, that group is more likely to succeed. Successful groups are perceived as "better" and, therefore, worthy of more resources. The others are perceived as "unworthy of our investment" or "a waste of our money."

The two institutions I chose to illustrate this archetype are the University of Texas (a PWI) and Huston-Tillotson University (an HBCU), both in Austin, Texas. These two universities, birthed during the same post-slavery period, from their inception had vastly different trajectories. Their very beginnings are the source of inequities that continue today.

Tillotson and Sam Huston were both created to educate newly freed slaves, students who were not allowed to attend White institutions of higher education. These schools merged in 1952 to become Huston-Tillotson College. UT was created to be the flagship Texas state college, with substantial state financial backing. It was institutionally racist, not admitting Blacks, thus creating the need for the continuation of HT, an HBCU created only years before UT.

HT and UT were established to serve different populations, but both had the mission of providing excellent education to their specific student body. Today UT is a PWI with extremely high visibility and status, while some people still ask the question, "Is Huston-Tillotson University in Houston, Texas?" indicating poor visibility and lack of perceived value. An analysis of these two institutions clearly supports the ideology that there are structural forces that makes UT more successful than HT. How one measures success and competence can, intentionally or unintentionally, favor UT over HT. These institutional norms or rules, in a racist society, tend to favor Whites over African Americans every time, and they still exist today, though more subtly.

The Success of the Successful pattern can be applied to HT (with its meager beginnings) and UT (with its resource-rich beginnings). Although both began within a few years of each other, from its inception UT received state sanction, state funds, societal acceptance, and normative entitlement; Tillotson and Sam Huston were poor in resources. Over the years, HT was overshadowed by UT, although HT is the oldest institution of higher learning in Austin. UT was historically considered more successful and impactful than HT. The definitions of success often applied to institutions of higher education include both student and faculty outcomes. Faculty success outcomes may include the number of publications in respected journals, books published, amount of funded research grants, and awards or advanced credentials given to faculty members. Student success outcomes often include postgraduate degrees, successful employment, and financial success of graduates. Both sets of measures are, consciously or unconsciously, biased in favor of PWIs. Thus, by defining success in terms of things that are less likely to be as available to non-White institutions, it's inevitable that White institutions like UT get perceived as more successful. Success is rewarded by more resources, yielding, in a competitive funding environment, fewer resources for those perceived as less successful, e.g. HT (as well as other HBCUs).

Inherent in this inequality is that the favored group is afforded privileges that the not-favored group lacks. And, when race is salient and highly differentiates the constituents within the universities, White privileges become the norm in the dissemination of resources. Thus, with UT being predominantly White and privileged and HT being predominantly Black and lacking similar privilege, the natural consequence is that the White, richer university gets richer and the Black, poorer university get poorer. Therefore, in a world where funding for higher education is limited and competitive, and in which many norms and rules favor Whites and White institutions, HBCUs have historically had fewer resources. Having fewer resources affects their success and that, in turn, leads to even fewer resources. More specifically, treatment of HBCUs within a White privilege environment may be further aggravated when PWIs woo competent personnel and students from HBCUs by giving them more resources at the PWIs that cannot be provided at the HBCUs. As an example: an HBCU highly talented institutional development officer, needed to execute an effective capital campaign, is offered an extremely high salary with benefits and job resources to do the same job at a PWI. The person takes the job, leaving the HBCU further in the hole (This happened several times at HT.) Likewise, the very students rejected by PWIs during the Jim Crow segregation era are now being recruited by PWIs to increase their minority student populations, which are often required to secure more government financial assistance. These examples highlight the snowball effect of the Success to the

Successful archetype. They also raise the question of how different HBCUs generally, and HT specially, would be if they were viewed as valuable as UT and were allotted status and resources comparable to those at UT.

The tough part about this archetype is that interventions need to happen on the larger system or institutional level, that is, at the level that determines success and provides resources. HBCUs, most affected by Success to the Successful archetype, usually do not have the authority or power to make the needed changes but depend on benefactors—government, philanthropists, and other organizations—to pave the way.[39] This means that peeling away the layer of racism, privilege, and classism must be a societal imperative. Changing institutional policies and societal injustices is required for more equitable treatment of HBCUs. First steps for the larger system are to examine and change the structures that define success and determine who and what are rewarded, and then create equitable pathways to achieve those rewards by HBCUs.

This archetype can also be applied to the lesser known HBCUs compared to those that are better known and endowed with greater financial resources due to their visibility and reputation.

Final Notes

Historically Black colleges and universities are still needed today despite PWIs' integration, especially in our current socioeconomic, political, and racial environment where old racist attitudes and behaviors are experiencing a resurgence. Blacks are disproportionately enslaved in prison systems and murdered at the hands of police officers; indeed, the cry "Black Lives Matter" is labeled as inciting hatred. Black students need a college or university where they don't have to be on guard 24/7, worrying about their physical and emotional safety. Many students and professors have said this very thing in my surveys and interviews. HBCUs provide Black students with one less thing to worry about, freeing them to concentrate on learning, engaging, and developing. Not every Black student needs a Black college, but for those who do, I hope that HBCUs' doors will remain open and ready to provide the best education possible. Changing societal attitudes about success and eradicating White privilege; partnerships with PWI institutions, successful forward-looking corporations, deep-pocket philanthropists, and financially supportive alumni; strong business and educational models; and committed leaders, tempered with family values, will grow our institutions and keep them viable not only for African Americans but for Hispanics, Asians, Whites, and anyone wanting an excellent education. The US Supreme Court provided another reason that HBCUs are still needed: it struck down affirmative action, disallowing universities from giving preferential acceptance of people of color.[40] Students who might have been admitted and received scholarships from PWIs under affirmative action policies might now apply to HBCUs.

A microscopic look at HT is instructive for understanding small HBCUs. Even with the many differences that exist among them, their similarities are striking. HBCU presidents are often mentors to each other as they meet annually sharing ideas and experiences, both good and bad. Each president returns to his or her institution armed with new insights on governing it. Presidents matter as they bring their knowledge, leadership skills, attitudes, personalities, and interpersonal skills to their institution. HT is relatable; one or more of HT's presidents have similar characteristics of presidents of other HBCUs. Each individual enters his or her presidency with the intent to create an environment suited for academic excellence for all students. Sometimes presidents lose sight of their mission and make decisions that derail goodwill on their campus. Many presidents of small HBCUs struggle to get the funding needed to keep their institution financially viable to underwrite student programs, faculty and staff salaries, operational costs, travel, and other expenses. Some HBCUs will be faced with reaccreditation difficulties, which might result in closure.

Too often our HBCUs are analyzed from a place where they are seen as inferior, not deserving to survive. That's an elitist perspective. Yet, when analyzed from the theory of Success to Successful, a new perspective emerges: an understanding that external, historical systems have been stacked against HBCUs. Institutional and systemic racism, both covert and overt, must be addressed by those with the resources to change the trajectory of HBCUs. These hard, courageous conversations about support for educating HBCUs' students are critical to the success of those schools and necessitate envisioning strategies to help HBCUs thrive. HBCUs can rise up by cultivating partnerships within their communities, partnerships with other HBCUs and PWIs, and collaborations with industries. Presidents that retreat inwards may not survive, but, in connecting deeply with other HBCUs, UNCF, PWIs, church-related funding sources, federal funders, philanthropists, and companies like Apple, HBCUs like HT will rise stronger and better than they are now, producing students who will continue to change the world for the better!

Therefore, we MUST tell our stories and make our institutions more visible, viable, and known to those who can help us keep our universities fully funded and open to all wanting a first-class education. Our stories should be told over and over again from different perspectives to different audiences at different times. Collectively, our voices will be heard to recruit more students, generate greater resources, yield deserved esteem, and provide more successful outcomes.

This book constitutes a single voice telling stories about four presidents and those whose lives they touched. Although not always pretty, the loud part of our HBCU stories proclaim, "We are here, we are resilient, and we fulfill our mission to educate amazing students who will do extraordinary things throughout their lives as they use their abilities in our diverse global society, making our world better, one life at a time."

EPILOGUE

New Beginnings

DR. KING AND DR. MCMILLAN ARE DECEASED. DR. EARVIN returned to Atlanta, was a vice president at SACSCOC, and retired in 2023.[1] Pierce Burnette retired from her HT presidency on June 30, 2022, to embark on a new profession as president and CEO of Newfield Museum in Indianapolis, Indiana, leaving HT without a permanent president for two months. Pierce-Burnette left Newfield Museum after being there for fifteen months and is now retired. HT's Provost and Vice President for Academic Affairs, Dr. Archibald Vanderpuye, was appointed to serve as interim president of Huston-Tillotson University beginning July 1, 2022. He served until a new president, Dr. Melva Williams (Wallace upon marriage), was selected by HT's Board of Trustees to be HT's seventh president and CEO, effective August 15, 2022.

Dr. Wallace is the fifth president with whom I worked, beginning her journey at HT within a year of me ending mine of fifty years. I was at HT longer than any faculty member in its 149 years—two-thirds of my life and one-third of the life of Huston-Tillotson University.

Wallace awarded me an honorary doctorate in Humane Letters and Professor Emerita at Huston-Tillotson's May 2023 commencement, recognizing me as a living legend. HT was more than my place of employment; it was a divine calling on my life. Now I await God's next calling.

This book is my last major act of love for my beloved institution; I was chosen by God and the universe to write it. I wanted to add my voice to existing books, articles, and narratives about HT. I used the stories of four presidents to tell their/my/our HT stories. My unique perspective and experiences are unmatched by those of anyone else, as are other voices in this book.

If you are connected to an HBCU, write your own story about it, as your voice is needed as well. Only then will our institutions cease to be invisible, as each page will highlight our amazing accounts of resilience, nurturing, growing, winning, and sharing. And add to your voice your dollars. Pay it forward by providing scholarships for today's generations and the generations to come. HT is still needed; HBCUs are still needed. We need you to keep our schools' doors open! Generations of students of all hues need us to give them a future far better than if they didn't come through our doorways.

Appendix

Comparison of Four Presidents

THIS APPENDIX PROVIDES A QUICK COMPARISON OF THE FOUR presidents on twelve key dimensions that I believe greatly impacted the institution's legacy and stability. Among the lessons learned in viewing this table are that presidents' vision often coincides with the university mission, although the mission has changed under different presidents. Despite their varied backgrounds and approaches, each president wanted HT to be a hub of educational excellence, preparing students to become contributing global citizens. Each president saw their presidential roles from their personal vantage point—their values and vision. These attributes spilled into how they served, creating a clearly distinctive environment. Their legacies have been left for all to see, not only in this book but in written, oral, and visual media. Yet, their successes did not rest totally on their leadership skills. Societal structures, culture, and norms impact HT's ability to grow and stay viable. As an HBCU, HT is intricately related to other HBCUs in many ways.

APPENDIX

Four Presidents Comparison

	Dr. King	Dr. McMillan	Dr. Earvin	Dr. Pierce Burnette
Education & Career Background Note: The presidents arrived from very different backgrounds.	King held a PhD in mathematics and statistics. He was the only president who climbed up through the HT academic ranks and the only president with military experience. He was deeply rooted in Austin and owned a family business. His presidential tenure was under highly segregated Texas and the US. He and his wife received an honorary HT doctorate in 1988 from Dr. McMillan.	McMillan held an EdD in higher education administration. He held leadership roles in United Church of Christ, including board liaison to HT. He had two honorary doctorates, one from HT in 1984 from Dr. King, before he became president. McMillan never taught at a university.	Earvin had a PhD in American Studies. He held key leadership roles with the accrediting body, SACSCOC. Earvin taught and was a former dean at Clark Atlanta University for many years, key educational experiences for being accepted as president at HT.	Pierce Burnette was an engineer with business experience and an EdD in higher education. She held a variety of both engineer and higher education leadership roles including IT, finance, vice president, and interim president prior to becoming president.
Mission Statements and Vision Note: HT's mission statement has evolved over the years, with some longer than others. The vision is not found in all documents that identify the mission. Presidents may inherit a mission statement and then change it, as was the case with Earvin.	MISSION (1983–87) Bulletin: Huston-Tillotson College is to provide educational opportunities to Black Americans and other ethnic groups who possess the desire and capabilities for achieving intellectual growth. The mission statement acknowledged HT's connection to its religious ties, UCC and UMC. VISION: Educating Black Americans not only intellectually but holistically.	MISSION: HT is a historically Black college with the United Methodist Church and the United Church of Christ. The mission of the university is to provide its increasingly diverse student body with an exemplary education that is grounded in the liberal arts and sciences, balanced with professional development and directed to public service and leadership. The university prepares students with the integrity and civility to thrive in a diverse society. It preserves and promotes interest in the accomplishments and experiences of the university's historic constituents and evolving population, and creates and sustains supportive relationships that advance the HT community.	MISSION (2014): HT nurtures a legacy of leadership and excellence in education, connecting knowledge, power, passion, and values. NOTE: Many constituents believe that this mission statement should change to include that it is an HBCU affiliated with its two religious groups. VISION: A connected world where diversity of thought matters.	MISSION (2014): HT nurtures a legacy of leadership and excellence in education, connecting knowledge, power, passion, and values. VISION: A connected world where diversity of thought matters.

APPENDIX

	Dr. King	Dr. McMillan	Dr. Earvin	Dr. Pierce Burnette
Leadership Qualities **Note:** Leadership styles are a result of education, personal values, and leadership philosophy.	King was regal, firm but a good listener. He was charismatic yet business minded. He led by example and was patriarchal. He was strong, open, inclusive, caring, and hands-on in his approach. He was strategic yet empowered others. He was democratic, recognizing the good in everyone. He used his knowledge of the community from moving through the ranks to inform his leadership style. Most students evaluated his leadership in very positive terms.	McMillan was charismatic and autocratic, with a "follow me" attitude, sometimes an over-the-top dictator. He was carefree, enthusiastic, and encouraging. Hands-on micromanager who put into place ways to "weed out" those considered not desirable. He was collaborative with chosen individuals but conflictual with others. He was controversial and viewed variously by his constituents. Overall, he was a top-down leader.	Earvin was resourceful, silent but professional. He was a visionary but led from afar. In his absence, he delegated responsibility to others. Authoritative and firm, he governed with a top-down approach. He was more interested in growing partners nationally than in Austin, which he later regretted. Most faculty believed that they needed to "stay in their lane," thus prohibiting innovation and creative changes needed for professional and student growth.	Pierce Burnette was stern but led by example. She was a visionary with a blueprint. She was open, supportive, and approachable to students, not always with faculty and staff. She surrounded herself with a hand-picked team. She was transformative, pushing the tenets of IDEAL (Integrity, Diversity, Excellence, Accountability, and Leadership), though she sometimes failed to practice those values herself. She took HT to the community, seeking partners and not handouts. She was selected to co-chair Mayor Adler's Task Force on Institutional Racism and Systemic Inequities, which aligned with her social justice passion.

APPENDIX

	Dr. King	Dr. McMillan	Dr. Earvin	Dr. Pierce Burnette
Students' Educational programs Note: Academic excellence was a goal for all four presidents. Each president envisioned excellent education in different ways as indicated by academic programs he/she advocated.	King envisioned building an institution that honored the ancestors of Sam Huston and Tillotson Colleges. During segregation, his K–12 education was excellent. He wanted HT to provide a first-rate liberal arts education to its primarily Black students, though a diverse student body existed. The survival of HT for students' success was paramount, even if another merger was needed. An art program was established under King's administration.	McMillan believed a revised core curriculum was the way to bring excellent education to students. He called for a "first-class institution" like Harvard or Yale. Yet, he did little to make that happen. He created a divide between faculty, staff, and students, sometimes pushing faculty to "give grades." Mixed evaluations of McMillan and his effectiveness.	Earvin changed HT from a college to a university, giving higher status to degrees awarded. Under his presidency the first graduate degree was established, an MEd program. He created the DuBois Honor Society and initiated the Adult Degree Program for older learners in the workforce. Earvin used research to inform new majors. Green Is the New Black, a student environmental group, was established.	Pierce Burnette expected excellence from all students and those who taught them. Experiential learning through paid and unpaid internships was emphasized. An MBA program was created in 2019. The existing MEd program lost ground. She called her students the Genius Generation, expecting faculty to kindle that genius from within. Students overall evaluated her positively. Pierce Burnette established numerous APPLE initiatives, including the 100 African American Male Teacher Imitative Leadership scholarships.
President Student Relationship Note: Leadership success depends on dynamic relationships built on mutual trust, respect, and understanding.	King served as a father figure to students on many levels: providing housing, money, and scholarships for some while being a character role model for all. He expected students to be self-determined. He promoted enrollment of international students, with at one time having about 30 percent enrolled. He traveled with the choir and communicated with students through newsletters. King fostered within them an "I can do" attitude.	McMillan called himself a "students' president." He was highly visible with students, knew their names, and promoted an open-door policy. Some saw him as being easygoing and tenacious. He sometimes interacted inappropriately with select students at social gatherings. Some students were harmed by his actions. Some students saw him as standoffish, messy, and rude, being partial to certain students, such as his frat brothers. Jamaican students thought well of him because of the scholarships and benefits he gave.	Earvin knew far fewer students on a personal level than the other three presidents. Some students reported in my online survey that they only saw him on special occasions such as Charter Day and graduation. Students often overlooked the good things he did because of his absenteeism. Others noticed structural and academic changes under his leadership and saw him as business-minded and not as a family member.	Pierce Burnette saw herself as a students' president, encouraging her "geniuses" to rise to that standard. She attended many student functions and often took students to community events to "show off their accomplishments." She was a strong role model for her female students to matriculate in STEM majors. She also highlighted her students on her social media platforms. Some saw her as being partial to certain students.

330

APPENDIX

	Dr. King	Dr. McMillan	Dr. Earvin	Dr. Pierce Burnette
Retention and Recruitment Strategies Note: A problem for each president was limited scholarships and difficulties in financial aid; each negatively impacted retention and recruitment.	King established committees to review recruitment and retention policies and established the first Office of Enrollment. Raising money for scholarships was a priority; he even contributed to scholarships. Many students attended HT due to segregation; others came because of family legacy. As PWIs opened to Blacks, HT had to work differently to get and keep students. Alumni from King's administration were many and were committed to assist with recruitment by bringing potential students to HT.	McMillan inherited low enrollment and overall was not able to grow it. There was inadequate scholarship money, although some students got a "free ride" based on presidential whim, while others got nothing, increasing inequity among students. A financial aid crisis caused by fraudulent behavior by some staff resulted in staff arrest and high student turnover. Many students did not return because of the president's moral character. Many alumni decided not to send their children to HT because of the bad experience they had under McMillan's presidency. Austin Black churches that supported King by sending students and money withdrew support and encouragement during McMillan's administration. Many alumni from his tenure did not participate or give back to HT due to bad feelings about him and his administration.	Earvin established DuBois Honors scholars who were given full, four-year scholarships. Most completed HT, having one of the highest rates of completion. The Adult Degree Program helped raise total enrollment to over 1,000. Turnover in the enrollment, provost, and institutional development offices was high, making recruitment difficult. Towards the end of Earvin's tenure another financial aid crisis emerged, resulting in the firing of staff and the hiring of consultants to "clean up the mess." There was a substantial drop in enrollment between Earvin's last year and Pierce Burnette's first year due to the inability to provide students with financial aid packages on a timely basis.	Pierce Burnette was met with a financial aid crisis from the previous administration resulting in major government paybacks and a reduction in traditional student enrollment. Her goal was to increase HT's enrollment to 3,000 by increasing both traditional and adult program students; this did not happen. There is now a slight increase in traditional students and a slight decrease in Adult Degree Program students. Financial aid is a barrier to completion for both groups. Covid-19 led to a drop in enrollment, but Pierce Burnette's last year saw enrollment increases. She raised substantial scholarship money to assist students. Covid-19 and philanthropists' monies paid off some students' debt, resulting in a higher retention rate.

APPENDIX

	Dr. King	Dr. McMillan	Dr. Earvin	Dr. Pierce Burnette
Relationship with Faculty & Faculty Governance Note: Having full faculty governance and naming the unit a "Faculty Senate" was disallowed by two of the presidents because of the inherent perceived faculty power in such a body.	King was committed to faculty. While being sorry for not being able to give them deserved raises, he initiated other benefits such as free tuition for employees' children, paid health care benefits, and release time to pursue advanced degrees. All future employees can thank King for these benefits. A Faculty Senate was organized in the 1970s but was not active throughout his presidency. He and the Board of Trustees honored faculty's longevity and gave them retirement parties and gifts befitting the service they rendered. He was the only one of the four presidents to systematically honor longevity. Faculty and staff who worked with him regarded him and his presidency positively.	Wanting immediate curriculum changes, McMillan bypassed faculty and top administrators. He perceived faculty to be an obstacle to success, resulting in low faculty morale. He did not support adding new tenure positions. He rejected the reorganization of a Faculty Senate, until a SACS representative encouraged him to allow faculty to organize. He appointed a Vice President for Academic Affairs without faculty input, resulting in a crisis that spilled into the community and ultimately his own demise as president. At a faculty meeting he said there were "snakes among us; we need to rise up and kill them," further alienating constituents. Some people were honored at retirement with an institutional party and substantial gifts, while others weren't.	Earvin's greatest contribution to faculty was enrolling HT in the Faculty Resource Network at NYU in New York to further faculty development. Some faculty believed Earvin favored the business department with higher salaries and greater resources and autonomy as he brought with him the person to become dean of that department. Earvin "tolerated" HT's Faculty Advisory Council (FAC), a substitute for a Faculty Senate, and barely interacted with FAC as an organization. He preferred top-down relationships, often referring faculty to immediate supervisors; he was not usually accessible to most faculty. Longevity was not valued, as indicated by poor salary and limited internal promotion. Institutional retirement parties mostly did not exist. Faculty and staff initiated and primarily paid for colleagues' retirement parties.	Some faculty felt that Pierce Burnette, a self-declared students' president, valued students over them. She disagreed with that assessment and told faculty they were central to students' education. Unlike previous presidents, she met monthly with the chairperson and secretary of the FAC to hear pressing faculty concerns. Some faculty members believed this was a token action as she appointed important academic positions without initial input from key faculty. However, most professors were impressed with her openness, despite the fact they did not always get what they wanted. Institutional retirement parties didn't exist. Faculty initiated and primarily paid for those parties. A few faculty members left HT during Covid-19 and received no HT acknowledgement. She was a strong president during Covid, resulting in faculty, staff, and students being safe online and in person.

APPENDIX

	Dr. King	Dr. McMillan	Dr. Earvin	Dr. Pierce Burnette
Financial Challenges and Fundraising Strategies Note: For all four presidents, deep-pocket board members with critical financial contributions or contacts with deep pockets appeared to be missing.	King called himself a "professional beggar." He, along with HT choir, traveled throughout Austin and Texas to solicit funds from alumni associations, churches, and organizations. He initiated several funding sources that exist today, including federal Title III and the United Negro College Funds. The dire financial need resulted in his board considering merging HT with two other Texas HBCUs. Despite five tuition increases, few raises were given, and student programs were limited. Occasionally he refused his salary. King made personal donations to cover salaries by placing his home up for collateral.	McMillan did not like raising money, although that is a university president's primary function. His Office of Institutional Development lacked strong leadership in fundraising. He insisted that faculty and staff write grants to pick up his slack. At times he misused the grants funds for unrelated costs. Major grants were received to strengthen the education department. His administration was plagued with financial aid corruption, resulting in staff going to jail. He sold land on his signature only. Poor financial management resulted in HT's being placed on warning by SACS.	Earvin raised more than $1.5 million before he was inaugurated. Establishing a sound fiscal basis, he was eventually able to meet SACSOCS financial guidelines for reaffirmation. He created the MASKED Ball as a major fundraiser, raising scholarship money. HT also benefited from his national organizational involvements, as through some of those contacts he was able to raise money for HT. The Office of Institutional Development was often vacant, limiting HT's capacity to raise new revenue strands. Earvin received $3 million from an alumna for a campus health clinic, to be named after her daughter. Despite his strong financial legacy, Earvin left HT with a huge financial aid crisis.	Pierce Burnette believed that HT's fiscal health was linked to HT's visibility and connection to the Austin community and beyond. Finding alternative funding sources was a priority. Opening the campus to community groups brought income for unrestricted expenses. Being intentional in seeking equitable partnerships, Pierce Burnette believed that marketing HT as a partner and a pipeline, and not a charity case, would bring the best dividends. She received anonymous funding to make HT an all-Steinway University. Pierce Burnette wants to be remembered for her longstanding and reciprocal collaborations with organizations. She told alumni that she retired with HT being in the black. Covid CARES money and philanthropists paid off students' debts and provided funds for technology, etc. As is the case with her predecessors, the Office of Institutional Development was often vacant with high turnover and limited fundraising, resulting in no real capital campaign activities.

APPENDIX

	Dr. King	Dr. McMillan	Dr. Earvin	Dr. Pierce Burnette
Reaffirmation Note: Reaffirmation occurs every ten years. The institution can get fully accredited, warning, probation, or not reaccredited.	King successfully took HT through two reaccreditations, in 1970 and 1980, and ended his presidency in 1988 at the beginning of his third reaccreditation, passed on to the next president. The reaccreditation process begins 2–3 years before it is due.	McMillan inherited the 1990 reaccreditation which resulted in reaffirmation with some recommendations needing to be addressed. His second reaffirmation process, in 2000, did not go as well. HT's finances were in such disarray that HT was placed on warning, which he passed to Earvin, his successor.	Earvin began his presidency with HT being on warning. He had a great deal of knowledge about the accreditation process as he worked with SACS previously. His initial presidential task was to bring HT faculty and staff together to do the hard lifting needed to become reaffirmed. Within his first year, HT moved from warning to probation; the next step would be "not reaffirmed." The downhill spiral was the result of unfinished McMillan work. Along with raising money and crafting excellent responses to SACSOCS, HT was taken off probation and was reaffirmed during Earvin's second year without recommendations. This was his greatest contribution to HT.	Pierce Burnette began her presidency during the fifth year of the ten-year reaccreditation cycle. She was responsible for the 2020 reaccreditation, during Covid. Doing most of the process online, the institution was reaccredited.
HT as a Family (fRAMily) Note: Historically, HT was viewed as a family away from home; that view is changing.	King was the president during segregation, which may have facilitated closeness of students, faculty, staff, and administration. The spirit of family was prevalent throughout King's presidency. He advocated for a new model that included a strong financial base while keeping the culture of family, which has proven to be a forecast of the future.	McMillan: During a time of integration, students had more choices. The student body was drawn from more diverse backgrounds and locations. Faculty and staff continued to foster a family environment, but not McMillan. He viewed HT more as a community, not a family, and not everyone was considered part of the community.	Since Earvin was viewed as an absentee president, students who responded to my survey evaluated him low on creating a family environment. However, perceiving HT as family had less to do with the president than with faculty and staff with whom students had frequent contact.	Pierce Burnette nurtured students as a parent would a child, with high expectations for them. Many student respondents reported that HT felt like a family, despite the problems they sometimes faced in dealing with systems and programs. Under her presidency, HT constituents were referred to as HT fRAMily, with HT mascot, the "Ram," embedded in family. As in all families there were ups and downs.

APPENDIX

	Dr. King	Dr. McMillan	Dr. Earvin	Dr. Pierce Burnette
Improving HT's Visibility Note: HT is the oldest institution of higher education in Austin but the least known. All presidents identified the lack of visibility as a problem.	King was deeply grounded in segregated East Austin; his family business was and still is located there. HT was often the place to go for programs and activities. Though visible in the Black community, HT was often invisible to the Austin community. King's presidency was primarily pre-internet/social media platforms. His efforts towards visibility were primarily relational: face-to-face or through letters and speeches. Some key connections included President Lyndon B. Johnson, Congressman Lloyd Doggett, military personnel, and the United Methodist Church. He had many alumni who became well-known, some of whom acknowledged HT's contributions to their success.	As McMillan was viewed as charismatic and an excellent speaker, HT and the community initially welcomed him. Early on he was invited to speak at different venues on behalf of HT. In later years, however, Austin's religious community and other organizations withdrew from HT when concerns arose about his activities with students and his negative image. There were many unfavorable newspaper articles on him and his leadership.	With a focus on national boards and involvement, Earvin did little to nurture positive relationships with partners in Austin. He was viewed as an absentee leader by many students, faculty, staff, and the community. During his presidency, many community leaders continued to back away from HT as he did not create a welcoming environment.	Pierce Burnette's major goal was to increase HT's visibility by focusing outward. She used Facebook, Instagram, LinkedIn, email, Twitter, and YouTube to reach HT constituents and the Austin community. She made HT more visible via community involvement, interviews, and written articles. As a sought-after speaker by community organizations, she welcomed opportunities to share her HT vision with a broad audience. She won accolades from many about the very positive way she presented HT to the community. Her efforts resulted in increased scholarship donations and internship opportunities. Pierce Burnette was able to bring the religious community back to HT with intentional activities. HT welcomed community organizations to have activities on campus. She received the 2021 Austinite of the Year award, giving evidence of making herself visible and indirectly making HT visible. A concern is whether her visibility could be translated to HT's visibility after her retirement. Her wish is that organizations and partnerships she nurtured will be available to the president who followed her.

APPENDIX

	Dr. King	Dr. McMillan	Dr. Earvin	Dr. Pierce Burnette
President's Relationship with the Board of Trustees Note: The Board of Trustees hires the president and CEO of HT. However, their relationship to the president differs.	King came through the ranks from teacher to dean to president. The board must have seen something in him to hand him the reins to HT. Reviewing board reports indicates that King and the board had a good professional relationship, although there were times he was disappointed with the board's involvement. King asked each board member to give at least $1,000 per year. Under King, a faculty could sit on the board's Education Committee meeting but could only speak if asked a question and did not have a vote. None of the other presidents even allowed that, although Faculty Senate requested a seat under each president.	McMillan was on the board when he was selected president. He had no prior administrative or teaching experience at a college or university. As a United Church of Christ representative to the board, the presidency was "given to him" because no former president was from that religious affiliation. McMillan controlled his board, giving it partial information which did not always depict real-time happenings. He also got the board to approve his buying and selling HT's property on his signature alone. McMillan's board president engaged in verbal confrontation with the faculty founders of Save HT. Seventeen years after McMillan's presidency, his board president stated that McMillan was not the best president for the college.	Earvin: Because of the conflict with the previous president, the HT board strongly voiced the need for faculty input in the presidential selection. Faculty members selected me and another to be on the search committee. The board president, a carryover from McMillan's board, did not want me on the committee and intentionally retaliated against me because of that. I was accused of sharing confidential information with non-committee members. I sent a letter to the board president to cease the harassment; it stopped. After Earvin was selected, the board told him negative things about me, including asking him to let me go. He did not do it, perhaps because I was tenured. Due to board influence, Earvin would not approve my moving into administrative positions under his leadership until his thirteenth year. With no one else capable of being Acting Dean for CAS (it had five deans in three years), Earvin asked me to do so for a few months, which lasted until he retired, seventeen months later.	Pierce Burnette was at HT only seven years but received exceptional support from the board. However, she began her presidency with a serious financial aid problem that even the board president was unaware of. Had she been told, Pierce Burnette said, her initial HT goals would have been different. She indicated that she was transparent, giving the board "the good, bad, and ugly" information on HT. During the 2023 graduation, the Board of Trustees named Pierce Burnette President Emerita.

Notes

Preface

1. Chrystine Shackles, *Reminiscences of Huston-Tillotson College* (Austin: Best Printing Co., 1973). Ms. Shackles left Atlanta to teach history at HT in 1928, with the intention of staying only one year. She retired from HT in 1968.
2. Bronté Denise Jones, "Restoring Accreditation in Two Private Texas Historically Black Colleges," online dissertation, May 2005, https://repositories.lib.utexas.edu/bitstream/handle/2152/1583/jonesb53400.pdf.
3. I also worked under Dr. Archie Vanderpuye, an interim president for three months. Dr. Vanderpuye served HT for over ten years, with his most recent titles being provost and vice president for academic affairs. He was interim president in 2022 from the time of Dr. Burnette's leaving to that of Dr. Wallace's hire as the new HT president and CEO. Vanderpuye's interim presidency will not be addressed in this book; Wallace's presidency will have minor notations.
4. Robert Smith, "The Financial Struggles Facing HBCUs and Students," Robert F. Smith blog, August 16, 2021, https://robertsmith.com/the-financial-struggles-.facing-hbcs-and-students/.
5. Jon Edelman, "Report Reveals a Differing Picture of Debt at HBCUs," *Diverse: Issues in Higher Education*, September 7, 2022, https://www.diverseeducation.com/institutions/hbcus/article/15296482/report-reveals-a-differing-picture-of-debt-at-hbcus.
6. Although at times staff data is included, it is not a focus of the book. Staff voices are important, and my hope is that someone else will capture theirs. For example, Mrs. Earnestine Strickland has been at HT eight months shy of my tenure: fifty years as registrar and in other capacities. She also graduated from HT while working there.
7. Peter M. Senge, *The Fifth Discipline: The Art & Practice of the Learning Organization* (New York: Crown Currency, 2010).
8. The announcement of our seventh president, Dr. Melva Williams (within months she got married and is now Wallace), was made in August 2023. The book doesn't contain much information about her, but it was important to include the name of the new president. When the book was submitted in July 2022, HT was in search of a president.
9. Mr. Buyers died in 2020.
10. Dr. Schwab died in May 2021.
11. Dr. McMillan was interviewed in November 2017.
12. The University Marshal carries the mace, which symbolizes the heritage of the university and

reaffirms the institution's continuing commitments. The most senior ranking member of the faculty is the University Marshal. I was University Marshal from 2001 to 2023, under three presidents. Under Presidents Earvin and Burnette, the Universal Marshal led the president into the formal events. Under Dr. Wallace (the newest president), the University Marshal begins, and the president ends, the procession.

13. Board members are critical to the success of an institution. To the extent they both support and hold presidents accountable, an institution thrives. When board members fail to fulfill their roles as fundraisers and overseers, institutions suffer. The latter happened under Dr. McMillan's administration.
14. Niche, https://www.niche.com/colleges/huston-tillotson-university/reviews/?category=Academics.
15. SurveyMonkey, https://www.surveymonkey.com/.

Acknowledgments

1. Huston-Tillotson College and Huston-Tillotson University are often referred to as HT in this document.
2. John Q. Taylor King (1921–2011).
3. King's daughter, Marjon Christopher (1949–2022).
4. Joseph T. McMillan (1944–2017).
5. Harriet Buxkemper (1928–2017).
6. Theodore Francis left HT in summer 2022 for a Predominantly White Institution (PWI) paying a higher salary and offering dedicated money for research.
7. Betty Etier (1927–2016).
8. The list of face-to-face participants is found in HT's archives.
9. Carolyn Collins (1941–2022).

Prologue

1. Frederick Douglass, *Narrative of the Life of Frederick Douglass, an American Slave* (Boston: Anti-Slavery Office, 1845).
2. The University of Texas, a privileged White institution, was established in 1883 in Austin, eight years after the founding of Tillotson College.
3. Chrystine Shackles, *Reminiscences of Huston-Tillotson College* (Austin: Best Printing Co., 1973), 6.
4. Chrystine Shackles, Huston-Tillotson website, https://www.sutori.com/story/huston-tillotson-university.
5. Huston-Tillotson College, *Faculty Handbook, 1989*. In HT Archives.
6. Texas State Historical Association, "Tillotson College" (1952, updated 2020), https://www.tshaonline.org/handbook/entries/tillotson-college.
7. James D. Richardson, *The Abolitionist's Journal: Memories of an American Antislavery Family* (Albuquerque: High Road Books/University of New Mexico Press, 2022), 3.
8. Ibid., 5.

9. Ibid., 185.
10. Ibid., 185. Lovinggood was the longest serving president (1900–1916) of Samuel Huston. His academic area was Greek and Latin; students had to take four years of Latin.
11. Shackles, *Reminiscences of Huston-Tillotson College*.
12. Jeff Miller, "The Undertold Story of Jackie Robinson's College Hoops Coaching Days," *Texas Monthly*, April 14, 2023, https://www.texasmonthly.com/arts-entertainment/jackie-robinson-hbcu-basketball-coach/.
13. Linda Jackson, "Jackie Robinson and Roland Harden—HT Connection," *Ram Magazine*, August 12, 2016, www.htu.edu, and "Jackie Robinson's Lasting Impact on the World and HT," Summer/Fall 2007, https://htu.edu/18168/ht-joins-to-world-in-celebration-of-jackie-robinson-day#fancybox-2. Jackson did not give the dates he was on the HT board.
14. "African Americans in Austin." You Are Here, ATX. https://www.youarehereatx.org/african-americans-in-austin/.
15. Shackles, *Reminiscences of Huston-Tillotson College*, 18. Shackles taught history at HT from 1928 to 1969. She published this book the same year I started teaching at HT.
16. Ibid.
17. Ibid., 16.
18. Huston-Tillotson College, *Catalogue 1961–1962, 1962–1963*, 12, HT Archives.
19. Ibid.
20. Huston-Tillotson University History, HT website, www.htu.edu.
21. In this research Huston-Tillotson will be referred to as a college until February 2005 when the institution was renamed a university. As a college, the abbreviation was HT-C; after its renaming to "university" it is HT. I will use HT throughout this research.
22. John Q. Taylor King, Board Report, March 12, 1967, HT Archives.
23. John Q. Taylor King, Board Report, March 25, 1969, HT Archives.

Chapter 1

1. John Q. Taylor King papers, "A Fisk Family: Four Generations of Faith and Leadership or The Allen-Woodson-King Tradition," n.d., HT archives.
2. David Williams, "Parallel and Crossover Lives: Texas before and after Desegregation," Humanities Texas, May 29, 2001, https://www.humanitiestexas.org/sites/default/files/page-attachment/King_John_Interview.pdf.
3. Williams, "Parallel and Crossover Lives."
4. Her children, Marjon Christopher and Stuart King, indicated that their mother was deeply hurt by the Board's decision, as teaching was one of her passions. Another passion was music; she played piano for a local church for many years.
5. Hal Drake. "Interview with Dr. King," *Pacific Stars and Stripes*, HT Archives.
6. John Q. Taylor King speech, "To Serve the Future Hour," *The Informer* 8, no. 4, May 1975, excerpts pp. 6–9, HT Archives.
7. Aristotle indicated that educating the mind without educating the heart is no education at all.
8. Wilhelmina Perry and Gus Swain, *Huston-Tillotson University Legacy: A Historical Treasure*, self-published, 2007.

NOTES

9. Alumni stories came from interviews, websites, newspapers, obituaries, and HT documents. Alumni SurveyMonkey was designed to specifically collect their quantitative and qualitative responses related to their time at HT. Their survey responses were pregnant with rich data.
10. Charles Akins (1932–2017).
11. Melissa B. Taboada, "BREAKING NEWS: Longtime Austin Educator Dr. Charles Akins Dies," *Austin American-Statesman*, March 29, 2017, https://www.statesman.com/story/news/2017/03/29/breaking-news-longtime-austin-educator-dr-charles-akins-dies/10395117007/.
12. Ada Anderson was interviewed on October 18, 2017; she died on June 5, 2021.
13. June Brewer (1925–2010).
14. *Sweatt v. Painter* (1946) was a case the NAACP took to the courts to force UT to provide legal education to a Black man, Heman Sweatt. Rather than integrating the law school, UT set aside a below-standard basement space with limited resources for Sweatt to be educated.
15. Reginald Christopher (1938–2023).
16. Marvin Kimbrough (1932–2010).
17. Bertha Means (1921–2021), former HT board member, died at age 100.
18. James Means (1910–2008) died at age 99.
19. UT allowed a cohort of six Black students to enter in 1956, the same year that Ms. Morton graduated from HT. https://precursors.utexas.edu/#:~:text=In%201956%20the%20first%20African,have%20attended%20this%20flagship%20institution. 2016.
20. Blackpast.com, An Online Reference Guide to African American History, https://blackpast.org/aah/morton-azie-taylor-1936-2003.
21. Wilhelmina Perry (1925–2022) died at age 97.
22. Austin Revitalization Authority, Dr. Charles E. Urdy Plaza, https://austinrev.org/projects/dr-charles-e-urdy-plaza/.
23. Coach Wilson (1936–2023).
24. John Q. Taylor King's Board reports are found in HT Archives.
25. Ibid.
26. John Q. Taylor King, Board Report, March 1969, HT Archives.
27. John Q. Taylor King, "Report on Christian Higher Education: Education for Responsible Living," n.d. (probably around 1974, a year before HT's 100-year anniversary), HT Archives.
28. Excerpts from King's Report of the Commission on Higher Education, n.d. (probably around 1974), HT Archives.
29. President's Report to the Board of Trustees, March 25, 1969, HT Archives.
30. HT bulletin, HT Archives.
31. Note how similar these skills are to those held personally by Dr. King.
32. 1983–1987 Bulletins in HT Archives.
33. Gary Job Corps Center: Job Corps is a no-cost education and career technical training program administered by the US Department of Labor to help young people ages 16–24 improve their lives and careers. For more information see http://www.sanmarcostx.gov/1085/Gary-Job-Corps-Center.
34. Yearbook is in HT Archives.
35. HT alumni responses, HT alumni magazine, "Celebrating Fondest Memories, the Class of

1967," HT Archives.
36. Student survey (SurveyMonkey), administered November 2017 to March 2018; see preface.
37. Alumni were interviewed face-to-face and by SurveyMonkey as described in the preface.
38. When I interviewed retired Dr. Arberenia Malone, she was the oldest HT faculty member at 96. She received a PhD in Business Administration from UT Austin during the early 1960s, one of the first Black students to do so. She died July 22, 2018, at 98. She was the chairperson of the Social Science Division when I was hired at HT.
39. Billy Harden (1953–2018).
40. Ada Harden and her son Billy Harden were interviewed by me together in November 2017.
41. Julie Hutchinson, "Keeping Faith: Huston-Tillotson University's King Gives Decades of Devotion," *Austin American-Statesman*, August 11, 1985.
42. John Q. Taylor King, Board of Trustees report, October 1973, HT Archives.
43. Michael Cardinenaz, "Students End Boycott," *Daily Texan*, March 3, 1976, Texas Humanities Archives.
44. Students in my Spring 1988 Community class interviewed HT students as a class assignment. Research was reported in numbers and percentages.
45. King's son, Stuart King, and daughter, Marjon Christopher, elaborated on the financial sacrifice that their family endured to supplement HT's financial deficit. It included King's foregoing or accepting a reduced salary some months; interview in November 2017.
46. Marjon Christopher and Stuart King called their father a "professional beggar"; I then found the same reference in two articles.
47. Hutchinson, "Keeping Faith."
48. Title III is a government-funded program that still exists today. An annual proposal is submitted containing the specific projects to be funded—faculty development activities, funds for communication, etc. For example, under Dr. King an art curriculum was funded (art major/minor programs no longer exist).
49. TRIO programs are federal outreach and student services for individuals from disadvantaged backgrounds. TRIO includes eight programs in the 1980s targeted to serve and assist low-income individuals, first-generation college students, and individuals with disabilities to progress through the academic pipeline from middle school to postbaccalaureate programs. It also included a training program for staff: https://www2.ed.gov/about/offices/list/ope/trio/index.html.
50. UNCF has various programs through which HBCU institutions apply for funds.
51. *Lou Rawls Parade of Stars* (later *An Evening of Stars*) was an annual telethon featuring pop singers and other celebrities. The twelve-hour event raised money for the UNCF, and the local colleges participated by getting people in its community to make pledges. HT participated in the telethon from its inception in 1979 until it ended in 2015. The amount of money raised locally affected the amount of money returned to the college. Dr. King often served on local TV as a cohost and/or a phone operator receiving pledges. Performing stars included Anita Baker, Bob Hope, Patti LaBelle, and Julio Iglesias: https://www.nytimes.com/1989/12/29/arts/lou-rawls-telethon.html.
52. Governor Mark White, President Lyndon B. Johnson, Senator Lloyd Doggett, Mayor Carole Keeton Rylander (1977–1983), etc.

53. John Q. Taylor King, Board Report, March 16, 1966, HT Archives.
54. Division of Higher Education, Board of Education, the United Methodist Church, Higher Education Report: Special Race Relations Sunday Issue, January–March 1971.
55. John Q. Taylor King, Board Report, March 19, 1971, HT Archives.
56. These Tier 1 universities changed their financial status through increased endowments, alumni support, and successful million-dollar capital campaigns. King advocated for all these strategies in many of his board reports, strongly insisting that board members and other constituents assist with fundraising.
57. John Q. Taylor King, Board Report, 1969, HT Archives.
58. John Q. Taylor King, Board Report, 1980, HT Archives.
59. John Q. Taylor King, Board Report, 1983, HT Archives.
60. John Q. Taylor King, Board Report, 1971 and 1973, HT Archives.
61. In 2017, TEG provided up to $3,364 but in unusual circumstances would pay as much as $5,042 to private colleges/universities.
62. Alumni News brochure, November 1982, HT Archives.
63. This occurred with the living gift of the Polk property (1973). In exchange for 105 acres, HT took care of Mr. Polk's taxes, home repairs, insurance, and health needs. Mr. Polk lived for ten more years, costing the college a considerable amount of money, and at times the bequest was contested by relatives. Other property "gifts" have also been contested by relatives.
64. John Q. Taylor King, Board Report, 1985, HT Archives.
65. In October 1985, a letter concerning a merger request was sent to King from Dr. Julius S. Bill Junior, Associate General Secretary of the Board (UMC), HT Archives.
66. John Q. Taylor King papers, 1987, HT Archives.
67. A guaranty agency insures federal loans by repaying the loan holder when a loan defaults.
68. GSL is Guarantee Student Loan. It is now replaced with Stafford loans, which are low-interest loans for eligible students to help cover the cost of higher education.
69. John Q. Taylor King, Board Report, October 1974, HT Archives.
70. Steve Reed, "Huston-Tillotson Seeking Support in the Wake of Cash-Flow Problems," *Austin American-Statesman*, April 11, 1987.
71. Huston-Tillotson "Make a Difference," 87–88 *Rams*, 1988 yearbook interview with Dr. John Q. Taylor King, HT Archives.
72. Consortia 1, 3, and 5–9 no longer exist. HT still participates in consortia 2 and 4. Information for them came from various board reports and some letters filed in my office, to be given to HT Archives. Information as to whether the consortia still exist came from various websites.
73. Many HT faculty members participated in research supported by Consortiums for Research Training (CRT). As the HT liaison, I collected the research and sent a copy to CTR and gave a copy to HT library to be placed in the archives.
74. From program, special business seminar, Striving for Excellence in Business and Education, sponsored by HT Department of Business Administration and Economics and BEEP of the National Urban League, November 1987.
75. King's Board Report, HT Archives. Additional information can be found on United Methodist Higher Education & Ministry website, https://www.gbhem.org/education-leaders/bcf-for-schools/list-of-bcf-schools/, retrieved on July 3, 2023.

NOTES

76. HT and ACC have new agreements (from President Earvin's tenure). One such is that if a student has an associate's degree that student does not have to take HT's required core curriculum. The student can go right to the major unless the major requires specific core courses not taken at ACC.
77. King, Board of Trustees Report, March 1966.
78. John Q. Taylor King, Board Report, 1967, HT Archives.
79. Ibid.
80. Dr. Waters (1972–2000) had academic and staff positions at HT under King and McMillan. Under Dr. King she was a professor of education and the Vice President of Academic Affairs. Under McMillan she was also VPAA and had other positions to be noted later. I interviewed her on October 24, 2017, at her home.
81. Coach Dubra met King as a student 1958–1964. He lived with King for a period as a student. King brought him to HT as a faculty to coach the women's basketball team from 1969–1988; he coached under McMillan; 1988–1999; returned 2005–2017.
82. John T. King, "Serving the Disadvantaged in Higher Education Report," Special Race Relations Sunday Issue, Division of Higher Education, Board of Education, United Methodist Church, January–March 1971, HT Archives.
83. See HT 1980 and 1985 Bulletins, HT Archives.
84. Currently, TRIO (2024) consists of six basic programs: https://www2.ed.gov/about/offices/list/ope/trio/index.html.
85. I created the field placement course in 1974, within the first year of my teaching at HT. My master's was in social work, and I brought the field placement course requirement from that major to the sociology major.
86. Throughout HT's history majors were created and then dismantled depending on specific funding. This is not unique to HT but to HBCUs and smaller PWIs that have limited discretionary funds, endowments, and capital funding activities. In 2023, with the large population of 65 and over, a major in gerontology would meet critical societal needs for programs for that population.
87. HT was accredited by Texas Education Agency, The University Senate of the United Methodist Church, The National Committee on Accrediting, the Council for Higher Education of the United Church of Christ, and more importantly Southern Association of Colleges and Schools as a Level II General postsecondary institution. Information found in Huston-Tillotson College Bulletin, 1983–1985, HT Archives.
88. It was under King's administration when HIV awareness led to the establishment of global health programs. Many Austin community organizations became involved in eradicating HIV among its varied populations.
89. Huston-Tillotson College Bulletin, 1978–1980, 14, HT Archives.
90. Huston-Tillotson College Bulletin, 1978–1980, 14, HT Archives.
91. Student/alumni survey conducted between November 2017 and March 2018.
92. Alumni survey responses under King's administration on HT SurveyMonkey. Some grammar was corrected, but content was not changed.
93. Robert Duncan, "King, John Quill Taylor, Sr.," https://tshaonline.org/handbook/online/articles/fki77.

94. John Q. Taylor King, "Excerpts from an Address Made to the United Methodist Black Colleges at a Crossroads," no date, HT Archives. HBCUs are further addressed in chapter 6.
95. Names for African Americans varied over time, given by Whites to undercut their status in the US.
96. National Archives, *Plessy v. Ferguson* (1896). The ruling in this Supreme Court case upheld a Louisiana state law that allowed for "equal but separate accommodations for the white and colored races." https://www.archives.gov/milestone-documents/plessy-v-ferguson.
97. Jean Van Delinder, "*Brown v Board of Education of Topeka*: A Landmark Case Unresolved Fifty Years Later," *Prologue Magazine* 36, no. 1 (Spring 2004), https://www.archives.gov/publications/prologue/2004/spring/brown-v-board-1.html#:~:text=The%20Topeka%20Brown%20case%20is,children%20of%20equal%20educational%20opportunities. The wording, 'all deliberate speed' was vague and subject to interpretation and much delay in desegregation.
98. Lyndon B. Johnson, "Civil Rights Act of 1964," National Archives, https://www.archives.gov/milestone-documents/civil-rights-act. This prohibited discrimination in public places, provided for the integration of schools and other public facilities, and made employment discrimination illegal. It was the most sweeping civil rights legislation since Reconstruction.
99. Austin History Center, "Integration Suit Filed on Austin," [AF-Segregation-Public Schools-S1700 (2)-1970; *Austin American-Statesman*, August 08, 1970]. https://austinlibrary.com/ahc/desegregation/index.cfm.
100. Humanities Texas, "Parallel and Crossover Lives: Texas Before and After Desegregation," https://www.humanitiestexas.org/sites/default/files/page-attachment/King_John_Interview.pdf.
101. Ibid.

Chapter 2

1. Joseph T. McMillan, "A President's Message," final report to the Board of Trustees, 2000, HT Archives.
2. I used the word "dash" for McMillan's entire presidency, 1988–2000.
3. Joseph T. McMillan, letter to HT Board of Trustees as part of the selection process for HT president, 1987.
4. McMillan memorial services, http://www.publicnow.com/view/226F9F75A54CFD3113DFDADDC869A1B92375376B.
5. The Evangelical and Reformed Church and the General Council of the Congregational Christian Churches united in 1957 to form the UCC.
6. Information on McMillan's awards came from his obituary from King-Tears website and *Austin American-Statesman* websites.
7. Ibid.
8. King's statement regarding the appointment of Dr. Joseph T. McMillan Jr. as president of Huston-Tillotson College, December 4, 1987.
9. A face-to-face interview with King's son and daughter was conducted in November 2017.
10. Joseph McMillan, President-Elect, Huston-Tillotson College, December 4, 1987, press release, HT Archives.

NOTES

11. Many of the documents quoted in McMillan's chapter were in my personal document collection that I gave to HT Archives after the completion of this book. McMillan's inaugural program is one of those documents.
12. Huston-Tillotson College *Alumni & Friends* magazine, inaugural issue, Spring 1989, HT Alumni.
13. HT alumni names came from various sources, including an online survey, face-to-face interviews, and Wilhelmina Perry and Gus Swain, *Huston-Tillotson University Legacy: A Historical Treasure*, self-published, 2007.
14. Merle Miles-Adams (1936–2017). She taught at HT from 1973 to 2000.
15. Texas Humanities, "Texas Originals – J. Mason Brewer," assessed November 25, 2017, https://www.humanitiestexas.org/programs/tx-originals/list/j-mason-brewer.
16. I interviewed Mr. Linder on August 27, 2017.
17. Johnnie M. Overton, "Overton, Volma Robert, Sr.," assessed January 16, 2019, https://tshaonline.org/handbook/online/articles/fov02.
18. General Marshall (1936–2020) died at age 84. I interviewed him in November 2017.
19. Austin Independent School District, "Middle School Naming Honors a Lifetime of Service," June 30, 2022, https://www.austinisd.org/announcements/2022/06/30/middle-school-naming-honors-lifetime-service-en-espanol.
20. I interviewed Curry-Jones on November 8, 2017.
21. Margaret Moser, "Keeping Up with the Joneses: A Way of Life Compressed into Two Lives," *Austin Chronicle*, June 18, 2010, https://www.austinchronicle.com/music/2010-06-18/1042038/; Texas Music Museum, www.texasmusicmuseum.org.
22. I interviewed Waters on October 24, 2017.
23. Harriet Buxkemper (1928–2017) was critical to the Save HT Committee's success.
24. Jennifer Davies completed one of the faculty surveys for this study. The quote came from the 2017 SurveyMonkey.
25. SACS institutions are found in Florida, Georgia, Kentucky, Louisiana, Mississippi, North Carolina, South Carolina, Alabama, Texas, and Virginia, as well as schools for US students in Mexico, the Caribbean, Central America, and South America. SACS had an organizational structural change resulting in a name change to SACS Commission on Colleges (SACSCOC).
26. I interviewed McMillan in November 2017.
27. Bronte Jones, "Restoring Accreditation in Two Private Texas Historically Black Colleges," Appendix A, 165–70, https://repositories.lib.utexas.edu/bitstream/handle/2152/1583/jonesb53400.pdf.
28. Ibid.
29. I interviewed Terry Smith in November 2017.
30. McMillan inherited a low student population of around 506 full-time equivalencies (FTE) in 1988; the next year, 1989, the enrollment had a 37 percent increase. In 1990 it increased to 700, a 2.2 percent increase. Enrollment dropped and in 1993 was 531 with a 13 percent increase (611) in 1994. Fall 1996 saw 701 students (the highest number), but spring 1997 saw a dip back to less than 700. Fall 1997 saw an enrollment of 696.
31. McMillan, "President's Task Force on Student Retention," April 25, 1989, HT Archives.
32. Memo from McMillan to members of the faculty, staff, and selected student leaders of HT,

NOTES

February 8, 1991, HT Archives.

33. *The Ram*, Huston-Tillotson College and Friends Magazine, Reunion Edition, Spring/Summer 1995, 3, HT Archives.
34. McMillan, "The Fate of the Old Administration Building," HT Archives.
35. My interview with a student who wanted to remain anonymous, 2017.
36. Bronté Jones phone interview, November 12, 2017. She worked in various capacities at HT, as an economics adjunct professor, assistant dean of Financial Services, director of Enrollment Management, VP of Financial Services, and consultant.
37. Jones interview, November 12, 2017. Information can also be found in her dissertation, "Restoring Accreditation in Two Private Texas Historically Black Colleges," 104.
38. I applied for the position of executive vice president to McMillan. Terry Smith also applied and got the position. McMillan said I was "not loyal to him." The emphasis was on him and not on HT.
39. McMillan denied this aggression in his July 16, 1999, response to a faculty member's July 14, 1999, letter to him. Letters were part of my collection, placed in HT Archives.
40. This is a quote from my September 2017 interview with McMillan.
41. McMillan's showed obvious love for the Alpha "brothers." Many Alphas received special treatment. His adopted son told me that McMillan's presidential archival material was left to his Alpha friend. None of that material was placed in the HT Archives.
42. King-Tears website, https://www.king-tearsmortuary.com/obituary/DrJoseph-McMillanJr.
43. Paul Anaejionu, Rosalee Martin, and Harriet Buxkemper, "Bill of Particulars: Accountability and Stewardship at Huston-Tillotson College," excerpts from a student interview for the document. The student came to HT the same year that McMillan began his presidency. The president, new to HT, changed long-standing Miss UNCF processes, resulting in crisis and confusion. Information for the Bill of Particulars came from persons who participated in an underground group, Save HT (1999), in HT Archives.
44. Consequences to changing the UNCF rules included alumni and community dissatisfaction and backlash, as a petition circulated for signatures that Miss UNCF be crowned based on funds raised alone as was historically the case.
45. Much more about the Save HT Committee is forthcoming.
46. Alexa Buxkemper's story is in the Bill of Particulars. She is the daughter of HT professor Harriet Buxkemper, one of the organizers of Save HT. As an older student, Alexa spoke to the City Council on behalf of the group. The group suspected that an HT request for zoning change might indicate that the board and president had motives not in the best interests of HT.
47. McMillan's inauguration speech, October 21–23, 1988, in *Alumni & Friends* Huston-Tillotson College magazine, inaugural issue, Spring 1989. Among my documents, placed in HT Archives.
48. Interview with Dr. McMillan, September 15, 2017.
49. Letter from McMillan dated February 9, 1991, that primarily focuses on academic affairs and curriculum revisions. It is among my papers, placed in HT Archives.
50. Educational Policy Council (EPC) is chaired by the Vice President of Academic Affairs; members are academic department heads, selected faculty and staff, and other administrators.
51. Lenora Waters, "Vision for Academic Affairs," HT Archives.

NOTES

52. Institutional Goal 2 is omitted because it doesn't refer to academic affairs.
53. Rosalee Martin Wingate (married name) was the chairperson for that division from 1983 to 1999.
54. Dee Seligman, May 3, 1992, letter to McMillan in response to his February 19, 1991, letter. It is among my papers in HT Archives.
55. The core competencies were: Effective Communication, Analysis/Problem Solving/Critical Thinking, Citizenship and Social Responsibility, Appreciation of Diversity in a Context of Global and Historical Awareness, Understanding and Applying Science, Wellness, Aesthetics, Ethical Reasoning and Behavior, and Effective Use of Technology.
56. Mary Ann Roser, "Teacher Training Is Under Scrutiny," *Austin American-Statesman*, September 29, 1999.
57. Judith Loredo was a former school superintendent and was very familiar with the workings of Texas education.
58. Joseph T. McMillan, Report to the Board of Trustees, May 21–22, 1998, HT Archives.
59. Ibid.
60. Instead of using his name, I use MT for McMillan's interim VPAA, the individual who was in the center of the conflict between HT faculty and the president. I do this to protect his identity and prevent any legal ramification regarding the individual.
61. A conversation I had with the hotel and restaurant management professor who quit teaching on the spot (1999).
62. Many professors believed that the action of MT resulted in the termination of the HT Hotel and Restaurant Management Program, but Earvin, in a memo to faculty, said that the decision to terminate the major was the result of a SACS recommendation. This statement was questioned because SACS does not dictate what programs to have but does insist that the institution have resources to sustain and assess programs according to institutional policy.
63. *The Ram* (newsletter), February 28, 1996, HT Archives.
64. My interview with Terry Smith was in 2017.
65. I interviewed Waters on October 24, 2017.
66. Texas continued to be an "at-will employment" state, meaning no reason has to be given for firing or quitting.
67. Faculty document and McMillan's response were among my papers, placed in HT Archives.
68. It should be noted that McMillan's assessment that faculty only worked half a year created tension between faculty and staff, as staff often resented faculty not having a regular forty-hour week. There were times this sentiment was actually expressed, especially when there was heavy staff work-crunch. Also, some of McMillan's response did not have anything to do with the faculty recommendation.
69. An in-depth discussion of the UNCF fiasco was previously discussed.
70. Reginald Christopher, "A Second-Class Institution," *NOKOA*, September 18–24, 1992.
71. Reginald Christopher, "WHOOPS," *NOKOA*, September 25–October 1, 1992.
72. Reginald Christopher, "If You Love Our College, Don't Stand Back and Watch," NOKOA editorial, October 2–8, 1992, 2.
73. Nancy Crayton '53, (1932–2022), "International Alumni Support HT's Administration," *NOKOA*, October 9–15, 1992.

NOTES

74. Anonymous student, "The Truth Lies within the Administration (Pun Well Intended)," *The Villager*, October 16–23, 1992.
75. Rosalee Martin, "Breaking the Silence," *NOKOA*, October 2–8, 1992.
76. Coretta Taylor and Chuck Lindell, "HT No Time for Nostalgia. At 40, Growing Pains for Huston-Tillotson University," *Austin American-Statesman*, 1992. Among my papers, given to HT Archives.
77. Jones decided to leave HT because she could not grow professionally. Later she worked as a consultant with Earvin.
78. Joseph McMillan, letter to academic departments and division chairs of HT, July 16, 1999, HT Archives.
79. The faculty expressed their issues regarding Dr. McMillan to the SACS visiting team and felt they were heard by them.
80. Waters was removed from her VPAA position without McMillan's consulting her; Dr. McMillan believed by giving her another title she wouldn't care about the move. She was furnished the title of Senior Vice President, Dean of the College, but given the job to lead HT's self-study even though McMillan knew she planned on retiring prior to the completion of the self-study. Many professors believed McMillan moved Waters from the VPAA position because he couldn't control her and because she sometimes supported faculty rather than him.
81. Joseph McMillan, Semi-Annual Report of the President to the Board of Trustees, November 1, 1990, HT Archives.
82. Attorney George's letter was among my papers, placed in HT Archives.
83. MT was not a "Dr." Part of the problem was that he did not hold that title.
84. Anaejionu's, Buxkemper's, and Attorney George's letters are among my personal papers given to HT Archives.
85. Rosalee Martin, "H-T Rebellion," *NOKOA*, September 9, 1999, front page.
86. Mary Ann Roser, "Huston-Tillotson's Crisis of Confidence: Fight Against President Divides the Campus," *Austin American-Statesman*, September 10, 1999, 1, 10. My copy of the article is in HT Archives.
87. My interview with Terry Smith.
88. August 17, 1999 petition, signed by twenty faculty members, is in HT Archives.
89. A letter was sent to Board President Attorney George on October 27, 1999, including many of the same concerns contained in this memo.
90. I believe as a retaliatory action, the field placement course, usually taught and supervised by me, was taken from me and given to a person not knowledgeable about the Austin community or the goals of the course. This course requires students to complete 156 hours in a social agency or an educational facility.
91. *Ram Magazine*, 1999, HT Archives.
92. This was an upbeat "I will be in this position indefinitely" type of message. Yet less than six months later, McMillan's tone and message were vastly different. Within that time, he had announced his "retirement."
93. This first Save HT meeting and all other meetings were audiotaped by me. The tape was later placed in HT Archives.
94. Reginald Christopher is the same outspoken individual who wrote several articles in *The*

Villager and *NOKOA* many years earlier.

95. Fannie Lawless was a former registrar and was related to the person named on our science building: Dickey-Lawless.
96. Anaejionu, Martin, Buxkemper, "The Bill of Particulars," 1999, HT Archives. The Bill of Particulars was cited in previous endnotes.
97. Fund for the Improvement of Postsecondary Education (FIPSE). See https://www2.ed.gov/about/offices/list/ope/fipse/index.html, retrieved July 5, 2023.
98. The Board of Trustees gave McMillan complete control over the buying and selling of HT's property (in the document titled Consent of Executive Committee and Certificate of Incumbency, filed September 1, 1988) when McMillan had only been president for two months; in HT Archives.
99. From an interview with Paul Anaejionu.
100. Paul Anaejionu and I had tenure, and there was no basis for our dismissal.
101. That person is not named as she still teaches at HT, now having a very different relationship with me. From 2014 to 2017, I was dean and became this person's supervisor. No retaliation occurred. In fact, we both worked well together.
102. *Ram Magazine*, Spring/Fall 2000, HT Archives.
103. Jones, "The first and second time around" references the 1989 and 1999 reaccreditation process, "Restoring Accreditation in Two Private Texas Historically Black Colleges," 103.
104. President's report to the Board, April 28, 2000, HT Archives.
105. On July 1999 under McMillan's leadership, and on June 2000, inherited by the new president, HT was placed on warning. Warning is a serious sanction, more serious than being on notice and one step before being placed on probation. HT was in trouble!
106. McMillan, President's Report to the Board, April 28, 2000, HT Archives.
107. This was probably the final interview he gave to anyone prior to his death on December 12, 2017.
108. My complete final letter to McMillan is in HT Archives.
109. I repeat this quote at this time; it was my introductory quote "I love it" referencing HT. In this chapter I have shared McMillan's "dash," that is, his actions and behaviors from the time he became president to the time he retired. It is not a complete story as there are other perspectives that differ from mine; those stories should be told as well.
110. Dianne Hayes, "HBCU Presidents at a New Crossroads," *Diverse: Issues in Higher Education*, October 29, 2013, https://www.diverseeducation.com/demographics/african-american/article/15093864/hbcu-presidents-at-a-new-crossroads.
111. Crystal Keels, "Investing in HBCU Leadership," *Diverse: Issues in Higher Education*, September 8, 2004, https://www.diverseeducation.com/institutions/hbcus/article/15080269/investing-in-hbcu-leadership.
112. Reginald Stuart, "HBCUs Facing Challenges Amid Efforts to Stay Financially Viable and Competitive," *Diverse: Issues in Higher Education*, October 29, 2013, https://www.diverseeducation.com/sports/article/15092212/hbcus-facing-challenges-amid-efforts-to-stay-financially-viable-and-competitive.

Chapter 3

1. I was seen as the troublemaker because of the part I played in "forcing" the board's decision to ask McMillan to retire; it was not because of anything I did while a member of the search committee.
2. Larry Earvin, "The President's Message," *Ram Magazine*, Fall/Winter 2000, HT Archives.
3. Larry Earvin, "Inaugural Address," *Ram Magazine*, Fall/Winter 2001, HT Archives.
4. Erik Rodriguez, "College Swears In, Lauds Newest President," *Austin American-Statesman*, Metro & State, October 27, 2001.
5. Larry Earvin, "A Job Well Done," memo to the HT Family, November 6, 2001. My personal memo was given to HT Archives.
6. Larry Earvin, article without bibliographic information, HT Archives.
7. Ibid.
8. Ibid.
9. Dr. Melva Williams (now Wallace) became the seventh president at HT in August 2022 and was inaugurated in March 2023.
10. Earvin, "The President's Message," HT Archives.
11. Larry Earvin, "Vice President SACSCOC," August 2015, https://events.bizzabo.com/CBESummit/agenda/speakers/162424.
12. Earvin, "Vice President SACSCOC."
13. "Joya Hayes Randle," Officer Profile, http://www.main.org/aspa/hayesprofile.htm.
14. Austintexas.gov, http://www.austintexas.gov/department/human-resources/about.
15. Interviews with Terry Smith, 2017.
16. *NOKOA* Business Section, November 1, 2001.
17. Lydia Lum, "Thinking Outside the Fundraising Box," *Diverse: Issues in Higher Education*, http://diverseeducation.com/article/13424/, August 20, 2009.
18. Roxanne Evans, "How Larry Earvin Sees Huston-Tillotson," Austin & Corporate Donors, *Our Texas*, 2001.
19. More details on the reaffirmation process will be found in another section of this chapter.
20. The Bill of Particulars was a written case against McMillan, with specific documentation supporting conclusions; discussed in the chapter on McMillan.
21. Documents will be placed in HT Archives.
22. The citations for these documents were noted in McMillan's chapter.
23. The actions of Save HT were described in the discussion of McMillan.
24. Sharon Jayson, "New President's Inauguration, Hope Prevails," *Austin American-Statesman*, October 24, 2001.
25. Earvin, "Redeeming the Promise," President's Report, 2003, HT Archives.
26. King Davis, Charter Day Keynote Address, 2003. Davis was the executive director of the Hogg Foundation for Mental Health and Robert Lee Sutherland Chair in Mental Health and Social Policy in the School of Social Work at the University of Texas. He retired in 2018.
27. Definition of "redeem" found in Random House dictionary of the English language.
28. Earvin, "Redeeming the Promise."
29. Earvin, "An Agenda for Excellence: Strategic Planning in the Context of Environment

NOTES

Scanning and Future Research," April 2001; the strategic plan is also found in many HT documents in HT Archives.
30. Ibid.
31. *Hopwood v. Texas*, 78 F.3rd 932 (5th Cir. 1996), was the first legal challenge to a university's affirmative action policy in student admissions since *Regents of the University of California v Bakke*. The Texas court held that UT School of Law may not use race as a factor in deciding which applicants to admit in order to achieve a diverse student population.
32. Earvin secured funding for renovating both the library and dormitories, including expansive technological capabilities and computer labs.
33. In 2023, HT's cable channel is no longer in operation. I have no date as to when it ceased operating.
34. Joseph McMillan, "Mission, Vision and Strategic Plan: Focus on the Future," September 1996.
35. Most of the information on HT's reaffirmation was provided by Dr. Bronté Jones in an interview and in her dissertation, "Restoring Accreditation in Two Private Texas Historically Black Colleges," University of Texas, 2005. Jones's dissertation can be found online at https://repositories.lib.utexas.edu/bitstream/handle/2152/1583/jonesb53400.pdf.
36. Jones, "Restoring Accreditation in Two Private Texas Historically Black Colleges."
37. Ibid., 169.
38. Ibid.
39. Ibid.
40. SACS provides recommendations either for change or to provide documentation. Some recommendations are easy fixes, but others, especially related to finances, are not. To be reaffirmed without recommendations is a president's dream but rarely happens.
41. Taken from Earvin's thank you letter for his inauguration.
42. Students' responses to survey questions on Earvin, SurveyMonkey.
43. My letter to Dr. Earvin, June 20, 2000, HT Archives.
44. Earvin's wife was killed on the day they were preparing to come to HT for his interview. Prior to leaving for the airport, his wife left home and crashed on her return. Rainy weather contributed to the accident. This letter can be found in HT Archives.
45. Earvin did not budge on his negative opinion about me. Rather than speaking to me before judging me, he listened to members of the Board of Trustees who resented that I and others pushed them to make a decision to ask McMillan to retire. Had they made that decision earlier, the faculty and others would not have had to do what they did to save HT from losing its accreditation.
46. When Earvin began his presidency at HT, the position of chairperson of the Social Science Division was open. The search committee established by McMillan asserted that I was the most qualified and was the committee's choice. Dr. Vaughn, VPAA, recommended to Earvin that I become the interim chair until he decided what he wanted to do. At first he agreed; after Vaughn informed me of my interim appointment, Earvin withdrew his support.
47. McMillan emphasized core curriculum revision as well and many changes occurred under his administration. Earvin wanted even more revisions. In both administrations there was the need to align core curriculum with that of state institutions to make for easy transfer from one institution to another. Changing the number of core courses required was an area for

consideration.
48. Faculty survey, SurveyMonkey: thirty-one faculty and twenty-three staff respondents.
49. Mr. Terry Smith received an honorary doctorate from President Earvin and later was called Dr. Terry Smith. Information came from face-to-face interview with Dr. Smith.
50. Earvin, "President's Update," Vol 1, Issue 1 (Spring 2005), HT Archives.
51. McMillan, with the approval of the Board of Trustees, removed tenure from the faculty handbook, resulting in the abolishment of policy.
52. Faculty letter sent to Dr. Earvin, May 10, 2003, HT Archives.
53. Dr. Peña's letter outlined in great detail the financial plight of long-term committed HT faculty members whose salary was so far below national standards, as compared to those of HT administrators. Without raises, it was a real sacrifice to continue to teach at HT. The letter also acknowledged that new faculty members begin at HT with higher salaries than those who have been part of HT legacy teaching.
54. Both letters sent to Earvin and eight-page document are found in HT Archives.
55. President's update, HT Archives.
56. "Was Earvin attempting to shut down dialogue?" was a question raised by many faculty members.
57. Earvin's solution to our concerns—for us to read and share articles—appears to be a delay tactic and reflected his being out of touch with his faculty and their needs and concerns.
58. This is what faculty wanted: an open and frank communication among persons who were treated with respect, and not based on selected readings.
59. Earvin was not transparent with faculty. He told Judith Loredo and Marian Elbert, not the faculty, that he didn't want a Faculty Senate.
60. How was the concept of Faculty Senate presented to the Board of Trustees? Was the board asked to read articles to support the value of a Faculty Senate? Was the board presented with Earvin's opinion related to the ills of an established Faculty Senate? In a face-to-face interview with a former board member, I was told that board members only got information the president wanted them to have. He said it this way: "The board only sees through the opening of a straw," meaning that they only get limited information.
61. Earvin advocated a top-down bureaucratic structure. That structure supports top-down decision-making.
62. The words "with the President" were missing in the actual letter. I added the word "president" as it seems to fit there: found in HT Archives.
63. Texas is an at-will state where the employer and employee can terminate employment at any time. Employers do not have to give reason. Non-tenured faculty members can be terminated at the will of the president.
64. The major difference between the Faculty Senate and the Faculty Advisory Committee is the line of command. Faculty Senate officers may go directly to the president with concerns, while Faculty Advisory Committee officers must initially go to the VPAA/Provost, consistent with the hierarchal structure that Earvin supported.
65. Faculty wanted the organization to be named "council," while the administration wanted it to be a "committee." The word "council" has more implied power than does "committee." Sometimes these words are used interchangeably in correspondence.

NOTES

66. There was a push, as had been the case with previous presidents, for faculty members to write grants to support their programs.
67. Notice a reference to Huston-Tillotson University, not College. Huston-Tillotson College became University in February 2005.
68. Faculty Resource Network is a program of New York University. All information came from https://facultyresourcenetwork.org/.
69. *Ram Magazine*, Spring 2006, 22, HT Archives.
70. Universities are a group of colleges within its structure; colleges are collections of disciplines/majors.
71. Copies of *900 Chicon* are in the library. As of 2023, there are eleven issues.
72. The 3/2 program is when a student takes three years at HT and two years of engineering courses at either Prairie View A&M or UT Austin. The student will receive a math degree from HT and an engineering degree from the other university.
73. Dean Steven Edmond, "Creating Leaders of the Future," Huston-Tillotson University School of Business magazine, 2013, HT Archives.
74. Professor Judith Loredo is the person faculty wanted to be VPAA rather than MT during McMillan's presidency.
75. *Ram Magazine*, Spring 2006, 22, HT Archives.
76. Sumler-Edmond was brought to Huston-Tillotson in 2001 by Earvin. Sumler-Edmond is the wife of Steven Edmond, Dean of the School of Business. She has both a PhD in history and a law degree. She taught in the history department before her retirement from HT as emerita.
77. Caviness was the director of the DuBois Scholars as well as director of the Center of Academic Excellence (appointment under Pierce Burnette). She is now Dr. Caviness and director of Marketing and Public Relations (2023).
78. HT website, http://htu.edu/enrollment/adultdegrees.
79. Amanda Masino and Karen Magid, "Green Is the New Black: Environmental Justice and HBCUs," *Second Nature*, December 18, 2015, https://secondnature.org/2015/12/18/green-new-black-environmental-justice-hbcus/.
80. Ibid.
81. The position of Dean of Freshman Studies was created for Wilson but ceased to exist after he left. A similar position existed under the administration of McMillan that lasted for years.
82. "Meet the Dumpster Project," http://dumpsterproject.org/.
83. "Graduating a New Class of Dumpster Residents," Dumpster Project, http://dumpsterproject.org/graduating-a-new-class-of-dumpster-residents/.
84. The Dumpster Project, "Meet the Team," http://dumpsterproject.org/#meet-the-team.
85. Nora Ankrum, "Austin's Sustainable Secret: Student-founded Green Is the New Black Makes Renewable Energy at Huston-Tillotson," *Austin Chronicle*, October 24, 2014, https://www.austinchronicle.com/news/2014-10-24/austins-sustainable-secret/.
86. "Tom Joyner Foundation Names Huston-Tillotson University as July School of the Month," 2014, https://tomjoynerfoundation.org/tom-joyner-foundation-names-hustontillotson-university-july-school-month/.
87. I interviewed Ada Anderson in 2017; she passed away in 2021 at age 98. She and husband, Andy Anderson, established the Anderson-Wormley Real Estate and Insurance Company,

NOTES

88. Some students protested when they found out that their financial aid was cut; more than usual didn't return.
89. Earvin, President's Board Report, VPAA Vanderpuye's update on financial aid, 2014–2015, HT Archives.
90. Ralph K. M. Haurwitz, "Huston-Tillotson President Larry Earvin to Retire in June 2015," *Austin American-Statesman*, March 22, 2014, https://www.statesman.com/story/news/local/2014/03/22/huston-tillotson-president-larry-earvin-to-retire-in-june-2015/9939493007/.
91. Formerly Southern Association of Colleges and Schools (SACS).
92. American Council of Trustees and Alumni, "Selecting a New President," retrieved June 30, 2023, https://www.goacta.org/wp-content/uploads/ee/download/selecting_a_new_president.pdf.
93. Mary Beth Marklein, "Black Colleges Examine Their Mission," *USA Today*, February 10, 2014, https://www.usatoday.com/story/news/nation/2014/02/10/black-colleges-mission/5374863/.
94. Sarah Butrymowicz, "Historically Black Colleges Are Becoming More White," *Time*, June 27, 2014, https://time.com/2907332/historically-black-colleges-increasingly-serve-white-students/.

Chapter 4

1. John L. Hanson, "Dr. Colette Pierce Burnette HT's Sixth President," KUT 90.5, December 14, 2016, http://kut.org/post/dr-colette-Pierce-Burnette-ht-s-sixth-president.
2. Interview with Pierce Burnette, September 25, 2017.
3. Ibid.
4. Mikela Floyd and Ramona Flume, "Women We Love: Colette Pierce Burnette," *Austin Monthly*, February 1, 2016, http://www.austinmonthly.com/AM/February-2016/Women-We-Love-Colette-Pierce-Burnette/.
5. Chrystine Shackles, *Reminiscences of Huston-Tillotson College* (Austin: Best Printing Co., 1973).
6. Oliver D. Brown and Michael Heintze, "Branch, Mary Elizabeth (1881–1944)," Texas State Historical Association, accessed April 5, 2020, https://www.tshaonline.org/handbook/entries/branch-mary-elizabeth.
7. Discover Black Austin [includes Pierce Burnette], retrieved September 18, 2018, https://www.discoverblackaustin.com/hidden-figures-of-austin/.
8. "Dr. Colette Pierce Burnette on Building Capacity," Big Brothers, Big Sisters of Central Texas, August 5, 2016, https://bigmentoring.wordpress.com/2016/08/05/dr-colette-Pierce-Burnette-on-building-capacity/.
9. Discover Black Austin, https://www.discoverblackaustin.com/hidden-figures-of-austin/.
10. Doyin Oyeniyi, "Colette Pierce Burnette Is in the Pilot's Seat," *Austin Woman*, July 31, 2017, http://atxwoman.com/in-the-pilots-seat/.
11. Michael Barnes, "Colette Pierce Burnette Named Austinite of the Year," *Austin*

NOTES

      American-Statesman, January 9, 2022, statesman.com.
12. HT press release, April 1, 2015.
13. Albert Hawkins, in his oral presentation of Dr. Burnette to the HT community as president-elect.
14. Interview of Pierce Burnette by author, September 27, 2017.
15. Pierce Burnette, "A Message to My Campus Community," HT email, June 3, 2020.
16. Oyeniyi, "Colette Pierce Burnette Is in the Pilot's Seat," 7.
17. Interview with Pierce Burnette, September 25, 2017.
18. Ibid.
19. Pierce Burnette, "Meet HT's Sixth President and CEO," *Ram Magazine*, 2016, HT Archives.
20. Interview with Pierce Burnette, September 25, 2017.
21. Anthony and Louise Viaer-Alumni Hall was formerly the old Administration Building renovated by Dr. Earvin. It was remodeled with funds from Anthony Viaer.
22. Pierce Burnette, Engagement Report, 2017–2018, HT Archives.
23. Pierce Burnette, *Ram Magazine*, 2016, HT Archives.
24. Interview with Pierce Burnette, September 25, 2017.
25. Kate McGee, "East Austin Is Growing, and Huston-Tillotson Hopes Its Roots Keep a Community Intact," KUT-FM, March 21, 2017.
26. Pierce Burnette, Board Report, November 3, 2017, 5, HT Archives.
27. Interview with Pierce Burnette, September 25, 2017.
28. Pierce Burnette, "Building Tomorrow's Leaders," fundraiser keynote, ACC Center for Public Policy and Political Studies (CPPPS), May 8, 2018, https://www.youtube.com/watch?v=wlYEp1V6V2U.
29. Mayor's Task Force on Institutional Racism and Systemic Inequities, Final Report, April 6, 2017, retrieved September 21, 2018, file:///F:/Dr.%20Pierce-Burnette/Mayor%20Task_Force_Report-Updated-4-6-17.pdf.
30. Will Anderson, "Colette Pierce Burnette Reflects on Huston-Tillotson CEO Tenure, Austin's Attempts to Right Historic Wrongs," Texas Business Minds Podcast, *Austin Business Journal*, March 4, 2021, bizjournals.com.
31. Michael Barnes, "Colette Pierce Burnette, President of Huston-Tillotson University, Named Austinite of the Year," *Austin American-Statesman*, January 9, 2022, https://www.statesman.com/story/news/2022/01/09/colette-Pierce-Burnette-named-austinite-year/8971929002/.
32. Ibid.
33. Ibid.
34. Julianne P. Hanckel, email, February 24, 2017.
35. Juli Fellows, email to Dr. Pierce Burnette, March 8, 2017.
36. "Black Austin Rally and March for Black Lives: Protesters March to the Capitol," fox7austin.com, June 7, 2020.
37. Pierce Burnette, email, June 3, 2020.
38. This July 25, 2015, email was sent twenty-nine days into her presidency; it established that student success was her priority.
39. Shawanda Stewart, English professor, email, December 2016.
40. Darrion Jamerson, biology major, class of 2019.

41. McGee, "East Austin Is Growing."
42. Spelman College is a women's HBCU in Atlanta, Georgia.
43. Business and Technology page, "China Study Abroad," retrieved October 18, 2018www.htu.edu.
44. Steven Edmond retired in summer 2021 as Dean Emeritus but came back to work on international programming.
45. Femi Alabi Onikeku, "Diki: Returning to Impact on Her Roots," *Guardian*, April 9, 2016, https://guardian.ng/saturday-magazine/diki-returning-to-impact-on-her-roots/#google_vignette
46. Information from HT Business website.
47. HT Office of Sponsored Programs journal, Inaugural Edition, Austin, Texas, 2022, 22–23, HT Archives.
48. Business and Technology page, CEI, www.htu.edu.
49. Ralph Haurwitz, "Huston-Tillotson Opening Expanded Entrepreneurship," *Austin American-Statesman*, October 17, 2018.
50. HT Office of Sponsored Programs Journal. The journal contains HT's programs and grants, 2020–2022, 32, in HT Archives.
51. "A New Generation of Black Male Teachers Starts Its Journey in Partnership with Apple," Apple Newsroom, May 13, 2021, https://www.apple.com/newsroom/2021/05/a-new-generation-of-black-male-teachers-starts-its-journey-in-partnership-with-apple/.
52. My interview with Pierce Burnette, 2017.
53. Apple Newsroom, "A New Generation of Black Male Teachers Starts Its Journey in Partnership with Apple."
54. US Department of Education, HT website, www.htu.edu.
55. Ibid.
56. Interview with Pierce Burnette, September 25, 2017.
57. Ibid.
58. I was interim dean of the College of Arts and Sciences (March 2014–July 2017) as a carryover from Dr. Earvin. I stayed in that position for Dr. Pierce Burnette's first two years. I asked Pierce Burnette to name me dean, as previous deans were appointed by the prior administration. Pierce Burnette wanted her new provost to conduct a search for the position of dean of CAS. I did not apply and went on sabbatical instead.
59. Mrs. Ericka Jones later became Dr. Ericka Jones.
60. Interview with Pierce Burnette, September 25, 2017.
61. Former HT employee, email, August 16, 2018.
62. Interview with Pierce Burnette, September 25, 2017.
63. Ibid.
64. "We Are You," January 22, 2019, https://www.youtube.com/watch?v=HIRMZqhqGsI. The theme is also on HT's website.
65. Interview with Pierce Burnette, September 25, 2017.
66. HT website, www.htu.edu.
67. SurveyMonkey, Student/Alumni, responses gathered November 2017–April 2018.
68. Ibid.
69. Huston-Tillotson University Review, 414 respondents. Freshmen responded December 2017.

NOTES

https://www.niche.com/colleges/huston-tillotson-university/reviews/.
70. Huston-Tillotson University (Join the Rams), April 26, 2021, https://www.youtube.com/watch?v=BXnmV8hjgX8.
71. Pierce Burnette, Board Report, 2017, HT Archives.
72. SurveyMonkey: HT Financial Instability, posted on April 20, 2018.
73. HT website, http://htu.edu/offices/ia/steinway.
74. HT Office of Sponsored Programs Journal, 2022, 70–71. Grants awarded for 2019 totaled $3,496,521.00; in 2020 (Covid year) total grants, not including CARES Act funds, were $3,543,636.00; and 2021–2022 grant funds (not including Transformation Project which might yield an addition $1.5 million) were $4,364,427.00. HT Archives.
75. Sharon D. Kruse, Shameem Rakha, and Shannon Calderone, "Developing Cultural Competency in Higher Education: An Agenda for Practice," *Teaching in Higher Education: Critical Perspectives* 23, no. 6 (2017): 733–50, https://eric.ed.gov/?id=EJ1183684.
76. I interviewed Schwab, Anaejionu, and Kamalvand in November 2017. We knew each other well and were in regular contact for decades at HT. When Schwab, Kamalvand, and I were chairpersons for our respective divisions at the same time, we met monthly in chairpersons' meetings with our dean.
77. Wilhelmina Perry and Gus Swain, *Huston-Tillotson University Legacy: A Historical Treasure*, self-published, 2007.
78. I had two interviews with Schwab in 2017.
79. Schwab was Wiley before her marriage.
80. Save HT was discussed in detail in McMillan's chapter.
81. QEP is a plan to implement and assess a focused set of initiatives designed to improve student learning across the university. The Southern Association of Colleges and Schools Commission on Colleges (SACSCOC) requires universities to have a QEP.
82. HT's 2023 QEP is on Professional Development, Career and Work Ethics. See HT's website on QEP, www.htu.edu.
83. Interview with Kamalvand, 2017.
84. Paul Anaejionu, Harriet Buxkemper, and I were the organizers of Save HT, and we authored the Bill of Particulars discussed in detail in the chapter on McMillan.
85. See information found in the chapter on McMillan.
86. Holman was hired by Earvin in 2014. She left for a higher paying job in 2021.
87. Bullock Museum, https://www.thestoryoftexas.com/discover/texas-story-project/texas-history-is-my-history.
88. Comments Oldmixon made during casual conversations and in Faculty Advisory Council meetings.
89. Taken from CAS report included in 2017 board report, HT Archives.
90. I am an artist and a poet as well as a sociologist and social worker. I have occasional art exhibits. Professor Hudson selected two of my pieces to become part of her collection.
91. Oldmixon, email, November 9, 2018.
92. Kraft, email, December 14, 2017.
93. Ibid.
94. Oldmixon, email, November 9, 2018.

NOTES

95. No formal faculty survey was conducted after 2018 to give input as to whether their perception of Pierce Burnette had changed; some faculty members informally made verbal comments.
96. FAC's membership is comprised of faculty only. Persons in ranks above that of chair of a department must be invited for specific meetings.
97. The president met with faculty at their monthly Faculty Advisory Meeting on January 9, 2019. In addition to President Pierce Burnette and faculty were Archibald Vanderpuye, Mike Hirsch, and Beverly Downing and administrators who were not members of FAC.
98. The March 6 and March 12 letters will be placed in HT Archives.
99. US Department of Education, Office of Post Secondary Education, "CARES Act: Higher Education Emergency Relief Fund," March 27, 2020, https://www2.ed.gov/about/offices/list/ope/caresact.html.
100. Ella Malena Feldman, "First United Methodist Church of Austin Eliminates Debt for HBCU Huston-Tillotson Students," *Austin American-Statesman*, August 8, 2021, https://www.statesman.com/story/news/2021/08/08/austins-first-united-methodist-church-pays-debt-hbcu-huston-tillotson-graduates/5519616001/.
101. Jennifer Stayton, "Outgoing Huston-Tillotson President Knows It's Wise to 'Leave the Party When You're Having Fun,'" KUT 90.5, June 29, 2022, https://www.kut.org/austin/2022-06-29/outgoing-huston-tillotson-president-knows-its-wise-to-leave-the-party-when-youre-having-fun.
102. Carol McDonald, "Huston-Tillotson University President Dr. Colette Pierce Burnette Announces Retirement," press release, December 2, 2021, https://htu.edu/wp-content/uploads/2021/12/President-Burnette-Retirement-Press-Release.pdf.
103. Stayton, "Outgoing Huston-Tillotson President."
104. Colette Pierce Burnette, Holiday Card, December 17, 2021, https://www.youtube.com/watch?v=1N6D7PmsVbA.
105. Robert D. Gratz and Philip J. Salem, "Organizational Communication and Higher Education," AAHE-ERICJ Higher Education Research Report No. 10, 1982, https://digital.library.txstate.edu/bitstream/handle/10877/2599/fulltext.pdf?sequence=1&isAllowed=y
106. I added emails as they were not commonly used at the writing of this article.
107. Jazmyn Burton, "Magnanimous Gift from MacKenzie Scott Bolsters Spelman College's Strategic Outcomes," Spelman News Release, July 28, 2020. Spelman received $20 million to go towards its strategic plan. https://www.spelman.edu/about-us/news-and-events/news-releases/2020/07/28/magnanimous-gift-from-mackenzie-scott-bolsters-spelman-college-s-strategic-outcomes.
108. Kelly Tyko, "Billionaire Robert F. Smith's $34 Million Gift to Morehouse Grads Includes Parent Loans," *USA Today*, September 20, 2019, https://www.usatoday.com/story/money/2019/09/20/morehouse-billionaire-gift-smith-donates-34-million-pay-off-loans/2392458001/. Robert Smith has an office in Austin, Texas and Presidents Earvin and Pierce Burnette tried to get him to give substantial contributions to HT. He gave HT a gift of $75,000, years ago.
109. Jenny Gathright, "Howard University's Largest Donation Ever Raises Questions About Who Gets Donor Coin," NPR, February 11, 2020, https://www.npr.org/2020/02/11/803572593/howard-universitys-largest-donation-ever-raises-questions-about-who-gets-donor-c.

NOTES

110. Tyko, "Billionaire Robert F. Smith's $34 Million Gift to Morehouse Grads."
111. US Department of Education, Office of Post Secondary Education, CARES Act: Higher Education Emergency Relief Fund, https://www2.ed.gov/about/offices/list/ope/caresact.html.
112. Liz Schlemmer, "HBCUs Got a Windfall of Federal COVID Relief. Here's How Colleges Are Spending It," September 22, 2022, https://www.npr.org/2022/09/20/1124142614/how-hbcus-are-spending-their-covid-19-relief-money.

Chapter 5

1. John Q. Taylor King, "Vision of Greatness," no date, HT Archives.
2. *Plessy v. Ferguson* was a landmark 1896 US Supreme Court decision that upheld the constitutionality of racial segregation under the "separate but equal" doctrine. *Brown v. Board of Education of Topeka* was a landmark 1954 Supreme Court case in which the justices ruled unanimously that racial segregation of children in public schools was unconstitutional.
3. Alexandra Hegji, Congressional Research Service, "Higher Education Act (HEA): A Primer," updated October 24, 2018, 7.
4. National Center for Educational Statistics, Historically Black Colleges and Universities, retrieved June 23, 2020, https://nces.ed.gov/fastfacts/display.asp?id=667.
5. US Department of Education, White House Initiative on Historically Black Colleges and Universities, retrieved June 25, 2020, https://sites.ed.gov/whhbcu/one-hundred-and-five-historically-black-colleges-and-universities/.
6. Complete reasons given by survey respondents for the need for HBCUs can be found in HT Archives.
7. UNCF, retrieved June 24, 2020, https://uncf.org/pages/Why-Choose-an-HBCU.
8. Brian Bridges, "African Americans and College Education by the Numbers," UNCF, retrieved July 17, 2023, https://uncf.org/the-latest/african-americans-and-college-education-by-the-numbers.
9. UNCF, "Why Choose an HBCU," retrieved June 24, 2020, https://uncf.org/pages/Why-Choose-an-HBCU.
10. UNCF, "The Numbers Don't Lie: HBCUs Are Changing the College Landscape," retrieved July 17, 2023, https://uncf.org/the-latest/the-numbers-dont-lie-hbcus-are-changing-the-college-landscape.
11. La'Raven Taylor, "Netflix CEO, Wife Donate Record $120 Million to Atlanta HBCUs, UNCF," updated August 13, 2020, https://www.gpb.org/news/2020/06/17/netflix-ceo-wife-donate-record-120-million-atlanta-hbcus-uncf. Morehouse and Spelman received $40 million from the CEO of Netflix in June 2020; $40 million was also given to UNCF to distribute to the other 99 HBCUs.
12. HBC editor, "HBCU Buzz," 2014, https://hbcubuzz.com/2014/02/the-civil-rights-movement-hbcus-and-you/.
13. #MeToo is a social movement and awareness campaign against sexual abuse, sexual harassment, and rape culture.
14. "A New Era of Protest Is Energizing HBCUs. But There are Challenges," *Time*, June 4, 2018,

https://time.com/5286691/hbcu-black-colleges-protest-activism/.
15. Ibid.
16. Ibid.
17. Black Lives Matter (BLM) is a decentralized political and social movement that seeks to highlight racism, discrimination, and racial inequality experienced by Black people. Its primary concerns are incidents of police brutality and racially motivated violence against Black people.
18. Daniel Kim, "What Is Your Organization's Core Theory of Success?" *Systems Thinker*, https://thesystemsthinker.com/what-is-your-organizations-core-theory-of-success/.
19. Gathering data for this research was to end in December 2018. However, the onset of Covid-19 during the end of 2019 will influence the future of HBCUs in ways that this research cannot identify.
20. Robert Smith, "Morehouse 2019 Graduates Received Their Total School Debt Payoff," May 20, 2019, https://www.cbsnews.com/news/who-is-morehouse-billionaire-robert-f-smith/.
21. Second survey on HT financial stability sent to HT constituents in 2018.
22. Peter Jacob, "There's an Unprecedented Crisis Facing America's Historically Black Colleges," *Business Insider*, March 30, 2015, retrieved June 24, 2020, https://www.businessinsider.com/hbcus-may-be-more-in-danger-of-closing-than-other-schools-2015-3.
23. Association of Governing Boards (AGB), "The Urgency of Now: HBCUs at a Crossroads," 2020, 3, https://agb.org/wp-content/uploads/2020/01/Kresge-Report_Urgency_of_Now.pdf.
24. The Covid-19 health crisis began outside my original research period of 1965 to 2018. However, I cannot overlook the effect of this virus on HBCUs. My research was extended to 2022.
25. Black America, "Covid-19 Closures Could Hit Historically Black Colleges Particularly Hard," retrieved June 25, 2020, https://blackamericaweb.com/2020/03/24/covid-19-closures-could-hit-historically-black-colleges-particularly-hard/.
26. Shailaja Neelakantan, "UNCF: $1 Billion for HBCUs, TCUs, MSIs in Federal Coronavirus Stimulus Package," March 2020, https://diverseeducation.com/article/171010/.
27. US Department of Education, Office of Post Secondary Education, "CARES Act: Higher Education Emergency Relief Fund," March 27, 2020, https://www2.ed.gov/about/offices/list/ope/caresact.html.
28. US Department of Education, "Secretary DeVos Delivers Nearly $1.4 Billion in Additional CARES Act Relief Funds to HBCUs, Minority Serving Institutions, and Colleges and Universities Serving Low-Income Students," April 30, 2020, https://sites.ed.gov/whhbcu/category/funding/.
29. Carolyn Thompson and Collins Binkley, "Harvard, MIT Sue to Block ICE Rule on International Students," ABC News, July 8, 2020, https://abcnews.go.com/Politics/wireStory/harvard-mit-sue-block-ice-rule-international-students-71670205.
30. Matthew Lynch, "5 Factors That Influence the Future of HBCUS," *The Edvocate*, September 18, 2016, https://www.theedadvocate.org/5-factors-that-influence-the-future-of-hbcus/.
31. Donna Owens, "HBCUs Are Our Future," *Essence*, May 26, 2020, https://www.essence.com/feature/hbcus-are-our-future/.
32. Katherine Frey, "Suspect Identified in Bomb Threats Against HBCUs," *Washington Post*, November 16, 2022, https://www.insidehighered.com/news/2022/11/17/fbi-says-most-bomb-threats-against-hbcus-made-minor; US Department of Education, "Additional Project SERV

Grants to HBCUs," May 31, 2023, https://www.ed.gov/news/press-releases/us-department-education-announces-additional-project-serv-grants-hbcus.
33. Association of Governing Boards, "The Urgency of Now."
34. Erica Greene, "Why Students Are Choosing HBCUs: 4 Years Being Seen as Family," *New York Times*, June 11, 2022, https://safesupportivelearning.ed.gov/news/why-students-are-choosing-hbcus-4-years-being-seen-family.
35. Ibid.
36. Matthew Lynch, "HBCU Enrollment on the Rise," *The Edvocate*, March 20, 2023, https://www.theedadvocate.org/hbcu-enrollment-on-the-rise/.
37. Peter M. Senge, *The Fifth Discipline: The Art & Practice of the Learning Organization* (New York: Crown Currency, 2010). Senge is a senior lecturer at the Massachusetts Institute of Technology. He is founding chair of the Society for Organizational Learning (SoL), a global community of corporations, researchers, and consultants dedicated to the "interdependent development of people and their institutions." https://www.goodreads.com/author/show/21072.Peter_M_Senge, retrieved July 17, 2023.
38. Kim Daniels, "Success to the Successful: Self-Fulfilling Prophecies," Systems Thinker, retrieved July 17, 2023, https://thesystemsthinker.com/success-to-the-successful-self-fulfilling-prophecies/#:~:text=The%20%E2%80%9CSuccess%20to%20the%20Successful%E2%80%9D%20archetype%20highlights%20how%20success%20can,viable%20(or%20even%20superior).
39. Juli Fellows helped me with the analysis of the "Success for the Successful" archetype.
40. Andre M. Perry, Hannah Stephens, and Manann Donoghoe, "The Supreme Court Decision to Strike Down Affirmative Action Means That HBCU Investment Is More Important Than Ever," Brookings, June 29, 2023, https://www.brookings.edu/articles/the-supreme-courts-decision-to-strike-down-affirmative-action-means-that-hbcu-investment-is-more-important-than-ever/.

Epilogue

1. I saw Earvin at Wallace's inauguration, March 2023. He retired June 2023, marking fifty years in higher education institutions.

Bibliography

"A New Generation of Black Male Teachers Starts Its Journey in Partnership with Apple." Apple Newsroom, May 13, 2021. https://www.apple.com/newsroom/2021/05/a-new-generation-of-black-male-teachers-starts-its-journey-in-partnership-with-apple/.

Adler, Steve. "Mayor Task Force on Institutional Racism and Systemic Inequities, Final Report." City of Austin, April 6, 2017. https://cityofaustin.github.io/institutional-racism/.

Admin, in Dumpster Blog. "Graduating a New Class of Dumpster Residents." August 24, 2015. http://dumpsterproject.org/graduating-a-new-class-of-dumpster-residents/.

"African Americans in Austin." You are Here ATX. https://www.youarehereatx.org/african-americans-in-austin/.

Anaejionu, Paul, and Rosalee Martin. "Accountability and Stewardship at Huston-Tillotson College." Unpublished manuscript, 1999. HT Archives.

———. "Bill of Particulars: Case Against Dr. McMillan." Unpublished manuscript, 1999. HT Archives.

Anderson, Will. "Colette Pierce Burnette Reflects on Huston-Tillotson CEO Tenure, Austin's Attempts to Right Historic Wrongs, Texas Business Minds Podcast." *Austin Business Journal*, March 4, 2021. bizjournals.com.

Ankrum, Nora. "Austin's Sustainable Secret: Student-founded Green Is the New Black Makes Renewable Energy at Huston-Tillotson." *Austin Chronicle*, October 24, 2015. https://www.austinchronicle.com/news/2014-10-24/austins-sustainable-secret/.

Anonymous student. "The Truth lies within the Administration (Pun Well Intended)." *The Villager*, October 16–23, 1992.

Association of Governing Boards (AGB). "The Urgency of Now: HBCUs at a Crossroads." https://agb.org/wp-content/uploads/2020/01/Kresge-Report_Urgency_of_Now.pdf.

Austintexas.gov. http://www.austintexas.gov/department/human-resources/about.

Barnes, Michael. "Colette Pierce Burnette Named Austinite of the Year." *Austin American-Statesman*, January 9, 2022.

Black America Wed. "Covid-19 Closures Could Hit Historically Black Colleges Particularly Hard." March 24, 2020. https://blackamericaweb.com/2020/03/24/covid-19-closures-could-hit-historically-black-colleges-particularly-hard/.

"Black Austin Rally and March for Black Lives: Protesters March to the Capitol." Fox 7, June 7, 2020. fox7austin.com.

Blackpast.com. "An Online Reference Guide to African American History." https://blackpast.

org/aah/morton-azie-taylor-1936-2003.

Bridges, Brian. "African Americans and College Education by the Numbers." UNCF. https://uncf.org/the-latest/african-americans-and-college-education-by-the-numbers.

Brown, Oliver D., and Michael Heintze. "Branch, Mary Elizabeth (1881–1944)." Texas State Historical Association. https://www.tshaonline.org/handbook/entries/branch-mary-elizabeth.

Burton, Jazmyn. "Magnanimous Gift from MacKenzie Scott Bolsters Spelman College's Strategic Outcomes." Spelman News Release, July 28, 2020. https://www.spelman.edu/about-us/news-and-events/news-releases2020/07/28/magnanimous-gift-from-mackenzie-scott-bolsters-spelman-college-s-strategic-outcomes.

Cardinenaz, Michael. "Students End Boycott." *Daily Texan*, March 3, 1976. Texas Humanities Archives.

Crayton, Nancy. "International Alumni Support HT's Administration." *NOKOA*, October 9–15, 1992.

Christopher, Reginal. "If You Love Our College, Don't Stand Back and Watch." *NOKOA* editorial, October 2–8, 1992.

———. "A Second-Class Institution." *NOKOA*, September 18–24, 1992.

———. "WHOOPS." *NOKOA*, September 25–October 1, 1992.

Daniels, Kim. "Success to the Successful: Self-Fulfilling Prophecies." Systems Thinker. Retrieved July 17, 2023. https://thesystemsthinker.com/success-to-the-successful-self-fulfilling-prophecies/#:~:text=The%20%E2%80%9CSuccess%20to%20the%20Successful%E2%80%9D%20archetype%20highlights%20how%20success%20can,viable%20(or%20even%20superior).

Discover Black Austin. https://discoverblackaustin.org/hidden-figures-of-austin [Dr. Pierce Burnette].

Douglass, Frederick. *Narrative of the Life of Frederick Douglas, an American Slave*. Boston: Anti-Slavery Office, 1845.

"Dr. Colette Pierce Burnette on Building Capacity." Big Brothers, Big Sisters of Central Texas, August 5, 2016. https://bigmentoring.wordpress.com/2016/08/05/dr-colette-Pierce-Burnette-on-building-capacity/.

Drabicky, Anne. "Middle School Naming Honors a Lifetime of Service." Austin Independent School District, June 30, 2022. https://www.austinisd.org/announcements/2022/06/30/middle-school-naming-honors-lifetime-service-en-espanol.

Drake, Hal. "Interview with Dr. John King." *Pacific Stars and Stripes* (military newspaper), n.d. HT archives.

Duignan, Brian. *Plessy v. Ferguson*. Encyclopedia Britannica. Updated June 21, 2023. https://www.britannica.com/event/Plessy-v-Ferguson-1896.

Dumpster Project, The. "Graduating a New Class of Dumpster Residents," August 24, 2015. http://dumpsterproject.org/graduating-a-new-class-of-dumpster-residents/.

———. "Meet the Team," August 25, 2015. http://dumpsterproject.org/#meet-the-team.

Duncan, Robert. "King, John Quill Taylor, Sr." Texas State Historical Association, July 3, 2013. https://tshaonline.org/handbook/online/articles/fki77.

Earvin, Larry. "Huston Tillotson College, An Agenda for Excellence: Strategic Planning in the Context of Environment Scanning and Future Research." Strategic Plan, April 2001.

BIBLIOGRAPHY

HT Archives.

———. "Inaugural Address." *RAM Magazine*, Fall/Winter 2001. HT Archives.

———. Panelist, UNC CBE Summit. https://events.bizzabo.com/CBESummit/agenda/speakers/162424. May 25, 2017.

———. "The President's Message." *RAM Magazine*, Fall/Winter 2000. HT Archives.

———. "Redeeming the Promise." President's Report, 2003. HT Archives.

Edelman, Jon. "Report Reveals a Differing Picture of Debt at HBCUs." *Diverse: Issues in Higher Education*, September 7, 2022. https://www.diverseeducation.com/institutions/hbcus/article/15296482/report-reveals-a-differing-picture-of-debt-at-hbcus.

Edmond, Steven. "Creating Leaders of the Future." *Huston-Tillotson University School of Business Magazine*, 2013.

Faculty Resource Network Website. (New York University.) https://facultyresourcenetwork.org/.

Feldman, Ella Malena. "First United Methodist Church of Austin Eliminates Debt for HBCU Huston-Tillotson students." *Austin American-Statesman*, August 8, 2021. https://www.statesman.com/story/news/2021/08/08/austins-first-united-methodist-church-pays-debt-hbcu-huston-tillotson-graduates/5519616001/.

Floyd, Mikela. "Women We Love: Colette Pierce-Burnette—The University President." *Austin Monthly*, February 1, 2016. http://www.austinmonthly.com/AM/February-2016/Women-We-Love-Colette-Pierce-Burnette/.

Frey, Katherine. "Suspect Identified in Bomb Threats Against HBCUs." *Washington Post*, November 16, 2022. https://www.insidehighered.com/news/2022/11/17/fbi-says-most-bomb-threats-against-hbcus-made-minor.

Gasman, Marybeth. *Envisioning Black Colleges: A History of the United Negro College Fund*. Baltimore: John Hopkins University Press. 2018.

Gathright, Jenny. "Howard University's Largest Donation Ever Raises Questions About Who Gets Donor Coin." NPR, February 11, 2020. https://www.npr.org/2020/02/11/803572593/howard-universitys-largest-donation-ever-raises-questions-about-who-gets-donor-c.

Greene, Erica. "Why Students Are choosing HBCUs: 4 Years Being Seen as Family." *New York Times*, June 11, 2022. nytimes.com.

Hanson, John L. "Dr. Colette Pierce-Burnette HT's Sixth President." Kut 90.5, December 14, 2016. http://kut.org/post/dr-colette-Pierce-Burnette-ht-s-sixth-president.

Haurwitz, Ralph. "Huston-Tillotson Opening Expanded Entrepreneurship." *Austin American-Statesmen*, October 17, 2018.

———. "Huston-Tillotson President Larry Earvin to Retire in June 2015." *Austin American-Statesman*, March 22, 2014. https://www.statesman.com/story/news/local/2014/03/22/huston-tillotson-president-larry-earvin-to-retire-in-june-2015/9939493007/.

Hayes, Dianne. "HBCU Presidents at a New Crossroads." *Diverse: Issues in Higher Education*, October 29, 2013. https://www.diverseeducation.com/demographics/african-american/article/15093864/hbcu-presidents-at-a-new-crossroads.

HBC editor. "HBCU Buzz." 2014. https://hbcubuzz.com/2014/02/the-civil-rights-movement-hbcus-and-you/.

Hegji, Alexandra. "Higher Education Act (HEA): A Primer." Congressional Research Service.

Updated October 24, 2018, 7.

Huston-Tillotson College. *Catalogues 1961–1962 and 1962–1963.* HT Archives.

———. *Catalogues 1978–1980.* HT Archives

———. "Celebrating Fondest Memories, the Class of 1967." *Huston-Tillotson Alumni Magazine*, 2017.

———. *Faculty Handbook* 1989. HT Archives.

———. *Huston-Tillotson College Alumni and Friends Magazine*, Inaugural Issue." Spring 1989. HT Archives.

———. *The Ram:* Huston-Tillotson College and Friends Magazine, Reunion Edition. Spring/Summer 1995.

Huston-Tillotson University. http://htu.edu/enrollment/adultdegrees.

———. "Huston-Tillotson University History." http://htu.edu.

———. "A Huston-Tillotson University Publication." *The RAM Magazine*, Spring 2006.

———. "Join the Rams." April 26, 2021. https://www.youtube.com/watch?v=BXnmV8hjgX8.

———. Niche reviews. https://www.niche.com/colleges/huston-tillotson-university/reviews/?category=Academics.

———. *Office of Sponsored Programs Journal*, Inaugural Edition, 2022.

———. Website, http://htu.edu/offices/ia/steinway.

Hutchinson, Julie. "Keeping Faith: Huston-Tillotson University's King Gives Decades of Devotion." *Austin American-Statesman*, August 11, 1985.

Jackson, Linda. "Jackie Robinson and Roland Harden—HT Connection." August 12, 2016. http://htu.edu.

Jackson, Linda. "Jackie Robinson's Lasting Impact on the World and HT." *Ram Magazine*, Summer/Fall 2007. https://htu.edu/18168/ht-joins-to-world-in-celebration-of-jackie-robinson-day#fancybox-2.

Jacob, Peter. "There's an Unprecedented Crisis Facing America's Historically Black Colleges." *Business Insider*, March 30, 2015. https://www.businessinsider.com/hbcus-may-be-more-in-danger-of-closing-than-other-schools-2015-3.

Jayson, Sharon. "With New President's Inauguration, Hope Prevails." *Austin American-Statesman* Metro & State, October 24, 2001.

Johnson, Lyndon Baines. "Civil Rights Act of 1964." National Archives. https://www.archives.gov/milestone-documents/civil-rights-act.

Jones, Bronté. "Restoring Accreditation in Two Private Texas Historically Black Colleges." PhD diss., University of Texas, 2005. https://repositories.lib.utexas.edu.

"Joya Hayes Randle." Officer Profile. Metropolitan Austin Interactive Network. http://www.main.org/aspa/hayesprofile.htm.

Keels, Crystal. "Investing in HBCU Leadership." *Diverse: Issues in Higher Education*, September 8, 2004. https://www.diverseeducation.com/institutions/hbcus/article/15080269/investing-in-hbcu-leadership.

Kim, Daniel. "What Is Your Organization's Core Theory of Success?" Systems Thinker. https://thesystemsthinker.com/what-is-your-organizations-core-theory-of-success/.

King, John Q. Taylor, Sr. "At a Crossroads. The United Methodist Black Colleges." Unpublished manuscript, n.d. HT Archives.

———. "A Fisk Family: Four Generations of Faith and Leadership." Unpublished manuscript. n.p., n.d. HT Archives.

———. Board Report, March 12, 1967. HT Archives.

———. Board Report, March 25, 1969. HT Archives.

———. Board Report, March 1971. HT archives.

———. "Make a Difference." Interview in 1988 Yearbook. HT Archives.

———. "Report on Christian Higher Education: Education for Responsible Living." Unpublished manuscript, n.d. HT Archives.

———. "Serving the Disadvantaged in Higher Education Report." Special Race Relations Sunday Issue. Unpublished manuscript, n.d. HT Archives.

———. "To Serve the Future Hour." *The Informer* 7, no. 4, (May 1975): 6–9.

———. "Vision of Greatness." Unpublished manuscript, n.d. HT Archives.

King-Tears Mortuary, "McMillan Memorial Services." http://www.publicnow.com/view/226F9F75A54CFD3113DFDADDC869A1B92375376B.

Kruse, Sharon D., Shameem Rakha, and Shannon Calderone. "Developing Cultural Competency in Higher Education: An Agenda for Practice." *Teaching in Higher Education: Critical Perspectives* 23, no. 1 (December 12, 2017): 1–18. https://www.researchgate.net/publication/321767296_Developing_cultural_competency_in_higher_education_an_agenda_for_practice/citation/download.

Lum, Lydia. "Thinking Outside the Fundraising Box." *Diverse: Issues in Higher Education*, August 20, 2009. http://diverseeducation.com/article/13424/.

Lynch, Matthew. "5 Factors That Influence the Future of HBCUs." *The Edvocate*, September 18, 2016. https://www.theedadvocate.org/5-factors-that-influence-the-future-of-hbcus/.

———. "HBCU Enrollment on the Rise." *The Edvocate*, March 20, 2023. https://www.theedadvocate.org/hbcu-enrollment-on-the-rise/.

Marklein, Mary Beth. "Black Colleges Examine Their Mission. *USA Today*, February 10, 2014. https://www.usatoday.com/story/news/nation/2014/02/10/black-colleges-mission/5374863/.

Martin, Rosalee. "Breaking the Silence." *NOKOA Observer*, October 2–8, 1992.

———. "H-T Rebellion." *NOKOA Observer*, September 9, 1999.

Masino, Amanda, and Karen Magid. "Green Is the New Black: Environmental Justice and HBCUs." *Second Nature*, December 18, 2015. https://secondnature.org/2015/12/18/green-new-black-environmental-justice-hbcus/.

McDonald, Carol. "Huston-Tillotson University President Dr. Colette Pierce Burnette Announces Retirement." Press release, December 2, 2021. https://htu.edu/wp-content/uploads/2021/12/President-Burnette-Retirement-Press-Release.pdf.

McGee, Kate. "East Austin Is Growing, and Huston-Tillotson Hopes Its Roots Keep a Community Intact." KUT-FM, March 21, 2017.

McMillan, Joseph. "[HT] Mission, Vision and Strategic Plan: Focus on the Future," September 1996. HT Archives.

———. "Inauguration Speech." *Huston-Tillotson College, Alumni and Friends Magazine*, Inaugural Issue, Spring 1989. HT Archives.

———. "Letter to Board of Trustees" (as part of the selection process), 1987. HT Archives.

———. "President-Elect, Huston Tillotson College." HT press release, December 4, 1987. HT Archives.

———. "A President's Message." Final Board Report, 2000. HT Archives.

———. Report to the Board of Trustees. May 21–22, 1998. HT Archives.

———. "Semi-Annual Report of the President to the Board of Trustees." November 1, 1990. HT Archives.

Miller, Jeff. "The Undertold Story of Jackie Robinson's College Hoops Coaching Days." *Texas Monthly*, April 14, 2023. https://www.texasmonthly.com/arts-entertainment/jackie-robinson-hbcu-basketball-coach/.

National Center for Education Statistics. "Historical Black Colleges and Universities." https://nces.ed.gov/fastfacts/display.asp?id=667.

Neelakantan, Shailaja. "UNCF: $1 Billion for HBCUs, TCUs, MSIs in Federal Coronavirus Stimulus Package," March 2020, https://diverseeducation.com/article/171010/.

NOKOA Observer Business Section, November 1, 2001.

Onikeku, Femi Alabi. "Diki: Returning to Impact on Her Roots." *Guardian*, April 13, 2016. http://m.guardian.ng/saturday-magazine/diki-returning-to-impact-on-her-roots/.

Owens, Donna. "HBCUs Are Our Future." *Essence*, May 26, 2020. https://www.essence.com/feature/hbcus-are-our-future/.

Oyeniyi, Doyin. "In the Pilot's Seat: Collette Pierce Burnette." *Austin Woman*, July 31, 2017. http://atxwoman.com/in-the-pilots-seat/.

Perry, Andre M., Hannah Stephens, and Manann Donoghoe. "The Supreme Court Decision to Strike Down Affirmative Action Means That HBCU Investment Is More Important Than Ever." Brookings, June 29, 2023. https://www.brookings.edu/articles/the-supreme-courts-decision-to-strike-down-affirmative-action-means-that-hbcu-investment-is-more-important-than-ever/.

Perry, Wilhelmina, and Gus Swain. *Huston-Tillotson University Legacy: A Historical Treasure*. Self-Published, 2007.

Pierce Burnette, Colette. Engagement Report, 2017–2018.

———. Holiday Card, December 17, 2021. https://www.youtube.com/watch?v=1N6D7PmsVbA.

———. "Meet HT's Sixth President and CEO." *Ram Magazine*, 2016.

———. "A Message to My Campus Community." Unpublished manuscript, June 3, 2020.

———. Report to the Board of Trustees, November 3, 2017.

Reed, Steve. "Huston-Tillotson Seeking Support in the Wake of Cash-Flow Problems." *Austin American-Statesman*, April 11, 1987.

Rhodan, Maya. "A New Era of Protest Is Energizing HBCUs. But There Are Challenges." *Time*, June 4, 2018. https://time.com/5286691/hbcu-black-colleges-protest-activism/.

Richardson, James. *The Abolitionist's Journal: Memories of an American Antislavery Family*. Albuquerque: High Road Books–University of New Mexico Books, 2022.

Roser, Mary Ann. "Huston-Tillotson's Crisis of Confidence: Fight Against President Divides the Campus." *Austin American-Statesman*, September 10, 1999.

———. "Teacher Training Is Under Scrutiny." *Austin American-Statesman* archives, September 28, 1999. https://statesman.newsbank.com/search?text=Mary%20Ann%20Roser%2C%20Teacher%20Training%20is%20Under%20Scrutiny%2C&content_added=&date_from=&date_to=&pub%5B0%5D=AASB.

Schlemmer, Liz. "HBCUs Got a Windfall of Federal COVID Relief. Here's How Colleges Are Spending It." NPR, September 22, 2022. https://www.npr.org/2022/09/20/1124142614/how-hbcus-are-spending-their-covid-19-relief-money.

Senge, Peter M. *The Fifth Discipline: The Art & Practice of the Learning Organization*. New York: Crown Currency, 2010.

Shackles, Chrystine. Huston-Tillotson website. htu.edu/about/history. https://www.sutori.com/story/huston-tillotson-University.

———. *Reminiscences of Huston-Tillotson College*. Austin: Best Printing, 1973.

Smith, Robert. "The Financial Struggles Facing HBCUs and Students." Robert F. Smith blog, August 16, 2021. https://robertsmith.com/blog/the-financial-struggles-facing-hbcs-and-students/.

———. "Morehouse 2019 Graduates Received Their Total School Debt Payoff." CBS News, May 20, 2019. https://www.cbsnews.com/news/who-is-morehouse-billionaire-robert-f-smith/.

———. "Who Is Morehouse Billionaire Robert F. Smith?" CBS News, March 20, 2019. https://www.cbsnews.com/news/who-is-morehouse-billionaire-robert-f-smith/.

Stayton, Jennifer. "Outgoing Huston Tillotson President Knows It's Wise To 'Leave the Party When You're Having Fun.'" KUT 90.5, June 29, 2022. https://www.kut.org/austin/2022-06-29/outgoing-huston-tillotson-president-knows-its-wise-to-leave-the-party-when-youre-having-fun.

Stuart, Reginald. "HBCUs Facing Challenges Amid Efforts to Stay Financially Viable and Competitive." *Diverse: Issues in Higher Education*, October 29, 2013. https://www.diverseeducation.com/sports/article/15092212/hbcus-facing-challenges-amid-efforts-to-stay-financially-viable-and-competitive.

Survey Monkey. "Create Online Surveys and Forms That Mean Business." https://www.surveymonkey.com/.

Taylor, Coretta, and Chuck Lindell. "HT No Time for Nostalgia: At 40, Growing Pains for Huston-Tillotson University." *Austin American-Statesman*, October 1992.

Taylor, La'Raven. "Netflix CEO, Wife Donate Record $120 Million to Atlanta HBCUs, UNCF." GPD News, updated August 13, 2020. https://www.gpb.org/news/2020/06/17/netflix-ceo-wife-donate-record-120-million-atlanta-hbcus-uncf.

Texas Humanities. "Texas Originals, J. Mason Brewer." https://www.humanitiestexas.org/programs/tx-originals/list/j-mason-brewer.

Texas State Historical Association. "Volma Robert Overton, Jr." Published August 15, 2013. https://www.tshaonline.org/handbook/entries/overton-volma-robert-sr.

Thompson, Carolyn, and Collins Binkley. "Harvard, MIT Sue to Block ICE Rule on International Students." ABC News, July 8, 2020. https://abcnews.go.com/Politics/wireStory/harvard-mit-sue-block-ice-rule-international-students-71670205.

"Tillotson College." Texas State Historical Association, 1952 (updated 2020). https://www.tshaonline.org/handbook/entries/tillotson-college.

Tom Joyner Foundation. "Names Huston-Tillotson University July School of the Month," 2014. https://tomjoynerfoundation.org/tom-joyner-foundation-names-hustontillotson-university-july-school-month/.

Tyko, Kelly. "Billionaire Robert F. Smith's $34 Million Gift to Morehouse Grads Includes Parent Loans." *USA Today*, September 20, 2019. https://www.usatoday.com/story/money/2019/09/20/morehouse-billionaire-gift-smith-donates-34-million-pay-off-loans/2392458001/.

UNCF. "Why Choose an HBCU." Retrieved June 24, 2020. https://uncf.org/pages/Why-Choose-an-HBCU.

US Department of Education. "Additional Project SERV Grants to HBCUs," May 31, 2023. https://www.ed.gov/news/press-releases/us-department-education-announces-additional-project-serv-grants-hbcus.

US Department of Education. "Secretary DeVos Delivers Nearly $1.4 Billion in Additional CARES Act Relief Funds to HBCUs, Minority Serving Institutions, and Colleges and Universities Serving Low-Income Students," April 30, 2020. https://sites.ed.gov/whhbcu/category/funding/.

US Department of Education. "White House Initiative on Historically Black Colleges and Universities." Retrieved June 35, 2020. https://sites.ed.gov/whhbcu/one-hundred-and-five-historically-black-colleges-and-universities/.

US Department of Education, Office of Post Secondary Education. "CARES Act: Higher Education Emergency Relief Fund," March 27, 2020. https://www2.ed.gov/about/offices/list/ope/caresact.html.

Van Delinder, Jean. "*Brown v. Board of Education of Topeka* a Landmark Case Unresolved Fifty Years Later." *National Archives* 36, no. 1, Spring 2004.

We are HT. January 22, 2019. https://www.youtube.com/watch?v=HIRMZqhqGsI.

Williams, David. "Parallel and Crossover Lives: Texas before and after Desegregation: An Interview with Dr. King." *Humanities Texas*, May 29, 2001. https://www.humanitiestexas.org/sites/default/files/page-attachment/King_John_Interview.pdf.

Index

academic affairs at Huston-Tillotson. *See also* Vice President for Academic Affairs (VPAA)
  Earvin's new programs for, 187–90
  McMillan's impact on, 82–90
Accountability System for Educator Preparation, 190
Accreditation Council for Business Schools and Programs (ACBSP), 187, 273
accreditation problems for Huston-Tillotson, 4, 34, 68–69, 95, 132–36, 151, 162–64, 254, 349n105
Achievements in Black Austin, 265, 273
ADAM Project, 271
Adams, Edward B., 56–57
Adams, Roger, 148
Adler, Steve, 213
Administration Building restoration project, 72–73, 152
Adult Degree Program (ADP), 151–52, 189, 240–42, 264
African American Women's Profiles of Prominence in Education, 136
Agard, Isaac, 3
Akins, Charles, 15
All-Star Academy. *See* IDEAL Academy
Alpha Kappa Alpha sorority, 45
alumni of Huston-Tillotson. *See also* specific alumni
  Earvin and, 148–50, 193–94
  giving programs for, 248–50
  King and, 35
  McMillan and, 61–64, 69–70, 90–92, 95–121
American Association of University Professors (AAUP), 95, 130
American College & University Presidents' Climate Commitment (ACUPCC), 190
American Council of Trustees and Alumni, 197
American Methodist Association (AMA), 38
American Missionary Association, 3
Anaejionu, Jane, 122, 124–25, 130, 154
Anaejionu, Paul (Dr.), 67, 89, 106–14, 121–33, 150, 154, 255, 258–59
Anderson, Ada Cecilia Collins, 15, 144, 249–50, 296
Angelou, Maya, 262
Apple and HT Partnerships for Teachers and Students' Success, 231
Applied Materials funding, 251
Ask Your Mama project, 215–17
Association of Applied and Clinical Sociology (AACS), 263–64
Association of Governing Boards of Universities and Colleges (ABG), 317
athletics at Huston-Tillotson, 45
AusPREP program, 64, 90, 251
Austin, Texas, Huston-Tillotson visibility in, 89, 210–15
Austin American-Statesman newspaper, 98–113, 124–25
Austin Chamber of Commerce Austinite of the Year Award, 214
Austin Community College (ACC), Huston-Tillotson and, 38, 90–92, 212–13, 343n76
Aziz, Sara, 226

Baha'i Symposium on Race, 263
Bandiera, Nancy, 127
Barnett, Herman A., III (Dr.), 15
Biden, Joseph, 317
Bill of Particulars (Save HT Committee), 125–32, 152–55, 346n43, 350n20
Black, Gloria, 44
Black educational institutions, in Reconstruction era, 3–4
Black Executive Exchange Program (BEEP), 38
Black Lives Matter (BLM), 216–18, 307, 322, 360n17
Bluebonnet Hill, 4
Blues in the Night gala, 252
Board of Trustees
  building renovations and, 72–73
  church connections of, 55
  curriculum reforms and, 194–95
  duties of, 338n13
  Earvin appointment and, 139–40, 196–97
  faculty communications with, 106–12
  financial contributions by, 32–33
  King's reports to, 19–25, 33–36, 39–40
  McMillan's relations with, 53, 106, 129–34, 349n98
  Pierce-Burnette appointment and, 204–5
  Pierce-Burnette reports to, 211–12
  student correspondence with, 119–21
  Wiley-Texas Colleges merger and, 35, 67
Boles, Maxine Kelly, 15
Bond-Huie, Stephanie, 182
Bradford, Carmen, 262
Branch, Mary E., 4, 15, 49, 200–202, 209–10, 289
Brewer, June H. (Dr.), 16, 128–29
Brewington, Donald (Rev.), 234, 267
Brooks, William E. (Rev.), 3
Brown v. Board of Education (1954), 50, 300, 315, 359n2
Brownlee, Fred L., 6
Building Green Justice Forum, 191, 251
Burnaman, Stephen, 261–62
Burnette, Daarel, 206
Buxkemper, Alexa, 66, 80–81, 344n46
Buxkemper, Harriet, 65–66, 106–14, 121–32, 136, 154, 344n46

Carbon Commitment, 190
Career Readiness Award for Students at Huston-Tillotson University, 273
CARES (Coronavirus Aid, Relief and Economic Security) Act, 281, 285, 297, 314–15
Carmichael, Stokely, 306
Cascos, Carlos, 216
Caviness, Autumn, 188–89
Celebration of the Right University, Right Community and Right Assignment Gala, 253–54
Center for Academic Excellence (CAE), 230
Center for Academic Innovation and Transformation (CAIT), 230
Center for Entrepreneurship Innovation (CEI), 228–29, 240–41
Center for Social Justice, 259
Center for Sustainability and Environmental Justice, 191
Center of Excellence in Teacher Education, 87
Ceresa, Robert (Dr.), 271–72
Cervantes, Carlos (Dr.), 232, 270–71
Chic 26, 45
China, Huston-Tillotson student travel to, 193, 226–27
Christopher, Marjon, 57
Christopher, Reginald (Dr.), 16, 96–98, 124–25, 348n94
church leadership, King's links to, 10–11
Cirella-Urrutia, Anne (Dr.), 272
Civil Rights Act of 1964, 300, 344n98
Civil Rights Movement, faculty at Historically Black Colleges and Universities and, 306–7
Cole, Thomas (Dr.), 145
College Industry Cluster, 38
College of Arts and Sciences (Huston-Tillotson University), establishment of, 185–86

371

INDEX

Committee on General Studies Competency, 83
consortia, with Huston-Tillotson, 37–38, 342n72
Consortium for Curriculum Change (CCC), 37–38, 43
Consortiums for Research Training (CRT), 37, 342n3
Cooperative Education program (Huston-Tillotson), 43
Core Curriculum Competency Program, 85–86
COVID-19 pandemic
  future of HBCUs and, 314
  Huston-Tillotson experience of, 217–18
  online HT programs during, 240
  Pierce Burnette's management of, 280–89, 297
Crayton-Jones, Nancy, 97
Cruz, Paul (Dr.), 213
Cuban American Political Culture and Civic Organizing: Tocqueville in Miami (Ceresa), 272
curriculum development at Huston-Tillotson
  Earvin and, 194–95, 351n47
  under King, 42–44, 343n86
  under McMillan, 81–90, 351n47
Curry, Marion (Dr.), 64
Curry, Martha, 64
Curry-Jones, Beulah Agnes (Dr.), 65

Davage, Matthew S. (Dr.), 6
Davies, Jennifer (Dr.), 66–67
Davis, King, 156
Dean of Academic Support, Earvin's creation of, 187
Dean of Student Affairs Office, 44, 46
Delco, Wilhelmina, 139, 151
Dell Corporation, 150–51
Delta Sigma Theta sorority, 45
Department of Business Administration, accreditation of, 187
DePaul University, King as student at, 10
desegregation, King's experiences with, 50–51
Dilworth, Ethel, 128
Diri, Dikibujiri (Diki), 227–28
Discover Law program, 189–90, 225, 271
Distinguished Brothers, 45
diversity initiatives
  Earvin's development of, 155
  Pierce Burnette's development of, 225–28
Douglass, Frederick, 3
Downs, Karl E., 5
Drake, Hal, 11
Dr. Jones Research Day, 185–86
DuBois, W. E. B., 188, 315
DuBois Honors program (DuBois Scholar), 150, 187–89, 227, 229–31
DuBois Lecture series, 188
Dubra, Charles, 41, 343n81
Dumpster Project, 191–92

Earvin, Allyson Valeria, 146
Earvin, Larry L.
  accreditation problems under, 151, 162–64, 293–94
  Administration Building restoration, 152
  alumni and, 148–50
  assets and liabilities as president, 147–55
  building renovations and construction, 194
  College of Arts and Sciences and, 185–86
  DuBois Honors program (DuBois Scholar) under, 150, 187–89
  early life and career, 146–47
  faculty hiring and relations under, 150, 155, 166–87, 262–72, 351n45, 352nn57–60
  financial instability and fundraising by, 72, 150–51, 159–62, 195, 198, 244, 351n32
  on Historically Black Colleges and Universities (HBCUs), 299
  Huston-Tillotson University established under, 184–85
  inaugural address of, 140–46
  institutional goals and missions and, 152–55, 197–98
  international initiatives under, 193
  legacy of, 195–98, 327–36
  missed opportunities during presidency of, 194–95
  photo of, 139
  Pierce Burnette appointment and, 205
  retirement of, 195, 204, 325
  Save HT Committee and, 152–55
  School of Business and Technology and, 186–87
  selection as HT president, 139–46
  strategic planning by, 155–62
  student enrollment and, 155, 193–94
  students' relationship with, 164–66
  sustainability efforts under, 190–93
Earvin, Valerie, 140
Earvin, William Jarrett, 146
École Supérieure des Affaires (ESA) (West Africa), 226
economic environment, curriculum planning and, 159–60
Edelman, Marion Wright, 315
Edmond, Steven (Dr.), 150, 182–83, 186–87, 193, 226–28, 234, 263
education, slavery as barrier to, 3
Educational Leadership, master's program in, 190
Educational Policy Committee / Council (EPC), 161–62, 194–95, 346n50
engineering program at Huston-Tillotson, 43
enrollment decline, growth, and retention
  data on, 36, 118–21, 151–52
  Earvin's initiatives for, 155, 193–94, 240
  at Historically Black Colleges and Universities, 301
  McMillan's tenure and, 70–72, 102–3, 345n30
  under Pierce Burnette, 239–44

Environmental Studies Major / Environmental Justice Major, 191
Equal Heart funding, 251
Esso Education Foundation Faculty Fellowship, 40
Evers, Medgar, 306

Faculty Advisory Council, 264–65, 278–80, 352nn64–65, 358n96
faculty at Historically Black Colleges and Universities
  motivations and difficulties of, 307–10
  survey of, 302–6
faculty at Huston-Tillotson. *See also* specific faculty members
  Earvin's relations with, 150, 155, 166–87, 262–72, 351n45, 352nn57–60
  governance structure for, 278–80
  King's relations with, 39–42, 255–60
  McMillan and, 260–62
  McMillan's dismissal of, 126–32
  McMillan's relations with, 64–67, 70, 73–74, 81–90, 92–95, 103–21, 132–36, 347n68
  Pierce-Burnette's relations with, 217–20, 236–39, 254–55, 274–78
  presidential selection process and, 139–41
  salary increases for, 73, 278–80
  Save HT Committee campaign and, 124–32
  student support from, 5
Faculty Resource Network (FRN) (New York University), 150, 183–84
Faculty Senate (Faculty Forum) (Huston-Tillotson College), 93–95, 352nn64–65
Fairley, Anthony, 274
family environment
  at HBCUs, 310–12
  at Huston-Tillotson College, 46–48, 210, 220
Fatima Jinnah Women University (Pakistan), 226, 264
Federal Family Education Loan (FFEL), 159
financial aid for students
  COVID-19 pandemic and, 280–89
  crisis under Pierce Burnette for, 244
  fraud in, 73–74
  at HBCUs, 312–19
  student loan and aid programs, 159–62
financial instability at Huston-Tillotson
  COVID-19 pandemic and, 280–89
  under Earvin, 150–51, 159–62, 195
  financial aid fraud, 73–74
  grants and funds secured under Pierce Burnette, 250–54
  under King, 31–38
  under McMillan, 68–74, 138
  Pierce Burnette's initiatives for solving, 244–54
financial instability of HBCUs, 312–19
First International Virtual Summit on Medical Sociology and Public

372

INDEX

Health, 226
Fisk University, King's attendance at, 10
Floyd, George, 216–18
Ford Foundation, 32, 40, 69
fRAMily (RAM family), Pierce Burnett's embrace of, 212, 220
Francis, Theodore, II (Dr.), 269
Fulbright funding, Huston-Tillotson recipients of, 193
Future Act, HT funding from, 251

gala events, fundraising with, 251–52
Gasman, Marybeth, 313–14
General Board of Higher Education & Ministry-Black College Board (GBHEM) Capital Fund, 251
George, Jim
 McMillan leadership crisis and, 107–15, 119–21, 133
 Save HT Committee and, 124–32
Geschke, Charles M., 315
Golden, Carolyn (Dr.), 272
Greek organizations, King and, 44–46
Green Apple Fellows Grant, 232
Greene, Erica, 318–19
Green Is the New Black (GITNB) program, 192
Guided Reading and Study Precepts Laboratory (GRASP), 43
Guys and Dolls, 45

Hackathon competition, 188–89
Hampton University, 312
Hanckel, Julianne, 211–12
Haney, Asia, 248
Harden, Ada, 29, 61–62
Harden, Anita, 61
Harden, Billy, 29, 61–62
Harden, Camisha, 61
Harden, Marilyn, 61
Harden, Roland, 252
Harris, Kamala, 306, 317
Hatton Sumners Grant, 251
Hawkins, Albert, 205, 244
Hayes, Dianne, 137
Hayes, Robert E. (Bishop), 62
"HBCUs and Writing Programs Critical Hip Hop Language Pedagogy and First-Year Student Success" (Hudson-Stone), 265
Heritage Foundation Preservation Grant, 251
Higher Education Act (1965), 301
Higher Education Emergency Relief Fund (HEERF), 314
Hill, E. E., 16
Hines, Marcet Alice. *See* King, Marcet Hines
Hirsch, Mike (Dr.), 195, 226, 234, 263
Historically Black Colleges and Universities (HBCUs)
 family environment at, 310–12
 financial pressures for, 138
 future of, 312–19
 Huston-Tillotson as, 49–50
 importance of, 299–324
 Pierce Burnette's views on, 202–4, 296–97
 survey of faculty at, 302–10

HIV epidemic
 emergence of, 51–52
 HT education programming on, 44, 89–90, 343n88
Hodges, J. T., 3
Holman, Andrea (Dr.), 261
Home Residency Program, 192
Hopwood v. Texas, 159, 351n31
Hotel and Restaurant Management program, 88, 347n62
Howard University, 54–55, 296, 302
HT Golden Apple Teacher, 231
HT RAM Check, 284–85
HT Research Journal, 186
HT Research Scholars program, 220
HT Strategic Plan, 155–62
HT Young Alumni (HTYA), 248
Hudson, Jullie (Dr.), 265, 271
Huffman, Laura, 214
Huston, Samuel, 4
Huston-Tillotson College
 accreditation-reaccreditation problems for, 64–67, 70, 73–74, 81–90, 92–95, 103–21, 132–36
 Administration Building restoration at, 72–73, 152
 campaign to save HT, 121–32
 distinguished alumni and faculty, 15–19
 Earvin as president of, 139–98
 enrollment declines and student retention at, 31, 36
 establishment of, 6, 320–22
 family environment at, 46–48
 international initiatives at, 193, 225–28
 King as president of, 14–52
 library and dormitory renovations, 194
 McMillan as president of, 53–138
 new name and structure for, 184–85
 online course development at, 161–62
 partnerships and consortia with, 37–38
 Pierce-Burnette as president of, 199–297
 presidential selection process at, 139–40
 student loan programs at, 159
 study abroad program, 193
Huston-Tillotson Continuing Education Department, 44
Huston-Tillotson University
 All-Steinway School status for, 251
 comparison of presidents at, 327–36
 COVID-19 epidemic and, 280–89
 establishment of, 185
 future of, 312–19
Huston-Tillotson University Legacy: A Historical Treasure, 14
Hutson, Alaine (Dr.), 226, 269

IDEAL Academy, 230, 235, 274, 277
Imaniman: Poets Writing in the Anzaldúan Borderlands, 266
Institute for Research Training (IRT), 89, 258–59
Institute of Justice and Equity, 225

institutional funding for
 Huston-Tillotson
 Pierce Burnette's initiatives for, 252–55
 struggle for, 31–36, 69
Institutional Racism and Systemic Inequities Task Force (Austin, Texas), 213
institutional self-studies, introduction at HT of, 67–68, 151
integration, King's advocacy for, 12, 50–51
Inter-College Faculty Exchange Program, 40
international study programs
 federal restrictions on, 315
 Hirsch's role in, 263–64
 Huston-Tillotson students China travel, 193
 Pierce Burnette's development of, 225–28

Jackson, Jesse (Rev.), 217–18, 306
Jackson, Linda, 5
Jacob, Peter, 313–14
Johnson, Magic, 151
Jones, Bronté (Dr.), 73–74, 102, 132, 346n36
Jones, Ericka, 234
Jones, Joseph (Dr.), 183, 185
Jones, William H. J., 4
Joyner, Tom, 192–93

Kamalvand, Ahmad, 232, 255, 257–58
Kane, Ruth (Dr.), 254, 274
Kansas City Monarchs, 5
Kappa Alpha Psi fraternity, 45
Kasita Company, 191
Keels, Crystal, 138
Kellogg, Robert (Dr.), 272
Kiara, Carment, 127–28
Kimbrough, Marvin (Dr.), 16
Kinesiology Department (Huston-Tillotson), 232
King, Breanna, 268
King, Charles B., Sr., 8
King, Edwina, 8
King, John Q. Taylor (Dr.), 32
 books written by, 13
 career of, 7
 curriculum development by, 42–44
 death of, 325
 early life and career, 8–10
 faculty hiring and relations under, 39–42, 255–60
 family environment at HT under, 46–47
 financial history of HT and, 31–38
 fundraising efforts by, 31–36, 341n51, 342n56
 on Historically Black Colleges and Universities (HBCUs), 299–301
 history of Huston-Tillotson College and, 6
 honors bestowed on, 13–14
 as Huston-Tillotson president, 14–52
 legacy of, 49–52, 327–36
 McMillan and, 55–57, 59
 military career of, 11

373

INDEX

mission and vision of, 20–31
moral compass of, 19–20
partnerships and consortia under, 37–38
photo, 7
retirement of, 49
segregation experiences of, 12–13
strengths and accomplishments of, 48–49
student activities and student affairs under, 44–48
students' relations with, 24–31
King, Marcet Hines, 10, 49, 339n4
King, Marjon Christopher, 57, 341nn45–46
King, Martin Luther, Jr., 11, 306
King, Stuart, 57, 341nn45–46
King, Stuart Hines, 10
Kirk, Willie Mae, 16
Knox, Wayne, 234
Kraft, James (Dr.), 267–69
Kresge Institutional Capacity Building (ICB) grant, 251
Krueger, Jennine, 217, 223, 265–66

Lands, Tishana, 248–49
Langston Hughes Project, 214–15
L. C. Anderson High School, King's memories of, 8–10
Lewis, John, 306
Lewis, Teresia, 126–27
Linder, Nelson, 62–63
Loredo, Judith (Dr.), 66, 87, 187
Lotfalian, Ardavan E., 260–61
Lou Rawls Parade of Stars (Evening of Stars) (UNCF telethon), 341n51
Love, Patrick B., 63
Lovinggood, Reuben S., 4
Lynch, Matthew, 316

Macfarland, Hector Gomez, 229
Magid, Karen (Dr.), 191
Maharry Medical College, 302
Manley, Audrey F., 315
Marshall, General (Dr.), 64, 90
Marshall, Thurgood, 315
Martin, Roland, 217–18
Martin, Rosalee
  administrative positions held by, 234, 356n58
  career at HT, 259–60
  as CAS dean, 186, 356n58
  core competency research by, 86–87
  curriculum development efforts of, 194–95
  doctorate in Humane Letters and Professor Emerita awarded to, 325
  Earvin and, 145–46, 150, 154, 351nn45–46
  HIV work by, 89–90
  international initiatives at HT and, 226
  Kiara case and, 127–28
  King's hiring of, 255
  McMillan and, 53, 93, 120, 130–31, 133–36, 348n90
  on presidential search committee, 139–41
  on race, 268–69

research on HBCUs by, 302–24
VPAA crisis recalled by, 107–12
Masino, Amanda (Dr.), 191, 220, 226, 232, 251, 269–70
McClendon, Dionte, 248
McCurdy, Ron, 214–15
McDonald, Carol (Dr.), 291–93
McGee, Kate, 220
MC Hammer, 145
McHaney, Robert, 126
McMillan, Joseph T., 43
McMillan, Joseph T., Jr.
  abdication of presidential duties by, 138
  accreditation problems and, 132–36
  Administration Building restoration campaign and, 72–73
  alumni relations with, 61–64, 69–70, 90–92, 95–121
  appointment as HT president, 55–61
  challenges during presidency of, 67–74, 293
  conflict mismanagement under, 137–38
  core and major curriculum initiatives under, 81–90
  death of, 325
  early life and career, 54–55
  enrollment and retention and, 70–72, 102–3
  faculty hiring and relations under, 64–67, 70, 73–74, 81–90, 92–95, 260–62, 347n68
  financial problems under, 68–74, 138
  on Historically Black Colleges and Universities (HBCUs), 299
  as Huston-Tillotson president, 53–138
  illness and death of, 136
  King and, 44
  leadership crises under, 95–121
  legacy of, 74–90, 137–38, 327–36
  photo of, 53
  retirement of, 133–36
  Save HT Committee campaign and, 121–32
  student view of, 70–72, 75–81, 97–103, 118–21, 164
McMillan, Olivia Cooper, 54
Means, Bertha Sadler (Dr.), 17
Means, James, 17
Mellon Foundation, 32
#MeToo movement, 307, 359n13
Miles-Adams, Merle (Dr.), 61, 67–68
military, King's service in, 11
Miss UNCF contest, 46, 78–80, 96, 346n44
missions statements for Huston-Tillotson College, of King, 22–25
Morehouse College, 203, 296, 302, 312
Morton, Virgie, 17–18
Morton-Taylor, Azie, 17–18, 315
Moton Development Consortium, 38
Mouton, Tommy, 266–67
Ms. HT contest, 46, 220–21
Murphy, Debra (Dr.), 194, 261

Nash, Ashley, 265

National Academy of Performing Arts (Karachi, Pakistan), 264
National Center for Educational Statistics, 301
national honor societies at Huston-Tillotson, 45
National Instruments funding, 251
National Science Foundation, 160
National Urban League, 38
National Women of Achievement, Inc., 136
Natural Sciences program, 241, 251
Negro Baseball League, 5, 252
"Negro" schools and colleges. *See* Black educational institutions; Historically Black Colleges and Universities (HBCUs)
Network Summer program, 183
Network Winter program, 183
"The New Depression in Higher Education: A Study of Financial Conditions at 41 Colleges and Universities" (Carnegie Commission report), 33
New York University (NYU), Faculty Resource Network programs, 183–84
Newfields Museum, 295
900 Chicon (magazine), 186, 264
NOKOA newspaper, 96–98, 112
Norman, G. W., 6

Office of International Programs (OIP), 227–28
Okpalaeze, Azubike (Dr.), 272
Oldmixon, Katherine (Dr.), 264–65, 267
Omega Psi Phi fraternity, 45
On Writing Hat Poems (Kimbrough), 16
100 African American Male Teacher Initiative, 231–32
Overton, Volma Robert Sr., 63, 307

Parks, Rosa, 306
Partnerships for Education Transformation Project, 241
partnerships with Huston-Tillotson, 37–38
Patton, Kim, 148–49
Pell Grants, 159
Peña, Horacio (Dr.), 67, 254, 352n53
Penn, I. Garland, 6
Perry, Wilhelmina (Dr.), 18
Phi Beta Sigma fraternity, 45
Pierce, Colon, 253
Pierce, Ruth, 253
Pierce Burnette, Colette
  administrative appointments by, 234–39
  affiliations, memberships, and awards for, 207–8
  appointment as HT president, 204–5
  building restoration and construction under, 251
  campus activities under, 214–18
  Center for Entrepreneurship Innovation and, 228–29
  challenges faced by, 233–54
  community involvement by, 208, 212–14

INDEX

conflicts with staff, 235–39
COVID-19 and presidency of, 280–89, 297
diversity and international initiatives under, 225–28
early life and career, 202–8
Earvin and, 186
educational philosophy of, 199–202
enrollment retention and growth initiatives under, 239–44
faculty hiring and relations under, 64, 67, 150, 217–20, 235–39, 254–55, 273–78
family support for, 205–7
financial aid crisis under, 244
financial stability initiatives under, 244–54
fundraising initiatives under, 250–54
goals of, 200–201
on Historically Black Colleges and Universities (HBCUs), 296–97, 299
King and, 49
leadership recruitment by, 233–39
legacy of, 295–97, 327–36
photo of, 199
post-retirement career of, 295
presidency of, 209–17
retirement of, 289–95, 325
STEM initiatives under, 209, 220, 232, 251, 316
student-centered programs developed by, 225–32
student relations with, 199–200, 218–25
UNCF Career Pathways Initiative and, 229–30
Pilsen Education Foundation, 32
Planned Parenthood, Huston-Tillotson partnership with, 89–90
Plessy v. Ferguson, 3, 344n96, 359n2
Prairie View A&M, 43
predominantly White institutions (PWIs)
barriers to Black student enrollment in, 50
Black faculty recruitment to, 269, 307–8, 318
Black student enrollment at, 138, 198, 303–6
Black student preference for HBCUs over, 301, 310–11
financial stability of, 318
Presidential Chain of Office, 59–60, 145
President's MASKED Ball, 151, 183–85
President's Task Force on Student Retention (Huston-Tillotson), 71–72
Primo, Abena (Dr.), 273
Project REACH (Regional Education on AIDS for Community Health), 44, 89–90

Quality Enhancement Plan (QEP), 255, 257–58
Quinlan, Gloria (Dr.), 261–62

RAM Career Connections Summer Program Pathway, 229–30

Ram Magazine, McMillan's messages in, 77–78, 120–21, 130–32
Randle, Joya Hayes, 149
Reach for a New Rhythm campaign, 251
reaffirmation of accreditation.
See accreditation problems for Huston-Tillotson
Redmond, Walter (Dr.), 128
religion and religious tradition
Black American colleges and schools link to, 5–6
King's focus on, 19–20, 46
Pierce Burnette's attachment to, 206–7
Richardson, George Warren (Rev.), 4
Richardson, James, 4
Richie, Lionel, 315
Rivers, Jesse (Dr.), 274
Robinson, Jackie, 5, 252
Rogers, James T., 68
Roser, Mary Ann, 87, 112–13
ROTC program at Huston-Tillotson, 43
Rouche, John (Dr.), 106–7

Safe Health Rams coordinator, 284–85
Samuel Huston College, 3–5, 320
church affiliation with, 4, 10
curricula and instruction in, 6
merger with Tillotson Collegiate and Normal School, 6
Samuels, Lorraine (Dr.), 194, 271
Sandra Joy Anderson Community Health and Wellness Center, 194
Sanford, Lajuana, 249
Santillanes, Sarah (Dr.), 274
Save HT Committee, 66, 121–32, 152–55
protests against, 80
School of Business and Technology (SBT), 186–87, 228–29
enrollment growth and, 240–41
Schwab, Kathy (Dr.), 67, 139–40, 255–57
Seabrook, John Jarvis (Dr.), 6
Second Nature program, 190
segregation
Black relocation due to, 5
King's experiences with, 11–12, 50–51
in military, 8, 11
Senge, Peter, 319
Septowski, Charles (Dr.), 128
"Serving the Disadvantaged" (King), 42
Sexual Assault Prevention Education, 261
Shackles, Chrystine, 5
Shaw University, 307
slavery, education barriers during, 3
Smith, Robert, 296
Smith, Terry, 69, 73, 113, 138, 150–51
social media, Pierce-Burnette's use of, 211–12, 222–25, 252–53
Social Welfare Consortium, 37
Southern Association of Colleges and Schools Commission on Colleges (SACSCOC), 196
Southern Association of Colleges and Secondary Schools (SACS), 4, 345n25, 351n40

Earvin on board of, 147
HT accreditation problems and, 34, 68–69, 95, 120, 132–36, 151, 162–64, 347n62
Southwestern Athletic Conference, 5
Speak Place Poetry Project, 266
Spelman College, 302, 307, 312
Spence, Devan, 77, 149
Stayton, Jennifer, 294
STEM programs
at HBCUs, 316–17
at Huston-Tillotson, 90, 191–92, 209, 220, 232
scholarships for, 251
"Stewardship of Huston-Tillotson College Property," (Save HT Committee), 129–30
Stewart, Shawanda, 219, 265–66, 271
Stone, Brian, 266
Stuart, Reginald, 138
student activities and organizations, 192
King's support for, 44–46
Pierce-Burnette's support for, 216–18
Student Ambassador program, 189
Student Government Association (SGA) at Huston-Tillotson, 45
student loan and aid programs, 159–62
Student Nonviolent Coordinating Committee (SNCC), 307
students at Huston-Tillotson College
assessment of King's effectiveness by, 26–31
Earvin's relations with, 164–66
Earvin's student enrollment initiatives, 155, 193–94
King's presidency and, 24–26
low enrollment issues and, 118–21, 151–52
McMillan and, 70–72, 75–81, 97–103, 118–21, 164
Pierce Burnette's relations with, 199–200, 218–25, 242–44
Student Support Service, 43
"Success to the Successful" (HBCU archetype), 319–22
Sumler-Edmond, Janice (Dr.), 150, 187–89, 263, 353n76
Summer and Semester Scholar-in-Residence program, 183–84
Superb Club, 45
Sweatt v. Painter, 16
Symposia series and institutes at NYU, 184

Talent Search, 43
Taylor, Alice Clinton Woodson, 8
Taylor, John Quill, 8
Teacher Certification Program, 88
Teacher Education program, 43, 87–90, 231–32
"Teacher Training Is Under Scrutiny" (Roser), 87
technology development at Huston-Tillotson, 161–62
Temporary Assistance to Needy Families (TANF), 159
Tennant, Aimee (Dr.), 258
Tenure Promotion Committee, 272

375

Terry, Tammy, 63
Texas Association of Developing Colleges, 37
Texas Conference of the United Methodist Church, 4
Texas HBCU Conference, 272
Texas Methodist Association, 37
Texas Workforce Commission, 159
Thompson, Rohan (Dr.), 228, 273
Thurgood Marshall College Fund (TMCF), 241
Tillotson, George Jeffrey, 3
Tillotson Collegiate and Normal School, 3, 5, 200, 320
  curricula and instruction in, 6
  merger with Samuel Huston College, 6
Title III funds
  Earvin's use of, 183–84
  HBCU grants from, 316–17
  HT Office of International Programs and, 227–28
  King's use of, 32, 40
  McMillan's use of, 69, 86
  Pierce Burnette's use of, 251–54
  program of, 341n48
Title IV funding, 159
"To Serve the Future Hour" (King speech), 12–13
Tom Joyner Foundation Recognition, 192–93
Topkara, Engin, 258
TRIO pre-college program, 32, 43, 341n49
Trump, Donald, 315–16
Tuition Equalization Grant (TEG), 34

United Church of Christ (UCC), Huston-Tillotson and, 54–55, 69, 139, 155
United Methodist Black College Fund, 38
United Methodist Black College Presidents, 11
United Methodist Black Colleges Consortium, 38
United Methodist Church, Huston-Tillotson and, 46, 69, 139, 155
United Negro College Fund (UNCF)
  Career Pathways Initiative, 229–30
  HT funding from, 69, 89–90, 160, 163, 241, 251, 341n51
University Associate program, 184
University of Texas (Austin), Huston-Tillotson partnership with, 37, 44, 46, 89, 189–90, 225, 263, 320–22
Upward Bound program, 32, 43, 69, 104
Urdy, Charles (Dr.), 18
US Constitutional Convention, 3

Vanderpuye, Archibald (Dr.), 234, 325, 337n3
Viaer, Anthony, 152, 249–50
Vice President for Academic Affairs (VPAA). *See also* academic affairs at Huston-Tillotson
  McMillan crisis involving, 88–90, 103–21
  Pierce Burnette's appointments to, 234

The Villager newspaper, 96, 112
"Vision for Academic Affairs" (Waters), 83–84
voter registration and voting drives
  HBCU involvement in, 306–7
  HT involvement in, 216

Wallace-Williams, Melva (Dr.), 146, 196, 325, 337n8
Waters, Lenora (Dr.)
  as Huston-Tillotson faculty member, 40, 65, 343n80
  Kiara case and, 127–28
  student retention and, 71
  as Vice President for Academic Affairs, 83–84, 90, 92–95, 104–5, 348n80
Webster, Jeremiah (Rev.), 4
WeCare Center, 273
Wesley Chapel Methodist Episcopal Church (Austin), 4, 10
West Texas Conference School, 4
"Why Students Are Choosing HBCUs: 4 Years Being Seen as Family" (Greene), 318–19
Wicks, Candace, 149–50
Wiley and Texas Colleges, proposed HT merger with, 35, 37, 67, 293
Williams, Cecil (Rev.), 18
Williams, David, 8
Wilson, James, 18–19
Wilson, Jeff (Dr.), 191
Wilson, Ora, 182
Woods, Prenza L., 72
Writers' Studio (Huston-Tillotson University), 274–75

Yildirim, Yusuf, 258

Zeta Phi Beta sorority, 45
Zodiac Club, 45

www.ingramcontent.com/pod-product-compliance
Lightning Source LLC
Chambersburg PA
CBHW032011300426
44117CB00008B/991